1591 S. Daniel. "Del

1594 H. Const

1599 M. D

Sonnet - Bliss Perry - Study of Poetry

p 293.

"A situation plus a thought gives a mood; or a mood plus an event gives a mental resolve.

p.292 Formula: "As" - for the octave - and "So" - for the sestet. or When and then.

Shakespeare's Sonnet - a threefold statement of the central thought, using a different image in each quatrain, and closing with a personal application of the idea.

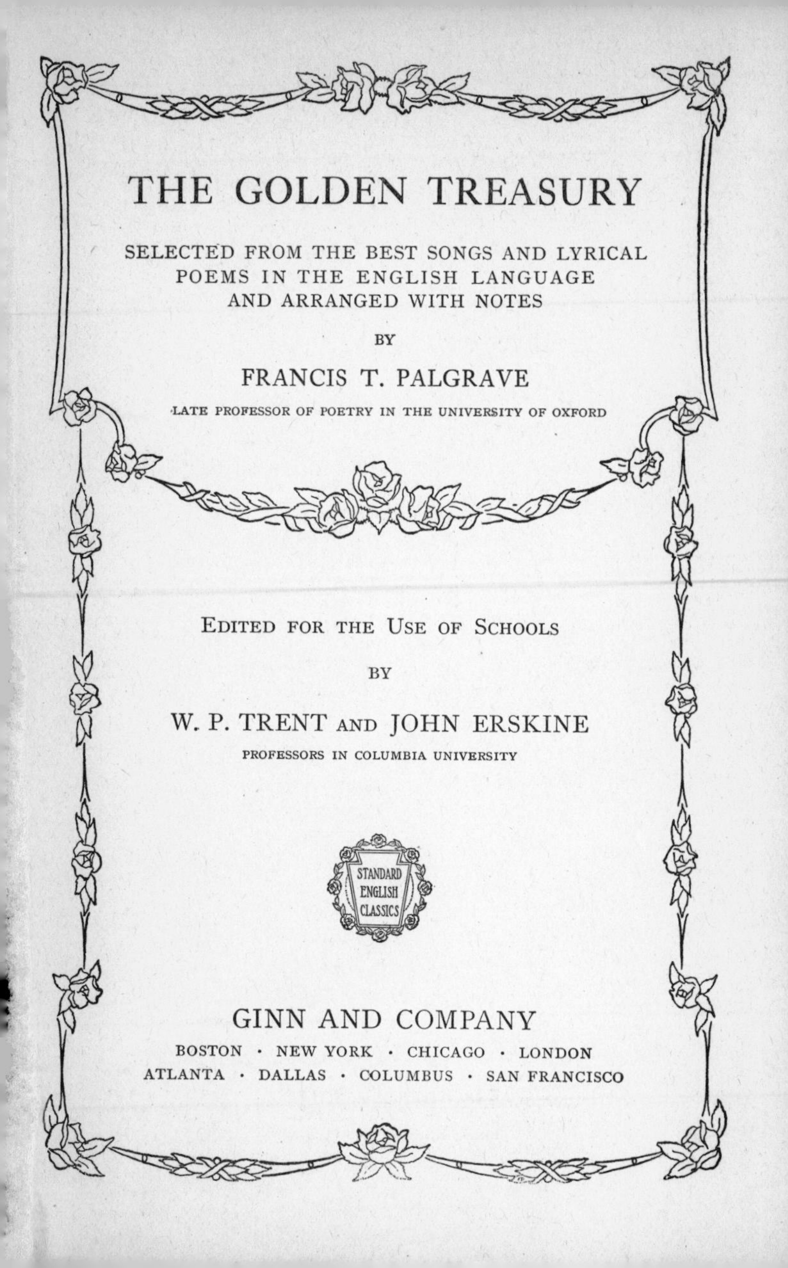

THE GOLDEN TREASURY

SELECTED FROM THE BEST SONGS AND LYRICAL POEMS IN THE ENGLISH LANGUAGE AND ARRANGED WITH NOTES

BY

FRANCIS T. PALGRAVE

LATE PROFESSOR OF POETRY IN THE UNIVERSITY OF OXFORD

EDITED FOR THE USE OF SCHOOLS

BY

W. P. TRENT AND JOHN ERSKINE

PROFESSORS IN COLUMBIA UNIVERSITY

GINN AND COMPANY

BOSTON · NEW YORK · CHICAGO · LONDON
ATLANTA · DALLAS · COLUMBUS · SAN FRANCISCO

618.11

The Athenæum Press
GINN AND COMPANY · PROPRIETORS · BOSTON · U.S.A.

EDITORIAL NOTE

This edition of the "Golden Treasury" is intended for high-school students and for the general reader. We have tried to let the poems speak for themselves, adding only such notes of information as one class of our readers or another might find helpful. For the most part we have avoided æsthetic criticism; where all is so excellent, the reader cannot go wrong if he makes his own choices and discoveries. In preparing the notes we have consulted the available annotations, and wish to acknowledge much serviceable guidance, especially from the elaborate commentary by Mr. J. H. Fowler and Mr. W. Bell, published by the Macmillan Company, and from the edition by Mr. Herbert Bates, published by Longmans, Green, and Co. In the omission of all metrical and of most etymological questions, we have wished to make clear to teachers and students what seem to us the more important steps in the approach to poetry.

W. P. T.
J. E.

CONTENTS

INTRODUCTION

I

Of all literary types the lyric is perhaps the easiest to recognize and the hardest to define. If we say that the lyric is a song, — a poem which is written to be sung or which sounds as if it might be sung, — we should have to include under our definition the old English or Scotch ballad, which has the suggestion of song, but which is narrative and belongs rather to the type of the short story. Palgrave chose for his anthology those poems which turned upon a single thought, feeling, or situation. Yet this formula did not represent his notion of the lyric; for he adds that he excluded narrative, descriptive, and didactic poems, "unless accompanied by rapidity of movement, brevity, and the coloring of human passion." The heart of his definition really lay in the last modest phrase, "the coloring of human passion."

For the lyric is essentially that literary type which expresses emotion, just as the drama and the novel express active experience, and the essay expresses thought. In his study of "The School of Giorgione" Walter Pater said that all art tends to become music, — that is, to stir emotions rather than to state intellectual ideas. A musician is annoyed when some one asks what the music "means"; to him it is a feeling, not a statement; it means no more than does the taste of sugar. So the painter is annoyed at the common attempt to read a story into a picture; to him the picture is a scheme of color and an arrangement of lines, — a sensation for the eye, as music is for the ear. But the average man looks for an idea, — especially in the United States, where "intellect" has unfortunately been rated higher than the gift and training to appreciate beauty; and in all art we see a certain struggle between the artist's desire to set out the loveliness of the world for man's enjoyment, and man's contrary desire that art shall say something that can be translated into words.

Pater in his famous saying meant that the best of art cannot be translated into words. When we hear a 'cello or violin, the tragic tones give us a luxurious sadness, although we have no reason to be sad, and cannot tell another man what the tone of the 'cello is like. The hurdy-gurdy in the street playing a dance tune sets the children to waltzing, and the drums and fifes of the military band make us feel like marching. These different emotions, we notice, can be indicated only by mentioning the instruments that stimulate them; if the reader has experienced the emotions, he will understand the reference, — otherwise it will mean nothing to him. So the lyric, nearest of all literary types to music, says to us many delicious things — recognizable but inexpressible emotions — which are over and above what the actual words mean.

The chief language, so to speak, which the lyric employs in addition to actual words is rhythm. Whether the beat of the lines is strong or weak, grave or merry; whether the measure befits a song or a dance tune or a military march, — we feel all this before we even attend to the intellectual message of the verse. The rhythm, the physical habit of the lyric, denotes the vital energy of its emotion. Poems with a strongly marked rhythm, like Jonson's "Hymn to Diana" (p. 87), suggest and stimulate a well-defined state of feeling wherein the emotion easily dominates — as in the lyric it should — the intellectual content. Such a poem, however, as Crashaw's "Wishes for the Supposed Mistress" (p. 87) indicates at once by its less definite rhythm that its emotional energy is relaxed and unimportant, almost secondary to the thoughts that make it a poem of intellectual conceits rather than of feeling. And in the fixed forms, like the sonnet, where the rhythm and the number of syllables and lines are prescribed, a reader of even slight experience detects differences of rhythmic energy between Shakespeare's "Let me not to the marriage of true minds" (p. 21), Milton's "When I consider how my life is spent" (p. 81), and Wordsworth's "The world is too much with us" (p. 359).

Within the single poem the rhythm may alter if it parallels some emotional change. Obviously such alterations occur most often in long poems. The changes in Dryden's "Song for St. Cecilia's Day" are necessary to express, as in page 67, line 30, the sensation roused by trumpet and drum; or, as in page 68, line 7, the feeling stirred by the soft, complaining flute. With Dryden and the other essentially classical poets the change of rhythm is formal and for a set purpose; the lyrics of this school therefore divide into sections, which vaguely resemble the movements of a sonata or symphony. In the romantic practice of Shelley, however, the changes are more subtle and seldom prepared for; the rhythm is more sensitive to veering moods, and accommodates itself to its subject like modern music, measure by measure, instead of prescribing the form its subject shall take. Line 16 of Shelley's famous verses "Written among the Euganean Hills" must, for example, be read by itself, not in the rhythm of the preceding lines; the effect is to express the sinking of the metaphorical ship:

> The tempest fleet
> Hurries on with lightning feet,
> Riving sail, and cord, and plank,
> Till the ship has almost drank
> Death from the o'er-brimming deep;
> And sínks dówn, dówn, líke that sléep
> When the dreamer seems to be
> Weltering through eternity.

Next after rhythm, time — the *tempo* of music — is the vehicle of lyric expression. It is an error to think of all verse or of all the lines in one poem as measured by fixed time beats. The first line of Burns's "To a Mouse" (p. 182) is appreciably slower than the second line or the third; and the stanzas of Gray's "On a Favorite Cat" (p. 148) may be compared with those of Wordsworth's "The Education of Nature" (p. 226), — the second generally slower in effect, full of musical *rallentandos*, although metrically the poems are alike. Like rhythm, the time may change with subtle variations, or more formally, as at the end of the introductions to "L'Allegro" (p. 124) and "Il Penseroso" (p. 128). The length of the syllable or the use of rests concerns the time of verse as vitally as the length of notes and rests concerns the tempo of music; without intelligence in these elementary divisions neither music nor verse can be read. Usually one can guess at the length of a syllable from its rhythmic or intellectual emphasis. In the line "Toll for the Brave" (p. 160) it is easy to see that the first word represents both a long and a short syllable, and the line has three beats, to correspond with the rhythm of the following lines:

> Tóll fór the Bráve!
>
> The bráve that áre no móre!

And in Coleridge's "Youth and Age" (p. 361), the reverberating words "young" and "old" at the end of lines 5, 22, and 43 occupy the attention that would elsewhere be given to half a line. But in line 3, page 68, of the "Song for St. Cecilia's Day" the effect of the stanza depends upon the correct reading of the twice-repeated "double." Unless these syllables represent very short notes, the well-defined rhythm is confused and there is no imitation of the drum roll:

> The trúmpet's loud clángor
>
> Excítes us to árms,
>
> With shríll notes of ánger
>
> And mórtal alárms.
>
> The dóuble double double béat
>
> Of the thúndering drúm
>
> Cries 'Hárk! The foes cóme;
>
> Chárge, chárge, 't is too láte to retréat!'

The third vehicle of lyric expression is tone, or what we often call in a loose way "musical quality." The same note played upon the piano and the flute and the violin has in each case a different appeal, which lies in the tone quality of the instrument. The melody would probably seem most appealing, most emotional, when played upon the violin, because that instrument has the most emotional tone. So the thought of a lyric stirs us to a greater degree when the very sound of the words is stirring. This word music depends upon the combination of vowels and consonants; the liquid consonants *l*, *m*, *n*, *r*, produce the most obvious effect of smoothness, as we see in many a haunting quotation:

> That last infirmity of noble mind. (p. 75, l. 22)
>
> He nothing common did or mean
> Upon that memorable scene. (p. 71, l. 17)
>
> From Harmony, from heavenly Harmony
> This universal frame began. (p. 67, l. 6)

The tone quality of a lyric is hard for some people to appreciate when the intellectual content of the poem is slight. Their problem is then much as if they were listening to pure music and trying to discover its "meaning." Marlowe's "Come live with me and be my Love" (p. 5) says very little intellectually; rhythmically, too, it is extremely simple; but the tone that distinguishes it from beginning to end, with a faultless consistency rare even in the best lyrics, has made it in some respects the most significant of Elizabethan songs — significant of the worship of ideal beauty and of the gift of music only at that time characteristic of the English race.

Because word rhythm and word melody are conveniently described in terms of music, some confusion is likely to result as to the relation between music and verse. The two arts, for practical purposes, are distinct, and cannot be confused without some loss to each or either. The fact that the lyric in Elizabeth's time was rich in melody and rhythm cannot be explained by the public ability at the time to play the lute, or the educated gentleman's ability to sing a part in a madrigal, any more than the frequent harshness of Browning's verse could be cited as proof that he was not an accomplished musician. We know, of course, that his skill in music was great; and that Tennyson, who excelled him in verse melody, knew nothing of music; and that Edward Fitz-Gerald, who translated "Omar" into liquid verse, was a musician. So all combinations of knowledge and ignorance in the two arts are possible, and there is no necessary relation. The speaking voice, for which poetry is composed, is essentially an instrument of percussion, like the piano, and its words must be uttered with a certain speed before they make their effect. Song or ordinary music is prolonged sound, and needs an instrument of sustained tone, like the singing voice or the organ. The old ballads were sung to tunes which now are forgotten, because the words were much more important. Yet the words show in certain rhythmic peculiarities that they were fitted to musical exigencies, as is the case with most of Shakespeare's songs, like "Come away, come away, Death" (p. 41). Had the words made no stronger appeal than the notes, they would not have found their way into this or any other anthology, but would have been preserved, if at all, as incidental to the music.

What music once accompanied the lyric is of little consequence to the young student. Of much greater importance is his ability to feel in the poem the expression of more than the words, — that approximation to the condition of music which is found in the rhythm, the time, and the tone. Oral readers of poetry may usually be classified according as they value the intellectual content of the verse, reducing it to prose, or the melody of it, turning it often into a chant. It is said that the great poets monotoned their lines in what might seem to be a singsong; so Tennyson, in particular, read. Whatever our taste in that matter, we should retain our grip on the one important truth that the lyric, above all other literature, is emotional; and we are not reading it wisely if it does not reach our emotions before it reaches our brain.

II

When a lyric is composed the process in the poet's mind is perhaps something like this: an emotion is aroused in him by some stimulus; that emotion possesses him until it begins to take a definite rhythm in his mind, as the photographic film is developed and takes form in the chemical bath; when the rhythm is unmistakable to his inner ear, the poet writes his lyric. To him the terms in the process are stimulus, emotion, and rhythm. To the reader, however, the poem must present itself in a different order. He perceives the rhythm first, and by the rhythm he is prepared for the emotion that produced it; by a solemn rhythm he is prepared for a solemn emotion; by a joyous rhythm he is prepared for joy. If the emotion is to be altogether intelligible, the reader must come at once upon some explanation of the stimulus; otherwise he cannot appropriate to himself imaginatively the poet's experience. Therefore the stimulus, in the average lyric, must be the second thing that the reader or hearer perceives. After the emotion has been felt and explained the lyric is occupied with developing it.

In the average successful lyric the stimulus is made clear in the opening lines. In Lovelace's "To Lucasta" (p. 94) it is evident that the lady has just accused the lover of unkindness, and the taunt has stirred him to this spirited defense. In the opening paragraph of "Lycidas" (p. 73) the occasion of the poet's grief is stated more elaborately; so the patriotic stimulus is announced at the beginning of Campbell's "Battle of the Baltic" (p. 255). The stimulus may be found in any human experience, — in conversation, as in Lovelace's song; in nature, as in Shelley's "Ode to the West Wind" (p. 353); or in art, as in Keats's "Ode on a Grecian Urn" (p. 360). In all these cases the reader is aware of the cause of the emotion in the poet, and it becomes the cause of emotion also in himself; it makes concrete and rational what would otherwise be only a vague atmosphere of feeling created by the rhythm.

The experience of an emotion, however, has sometimes other phenomena, which to the poet seem more important even than its stimulus. For example, he may find some aspect of nature in remarkable sympathy with an habitual emotional state of his, and that sympathy may appear to him of vastly more importance than the original cause of his mood. To express his mood he may then depend upon the rhythm and the context of the poem; he perhaps will not try to explain it. In the "Ode to a Nightingale" (p. 302) Keats tells us that he is extremely unhappy, and that the nightingale singing near by seems to be the very voice of his soul. The intention of the poem is to make us feel Keats's recognition of his own mood and aspirations in the nightingale. We know from other sources that the sorrow which beset him at the moment was the death of a favorite brother, but that fact is not important to the poem, and is therefore omitted. In Wordsworth's "The Daffodils" (p. 314) the poet's mood, before the daffodils have gladdened him, is peculiarly empty. He was walking alone, we are told, but whether he was sad or gay or just absent-minded, we are not told; it is not necessary to the poem.

Lyrics intended to be sung in drama often omit the stimulus altogether, because it is implied in the dramatic situation or explained in the character of the singer. Such lyrics of course would be unintelligible if we were not thoroughly familiar with the play; the two fairy songs from "The Tempest" (p. 2) would seem the most arrant nonsense if we did not know Ariel and the other characters in that most poetic drama; and what verdict would a fearless reader pass upon the famous "Tell me where is fancy bred" (p. 44), if he did not know of Portia's desperate craft to evade her father's command and hint to Bassanio the relative worth of the caskets?

Some very short poems are classed as lyrics which not only are narrative but seem at first to be absolutely without emotion, — poems like Scott's "Proud Maisie is in the wood" (p. 279), or Campbell's "Earl March look'd on his dying child" (p. 246). The fact is, this type of lyric consists of the expression of the stimulus rather than of the emotion it stimulates. The most important part of the lyric is in the feelings of the reader. To be sure, all art arouses emotion in the beholder or hearer, and to that extent all art is lyrical; but the apparent detachment of this kind of song, the impersonal manner that at first appears to be the very absence of feeling, is the actor's skill in making the spectator live the part. Success in this kind of lyric is rare, and the examples of it included in "The Golden Treasury," especially the selections from Scott, are among the most artistic lyrics in the language.

Important as the stimulus is in the inward structure of the lyric, the development of the emotion is usually, of course, the chief object of the poem. Any emotion is short-lived; it subsides gradually until the mind is reëstablished in a state of normal calm. Therefore the record of the development of emotion in the lyric must be brief, and it concerns itself with the reëstablishment of the intellect over the feelings. As the lyric progresses, the emotion is likely to run thin, and unless the poet has the taste to stop in time, the end of his song will be didactic or moralizing or narrative, — anything but lyrical. Our habitual ways of thought are matters of convention; we think correctly on the great subjects; therefore our cold-blooded pronouncements on those subjects differ from age to age, as the fashions change, and those cold-blooded conventions make their appearance at the end of the lyrics. In the least controlled part of the emotional experience, the immediate reaction to the stimulus, the poet reveals most of himself; yet, strange as it may seem, the lyric in that personal revelation changes least from century to century, from land to land; for men are of one blood in their genuine feelings, and they are estranged chiefly by artificial habits of thought. The sonnets of Shakespeare and the love songs of Burns have often the same stimulus, and where either speaks his true emotion he is contemporary to the other; they differ in the use to which they put their emotions and the way in which their natures recover their normal state.

The best illustration of this analysis of the lyric can be found in the funeral poem or elegy, which from the lament of Moschus over Bion has had a traditional career in the poetry of Europe and a very brilliant career in English poetry. This type of lyric, expressing grief for a dead friend, begins with a statement of the cause of the sorrow, — the stimulus of the emotion. As the grief subsides, those questions suggest themselves which are common to all human loss, — Why was this man taken and another left? or, Why should we strive for our ideals, if the accidents of life so cruelly defeat us? In the third section of the elegy the poet's habitual reason is again in control of his emotion, and he comforts himself in the conventions of his time and country. The first and second portions of the elegy in English are, for all the famous illustrations, practically the same; "Lycidas" (p. 73), in the opinion of many competent critics, is the noblest example of the English type. The third section, giving the consolation, is very individual in each elegy. Milton has hope of Christian immortality; Shelley, in "Adonais," has a glimpse of the immortality of beauty; Tennyson, in "In Memoriam," comforts himself with the general promise of evolution; Arnold, in "Thyrsis," turns to the prospect of a heroic culture. These resemblances and differences are as true of other kinds of lyric as of the elegy.

We could put the matter in a slightly different way by saying that the possible stimuli of the lyric are very few; there are few primary emotions, and few occasions in any one man's life when his feelings are deeply stirred. Therefore the originality of the lyric is to be sought not in the stimulus but in the character of the poet upon whom the stimulus acts. We read a love song by Burns and one by Byron, and the charming one, say, by Graham of Gartmore (p. 166). The stimulus in all three is the same, but the poems express Burns and Byron and Graham. Therefore it has been the fashion of recent decades to emphasize the subjective, personal note in the definition of the lyric, and at least so much truth is in the convention as is here indicated; the difficulty with the point of view is that to-day many other kinds of literature besides the lyric are subjective.

An emotion, a mere feeling, is the most fleeting of human experiences, no matter how permanent its effect. The lyric poets instinctively try to give their emotions a kind of immortality in the close of the song. Their methods are infinite in variety; it is important only to be aware of the attempt and to match the instinct in our own feelings. In his poem to "The Highland Girl" (p. 308) Wordsworth ends with the imperishable landscape picture which is his memory of the incident; in "The Reaper" (p.310) he bears a song in his heart just as imperishably; Burns creates a similar immortality for his "Highland Mary," and Keats in his great odes closes upon a general truth or a state of mind which justly immortalizes our experience of the poem. It is this passion of all artists — and most of the lyric poets — to make permanent a beauty that is learned only in its vanishing, which Shelley expresses in the little song aptly set at the end of this anthology:

> Music, when soft voices die,
> Vibrates in the memory —
> Odors, when sweet violets sicken,
> Live within the sense they quicken.
>
> Rose leaves, when the rose is dead,
> Are heap'd for the beloved's bed;
> And so thy thoughts, when Thou art gone,
> Love itself shall slumber on.

TO

ALFRED TENNYSON

POET LAUREATE

This book in its progress has recalled often to my memory a man with whose friendship we were once honored, to whom no region of English literature was unfamiliar, and who, whilst rich in all the noble gifts of nature, was most eminently distinguished by the noblest and the rarest, — just judgment and high-hearted patriotism. It would have been hence a peculiar pleasure and pride to dedicate what I have endeavored to make a true national anthology of three centuries to Henry Hallam.[1] But he is beyond the reach of any human tokens of love and reverence; and I desire therefore to place before it a name united with his by associations which, while poetry retains her hold on the minds of Englishmen, are not likely to be forgotten.

Your encouragement, given while traversing the wild scenery of Treryn Dinas,[2] led me to begin the work, and it has been completed under your advice and assistance. For the favor now asked I have thus a second reason; and to this I may add the homage which is your right as poet, and the gratitude due to a friend, whose regard I rate at no common value.

Permit me then to inscribe to yourself a book which, I hope, may be found by many a lifelong fountain of innocent and exalted pleasure; a source of animation to friends when they meet; and able to sweeten solitude itself with best society, — with the companionship of the wise

1 The well-known English historian (1777–1859), author of "View of the State of Europe during the Middle Ages," "Constitutional History of England," "Introduction to the Literature of Europe in the 15th, 16th, and 17th Centuries," and father of Arthur Hallam, the subject of Tennyson's "In Memoriam."

2 On the west coast of Cornwall.

and the good, with the beauty which the eye cannot see, and the music only heard in silence. If this collection proves a storehouse of delight to labor and to poverty, if it teaches those indifferent to the poets to love them, and those who love them to love them more, the aim and the desire entertained in framing it will be fully accomplished.

F. T. P.

May, 1861

PREFACE

This little collection differs, it is believed, from others in the attempt made to include in it all the best original lyrical pieces and songs in our language (save a very few regretfully omitted on account of length), by writers not living, — and none besides the best. Many familiar verses will hence be met with; many also which should be familiar. The editor will regard as his fittest readers those who love poetry so well that he can offer them nothing not already known and valued.

The editor is acquainted with no strict and exhaustive definition of lyrical poetry; but he has found the task of practical decision increase in clearness and in facility as he advanced with the work, whilst keeping in view a few simple principles. "Lyrical" has been here held essentially to imply that each poem shall turn on some single thought, feeling, or situation. In accordance with this, narrative, descriptive, and didactic poems — unless accompanied by rapidity of movement, brevity, and the coloring of human passion — have been excluded. Humorous poetry, except in the very unfrequent instances where a truly poetical tone pervades the whole, with what is strictly personal, occasional, and religious, has been considered foreign to the idea of the book. Blank verse and the ten-syllable couplet, with all pieces markedly dramatic, have been rejected as alien from what is commonly understood by "song," and rarely conforming to lyrical conditions in treatment. But it is not anticipated, nor is it possible, that all readers shall think the line accurately drawn. Some poems, as Gray's "Elegy," the "Allegro" and "Penseroso," Wordsworth's "Ruth" or Campbell's "Lord Ullin," might be claimed with perhaps equal justice for a narrative or descriptive selection; whilst with reference especially to ballads and sonnets, the editor can only state that he has taken his utmost pains to decide without caprice or partiality.

This also is all he can plead in regard to a point even more liable to question, — What degree of merit should give rank among the best. That a poem shall be worthy of the writer's genius; that it shall reach a perfection commensurate with its aim; that we should require finish in proportion to brevity; that passion, color, and originality cannot atone for serious imperfections in clearness, unity, or truth; that a few good lines do not make a good poem; that popular estimate is serviceable as a guidepost more than as a compass; above all, that excellence should be looked for rather in the whole than in the parts, — such and other such canons have been always steadily regarded. He may, however, add that the pieces chosen, and a far larger number rejected, have been carefully and repeatedly considered; and that he has been aided throughout by two friends of independent and exercised judgment, besides the distinguished person addressed in the Dedication. It is hoped that by this procedure the volume has been freed from that one-sidedness which must beset individual decisions; but for the final choice the editor is alone responsible.

Chalmers's vast collection,[1] with the whole works of all accessible poets not contained in it, and the best anthologies of different periods, have been twice systematically read through; and it is hence improbable that any omissions which may be regretted are due to oversight. The poems are printed entire, except in a very few instances where a stanza or passage has been omitted. These omissions have been risked only when the piece could be thus brought to a closer lyrical unity; and, as essentially opposed to this unity, extracts, obviously such, are excluded. In regard to the text, the purpose of the book has appeared to justify the choice of the most poetical version, wherever more than one exists; and much labor has been given to present each poem, in disposition, spelling, and punctuation, to the greatest advantage.

In the arrangement the most poetically effective order has been attempted. The English mind has passed through phases of thought and cultivation so various and so opposed during these three centuries

[1] Alexander Chalmers (1759–1834) collected the works of a large number of British poets in twenty-one volumes, published in 1810.

of poetry, that a rapid passage between old and new, like rapid alteration of the eye's focus in looking at the landscape, will always be wearisome and hurtful to the sense of beauty. The poems have been therefore distributed into books corresponding, I, to the ninety years closing about 1616; II, thence to 1700; III, to 1800; IV, to the half century just ended. Or, looking at the poets who more or less give each portion its distinctive character, they might be called the books of Shakespeare, Milton, Gray, and Wordsworth. The volume in this respect, so far as the limitations of its range allow, accurately reflects the natural growth and evolution of our poetry. A rigidly chronological sequence, however, rather fits a collection aiming at instruction than at pleasure, and the wisdom which comes through pleasure; within each book the pieces have therefore been arranged in gradations of feeling or subject. And it is hoped that the contents of this Anthology will thus be found to present a certain unity, "as episodes," in the noble language of Shelley, "to that great poem which all poets, like the coöperating thoughts of one great mind, have built up since the beginning of the world." [1]

As he closes his long survey the editor trusts he may add without egotism that he has found the vague general verdict of popular fame more just than those have thought, who, with too severe a criticism, would confine judgments on poetry to "the selected few of many generations." Not many appear to have gained reputation without some gift or performance that, in due degree, deserved it; and if no verses by certain writers who show less strength than sweetness, or more thought than mastery of expression, are printed in this volume, it should not be imagined that they have been excluded without much hesitation and regret, — far less that they have been slighted. Throughout this vast and pathetic array of singers now silent, few have been honored with the name poet, and have not possessed a skill in words, a sympathy with beauty, a tenderness of feeling, or seriousness in reflection, which render their works — although never perhaps attaining that loftier and finer excellence here required — better worth reading than much of what fills the scanty hours that

[1] From "A Defense of Poetry," by the English lyrical poet Percy Bysshe Shelley. See A. S. Cook's edition (Ginn and Company), p. 23.

most men spare for self-improvement, or for pleasure in any of its more elevated and permanent forms. And if this be true of even mediocre poetry, for how much more are we indebted to the best! Like the fabled fountain of the Azores,[1] but with a more various power, the magic of this art can confer on each period of life its appropriate blessing: on early years, experience; on maturity, calm; on age, youthfulness. Poetry gives treasures "more golden than gold," leading us in higher and healthier ways than those of the world, and interpreting to us the lessons of nature. But she speaks best for herself. Her true accents, if the plan has been executed with success, may be heard throughout the following pages; wherever the poets of England are honored, wherever the dominant language of the world is spoken, it is hoped that they will find fit audience.

1861

Some poems, especially in Book I, have been added, — either on better acquaintance, in deference to critical suggestions, or unknown to the editor when first gathering his harvest. For aid in these after-gleanings he is specially indebted to the excellent reprints of rare early verse given us by Dr. Hannah, Dr. Grosart, Mr. Arber, Mr. Bullen,[2] and others; and (in regard to the additions of 1883) to the advice of that distinguished friend, by whom the final choice has been so largely guided.[3] The text has also been carefully revised from authoritative sources. It has still seemed best, for many reasons, to retain the original limit by which the selection was confined to those then no longer living. But the editor hopes that, so far as in him lies, a complete and definitive collection of our best lyrics, to the central year of this fast-closing century, is now offered.

1883–1890–1891 [PALGRAVE]

[1] The editors have been unable to locate this reference.

[2] Noted English scholars and anthologists, the first two of whom died before 1911.

[3] Lord Tennyson.

Εἰς τὸν λειμῶνα καθίσας,
ἔδρεπεν ἕτερον ἐφ' ἑτέρῳ
αἰρόμενος ἄγρευμ' ἀνθέων
ἁδομένᾳ ψυχᾷ ——

Sitting in the meadow he gathered spoil of flowers,
plucking one after another, with happy heart.

Euripides, Fragment 754

THE GOLDEN TREASURY

BOOK FIRST

The Elizabethan poetry, as it is rather vaguely termed, forms the substance of this Book, which contains pieces from Wyat, under Henry VIII, to Shakespeare midway through the reign of James I, and Drummond, who carried on the early manner to a still later period. There is here a wide range of style,—from simplicity expressed in a language hardly yet broken-in to verse, through the pastoral fancies and Italian conceits of the strictly Elizabethan time, to the passionate reality of Shakespeare; yet a general uniformity of tone prevails. Few readers can fail to observe the natural sweetness of the verse, the single-hearted straightforwardness of the thoughts; nor less, the limitation of subject to the many phases of one passion, which then characterized our lyrical poetry, unless when, as in especial with Shakespeare, the "purple light of love"[1] is tempered by a spirit of sterner reflection. For the didactic verse of the century, although lyrical in form, yet very rarely rises to the pervading emotion, the golden cadence, proper to the lyric.

It should be observed that this and the following summaries apply in the main to the collection here presented, in which (besides its restriction to lyrical poetry) a strictly representative or historical anthology has not been aimed at. Great excellence, in human art as in human character, has from the beginning of things been even more uniform than mediocrity, by virtue of the closeness of its approach to nature; and so far as the standard of excellence kept in view has been attained in this volume, a comparative absence of extreme contemporary phases in style, a similarity of tone and manner, will be found throughout,—something neither modern nor ancient, but true and speaking to the heart of man alike throughout all ages.—*Transferred from Palgrave's Notes.*

I

SPRING

Spring, the sweet Spring, is the year's pleasant king;
Then blooms each thing, then maids dance in a ring,
Cold doth not sting, the pretty birds do sing,
  Cuckoo, jug-jug, pu-we, to-witta-woo!

[1] For this phrase see *infra*, p. 171, Gray's "Progress of Poesy."

The palm and may make country houses gay,
Lambs frisk and play, the shepherds pipe all day,
And we hear aye birds tune this merry lay,
Cuckoo, jug-jug, pu-we, to-witta-woo.

The fields breathe sweet, the daisies kiss our feet, 5
Young lovers meet, old wives a-sunning sit,
In every street these tunes our ears do greet,
Cuckoo, jug-jug, pu-we, to-witta-woo!
Spring! the sweet Spring!

T. Nash

II

THE FAIRY LIFE

I

Where the bee sucks, there suck I: 10
In a cowslip's bell I lie;
There I couch, when owls do cry:
On the bat's back I do fly
After summer merrily.
Merrily, merrily, shall I live now, 15
Under the blossom that hangs on the bough!

III

2

Come unto these yellow sands,
And then take hands:
Courtsied when you have, and kiss'd
The wild waves whist, 20
Foot it featly here and there;
And, sweet Sprites, the burthen bear.
Hark, hark!
Bow-bow.
The watch-dogs bark: 25
Bow-wow.

Hark, hark! I hear
The strain of strutting chanticleer
Cry, Cock-a-diddle-dow!

W. Shakespeare

IV

SUMMONS TO LOVE

Phœbus, arise!
And paint the sable skies 5
With azure, white, and red:
Rouse Memnon's mother from her Tithon's bed
That she may thy career with roses spread:
The nightingales thy coming each-where sing:
Make an eternal Spring! 10
Give life to this dark world which lieth dead;
Spread forth thy golden hair
In larger locks than thou wast wont before,
And emperor-like decore
With diadem of pearl thy temples fair: 15
Chase hence the ugly night
Which serves but to make dear thy glorious light.

— This is that happy morn,
That day, long-wishéd day
Of all my life so dark, 20
(If cruel stars have not my ruin sworn
And fates my hopes betray),
Which, purely white, deserves
An everlasting diamond should it mark.
This is the morn should bring unto this grove 25
My Love, to hear and recompense my love.
Fair King, who all preserves,
But show thy blushing beams,
And thou two sweeter eyes
Shalt see than those which by Penéus' streams 30
Did once thy heart surprise.

Now, Flora, deck thyself in fairest guise:
If that ye winds would hear
A voice surpassing far Amphion's lyre,
Your furious chiding stay;
Let Zephyr only breathe, 5
And with her tresses play.
— The winds all silent are,
And Phœbus in his chair
Ensaffroning sea and air
Makes vanish every star: 10
Night like a drunkard reels
Beyond the hills, to shun his flaming wheels:
The fields with flowers are deck'd in every hue,
The clouds with orient gold spangle their blue;
Here is the pleasant place — 15
And nothing wanting is, save She, alas!

W. Drummond
of Hawthornden

V

TIME AND LOVE

I

When I have seen by Time's fell hand defaced
The rich proud cost of outworn buried age;
When sometime lofty towers I see down-razed,
And brass eternal slave to mortal rage; 20

When I have seen the hungry ocean gain
Advantage on the kingdom of the shore,
And the firm soil win of the watery main,
Increasing store with loss, and loss with store;

When I have seen such interchange of state, 25
Or state itself confounded to decay,
Ruin hath taught me thus to ruminate —
That Time will come and take my Love away:

This thought is as a death, which cannot choose
But weep to have that which it fears to lose.

W. Shakespeare

VI

2

Since brass, nor stone, nor earth, nor boundless sea,
But sad mortality o'ersways their power,
How with this rage shall beauty hold a plea, 5
Whose action is no stronger than a flower?

O how shall summer's honey breath hold out
Against the wreckful siege of battering days,
When rocks impregnable are not so stout
Nor gates of steel so strong, but time decays? 10

O fearful meditation! where, alack!
Shall Time's best jewel from Time's chest lie hid?
Or what strong hand can hold his swift foot back,
Or who his spoil of beauty can forbid?

O! none, unless this miracle have might, 15
That in black ink my love may still shine bright.

W. Shakespeare

VII

THE PASSIONATE SHEPHERD TO HIS LOVE

Come live with me and be my Love,
And we will all the pleasures prove
That hills and valleys, dale and field,
And all the craggy mountains yield. 20

There will we sit upon the rocks
And see the shepherds feed their flocks,
By shallow rivers, to whose falls
Melodious birds sing madrigals.

There will I make thee beds of roses 25
And a thousand fragrant posies,

A cap of flowers, and a kirtle
Embroider'd all with leaves of myrtle.

A gown made of the finest wool,
Which from our pretty lambs we pull,
Fair linéd slippers for the cold, 5
With buckles of the purest gold.

A belt of straw and ivy buds
With coral clasps and amber studs:
And if these pleasures may thee move,
Come live with me and be my Love. 10

Thy silver dishes for thy meat
As precious as the gods do eat,
Shall on an ivory table be
Prepared each day for thee and me.

The shepherd swains shall dance and sing 15
For thy delight each May-morning:
If these delights thy mind may move,
Then live with me and be my Love.

C. Marlowe

VIII

OMNIA VINCIT[1]

Fain would I change that note
To which fond Love hath charm'd me 20
Long long to sing by rote,
Fancying that that harm'd me:
Yet when this thought doth come
"Love is the perfect sum
    Of all delight," 25
I have no other choice
Either for pen or voice
    To sing or write.

1 From a Jacobean songbook, Tobias Hume's "The First Part of Airs French, Polish, and others together," 1605.

O Love! they wrong thee much
That say thy sweet is bitter,
When thy rich fruit is such
As nothing can be sweeter.
Fair house of joy and bliss, 5
Where truest pleasure is,
    I do adore thee:
I know thee what thou art,
I serve thee with my heart,
    And fall before thee! 10

Anon.

IX

A MADRIGAL

Crabbed Age and Youth
Cannot live together:
Youth is full of pleasance,
Age is full of care;
Youth like summer morn, 15
Age like winter weather,
Youth like summer brave,
Age like winter bare:
Youth is full of sport,
Age's breath is short, 20
Youth is nimble, Age is lame:
Youth is hot and bold,
Age is weak and cold,
Youth is wild, and Age is tame:—
Age, I do abhor thee, 25
Youth, I do adore thee;
O! my Love, my Love is young!
Age, I do defy thee—
O sweet shepherd, hie thee,
For methinks thou stay'st too long. 30

W. Shakespeare

X

Under the greenwood tree
Who loves to lie with me,
And turn his merry note
Unto the sweet bird's throat—
Come hither, come hither, come hither! 5
Here shall he see
No enemy
But winter and rough weather.

Who doth ambition shun
And loves to live i' the sun, 10
Seeking the food he eats
And pleased with what he gets—
Come hither, come hither, come hither!
Here shall he see
No enemy 15
But winter and rough weather.

W. Shakespeare

XI

It was a lover and his lass
With a hey and a ho, and a hey nonino!
That o'er the green cornfield did pass
In the springtime, the only pretty ring time, 20
When birds do sing hey ding a ding:
Sweet lovers love the Spring.

Between the acres of the rye
These pretty country folks would lie:
This carol they began that hour, 25
How that life was but a flower:

And therefore take the present time
With a hey and a ho and a hey nonino!
For love is crownéd with the prime
In springtime, the only pretty ring time, 30

When birds do sing hey ding a ding:
  Sweet lovers love the Spring.

W. Shakespeare

XII

PRESENT IN ABSENCE

Absence, hear thou this protestation
    Against thy strength,
    Distance, and length; 5
Do what thou canst for alteration:
  For hearts of truest mettle
Absence doth join, and Time doth settle.

Who loves a mistress of such quality,
    His mind hath found 10
    Affection's ground
Beyond time, place, and mortality.
  To hearts that cannot vary
Absence is present, Time doth tarry.

By absence this good means I gain, 15
    That I can catch her,
    Where none can match her,
In some close corner of my brain:
  There I embrace and kiss her;
And so I both enjoy and miss her. 20

J. Donne

XIII

VIA AMORIS

Highway, since you my chief Parnassus be,
And that my Muse, to some ears not unsweet,
Tempers her words to trampling horses' feet
More oft than to a chamber melody,—

Now, blessèd you bear onward blessèd me 25
To her, where I my heart, safe-left, shall meet;

My Muse and I must you of duty greet
With thanks and wishes, wishing thankfully;

Be you still fair, honor'd by public heed;
By no encroachment wrong'd, nor time forgot;
Nor blamed for blood, nor shamed for sinful deed; 5
And that you know I envy you no lot

Of highest wish, I wish you so much bliss, —
Hundreds of years you Stella's feet may kiss!

Sir P. Sidney

XIV

ABSENCE

Being your slave, what should I do but tend
Upon the hours and times of your desire? 10
I have no precious time at all to spend
Nor services to do, till you require:

Nor dare I chide the world-without-end hour
Whilst I, my sovereign, watch the clock for you,
Nor think the bitterness of absence sour 15
When you have bid your servant once adieu:

Nor dare I question with my jealous thought
Where you may be, or your affairs suppose,
But like a sad slave, stay and think of nought
Save, where you are, how happy you make those; — 20

So true a fool is love, that in your will
Though you do anything, he thinks no ill.

W. Shakespeare

XV

How like a winter hath my absence been
From Thee, the pleasure of the fleeting year!
What freezings have I felt, what dark days seen, 25
What old December's bareness everywhere!

And yet this time removed was summer's time:
The teeming autumn, big with rich increase,
Bearing the wanton burden of the prime
Like widow'd wombs after their lords' decease:

Yet this abundant issue seem'd to me 5
But hope of orphans, and unfather'd fruit;
For summer and his pleasures wait on thee,
And, thou away, the very birds are mute;

Or if they sing, 't is with so dull a cheer,
That leaves look pale, dreading the winter 's near. 10

W. Shakespeare

XVI

A CONSOLATION

When in disgrace with fortune and men's eyes
I all alone beweep my outcast state,
And trouble deaf heaven with my bootless cries,
And look upon myself, and curse my fate;

Wishing me like to one more rich in hope, 15
Featured like him, like him with friends possest,
Desiring this man's art, and that man's scope,
With what I most enjoy contented least;

Yet in these thoughts myself almost despising,
Haply I think on Thee — and then my state, 20
Like to the lark at break of day arising
From sullen earth, sings hymns at heaven's gate;

For thy sweet love remember'd, such wealth brings
That then I scorn to change my state with kings.

W. Shakespeare

XVII

THE UNCHANGEABLE

O never say that I was false of heart,
Though absence seem'd my flame to qualify:
As easy might I from myself depart
As from my soul, which in thy breast doth lie;

That is my home of love; if I have ranged, 5
Like him that travels, I return again,
Just to the time, not with the time exchanged,
So that myself bring water for my stain.

Never believe, though in my nature reign'd
All frailties that besiege all kinds of blood, 10
That it could so preposterously be stain'd
To leave for nothing all thy sum of good:

For nothing this wide universe I call,
Save thou, my rose: in it thou art my all.

W. Shakespeare

XVIII

To me, fair Friend, you never can be old, 15
For as you were when first your eye I eyed
Such seems your beauty still. Three winters cold
Have from the forests shook three summers' pride;

Three beauteous springs to yellow autumn turn'd
In process of the seasons have I seen, 20
Three April perfumes in three hot Junes burn'd,
Since first I saw you fresh, which yet are green.

Ah! yet doth beauty, like a dial hand,
Steal from his figure, and no pace perceived;
So your sweet hue, which methinks still doth stand, 25
Hath motion, and mine eye may be deceived:

For fear of which, hear this, thou age unbred,—
Ere you were born, was beauty's summer dead.

W. Shakespeare

XIX

ROSALINE

Like to the clear in highest sphere
Where all imperial glory shines,
Of selfsame color is her hair
Whether unfolded, or in twines:
  Heigh ho, fair Rosaline! 5
Her eyes are sapphires set in snow,
Resembling heaven by every wink;
The Gods do fear whenas they glow,
And I do tremble when I think
  Heigh ho, would she were mine! 10

Her cheeks are like the blushing cloud
That beautifies Aurora's face,
Or like the silver crimson shroud
That Phœbus' smiling looks doth grace;
  Heigh ho, fair Rosaline! 15
Her lips are like two budded roses
Whom ranks of lilies neighbor nigh,
Within which bounds she balm encloses
Apt to entice a deity:
  Heigh ho, would she were mine! 20

Her neck is like a stately tower
Where Love himself imprison'd lies,
To watch for glances every hour
From her divine and sacred eyes:
  Heigh ho, for Rosaline! 25
Her paps are centers of delight,
Her breasts are orbs of heavenly frame,
Where Nature molds the dew of light
To feed perfection with the same:
  Heigh ho, would she were mine! 30

With orient pearl, with ruby red,
With marble white, with sapphire blue

Her body every way is fed,
Yet soft in touch and sweet in view:
  Heigh ho, fair Rosaline!
Nature herself her shape admires;
The Gods are wounded in her sight; 5
And Love forsakes his heavenly fires
And at her eyes his brand doth light:
  Heigh ho, would she were mine!

Then muse not, Nymphs, though I bemoan
The absence of fair Rosaline, 10
Since for a fair there 's fairer none,
Nor for her virtues so divine:
  Heigh ho, fair Rosaline!
Heigh ho, my heart! would God that she were mine!

T. Lodge

XX

COLIN

Beauty sat bathing by a spring 15
  Where fairest shades did hide her;
The winds blew calm, the birds did sing,
  The cool streams ran beside her.
My wanton thoughts enticed mine eye
  To see what was forbidden: 20
But better memory said, fie!
  So vain desire was chidden:—
      Hey nonny nonny O!
      Hey nonny nonny!

Into a slumber then I fell, 25
  When fond imagination
Seeméd to see, but could not tell
  Her feature or her fashion.
But ev'n as babes in dreams do smile,
  And sometimes fall a-weeping, 30

So I awaked, as wise this while
  As when I fell a-sleeping:—
      Hey nonny nonny O!
      Hey nonny nonny!

The Shepherd Tonie

XXI

A PICTURE[1]

Sweet Love, if thou wilt gain a monarch's glory, 5
Subdue her heart, who makes me glad and sorry:
  Out of thy golden quiver
  Take thou thy strongest arrow
  That will through bone and marrow,
And me and thee of grief and fear deliver:— 10
But come behind, for if she look upon thee,
Alas! poor Love! then thou art woe-begone thee!

Anon.

XXII

A SONG FOR MUSIC[2]

Weep you no more, sad fountains:—
  What need you flow so fast?
Look how the snowy mountains 15
  Heaven's sun doth gently waste!
    But my Sun's heavenly eyes
      View not your weeping,
      That now lies sleeping
  Softly, now softly lies, 20
        Sleeping.

Sleep is a reconciling,
  A rest that peace begets:—
Doth not the sun rise smiling,
  When fair at even he sets? 25

[1] From John Wilbye's "First Set of English Madrigals," 1598.
[2] From John Dowland's "Third and Last Book of Songs or Airs," 1603.

— Rest you, then, rest, sad eyes!
Melt not in weeping!
While She lies sleeping
Softly, now softly lies,
Sleeping! 5

Anon.

XXIII

TO HIS LOVE

Shall I compare thee to a summer's day?
Thou art more lovely and more temperate:
Rough winds do shake the darling buds of May,
And summer's lease hath all too short a date:

Sometime too hot the eye of heaven shines, 10
And often is his gold complexion dimm'd:
And every fair from fair sometime declines,
By chance, or nature's changing course, untrimm'd.

But thy eternal summer shall not fade
Nor lose possession of that fair thou owest; 15
Nor shall Death brag thou wanderest in his shade,
When in eternal lines to time thou growest:—

So long as men can breathe, or eyes can see,
So long lives this, and this gives life to thee.

W. Shakespeare

XXIV

TO HIS LOVE

When in the chronicle of wasted time 20
I see descriptions of the fairest wights,
And beauty making beautiful old rhyme
In praise of ladies dead, and lovely knights;

Then in the blazon of sweet beauty's best
Of hand, of foot, of lip, of eye, of brow, 25

I see their antique pen would have exprest
Ev'n such a beauty as you master now.

So all their praises are but prophecies
Of this our time, all, you prefiguring;
And for they look'd but with divining eyes, 5
They had not skill enough your worth to sing:

For we, which now behold these present days,
Have eyes to wonder, but lack tongues to praise.

W. Shakespeare

XXV

BASIA

Turn back, you wanton flyer,
And answer my desire 10
With mutual greeting.
Yet bend a little nearer, —
True beauty still shines clearer
In closer meeting!
Hearts with hearts delighted 15
Should strive to be united,
Each other's arms with arms enchaining, —
Hearts with a thought,
Rosy lips with a kiss still entertaining.

What harvest half so sweet is 20
As still to reap the kisses
Grown ripe in sowing?
And straight to be receiver
Of that which thou art giver,
Rich in bestowing? 25
There is no strict observing
Of times' or seasons' swerving,
There is ever one fresh spring abiding; —
Then what we sow with our lips
Let us reap, love's gains dividing. 30

T. Campion

XXVI

ADVICE TO A GIRL

Never love unless you can
Bear with all the faults of man!
Men sometimes will jealous be
Though but little cause they see,
And hang the head as discontent, 5
And speak what straight they will repent.

Men, that but one Saint adore,
Make a show of love to more;
Beauty must be scorn'd in none,
Though but truly served in one: 10
For what is courtship but disguise?
True hearts may have dissembling eyes.

Men, when their affairs require,
Must awhile themselves retire;
Sometimes hunt, and sometimes hawk, 15
And not ever sit and talk:—
If these and such-like you can bear,
Then like, and love, and never fear!

T. Campion

XXVII

LOVE'S PERJURIES

On a day, alack the day!
Love, whose month is ever May, 20
Spied a blossom passing fair
Playing in the wanton air:
Through the velvet leaves the wind,
All unseen, 'gan passage find;
That the lover, sick to death, 25
Wish'd himself the heaven's breath.
Air, quoth he, thy cheeks may blow;
Air, would I might triumph so!

But, alack, my hand is sworn
Ne'er to pluck thee from thy thorn:
Vow, alack, for youth unmeet;
Youth so apt to pluck a sweet.
Do not call it sin in me 5
That I am forsworn for thee:
Thou for whom Jove would swear
Juno but an Ethiope were,
And deny himself for Jove,
Turning mortal for thy love. 10

W. Shakespeare

XXVIII

A SUPPLICATION

Forget not yet the tried intent
Of such a truth as I have meant;
My great travail so gladly spent,
Forget not yet!

Forget not yet when first began 15
The weary life ye know, since whan
The suit, the service none tell can;
Forget not yet!

Forget not yet the great assays,
The cruel wrong, the scornful ways, 20
The painful patience in delays,
Forget not yet!

Forget not! O, forget not this,
How long ago hath been, and is
The mind that never meant amiss — 25
Forget not yet!

Forget not then thine own approved
The which so long hath thee so loved,
Whose steadfast faith yet never moved —
Forget not this! 30

Sir T. Wyat

XXIX

TO AURORA

O if thou knew'st how thou thyself dost harm,
And dost prejudge thy bliss, and spoil my rest;
Then thou would'st melt the ice out of thy breast
And thy relenting heart would kindly warm.

O if thy pride did not our joys control, 5
What world of loving wonders should'st thou see!
For if I saw thee once transform'd in me,
Then in thy bosom I would pour my soul;

Then all my thoughts should in thy visage shine,
And if that aught mischanced thou should'st not moan 10
Nor bear the burden of thy griefs alone;
No, I would have my share in what were thine:

And whilst we thus should make our sorrows one,
This happy harmony would make them none.

W. Alexander,
Earl of Sterline

XXX

IN LACRIMAS[1]

I saw my Lady weep, 15
And Sorrow proud to be advancéd so
In those fair eyes where all perfections keep.
Her face was full of woe,
But such a woe (believe me) as wins more hearts
Than Mirth can do with her enticing parts. 20

Sorrow was there made fair,
And Passion, wise; Tears, a delightful thing;
Silence, beyond all speech, a wisdom rare:
She made her sighs to sing,
And all things with so sweet a sadness move 25
As made my heart at once both grieve and love.

[1] From John Dowland's "Second Book of Songs or Airs," 1600.

O fairer than aught else
The world can show, leave off in time to grieve!
Enough, enough: your joyful look excels:
Tears kill the heart, believe.
O strive not to be excellent in woe, 5
Which only breeds your beauty's overthrow.

Anon.

XXXI

TRUE LOVE

Let me not to the marriage of true minds
Admit impediments. Love is not love
Which alters when it alteration finds,
Or bends with the remover to remove:— 10

O no! it is an ever-fixéd mark
That looks on tempests, and is never shaken;
It is the star to every wandering bark,
Whose worth 's unknown, although his height be taken.

Love 's not Time's fool, though rosy lips and cheeks 15
Within his bending sickle's compass come;
Love alters not with his brief hours and weeks,
But bears it out ev'n to the edge of doom:—

If this be error, and upon me proved,
I never writ, nor no man ever loved. 20

W. Shakespeare

XXXII

A DITTY

My true-love hath my heart, and I have his,
By just exchange one for another given:
I hold his dear, and mine he cannot miss,
There never was a better bargain driven:
My true-love hath my heart, and I have his. 25

His heart in me keeps him and me in one,
My heart in him his thoughts and senses guides:
He loves my heart, for once it was his own,
I cherish his because in me it bides:
My true-love hath my heart, and I have his. 5

Sir P. Sidney

XXXIII

LOVE'S INSIGHT[1]

Though others may Her brow adore
Yet more must I, that therein see far more
Than any other's eyes have power to see:
She is to me
More than to any others she can be! 10
I can discern more secret notes
That in the margin of her cheeks Love quotes,
Than any else besides have art to read:
No looks proceed
From those fair eyes but to me wonder breed. 15

Anon.

XXXIV

LOVE'S OMNIPRESENCE

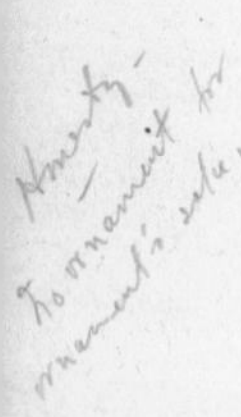

Were I as base as is the lowly plain,
And you, my Love, as high as heaven above,
Yet should the thoughts of me your humble swain
Ascend to heaven, in honor of my Love.

Were I as high as heaven above the plain, 20
And you, my Love, as humble and as low
As are the deepest bottoms of the main,
Whereso'er you were, with you my love should go.

[1] From John Daniel's "Songs for the Lute, Viol, & Voice," 1606. This is a portion of a song beginning, "Let not Chloris think, because She hath envassel'd me." John Daniel was the brother of Samuel Daniel, and it is not impossible that the latter wrote these lines.

Were you the earth, dear Love, and I the skies,
My love should shine on you like to the sun,
And look upon you with ten thousand eyes
Till heaven wax'd blind, and till the world were done.

Whereso'er I am, below, or else above you, 5
Whereso'er you are, my heart shall truly love you.

J. Sylvester

XXXV

CARPE DIEM

O Mistress mine, where are you roaming?
O stay and hear! your true-love 's coming
That can sing both high and low;
Trip no further, pretty sweeting, 10
Journeys end in lovers meeting —
Every wise man's son doth know.

What is love? 't is not hereafter;
Present mirth hath present laughter;
What 's to come is still unsure: 15
In delay there lies no plenty, —
Then come kiss me, Sweet-and-twenty,
Youth 's a stuff will not endure.

W. Shakespeare

XXXVI

AN HONEST AUTOLYCUS[1]

Fine knacks for ladies, cheap, choice, brave, and new,
Good pennyworths, — but money cannot move: 20
I keep a fair but for the Fair to view;
A beggar may be liberal of love.
Though all my wares be trash, the heart is true —
The heart is true.

[1] From John Dowland's "Second Book of Songs or Airs," 1600.

Great gifts are guiles and look for gifts again;
My trifles come as treasures from my mind;
It is a precious jewel to be plain;
Sometimes in shell the orient'st pearls we find;—
Of others take a sheaf, of me a grain! 5
Of me a grain!

Anon.

XXXVII

WINTER

When icicles hang by the wall
And Dick the shepherd blows his nail,
And Tom bears logs into the hall,
And milk comes frozen home in pail; 10
When blood is nipt, and ways be foul,
Then nightly sings the staring owl
Tu-whit!
To-who! A merry note!
While greasy Joan doth keel the pot. 15

When all about the wind doth blow,
And coughing drowns the parson's saw,
And birds sit brooding in the snow,
And Marian's nose looks red and raw;
When roasted crabs hiss in the bowl— 20
Then nightly sings the staring owl
Tu-whit!
To-who! A merry note!
While greasy Joan doth keel the pot.

W. Shakespeare

XXXVIII

That time of year thou may'st in me behold 25
When yellow leaves, or none, or few, do hang
Upon those boughs which shake against the cold,
Bare ruin'd choirs, where late the sweet birds sang:

In me thou see'st the twilight of such day
As after sunset fadeth in the west,
Which by and by black night doth take away,
Death's second self, that seals up all in rest:

In me thou see'st the glowing of such fire, 5
That on the ashes of his youth doth lie
As the deathbed whereon it must expire,
Consumed with that which it was nourish'd by:

— This thou perceiv'st, which makes thy love more strong,
To love that well which thou must leave ere long. 10

W. Shakespeare

XXXIX

MEMORY

When to the sessions of sweet silent thought
I summon up remembrance of things past,
I sigh the lack of many a thing I sought,
And with old woes new wail my dear time's waste;

Then can I drown an eye, unused to flow, 15
For precious friends hid in death's dateless night,
And weep afresh love's long-since-cancel'd woe,
And moan the expense of many a vanish'd sight.

Then can I grieve at grievances foregone,
And heavily from woe to woe tell o'er 20
The sad account of fore-bemoanéd moan,
Which I new pay as if not paid before:

— But if the while I think on thee, dear Friend,
All losses are restored, and sorrows end.

W. Shakespeare

XL

SLEEP

Come, Sleep: O Sleep! the certain knot of peace,
The baiting place of wit, the balm of woe,
The poor man's wealth, the prisoner's release,
Th' indifferent judge between the high and low;

With shield of proof shield me from out the prease 5
Of those fierce darts Despair at me doth throw:
O make in me those civil wars to cease;
I will good tribute pay, if thou do so.

Take thou of me smooth pillows, sweetest bed,
A chamber deaf of noise and blind of light, 10
A rosy garland and a weary head:
And if these things, as being thine in right,

Move not thy heavy grace, thou shalt in me,
Livelier than elsewhere, Stella's image see.

Sir P. Sidney

XLI

REVOLUTIONS

Like as the waves make towards the pebbled shore 15
So do our minutes hasten to their end;
Each changing place with that which goes before,
In sequent toil all forwards do contend.

Nativity, once in the main of light,
Crawls to maturity, wherewith being crown'd, 20
Crooked eclipses 'gainst his glory fight,
And Time that gave, doth now his gift confound.

Time doth transfix the flourish set on youth,
And delves the parallels in beauty's brow;

Feeds on the rarities of nature's truth,
And nothing stands but for his scythe to mow: —
And yet, to times in hope, my verse shall stand
Praising Thy worth, despite his cruel hand.

W. Shakespeare

XLII

Farewell! thou art too dear for my possessing, 5
And like enough thou know'st thy estimate:
The charter of thy worth gives thee releasing;
My bonds in thee are all determinate.

For how do I hold thee but by thy granting?
And for that riches where is my deserving? 10
The cause of this fair gift in me is wanting,
And so my patent back again is swerving.

Thyself thou gav'st, thy own worth then not knowing,
Or me, to whom thou gav'st it, else mistaking;
So thy great gift, upon misprision growing, 15
Comes home again, on better judgment making.

Thus have I had thee as a dream doth flatter;
In sleep, a king; but waking, no such matter.

W. Shakespeare

XLIII

THE LIFE WITHOUT PASSION

They that have power to hurt, and will do none,
That do not do the thing they most do show, 20
Who, moving others, are themselves as stone,
Unmovéd, cold, and to temptation slow, —

They rightly do inherit heaven's graces,
And husband nature's riches from expense;
They are the lords and owners of their faces, 25
Others, but stewards of their excellence.

The summer's flower is to the summer sweet,
Though to itself it only live and die;
But if that flower with base infection meet,
The basest weed outbraves his dignity:

For sweetest things turn sourest by their deeds; 5
Lilies that fester smell far worse than weeds.

W. Shakespeare

XLIV

THE LOVER'S APPEAL

And wilt thou leave me thus?
Say nay! say nay! for shame,
To save thee from the blame
Of all my grief and grame. 10
And wilt thou leave me thus?
Say nay! say nay!

And wilt thou leave me thus,
That hath loved thee so long
In wealth and woe among: 15
And is thy heart so strong
As for to leave me thus?
Say nay! say nay!

And wilt thou leave me thus,
That hath given thee my heart 20
Never for to depart
Neither for pain nor smart:
And wilt thou leave me thus?
Say nay! say nay!

And wilt thou leave me thus, 25
And have no more pity
Of him that loveth thee?
Alas! thy cruelty!
And wilt thou leave me thus?
Say nay! say nay! 30

Sir T. Wyat

XLV

THE NIGHTINGALE

As it fell upon a day
In the merry month of May,
Sitting in a pleasant shade
Which a grove of myrtles made,
Beasts did leap and birds did sing, 5
Trees did grow and plants did spring;
Everything did banish moan
Save the Nightingale alone.
She, poor bird, as all forlorn,
Lean'd her breast up-till a thorn, 10
And there sung the dolefull'st ditty
That to hear it was great pity.
Fie, fie, fie, now would she cry;
Teru, teru, by and by:
That to hear her so complain 15
Scarce I could from tears refrain;
For her griefs so lively shown
Made me think upon mine own.
— Ah, thought I, thou mourn'st in vain,
None takes pity on thy pain: 20
Senseless trees, they cannot hear thee,
Ruthless beasts, they will not cheer thee;
King Pandion, he is dead,
All thy friends are lapp'd in lead:
All thy fellow birds do sing 25
Careless of thy sorrowing:
Even so, poor bird, like thee
None alive will pity me.

R. Barnefield

XLVI

Care-charmer Sleep, son of the sable Night,
Brother to Death, in silent darkness born,
Relieve my languish, and restore the light;
With dark forgetting of my care return.

And let the day be time enough to mourn 5
The shipwreck of my ill-adventured youth:
Let waking eyes suffice to wail their scorn,
Without the torment of the night's untruth.

Cease, dreams, the images of day-desires,
To model forth the passions of the morrow; 10
Never let rising Sun approve you liars,
To add more grief to aggravate my sorrow:

Still let me sleep, embracing clouds in vain,
And never wake to feel the day's disdain.

S. Daniel

XLVII

The nightingale, as soon as April bringeth 15
Unto her rested sense a perfect waking,
While late-bare earth, proud of new clothing, springeth,
Sings out her woes, a thorn her songbook making;
And mournfully bewailing,
Her throat in tunes expresseth 20
What grief her breast oppresseth
For Tereus' force on her chaste will prevailing.

O Philomela fair, O take some gladness,
That here is juster cause of plaintful sadness:
Thine earth now springs, mine fadeth; 25
Thy thorn without, my thorn my heart invadeth.

Alas, she hath no other cause of anguish
But Tereus' love, on her by strong hand wroken,

Wherein she suffering, all her spirits languish,
  Full womanlike complains her will was broken.
    But I, who, daily craving,
    Cannot have to content me,
    Have more cause to lament me, 5
Since wanting is more woe than too much having.

O Philomela fair, O take some gladness
That here is juster cause of plaintful sadness:
    Thine earth now springs, mine fadeth;
Thy thorn without, my thorn my heart invadeth. 10

Sir P. Sidney

XLVIII

FRUSTRA

Take, O take those lips away
That so sweetly were forsworn,
And those eyes, the break of day,
Lights that do mislead the morn:
But my kisses bring again, 15
    Bring again —
Seals of love, but seal'd in vain,
    Seal'd in vain!

W. Shakespeare

XLIX

LOVE'S FAREWELL

Since there 's no help, come let us kiss and part, —
Nay I have done, you get no more of me; 20
And I am glad, yea, glad with all my heart,
That thus so cleanly I myself can free;

Shake hands forever, cancel all our vows,
And when we meet at any time again,
Be it not seen in either of our brows 25
That we one jot of former love retain.

Now at the last gasp of love's latest breath,
When his pulse failing, passion speechless lies,
When faith is kneeling by his bed of death,
And innocence is closing up his eyes,

—Now if thou would'st, when all have given him over, 5
From death to life thou might'st him yet recover!

M. Drayton

L

IN IMAGINE PERTRANSIT HOMO

Follow thy fair sun, unhappy shadow!
  Though thou be black as night
  And she made all of light,
Yet follow thy fair sun, unhappy shadow! 10

Follow her, whose light thy light depriveth!
  Though here thou liv'st disgraced,
  And she in heaven is placed,
Yet follow her whose light the world reviveth!

Follow those pure beams, whose beauty burneth, 15
  That so have scorchéd thee
  As thou still black must be
Till her kind beams thy black to brightness turneth.

Follow her, while yet her glory shineth!
  There comes a luckless night 20
  That will dim all her light;
— And this the black unhappy shade divineth.

Follow still, since so thy fates ordainéd!
  The sun must have his shade,
  Till both at once do fade, — 25
The sun still proved, the shadow still disdainéd.

T. Campion

LI

BLIND LOVE

O me! what eyes hath Love put in my head
Which have no correspondence with true sight:
Or if they have, where is my judgment fled
That censures falsely what they see aright?

If that be fair whereon my false eyes dote, 5
What means the world to say it is not so?
If it be not, then love doth well denote
Love's eye is not so true as all men's: No,

How can it? O how can love's eye be true,
That is so vexed with watching and with tears? 10
No marvel then though I mistake my view:
The sun itself sees not till heaven clears.

O cunning Love! with tears thou keep'st me blind,
Lest eyes well-seeing thy foul faults should find!

W. Shakespeare

LII

Sleep, angry beauty, sleep and fear not me! 15
For who a sleeping lion dares provoke?
It shall suffice me here to sit and see
Those lips shut up that never kindly spoke:
What sight can more content a lover's mind
Than beauty seeming harmless, if not kind? 20

My words have charm'd her, for secure she sleeps,
Though guilty much of wrong done to my love;
And in her slumber, see! she close-eyed weeps:
Dreams often more than waking passions move.
Plead, Sleep, my cause, and make her soft like thee: 25
That she in peace may wake and pity me.

T. Campion

LIII

THE UNFAITHFUL SHEPHERDESS[1]

While that the sun with his beams hot
Scorchéd the fruits in vale and mountain,
Philon the shepherd, late forgot,
Sitting beside a crystal fountain,
  In shadow of a green oak tree 5
  Upon his pipe this song play'd he:
Adieu, Love, adieu, Love, untrue Love,
Untrue Love, untrue Love, adieu, Love;
Your mind is light, soon lost for new love.

So long as I was in your sight 10
I was your heart, your soul, and treasure;
And evermore you sobb'd and sigh'd
Burning in flames beyond all measure:
  —Three days endured your love to me,
  And it was lost in other three! 15
Adieu, Love, adieu, Love, untrue Love,
Untrue Love, untrue Love, adieu, Love;
Your mind is light, soon lost for new love.

Another Shepherd you did see
To whom your heart was soon enchainéd; 20
Full soon your love was leapt from me,
Full soon my place he had obtainéd.
  Soon came a third, your love to win,
  And we were out and he was in.
Adieu, Love, adieu, Love, untrue Love, 25
Untrue Love, untrue Love, adieu, Love;
Your mind is light, soon lost for new love.

Sure you have made me passing glad
That you your mind so soon removéd,
Before that I the leisure had 30
To choose you for my best belovéd:

[1] From William Byrd's "Songs of Sundry Natures," 1589. It was reprinted in "England's Helicon," 1600.

For all your love was past and done
Two days before it was begun: —
Adieu, Love, adieu, Love, untrue Love,
Untrue Love, untrue Love, adieu, Love;
Your mind is light, soon lost for new love. 5

Anon.

LIV

ADVICE TO A LOVER[1]

The sea hath many thousand sands,
The sun hath motes as many;
The sky is full of stars, and Love
As full of woes as any:
Believe me, that do know the elf, 10
And make no trial by thyself!

It is in truth a pretty toy
For babes to play withal: —
But O! the honeys of our youth
Are oft our age's gall! 15
Self-proof in time will make thee know
He was a prophet told thee so;

A prophet that, Cassandra-like,
Tells truth without belief;
For headstrong Youth will run his race, 20
Although his goal be grief: —
Love's Martyr, when his heat is past,
Proves Care's Confessor at the last.

Anon.

LV

A RENUNCIATION

Thou art not fair, for all thy red and white,
For all those rosy ornaments in thee, — 25
Thou art not sweet, though made of mere delight,
Nor fair, nor sweet — unless thou pity me!

[1] From Robert Jones's "The Muses' Garden of Delights," 1610.

I will not soothe thy fancies; thou shalt prove
That beauty is no beauty without love.

—Yet love not me, nor seek not to allure
  My thoughts with beauty, were it more divine:
Thy smiles and kisses I cannot endure, 5
  I 'll not be wrapp'd up in those arms of thine:
—Now show it, if thou be a woman right—
Embrace and kiss and love me in despite!

T. Campion

LVI

Blow, blow, thou winter wind,
Thou art not so unkind 10
As man's ingratitude;
Thy tooth is not so keen
Because thou art not seen,
Although thy breath be rude.
Heigh ho! sing heigh ho! unto the green holly: 15
Most friendship is feigning, most loving mere folly:
Then, heigh ho! the holly!
This life is most jolly.

Freeze, freeze, thou bitter sky,
Thou dost not bite so nigh 20
As benefits forgot:
Though thou the waters warp,
Thy sting is not so sharp
As friend remember'd not.
Heigh ho! sing heigh ho! unto the green holly: 25
Most friendship is feigning, most loving mere folly:
Then, heigh ho! the holly!
This life is most jolly.

W. Shakespeare

LVII

A SWEET LULLABY[1]

Come little babe, come silly soul,
Thy father's shame, thy mother's grief,
Born as I doubt to all our dole,
And to thy self unhappy chief:
    Sing Lullaby and lap it warm, 5
    Poor soul that thinks no creature harm.

Thou little think'st and less dost know,
The cause of this thy mother's moan,
Thou want'st the wit to wail her woe,
And I myself am all alone: 10
    Why dost thou weep? why dost thou wail?
    And knowest not yet what thou dost ail.

Come little wretch, ah silly heart,
Mine only joy, what can I more?
If there be any wrong thy smart 15
That may the destinies implore:
    'T was I, I say, against my will,
    I wail the time, but be thou still.

And dost thou smile, oh thy sweet face!
Would God Himself He might thee see, 20
No doubt thou would'st soon purchase grace,
I know right well, for thee and me:
    But come to mother, babe, and play,
    For father false is fled away.

Sweet boy, if it by fortune chance, 25
Thy father home again to send,
If death do strike me with his lance,
Yet mayst thou me to him commend:
    If any ask thy mother's name,
    Tell how by love she purchased blame. 30

[1] From Nicholas Breton's "Arbor of Amorous Devices," 1593–1594.

Then will his gentle heart soon yield,
I know him of a noble mind,
Although a Lion in the field,
A Lamb in town thou shalt him find:
Ask blessing, babe, be not afraid, 5
His sugar'd words hath me betray'd.

Then mayst thou joy and be right glad,
Although in woe I seem to moan,
Thy father is no rascal lad,
A noble youth of blood and bone: 10
His glancing looks, if he once smile,
Right honest women may beguile.

Come, little boy, and rock asleep,
Sing lullaby and be thou still;
I that can do naught else but weep, 15
Will sit by thee and wail my fill:
God bless my babe, and lullaby
From this thy father's quality!

Anon.

LVIII

With how sad steps, O Moon, thou climb'st the skies!
How silently, and with how wan a face! 20
What, may it be that e'en in heavenly place
That busy archer his sharp arrows tries!

Sure, if that long-with-love-acquainted eyes
Can judge of love, thou feel'st a lover's case,
I read it in thy looks; thy languish'd grace, 25
To me, that feel the like, thy state descries.

Then, e'en of fellowship, O Moon, tell me,
Is constant love deem'd there but want of wit?
Are beauties there as proud as here they be?
Do they above love to be loved, and yet 30

Those lovers scorn whom that love doth possess?
Do they call virtue, there, ungratefulness?

Sir P. Sidney

LIX

O CRUDELIS AMOR

When thou must home to shades of underground,
And there arrived, a new admired guest,
The beauteous spirits do engirt thee round, 5
White Iopé, blithe Helen, and the rest,
To hear the stories of thy finish'd love
From that smooth tongue whose music hell can move;

Then wilt thou speak of banqueting delights,
Of masques and revels which sweet youth did make, 10
Of tourneys and great challenges of Knights,
And all these triumphs for thy beauty's sake:
When thou hast told these honors done to thee,
Then tell, O tell, how thou didst murder me!

T. Campion

LX

SEPHESTIA'S SONG TO HER CHILD

Weep not, my wanton, smile upon my knee; 15
When thou art old, there 's grief enough for thee.
Mother's wag, pretty boy,
Father's sorrow, father's joy;
When thy father first did see
Such a boy by him and me, 20
He was glad, I was woe,
Fortune changéd made him so,
When he left his pretty boy
Last his sorrow, first his joy.

Weep not, my wanton, smile upon my knee; 25
When thou art old, there 's grief enough for thee.

Streaming tears that never stint,
Like pearl drops from a flint,
Fell by course from his eyes,
That one another's place supplies;
Thus he grieved in every part, 5
Tears of blood fell from his heart,
When he left his pretty boy,
Father's sorrow, father's joy.

Weep not, my wanton, smile upon my knee;
When thou art old, there 's grief enough for thee. 10
The wanton smiled, father wept,
Mother cried, baby leapt;
More he crow'd, more we cried,
Nature could not sorrow hide:
He must go, he must kiss 15
Child and mother, baby bless,
For he left his pretty boy,
Father's sorrow, father's joy.
Weep not, my wanton, smile upon my knee,
When thou art old, there 's grief enough for thee. 20

R. Greene

LXI

A LAMENT

My thoughts hold mortal strife;
I do detest my life,
And with lamenting cries
Peace to my soul to bring
Oft call that prince which here doth monarchize: 25
—But he, grim grinning King,
Who caitiffs scorns, and doth the blest surprise,
Late having deck'd with beauty's rose his tomb,
Disdains to crop a weed, and will not come.

W. Drummond

LXII

DIRGE OF LOVE

Come away, come away, Death,
And in sad cypress let me be laid;
Fly away, fly away, breath;
I am slain by a fair cruel maid.
My shroud of white, stuck all with yew, 5
O prepare it!
My part of death, no one so true
Did share it.

Not a flower, not a flower sweet
On my black coffin let there be strown; 10
Not a friend, not a friend greet
My poor corpse, where my bones shall be thrown:
A thousand thousand sighs to save,
Lay me, O where
Sad true lover never find my grave, 15
To weep there.

W. Shakespeare

LXIII

TO HIS LUTE

My lute, be as thou wert when thou didst grow
With thy green mother in some shady grove,
When immelodious winds but made thee move,
And birds their ramage did on thee bestow. 20

Since that dear Voice which did thy sounds approve,
Which wont in such harmonious strains to flow,
Is reft from Earth to tune those spheres above,
What art thou but a harbinger of woe?

Thy pleasing notes be pleasing notes no more, 25
But orphans' wailings to the fainting ear;
Each stroke a sigh, each sound draws forth a tear;
For which be silent as in woods before:

Or if that any hand to touch thee deign,
Like widow'd turtle, still her loss complain.

W. Drummond

LXIV

FIDELE

Fear no more the heat o' the sun
Nor the furious winter's rages;
Thou thy worldly task hast done, 5
Home art gone and ta'en thy wages:
Golden lads and girls all must,
As chimney sweepers, come to dust.

Fear no more the frown o' the great,
Thou art past the tyrant's stroke; 10
Care no more to clothe and eat;
To thee the reed is as the oak:
The scepter, learning, physic, must
All follow this, and come to dust.

Fear no more the lightning flash 15
Nor the all-dreaded thunderstone;
Fear not slander, censure rash;
Thou hast finish'd joy and moan:
All lovers young, all lovers must
Consign to thee, and come to dust. 20

W. Shakespeare

LXV

A SEA DIRGE

Full fathom five thy father lies:
Of his bones are coral made;
Those are pearls that were his eyes:
Nothing of him that doth fade,
But doth suffer a sea-change 25
Into something rich and strange.

Sea nymphs hourly ring his knell:
Hark! now I hear them, —
Ding, dong, bell.

W. Shakespeare

LXVI

A LAND DIRGE

Call for the robin-redbreast and the wren,
Since o'er shady groves they hover 5
And with leaves and flowers do cover
The friendless bodies of unburied men.
Call unto his funeral dole
The ant, the field mouse, and the mole
To rear him hillocks that shall keep him warm 10
And (when gay tombs are robb'd) sustain no harm;
But keep the wolf far thence, that 's foe to men,
For with his nails he 'll dig them up again.

J. Webster

LXVII

POST MORTEM

If Thou survive my well-contented day
When that churl Death my bones with dust shall cover, 15
And shalt by fortune once more resurvey
These poor rude lines of thy deceasèd lover;

Compare them with the bettering of the time,
And though they be outstripp'd by every pen,
Reserve them for my love, not for their rhyme 20
Exceeded by the height of happier men.

O then vouchsafe me but this loving thought —
"Had my friend's Muse grown with this growing age,
A dearer birth than this his love had brought,
To march in ranks of better equipage: 25

But since he died, and poets better prove,
Theirs for their style I 'll read, his for his love."

W. Shakespeare

LXVIII

THE TRIUMPH OF DEATH

No longer mourn for me when I am dead
Than you shall hear the surly sullen bell
Give warning to the world, that I am fled
From this vile world, with vilest worms to dwell;

Nay, if you read this line, remember not 5
The hand that writ it; for I love you so,
That I in your sweet thoughts would be forgot
If thinking on me then should make you woe.

O if, I say, you look upon this verse
When I perhaps compounded am with clay, 10
Do not so much as my poor name rehearse,
But let your love even with my life decay;

Lest the wise world should look into your moan,
And mock you with me after I am gone.

W. Shakespeare

LXIX

YOUNG LOVE

Tell me where is Fancy bred, 15
Or in the heart, or in the head?
How begot, how nourishéd?
Reply, reply.

It is engender'd in the eyes;
With gazing fed; and Fancy dies 20
In the cradle where it lies:
Let us all ring Fancy's knell;
I 'll begin it, — Ding, dong, bell.
— Ding, dong, bell.

W. Shakespeare

LXX

A DILEMMA[1]

Lady, when I behold the roses sprouting
Which clad in damask mantles deck the arbors,
And then behold your lips where sweet love harbors,
My eyes present me with a double doubting:
For viewing both alike, hardly my mind supposes 5
Whether the roses be your lips, or your lips the roses.

Anon.

LXXI

ROSALYND'S MADRIGAL

Love in my bosom, like a bee,
Doth suck his sweet;
Now with his wings he plays with me,
Now with his feet. 10
Within mine eyes he makes his nest,
His bed amidst my tender breast;
My kisses are his daily feast,
And yet he robs me of my rest:
Ah! wanton, will ye? 15

And if I sleep, then percheth he
With pretty flight,
And makes his pillow of my knee
The livelong night.
Strike I my lute, he tunes the string; 20
He music plays if so I sing;
He lends me every lovely thing,
Yet cruel he my heart doth sting:
Whist, wanton, will ye?

Else I with roses every day 25
Will whip you hence,

[1] From John Wilbye's "First Set of English Madrigals," 1598.

And bind you, when you long to play,
For your offence;
I 'll shut my eyes to keep you in;
I 'll make you fast it for your sin;
I 'll count your power not worth a pin; 5
—Alas! what hereby shall I win,
If he gainsay me?

What if I beat the wanton boy
With many a rod?
He will repay me with annoy, 10
Because a god.
Then sit thou safely on my knee,
And let thy bower my bosom be;
Lurk in mine eyes, I like of thee,
O Cupid! so thou pity me, 15
Spare not, but play thee!

T. Lodge

LXXII

CUPID AND CAMPASPE

Cupid and my Campaspé play'd
At cards for kisses; Cupid paid:
He stakes his quiver, bow, and arrows,
His mother's doves, and team of sparrows; 20
Loses them too; then down he throws
The coral of his lip, the rose
Growing on 's cheek (but none knows how);
With these, the crystal of his brow,
And then the dimple on his chin; 25
All these did my Campaspé win:
And last he set her both his eyes—
She won, and Cupid blind did rise.
O Love! has she done this to thee?
What shall, alas! become of me? 30

J. Lylye

LXXIII

Pack, clouds, away, and welcome day,
  With night we banish sorrow;
Sweet air blow soft, mount larks aloft
  To give my Love good morrow!
Wings from the wind to please her mind, 5
  Notes from the lark I 'll borrow;
Bird, prune thy wing, nightingale sing,
  To give my Love good morrow;
    To give my Love good morrow
    Notes from them both I 'll borrow. 10

Wake from thy nest, Robin-red-breast,
  Sing, birds, in every furrow;
And from each hill, let music shrill
  Give my fair Love good morrow!
Blackbird and thrush in every bush, 15
  Stare, linnet, and cock sparrow!
You pretty elves, amongst yourselves
  Sing my fair Love good morrow;
    To give my Love good morrow
    Sing, birds, in every furrow! 20

T. Heywood

LXXIV

PROTHALAMION

Calm was the day, and through the trembling air
Sweet-breathing Zephyrus did softly play —
A gentle spirit, that lightly did delay
Hot Titan's beams, which then did glister fair;
When I (whom sullen care, 25
Through discontent of my long fruitless stay
In princes' court, and expectation vain
Of idle hopes, which still do fly away
Like empty shadows, did afflict my brain)

Walk'd forth to ease my pain
Along the shore of silver-streaming Thames;
Whose rutty bank, the which his river hems,
Was painted all with variable flowers,
And all the meads adorn'd with dainty gems 5
Fit to deck maidens' bowers,
And crown their paramours
Against the bridal day, which is not long:
Sweet Thames! run softly, till I end my song.

There in a meadow by the river's side 10
A flock of nymphs I chancéd to espy,
All lovely daughters of the flood thereby,
With goodly greenish locks all loose untied
As each had been a bride;
And each one had a little wicker basket 15
Made of fine twigs, entrailéd curiously.
In which they gather'd flowers to fill their flasket,
And with fine fingers cropt full feateously
The tender stalks on high.
Of every sort which in that meadow grew 20
They gather'd some; the violet, pallid blue,
The little daisy that at evening closes,
The virgin lily and the primrose true,
With store of vermeil roses,
To deck their bridegrooms' posies 25
Against the bridal day, which was not long:
Sweet Thames! run softly, till I end my song.

With that I saw two Swans of goodly hue
Come softly swimming down along the Lee;
Two fairer birds I yet did never see; 30
The snow which doth the top of Pindus strow
Did never whiter show,
Nor Jove himself, when he a swan would be
For love of Leda, whiter did appear;

Yet Leda was (they say) as white as he,
Yet not so white as these, nor nothing near;
So purely white they were
That even the gentle stream, the which them bare,
Seem'd foul to them, and bade his billows spare 5
To wet their silken feathers, lest they might
Soil their fair plumes with water not so fair,
And mar their beauties bright
That shone as Heaven's light
Against their bridal day, which was not long: 10
Sweet Thames! run softly, till I end my song.

Eftsoons the nymphs, which now had flowers their fill,
Ran all in haste to see that silver brood
As they came floating on the crystal flood;
Whom when they saw, they stood amazéd still 15
Their wondering eyes to fill;
Them seem'd they never saw a sight so fair
Of fowls, so lovely, that they sure did deem
Them heavenly born, or to be that same pair
Which through the sky draw Venus' silver team; 20
For sure they did not seem
To be begot of any earthly seed,
But rather Angels, or of Angels' breed;
Yet were they bred of summer's heat, they say,
In sweetest season, when each flower and weed 25
The earth did fresh array;
So fresh they seem'd as day,
Ev'n as their bridal day, which was not long:
Sweet Thames! run softly, till I end my song.

Then forth they all out of their baskets drew 30
Great store of flowers, the honor of the field,
That to the sense did fragrant odors yield,
All which upon those goodly birds they threw
And all the waves did strew,

That like old Peneus' waters they did seem
When down along by pleasant Tempe's shore
Scatter'd with flowers, through Thessaly they stream,
That they appear, through lilies' plenteous store,
Like a bride's chamber floor. 5
Two of those nymphs meanwhile two garlands bound
Of freshest flowers which in that mead they found,
The which presenting all in trim array,
Their snowy foreheads therewithal they crown'd;
Whilst one did sing this lay 10
Prepared against that day,
Against their bridal day, which was not long:
Sweet Thames! run softly, till I end my song.

"Ye gentle birds! the world's fair ornament,
And Heaven's glory, whom this happy hour 15
Doth lead unto your lovers' blissful bower,
Joy may you have, and gentle heart's content
Of your love's couplement;
And let fair Venus, that is queen of love,
With her heart-quelling son upon you smile, 20
Whose smile, they say, hath virtue to remove
All love's dislike, and friendship's faulty guile
Forever to assoil.
Let endless peace your steadfast hearts accord,
And blesséd plenty wait upon your board; 25
And let your bed with pleasures chaste abound,
That fruitful issue may to you afford
Which may your foes confound,
And make your joys redound
Upon your bridal day, which is not long: 30
Sweet Thames! run softly, till I end my song."

So ended she; and all the rest around
To her redoubled that her undersong,
Which said their bridal day should not be long:

And gentle Echo from the neighbor ground
Their accents did resound.
So forth those joyous birds did pass along
Adown the Lee that to them murmur'd low,
As he would speak but that he lack'd a tongue; 5
Yet did by signs his glad affection show,
Making his stream run slow.
And all the fowl which in his flood did dwell
'Gan flock about these twain, that did excel
The rest, so far as Cynthia doth shend 10
The lesser stars. So they, enrangéd well,
Did on those two attend,
And their best service lend
Against their wedding day, which was not long:
Sweet Thames! run softly, till I end my song. 15

At length they all to merry London came,
To merry London, my most kindly nurse,
That to me gave this life's first native source,
Though from another place I take my name,
An house of ancient fame: 20
There when they came whereas those bricky towers
The which on Thames' broad agéd back do ride,
Where now the studious lawyers have their bowers,
There whilom wont the Templar knights to bide,
Till they decay'd through pride; 25
Next whereunto there stands a stately place,
Where oft I gainéd gifts and goodly grace
Of that great lord, which therein wont to dwell,
Whose want too well now feels my friendless case;
But ah! here fits not well 30
Old woes, but joys to tell
Against the bridal day, which is not long:
Sweet Thames! run softly, till I end my song.

Yet therein now doth lodge a noble peer,
Great England's glory and the world's wide wonder, 35

Whose dreadful name late through all Spain did thunder,
And Hercules' two pillars standing near
Did make to quake and fear:
Fair branch of honor, flower of chivalry!
That fillest England with thy triumphs' fame, 5
Joy have thou of thy noble victory,
And endless happiness of thine own name
That promiseth the same;
That through thy prowess and victorious arms
Thy country may be freed from foreign harms, 10
And great Elisa's glorious name may ring
Through all the world, fill'd with thy wide alarms,
Which some brave Muse may sing
To ages following:
Upon the bridal day, which is not long: 15
Sweet Thames! run softly, till I end my song.

From those high towers this noble lord issúing
Like radiant Hesper, when his golden hair
In th' ocean billows he hath bathéd fair,
Descended to the river's open viewing 20
With a great train ensuing.
Above the rest were goodly to be seen
Two gentle knights of lovely face and feature,
Beseeming well the bower of any queen,
With gifts of wit and ornaments of nature, 25
Fit for so goodly stature,
That like the twins of Jove they seem'd in sight
Which deck the baldric of the Heavens bright;
They two, forth pacing to the river's side,
Received those two fair brides, their love's delight; 30
Which, at th' appointed tide,
Each one did make his bride
Against their bridal day, which is not long:
Sweet Thames! run softly, till I end my song.

E. Spenser

LXXV

THE HAPPY HEART

Art thou poor, yet hast thou golden slumbers?
O sweet content!
Art thou rich, yet is thy mind perplex'd?
O punishment!
Dost thou laugh to see how fools are vex'd 5
To add to golden numbers, golden numbers?
O sweet content! O sweet, O sweet content!
Work apace, apace, apace, apace;
Honest labor bears a lovely face;
Then hey nonny nonny, hey nonny nonny! 10

Canst drink the waters of the crispéd spring?
O sweet content!
Swimm'st thou in wealth, yet sink'st in thine own tears?
O punishment!
Then he that patiently want's burden bears 15
No burden bears, but is a king, a king!
O sweet content! O sweet, O sweet content!
Work apace, apace, apace, apace;
Honest labor bears a lovely face;
Then hey nonny nonny, hey nonny nonny! 20

T. Dekker

LXXVI

SIC TRANSIT

Come, cheerful day, part of my life to me;
For while thou view'st me with thy fading light
Part of my life doth still depart with thee,
And I still onward haste to my last night:
Time's fatal wings do ever forward fly— 25
So every day we live, a day we die.

But O ye nights, ordain'd for barren rest,
How are my days deprived of life in you

When heavy sleep my soul hath dispossest,
By feignéd death life sweetly to renew!
Part of my life, in that, you life deny:
So every day we live, a day we die.

T. Campion

LXXVII

This Life, which seems so fair, 5
Is like a bubble blown up in the air
By sporting children's breath,
Who chase it everywhere
And strive who can most motion it bequeath.
And though it sometimes seem of its own might 10
Like to an eye of gold to be fix'd there,
And firm to hover in that empty height,
That only is because it is so light.
— But in that pomp it doth not long appear;
For when 't is most admired, in a thought, 15
Because it erst was naught, it turns to naught.

W. Drummond

LXXVIII

SOUL AND BODY

Poor Soul, the center of my sinful earth,
[Foil'd by] those rebel powers that thee array,
Why dost thou pine within, and suffer dearth,
Painting thy outward walls so costly gay? 20

Why so large cost, having so short a lease,
Dost thou upon thy fading mansion spend?
Shall worms, inheritors of this excess,
Eat up thy charge? is this thy body's end?

Then, Soul, live thou upon thy servant's loss, 25
And let that pine to aggravate thy store;

Buy terms divine in selling hours of dross;
Within be fed, without be rich no more:—

So shalt thou feed on death, that feeds on men,
And death once dead, there 's no more dying then.

W. Shakespeare

LXXIX

The man of life upright, 5
Whose guiltless heart is free
From all dishonest deeds,
Or thought of vanity;

The man whose silent days
In harmless joys are spent, 10
Whom hopes cannot delude
Nor sorrow discontent:

That man needs neither towers
Nor armor for defence,
Nor secret vaults to fly 15
From thunder's violence:

He only can behold
With unaffrighted eyes
The horrors of the deep
And terrors of the skies. 20

Thus scorning all the cares
That fate or fortune brings,
He makes the heaven his book,
His wisdom heavenly things;

Good thoughts his only friends, 25
His wealth a well-spent age,
The earth his sober inn
And quiet pilgrimage.

T. Campion

LXXX

THE LESSONS OF NATURE

Of this fair volume which we World do name
If we the sheets and leaves could turn with care,
Of Him who it corrects, and did it frame,
We clear might read the art and wisdom rare:

Find out His power which wildest powers doth tame, 5
His providence extending everywhere,
His justice which proud rebels doth not spare,
In every page, no period of the same.

But silly we, like foolish children, rest
Well pleased with color'd vellum, leaves of gold, 10
Fair dangling ribbons, leaving what is best,
On the great Writer's sense ne'er taking hold;

Or if by chance we stay our minds on aught,
It is some picture on the margin wrought.

W. Drummond

LXXXI

Doth then the world go thus, doth all thus move? 15
Is this the justice which on earth we find?
Is this that firm decree which all doth bind?
Are these your influences, Powers above?

Those souls which vice's moody mists most blind,
Blind Fortune, blindly, most their friend doth prove; 20
And they who thee, poor idol Virtue! love,
Ply like a feather toss'd by storm and wind.

Ah! if a Providence doth sway this all
Why should best minds groan under most distress?
Or why should pride humility make thrall, 25
And injuries the innocent oppress?

Heavens! hinder, stop this fate; or grant a time
When good may have, as well as bad, their prime!

W. Drummond

LXXXII

THE WORLD'S WAY

Tired with all these, for restful death I cry —
As, to behold desert a beggar born,
And needy nothing trimm'd in jollity,
And purest faith unhappily forsworn,

And gilded honor shamefully misplaced, 5
And maiden virtue rudely strumpeted,
And right perfection wrongfully disgraced,
And strength by limping sway disabled,

And art made tongue-tied by authority,
And folly, doctor-like, controlling skill, 10
And simple truth miscall'd simplicity,
And captive Good attending captain Ill: —

— Tired with all these, from these would I be gone,
Save that, to die, I leave my Love alone.

W. Shakespeare

LXXXIII

A WISH

Happy were he could finish forth his fate 15
In some unhaunted desert, where, obscure
From all society, from love and hate
Of worldly folk, there should he sleep secure;

Then wake again, and yield God ever praise;
Content with hip, with haws, and brambleberry; 20
In contemplation passing still his days,
And change of holy thoughts to make him merry:

Who, when he dies, his tomb might be the bush
Where harmless robin resteth with the thrush:
— Happy were he! 25

R. Devereux,
Earl of Essex

LXXXIV

SAINT JOHN BAPTIST

The last and greatest Herald of Heaven's King
Girt with rough skins, hies to the deserts wild,
Among that savage brood the woods forth bring,
Which he more harmless found than man, and mild.

His food was locusts, and what there doth spring, 5
With honey that from virgin hives distill'd;
Parch'd body, hollow eyes, some uncouth thing
Made him appear, long since from earth exiled.

There burst he forth: All ye whose hopes rely
On God, with me amidst these deserts mourn, 10
Repent, repent, and from old errors turn!
— Who listen'd to his voice, obey'd his cry?

Only the echoes, which he made relent,
Rung from their flinty caves, Repent! Repent!

W. Drummond

BOOK SECOND

This division, embracing generally the latter eighty years of the seventeenth century, contains the close of our early poetical style and the commencement of the modern. In Dryden we see the first master of the new; in Milton, whose genius dominates here as Shakespeare's in the former book, the crown and consummation of the early period. Their splendid odes are far in advance of any prior attempts, Spenser's excepted; they exhibit that wider and grander range which years and experience and the struggles of the time conferred on poetry. Our Muses now give expression to political feeling, to religious thought, to a high philosophic statesmanship in writers such as Marvell, Herbert, and Wotton; whilst in Marvell and Milton, again, we find noble attempts, hitherto rare in our literature, at pure description of nature, destined in our own age to be continued and equaled. Meanwhile the poetry of simple passion, although before 1660 often deformed by verbal fancies and conceits of thought, and afterwards by levity and an artificial tone, produced in Herrick and Waller some charming pieces of more finished art than the Elizabethan, until in the courtly compliments of Sedley it seems to exhaust itself and lie almost dormant for the hundred years between the days of Wither and Suckling and the days of Burns and Cowper. That the change from our early style to the modern brought with it at first a loss of nature and simplicity is undeniable; yet the bolder and wider scope which poetry took between 1620 and 1700, and the successful efforts then made to gain greater clearness in expression, in their results have been no slight compensation.—*Transferred from Palgrave's Notes.*

LXXXV

ODE ON THE MORNING OF CHRIST'S NATIVITY

This is the month, and this the happy morn
Wherein the Son of Heaven's Eternal King
Of wedded maid and virgin mother born,
Our great redemption from above did bring;
For so the holy sages once did sing 5
That He our deadly forfeit should release,
And with His Father work us a perpetual peace.

That glorious Form, that Light unsufferable,
And that far-beaming blaze of Majesty
Wherewith He wont at Heaven's high council table
To sit the midst of Trinal Unity,
He laid aside; and, here with us to be, 5
Forsook the courts of everlasting day,
And chose with us a darksome house of mortal clay.

Say, heavenly Muse, shall not thy sacred vein
Afford a present to the Infant God?
Hast thou no verse, no hymn, or solemn strain 10
To welcome Him to this His new abode,
Now while the heaven, by the sun's team untrod,
Hath took no print of the approaching light,
And all the spangled host keep watch in squadrons bright?

See how from far, upon the eastern road, 15
The star-led wizards haste with odors sweet:
O run, prevent them with thy humble ode
And lay it lowly at His blessed feet;
Have thou the honor first thy Lord to greet,
And join thy voice unto the Angel quire 20
From out His secret altar touch'd with hallow'd fire.

THE HYMN

It was the winter wild
While the heaven-born Child
All meanly wrapt in the rude manger lies;
Nature in awe to Him 25
Had doff'd her gaudy trim,
With her great Master so to sympathize:
It was no season then for her
To wanton with the sun, her lusty paramour.

Only with speeches fair 30
She woos the gentle air
To hide her guilty front with innocent snow;

And on her naked shame,
Pollute with sinful blame,
The saintly veil of maiden white to throw;
Confounded, that her Maker's eyes
Should look so near upon her foul deformities. 5

But He, her fears to cease,
Sent down the meek-eyed Peace;
She, crown'd with olive green, came softly sliding
Down through the turning sphere,
His ready harbinger, 10
With turtle wing the amorous clouds dividing;
And waving wide her myrtle wand,
She strikes a universal peace through sea and land.

No war or battle's sound
Was heard the world around: 15
The idle spear and shield were high uphung;
The hookéd chariot stood
Unstain'd with hostile blood;
The trumpet spake not to the arméd throng;
And kings sat still with awful eye, 20
As if they surely knew their sovran Lord was by.

But peaceful was the night
Wherein the Prince of Light
His reign of peace upon the earth began:
The winds, with wonder whist, 25
Smoothly the waters kist,
Whispering new joys to the mild oceán —
Who now hath quite forgot to rave,
While birds of calm sit brooding on the charméd wave.

The stars, with deep amaze, 30
Stand fix'd in steadfast gaze,
Bending one way their precious influence;
And will not take their flight

For all the morning light,
Or Lucifer that often warn'd them thence;
But in their glimmering orbs did glow
Until their Lord Himself bespake, and bid them go.

And though the shady gloom 5
Had given day her room,
The sun himself withheld his wonted speed,
And hid his head for shame,
As his inferior flame
The new-enlighten'd world no more should need; 10
He saw a greater Sun appear
Than his bright throne, or burning axletree could bear.

The shepherds on the lawn
Or ere the point of dawn
Sate simply chatting in a rustic row; 15
Full little thought they than
That the mighty Pan
Was kindly come to live with them below;
Perhaps their loves, or else their sheep
Was all that did their silly thoughts so busy keep:— 20

When such music sweet
Their hearts and ears did greet
As never was by mortal finger strook—
Divinely-warbled voice
Answering the stringéd noise, 25
As all their souls in blissful rapture took:
The air, such pleasure loth to lose,
With thousand echoes still prolongs each heavenly close.

Nature, that heard such sound
Beneath the hollow round 30
Of Cynthia's seat the airy region thrilling,
Now was almost won
To think her part was done,
And that her reign had here its last fulfilling;

She knew such harmony alone
Could hold all Heaven and Earth in happier union.

At last surrounds their sight
A globe of circular light
That with long beams the shamefaced night array'd; 5
The helméd Cherubim
And sworded Seraphim
Are seen in glittering ranks with wings display'd,
Harping in loud and solemn quire
With unexpressive notes, to Heaven's newborn Heir. 10

Such music (as 't is said)
Before was never made
But when of old the Sons of Morning sung,
While the Creator great
His constellations set 15
And the well-balanced world on hinges hung;
And cast the dark foundations deep,
And bid the weltering waves their oozy channel keep.

Ring out, ye crystal spheres!
Once bless our human ears, 20
If ye have power to touch our senses so;
And let your silver chime
Move in melodious time;
And let the bass of heaven's deep organ blow;
And with your ninefold harmony 25
Make up full consort to the angelic symphony.

For if such holy song
Enwrap our fancy long,
Time will run back, and fetch the age of gold;
And speckled Vanity 30
Will sicken soon and die,
And leprous Sin will melt from earthly mold;
And Hell itself will pass away,
And leave her dolorous mansions to the peering day.

Yea, Truth and Justice then
Will down return to men,
Orb'd in a rainbow; and, like glories wearing,
Mercy will sit between
Throned in celestial sheen, 5
With radiant feet the tissued clouds down steering;
And Heaven, as at some festival,
Will open wide the gates of her high palace hall.

But wisest Fate says No;
This must not yet be so; 10
The Babe yet lies in smiling infancy
That on the bitter cross
Must redeem our loss;
So both Himself and us to glorify:
Yet first, to those ychain'd in sleep 15
The wakeful trump of doom must thunder through the
deep;

With such a horrid clang
As on Mount Sinai rang
While the red fire and smoldering clouds outbrake:
The aged Earth aghast 20
With terror of that blast
Shall from the surface to the center shake,
When, at the world's last sessión,
The dreadful Judge in middle air shall spread His
throne.

And then at last our bliss 25
Full and perfect is,
But now begins; for from this happy day
The old Dragon underground,
In straiter limits bound,
Not half so far casts his usurpéd sway; 30
And, wroth to see his kingdom fail,
Swinges the scaly horror of his folded tail.

The Oracles are dumb;
No voice or hideous hum
Runs through the archéd roof in words deceiving.
Apollo from his shrine
Can no more divine, 5
With hollow shriek the steep of Delphos leaving:
No nightly trance or breathéd spell
Inspires the pale-eyed priest from the prophetic cell.

The lonely mountains o'er
And the resounding shore 10
A voice of weeping heard, and loud lament;
From haunted spring and dale
Edged with poplar pale
The parting Genius is with sighing sent;
With flower-inwoven tresses torn 15
The Nymphs in twilight shade of tangled thickets mourn.

In consecrated earth
And on the holy hearth
The Lars and Lemurés moan with midnight plaint;
In urns, and altars round 20
A drear and dying sound
Affrights the Flamens at their service quaint;
And the chill marble seems to sweat,
While each peculiar Power forgoes his wonted seat.

Peor and Baalim 25
Forsake their temples dim,
With that twice-batter'd god of Palestine;
And moonéd Ashtaroth
Heaven's queen and mother both,
Now sits not girt with tapers' holy shine; 30
The Lybic Hammon shrinks his horn:
In vain the Tyrian maids their wounded Thammuz mourn.

And sullen Moloch, fled,
Hath left in shadows dread

His burning idol all of blackest hue;
In vain with cymbals' ring
They call the grisly king,
In dismal dance about the furnace blue;
The brutish gods of Nile as fast, 5
Isis, and Orus, and the dog Anubis, haste.

Nor is Osiris seen
In Memphian grove, or green,
Trampling the unshower'd grass with lowings loud:
Nor can he be at rest 10
Within his sacred chest;
Nought but profoundest Hell can be his shroud;
In vain with timbrel'd anthems dark
The sable-stolèd sorcerers bear his worshipt ark.

He feels from Juda's land 15
The dreaded Infant's hand;
The rays of Bethlehem blind his dusky eyn;
Nor all the gods beside
Longer dare abide,
Not Typhon huge ending in snaky twine: 20
Our Babe, to show His Godhead true,
Can in His swaddling bands control the damnèd crew.

So, when the sun in bed
Curtain'd with cloudy red
Pillows his chin upon an orient wave, 25
The flocking shadows pale
Troop to the infernal jail,
Each fetter'd ghost slips to his several grave;
And the yellow-skirted fays
Fly after the night steeds, leaving their moon-loved
maze. 30

But see! the Virgin blest
Hath laid her Babe to rest;
Time is, our tedious song should here have ending:

Heaven's youngest-teemèd star
Hath fix'd her polish'd car,
Her sleeping Lord with handmaid lamp attending:
And all about the courtly stable
Bright-harness'd Angels sit in order serviceable. 5

J. Milton

LXXXVI

SONG FOR ST. CECILIA'S DAY, 1687

From Harmony, from heavenly Harmony
This universal frame began:
When Nature underneath a heap
Of jarring atoms lay
And could not heave her head, 10
The tuneful voice was heard from high,
Arise, ye more than dead!
Then cold and hot and moist and dry
In order to their stations leap,
And Music's power obey.— 15
From harmony, from heavenly harmony
This universal frame began:
From harmony to harmony
Through all the compass of the notes it ran,
The diapason closing full in Man. 20

What passion cannot Music raise and quell?
When Jubal struck the chorded shell
His listening brethren stood around,
And, wondering, on their faces fell
To worship that celestial sound. 25
Less than a god they thought there could not dwell
Within the hollow of that shell
That spoke so sweetly and so well.
What passion cannot Music raise and quell?

The trumpet's loud clangor 30
Excites us to arms,

With shrill notes of anger
And mortal alarms.
The double double double beat
Of the thundering drum —
Cries "Hark! the foes come; 5
Charge, charge, 't is too late to retreat!"

The soft complaining flute
In dying notes discovers
The woes of hopeless lovers,
Whose dirge is whisper'd by the warbling lute. 10

Sharp violins proclaim
Their jealous pangs and desperation,
Fury, frantic indignation,
Depth of pains, and height of passion
For the fair disdainful dame. 15

But oh! what art can teach,
What human voice can reach
The sacred organ's praise?
Notes inspiring holy love,
Notes that wing their heavenly ways 20
To mend the choirs above.

Orpheus could lead the savage race,
And trees unrooted left their place
Sequacious of the lyre:
But bright Cecilia raised the wonder higher: 25
When to her Organ vocal breath was given
An Angel heard, and straight appear'd —
Mistaking Earth for Heaven.

GRAND CHORUS

As from the power of sacred lays
The spheres began to move, 30
And sung the great Creator's praise
To all the blest above;
So when the last and dreadful hour

This crumbling pageant shall devour,
The trumpet shall be heard on high,
The dead shall live, the living die,
And Music shall untune the sky.

J. Dryden

LXXXVII

ON THE LATE MASSACRE IN PIEDMONT

Avenge, O Lord! Thy slaughter'd saints, whose bones 5
Lie scatter'd on the Alpine mountains cold;
Even them who kept Thy truth so pure of old
When all our fathers worshipt stocks and stones,
Forget not: In Thy book record their groans
Who were Thy sheep, and in their ancient fold 10
Slain by the bloody Piemontese that roll'd
Mother with infant down the rocks. Their moans

The vales redoubled to the hills, and they
To Heaven. Their martyr'd blood and ashes sow
O'er all the Italian fields, where still doth sway 15

The triple Tyrant: that from these may grow
A hundredfold, who, having learnt Thy way,
Early may fly the Babylonian woe.

J. Milton

LXXXVIII

HORATION ODE UPON CROMWELL'S RETURN FROM IRELAND

The forward youth that would appear,
Must now forsake his Muses dear, 20
Nor in the shadows sing
His numbers languishing.

'T is time to leave the books in dust,
And oil the unuséd armor's rust,
Removing from the wall 25
The corslet of the hall.

So restless Cromwell could not cease
In the inglorious arts of peace,
But through adventurous war
Urgéd his active star:

And like the three-fork'd lightning, first 5
Breaking the clouds where it was nurst,
Did thorough his own Side
His fiery way divide:

For 't is all one to courage high,
The emulous, or enemy; 10
And with such, to inclose
Is more than to oppose;

Then burning through the air he went
And palaces and temples rent;
And Cæsar's head at last 15
Did through his laurels blast.

'T is madness to resist or blame
The face of angry heaven's flame;
And if we would speak true,
Much to the Man is due 20

Who, from his private gardens, where
He lived reservéd and austere,
(As if his highest plot
To plant the bergamot),

Could by industrious valor climb 25
To ruin the great work of time,
And cast the Kingdoms old
Into another mold;

Though Justice against Fate complain,
And plead the ancient Rights in vain — 30
But those do hold or break
As men are strong or weak;

Nature, that hateth emptiness,
Allows of penetration less,
And therefore must make room
Where greater spirits come.

What field of all the civil war 5
Where his were not the deepest scar?
And Hampton shows what part
He had of wiser art,

Where, twining subtle fears with hope,
He wove a net of such a scope 10
That Charles himself might chase
To Carisbrook's narrow case,

That thence the Royal actor borne
The tragic scaffold might adorn:
While round the arméd bands 15
Did clap their bloody hands.

He nothing common did or mean
Upon that memorable scene,
But with his keener eye
The ax's edge did try; 20

Nor call'd the Gods, with vulgar spite,
To vindicate his helpless right;
But bow'd his comely head
Down, as upon a bed.

— This was that memorable hour 25
Which first assured the forcéd power:
So when they did design
The Capitol's first line,

A Bleeding Head, where they begun,
Did fright the architects to run; 30
And yet in that the State
Foresaw its happy fate!

And now the Irish are ashamed
To see themselves in one year tamed:
    So much one man can do
    That does both act and know.

They can affirm his praises best, 5
And have, though overcome, confest
    How good he is, how just
    And fit for highest trust.

Nor yet grown stiffer with command,
But still in the Republic's hand— 10
    How fit he is to sway
    That can so well obey!

He to the Commons' feet presents
A Kingdom for his first year's rents,
    And (what he may) forbears 15
    His fame, to make it theirs:

And has his sword and spoils ungirt
To lay them at the Public's skirt.
    So when the falcon high
    Falls heavy from the sky, 20

She, having kill'd, no more doth search
But on the next green bough to perch,
    Where, when he first does lure,
    The falconer has her sure.

—What may not then our Isle presume 25
While victory his crest does plume?
    What may not others fear
    If thus he crowns each year?

As Cæsar he, erelong, to Gaul,
To Italy an Hannibal, 30
    And to all States not free
    Shall climacteric be.

The Pict no shelter now shall find
Within his parti-color'd mind,
But from this valor sad
Shrink underneath the plaid—

Happy, if in the tufted brake 5
The English hunter him mistake,
Nor lay his hounds in near
The Caledonian deer.

But Thou, the War's and Fortune's son,
March indefatigably on; 10
And for the last effect
Still keep the sword erect:

Besides the force it has to fright
The spirits of the shady night,
The same arts that did gain 15
A power, must it maintain.

A. Marvell

LXXXIX

LYCIDAS

(Elegy on a Friend drowned in the Irish Channel, 1637)

Yet once more, O ye laurels, and once more
Ye myrtles brown, with ivy never sere,
I come to pluck your berries harsh and crude,
And with forced fingers rude 20
Shatter your leaves before the mellowing year.
Bitter constraint and sad occasion dear
Compels me to disturb your season due:
For Lycidas is dead, dead ere his prime,
Young Lycidas, and hath not left his peer. 25
Who would not sing for Lycidas? he knew
Himself to sing, and build the lofty rime.
He must not float upon his watery bier
Unwept, and welter to the parching wind,
Without the meed of some melodious tear. 30

Begin then, Sisters of the sacred well
That from beneath the seat of Jove doth spring;
Begin, and somewhat loudly sweep the string.
Hence with denial vain and coy excuse:
So may some gentle Muse 5
With lucky words favor my destined urn;
And as he passes, turn
And bid fair peace be to my sable shroud.

For we were nursed upon the selfsame hill,
Fed the same flock by fountain, shade, and rill: 10
Together both, ere the high lawns appear'd
Under the opening eyelids of the Morn,
We drove afield, and both together heard
What time the gray-fly winds her sultry horn,
Battening our flocks with the fresh dews of night, 15
Oft till the star that rose at evening bright
Toward heaven's descent had sloped his westering wheel.
Meanwhile the rural ditties were not mute;
Temper'd to the oaten flute
Rough Satyrs danced, and Fauns with cloven heel 20
From the glad sound would not be absent long;
And old Damœtas loved to hear our song.

But, oh! the heavy change, now thou art gone,
Now thou art gone, and never must return!
Thee, Shepherd, thee the woods and desert caves 25
With wild thyme and the gadding vine o'ergrown,
And all their echoes, mourn:
The willows and the hazel copses green
Shall now no more be seen
Fanning their joyous leaves to thy soft lays:— 30
As killing as the canker to the rose,
Or taintworm to the weanling herds that graze,
Or frost to flowers, that their gay wardrobe wear
When first the whitethorn blows;
Such, Lycidas, thy loss to shepherd's ear. 35

Where were ye, Nymphs, when the remorseless deep
Closed o'er the head of your loved Lycidas?
For neither were ye playing on the steep
Where your old bards, the famous Druids, lie,
Nor on the shaggy top of Mona high, 5
Nor yet where Deva spreads her wizard stream:
Ay me! I fondly dream —
Had ye been there . . . For what could that have done?
What could the Muse herself that Orpheus bore,
The Muse herself, for her enchanting son, 10
Whom universal nature did lament,
When by the rout that made the hideous roar
His gory visage down the stream was sent,
Down the swift Hebrus to the Lesbian shore?

Alas! what boots it with uncessant care 15
To tend the homely, slighted, shepherd's trade
And strictly meditate the thankless Muse?
Were it not better done, as others use,
To sport with Amaryllis in the shade,
Or with the tangles of Neæra's hair? 20
Fame is the spur that the clear spirit doth raise
(That last infirmity of noble mind)
To scorn delights, and live laborious days;
But the fair guerdon when we hope to find,
And think to burst out into sudden blaze, 25
Comes the blind Fury with the abhorréd shears
And slits the thin-spun life. "But not the praise"
Phœbus replied, and touch'd my trembling ears;
"Fame is no plant that grows on mortal soil,
Nor in the glistering foil 30
Set off to the world, nor in broad rumor lies:
But lives and spreads aloft by those pure eyes
And perfect witness of all-judging Jove;
As he pronounces lastly on each deed,
Of so much fame in heaven expect thy meed." 35

O fountain Arethuse, and thou honor'd flood
Smooth-sliding Mincius, crown'd with vocal reeds,
That strain I heard was of a higher mood.
But now my oat proceeds,
And listens to the herald of the sea 5
That came in Neptune's plea;
He ask'd the waves, and ask'd the felon winds,
What hard mishap hath doom'd this gentle swain?
And question'd every gust of rugged wings
That blows from off each beakéd promontory: 10
They knew not of his story;
And sage Hippotadés their answer brings,
That not a blast was from his dungeon stray'd;
The air was calm, and on the level brine
Sleek Panopé with all her sisters play'd. 15
It was that fatal and perfidious bark
Built in the eclipse, and rigg'd with curses dark,
That sunk so low that sacred head of thine.

Next Camus, reverend sire, went footing slow,
His mantle hairy, and his bonnet sedge 20
Inwrought with figures dim, and on the edge
Like to that sanguine flower inscribed with woe:
"Ah! who hath reft," quoth he, "my dearest pledge!"
Last came, and last did go
The Pilot of the Galilean lake; 25
Two massy keys he bore of metals twain
(The golden opes, the iron shuts amain);
He shook his mitered locks, and stern bespake:
"How well could I have spared for thee, young swain,
Enow of such, as for their bellies' sake 30
Creep and intrude and climb into the fold!
Of other care they little reckoning make
Than how to scramble at the shearers' feast,
And shove away the worthy bidden guest.
Blind mouths! that scarce themselves know how to hold 35

A sheephook, or have learn'd aught else the least
That to the faithful herdman's art belongs!
What recks it them? What need they? They are sped;
And when they list, their lean and flashy songs
Grate on their scrannel pipes of wretched straw; 5
The hungry sheep look up, and are not fed,
But swoln with wind and the rank mist they draw
Rot inwardly, and foul contagion spread:
Besides what the grim wolf with privy paw
Daily devours apace, and nothing said: 10
— But that two-handed engine at the door
Stands ready to smite once, and smite no more."

Return, Alphéus; the dread voice is past
That shrunk thy streams; return, Sicilian Muse,
And call the vales, and bid them hither cast 15
Their bells and flowerets of a thousand hues.
Ye valleys low, where the mild whispers use
Of shades, and wanton winds, and gushing brooks
On whose fresh lap the swart star sparely looks;
Throw hither all your quaint enamel'd eyes 20
That on the green turf suck the honey'd showers
And purple all the ground with vernal flowers.
Bring the rathe primrose that forsaken dies,
The tufted crow-toe, and pale jessamine,
The white pink, and the pansy freak'd with jet, 25
The glowing violet,
The musk rose, and the well-attired woodbine,
With cowslips wan that hang the pensive head,
And every flower that sad embroidery wears:
Bid amaranthus all his beauty shed, 30
And daffodillies fill their cups with tears
To strew the laureat hearse where Lycid lies.
For so to interpose a little ease,
Let our frail thoughts dally with false surmise: —
Ay me! whilst thee the shores and sounding seas 35

Wash far away, — where'er thy bones are hurl'd,
Whether beyond the stormy Hebrides
Where thou perhaps, under the whelming tide,
Visitest the bottom of the monstrous world;
Or whether thou, to our moist vows denied, 5
Sleep'st by the fable of Bellerus old,
Where the great Vision of the guarded mount
Looks toward Namancos and Bayona's hold,
— Look homeward, Angel, now, and melt with ruth:
— And, O ye dolphins, waft the hapless youth! 10

Weep no more, woeful shepherds, weep no more,
For Lycidas, your sorrow, is not dead,
Sunk though he be beneath the watery floor:
So sinks the day star in the ocean bed,
And yet anon repairs his drooping head 15
And tricks his beams, and with new-spangled ore
Flames in the forehead of the morning sky:
So Lycidas sunk low, but mounted high
Through the dear might of Him that walk'd the waves;
Where, other groves and other streams along, 20
With nectar pure his oozy locks he laves,
And hears the unexpressive nuptial song
In the blest kingdoms meek of joy and love.
There entertain him all the Saints above
In solemn troops, and sweet societies, 25
That sing, and singing, in their glory move,
And wipe the tears forever from his eyes.
Now, Lycidas, the shepherds weep no more;
Henceforth thou art the Genius of the shore
In thy large recompense, and shalt be good 30
To all that wander in that perilous flood.

Thus sang the uncouth swain to the oaks and rills,
While the still morn went out with sandals gray;
He touch'd the tender stops of various quills,
With eager thought warbling his Doric lay: 35

And now the sun had stretch'd out all the hills,
And now was dropt into the western bay:
At last he rose, and twitch'd his mantle blue:
To-morrow to fresh woods, and pastures new.

J. Milton

XC

ON THE TOMBS IN WESTMINSTER ABBEY

Mortality, behold and fear 5
What a change of flesh is here!
Think how many royal bones
Sleep within these heaps of stones;
Here they lie, had realms and lands,
Who now want strength to stir their hands, 10
Where from their pulpits seal'd with dust
They preach, "In greatness is no trust."
Here 's an acre sown indeed
With the richest royalest seed
That the earth did e'er suck in 15
Since the first man died for sin:
Here the bones of birth have cried
"Though gods they were, as men they died!"
Here are sands, ignoble things,
Dropt from the ruin'd sides of kings: 20
Here 's a world of pomp and state
Buried in dust, once dead by fate.

F. Beaumont

XCI

THE LAST CONQUEROR

Victorious men of earth, no more
  Proclaim how wide your empires are;
Though you bind-in every shore 25
  And your triumphs reach as far
    As night or day,
  Yet you, proud monarchs, must obey

And mingle with forgotten ashes, when
Death calls ye to the crowd of common men.

Devouring Famine, Plague, and War
  Each able to undo mankind,
Death's servile emissaries are; 5
  Nor to these alone confined,
    He hath at will
  More quaint and subtle ways to kill;
A smile or kiss, as he will use the art,
Shall have the cunning skill to break a heart. 10

J. Shirley

XCII

DEATH THE LEVELER

The glories of our blood and state
  Are shadows, not substantial things;
There is no armor against fate;
  Death lays his icy hand on kings:
    Scepter and Crown 15
    Must tumble down,
And in the dust be equal made
With the poor crooked scythe and spade.

Some men with swords may reap the field,
  And plant fresh laurels where they kill: 20
But their strong nerves at last must yield;
  They tame but one another still:
    Early or late
    They stoop to fate,
And must give up their murmuring breath 25
When they, pale captives, creep to death.

The garlands wither on your brow;
  Then boast no more your mighty deeds;
Upon Death's purple altar now
  See where the victor-victim bleeds: 30

Your heads must come
To the cold tomb;
Only the actions of the just
Smell sweet, and blossom in their dust.

J. Shirley

XCIII

WHEN THE ASSAULT WAS INTENDED TO THE CITY

Captain, or Colonel, or Knight in Arms, 5
Whose chance on these defenseless doors may seize,
If deed of honor did thee ever please,
Guard them, and him within protect from harms.

He can requite thee; for he knows the charms
That call fame on such gentle acts as these, 10
And he can spread thy name o'er lands and seas,
Whatever clime the sun's bright circle warms.

Lift not thy spear against the Muses' bower:
The great Emathian conqueror bid spare
The house of Pindarus, when temple and tower 15
Went to the ground: and the repeated air
Of sad Electra's poet had the power
To save the Athenian walls from ruin bare.

J Milton

XCIV

ON HIS BLINDNESS

When I consider how my light is spent
Ere half my days, in this dark world and wide, 20
And that one talent which is death to hide
Lodged with me useless, though my soul more bent

To serve therewith my Maker, and present
My true account, lest He returning chide,—
Doth God exact day-labor, light denied? 25
I fondly ask:— But Patience, to prevent

That murmur, soon replies; God doth not need
Either man's work, or His own gifts: who best
Bear His mild yoke, they serve Him best: His state

Is kingly; thousands at His bidding speed
And post o'er land and ocean without rest:— 5
They also serve who only stand and wait.

J. Milton

XCV

CHARACTER OF A HAPPY LIFE

How happy is he born and taught
That serveth not another's will;
Whose armor is his honest thought
And simple truth his utmost skill! 10

Whose passions not his masters are,
Whose soul is still prepared for death,
Untied unto the world by care
Of public fame, or private breath;

Who envies none that chance doth raise 15
Nor vice; who never understood
How deepest wounds are given by praise;
Nor rules of state, but rules of good:

Who hath his life from rumors freed,
Whose conscience is his strong retreat; 20
Whose state can neither flatterers feed,
Nor ruin make oppressors great;

Who God doth late and early pray
More of His grace than gifts to lend;
And entertains the harmless day 25
With a religious book or friend;

—This man is freed from servile bands
Of hope to rise, or fear to fall;

Lord of himself, though not of lands;
And having nothing, yet hath all.

Sir H. Wotton

XCVI

THE NOBLE NATURE

It is not growing like a tree
In bulk, doth make Man better be;
Or standing long an oak, three hundred year, 5
To fall a log at last, dry, bald, and sere:
A lily of a day
Is fairer far in May,
Although it fall and die that night—
It was the plant and flower of Light. 10
In small proportions we just beauties see;
And in short measures life may perfect be.

B. Jonson

XCVII

THE GIFTS OF GOD

When God at first made Man,
Having a glass of blessings standing by;
Let us (said He) pour on him all we can: 15
Let the world's riches, which dispersèd lie,
Contract into a span.

So strength first made a way;
Then beauty flow'd, then wisdom, honor, pleasure:
When almost all was out, God made a stay, 20
Perceiving that alone, of all His treasure,
Rest in the bottom lay.

For if I should (said He)
Bestow this jewel also on My creature,
He would adore My gifts instead of Me, 25
And rest in Nature, not the God of Nature.
So both should losers be.

Yet let him keep the rest,
But keep them with repining restlessness:
Let him be rich and weary, that at least,
If goodness lead him not, yet weariness
May toss him to My breast. 5

G. Herbert

XCVIII

THE RETREAT

Happy those early days, when I
Shined in my Angel-infancy!
Before I understood this place
Appointed for my second race,
Or taught my soul to fancy aught 10
But a white, celestial thought;
When yet I had not walk'd above
A mile or two from my first Love,
And looking back, at that short space
Could see a glimpse of His bright face; 15
When on some gilded cloud or flower
My gazing soul would dwell an hour,
And in those weaker glories spy
Some shadows of eternity;
Before I taught my tongue to wound 20
My conscience with a sinful sound,
Or had the black art to dispense
A several sin to every sense,
But felt through all this fleshly dress
Bright shoots of everlastingness. 25

O how I long to travel back,
And tread again that ancient track!
That I might once more reach that plain
Where first I left my glorious train;
From whence th' enlighten'd spirit sees 30
That shady City of palm trees!

But ah! my soul with too much stay
Is drunk, and staggers in the way: —
Some men a forward motion love,
But I by backward steps would move;
And when this dust falls to the urn, 5
In that state I came, return.

H. Vaughan

XCIX

TO MR. LAWRENCE

Lawrence, of virtuous father virtuous son,
Now that the fields are dank and ways are mire,
Where shall we sometimes meet, and by the fire
Help waste a sullen day, what may be won 10

From the hard season gaining? Time will run
On smoother, till Favonius re-inspire
The frozen earth, and clothe in fresh attire
The lily and rose, that neither sow'd nor spun.

What neat repast shall feast us, light and choice, 15
Of Attic taste, with wine, whence we may rise
To hear the lute well touch'd, or artful voice

Warble immortal notes and Tuscan air?
He who of those delights can judge, and spare
To interpose them oft, is not unwise. 20

J. Milton

C

TO CYRIACK SKINNER

Cyriack, whose grandsire, on the royal bench
Of British Themis, with no mean applause
Pronounced, and in his volumes taught, our laws,
Which others at their bar so often wrench;

To-day deep thoughts resolve with me to drench 25
In mirth, that after no repenting draws;

Let Euclid rest, and Archimedes pause,
And what the Swede intend, and what the French.

To measure life learn thou betimes, and know
Toward solid good what leads the nearest way;
For other things mild Heaven a time ordains, 5

And disapproves that care, though wise in show,
That with superfluous burden loads the day,
And, when God sends a cheerful hour, refrains.

J. Milton

CI

A HYMN IN PRAISE OF NEPTUNE

Of Neptune's empire let us sing,
At whose command the waves obey; 10
To whom the rivers tribute pay,
Down the high mountains sliding;
To whom the scaly nation yields
Homage for the crystal fields
Wherein they dwell; 15
And every sea-god pays a gem
Yearly out of his watery cell,
To deck great Neptune's diadem.

The Tritons dancing in a ring,
Before his palace gates do make 20
The water with their echoes quake,
Like the great thunder sounding:
The sea-nymphs chant their accents shrill,
And the Sirens taught to kill
With their sweet voice, 25
Make every echoing rock reply,
Unto their gentle murmuring noise,
The praise of Neptune's empery.

T. Campion

CII

HYMN TO DIANA

Queen and Huntress, chaste and fair,
Now the sun is laid to sleep,
Seated in thy silver chair
State in wonted manner keep:
Hesperus entreats thy light, 5
Goddess excellently bright.

Earth, let not thy envious shade
Dare itself to interpose;
Cynthia's shining orb was made
Heaven to clear when day did close: 10
Bless us then with wishéd sight,
Goddess excellently bright.

Lay thy bow of pearl apart
And thy crystal-shining quiver;
Give unto the flying hart 15
Space to breathe, how short soever:
Thou that mak'st a day of night,
Goddess excellently bright!

B. Jonson

CIII

WISHES FOR THE SUPPOSED MISTRESS

Whoe'er she be,
That not impossible She 20
That shall command my heart and me;

Where'er she lie,
Lock'd up from mortal eye
In shady leaves of destiny:

Till that ripe birth 25
Of studied Fate stand forth,
And teach her fair steps tread our earth;

Till that divine
Idea take a shrine
Of crystal flesh, through which to shine:

— Meet you her, my Wishes,
Bespeak her to my blisses, 5
And be ye call'd, my absent kisses.

I wish her beauty
That owes not all its duty
To gaudy tire, or glist'ring shoe-tie:

Something more than 10
Taffeta or tissue can,
Or rampant feather, or rich fan.

A face that's best
By its own beauty drest,
And can alone commend the rest: 15

A face made up
Out of no other shop
Than what Nature's white hand sets ope.

Sidneian showers
Of sweet discourse, whose powers 20
Can crown old Winter's head with flowers.

Whate'er delight
Can make day's forehead bright
Or give down to the wings of night.

Soft silken hours, 25
Open suns, shady bowers;
'Bove all, nothing within that lowers.

Days, that need borrow
No part of their good morrow
From a fore-spent night of sorrow: 30

Days, that in spite
Of darkness, by the light
Of a clear mind are day all night.

Life, that dares send
A challenge to his end, 5
And when it comes, say, "Welcome, friend."

I wish her store
Of worth may leave her poor
Of wishes; and I wish — no more.

Now, if Time knows 10
That Her, whose radiant brows
Weave them a garland of my vows;

Her that dares be
What these lines wish to see:
I seek no further, it is She. 15

'T is She, and here
Lo! I unclothe and clear
My wishes' cloudy character.

Such worth as this is
Shall fix my flying wishes, 20
And determine them to kisses.

Let her full glory,
My fancies, fly before ye;
Be ye my fictions: — but her story.

R. Crashaw

CIV

THE GREAT ADVENTURER[1]

Over the mountains 25
And over the waves,
Under the fountains
And under the graves;

[1] Preserved in Bishop Percy's "Reliques of English Poetry," 1765.

Under floods that are deepest,
Which Neptune obey;
Over rocks that are steepest
Love will find out the way.

Where there is no place 5
For the glow-worm to lie;
Where there is no space
For receipt of a fly;
Where the midge dares not venture
Lest herself fast she lay; 10
If love come, he will enter
And soon find out his way.

You may esteem him
A child for his might;
Or you may deem him 15
A coward from his flight;
But if she whom love doth honor
Be conceal'd from the day,
Set a thousand guards upon her,
Love will find out the way. 20

Some think to lose him
By having him confined;
And some do suppose him,
Poor thing, to be blind;
But if ne'er so close ye wall him, 25
Do the best that you may,
Blind love, if so ye call him,
Will find out his way.

You may train the eagle
To stoop to your fist; 30
Or you may inveigle
The phœnix of the east;
The lioness, ye may move her

To give o'er her prey;
But you 'll ne'er stop a lover:
He will find out his way.

Anon.

CV

THE PICTURE OF LITTLE T. C. IN A PROSPECT OF FLOWERS

See with what simplicity
This nymph begins her golden days! 5
In the green grass she loves to lie,
And there with her fair aspect tames
The wilder flowers, and gives them names;
But only with the roses plays,
And them does tell 10
What colors best become them, and what smell.

Who can foretell for what high cause
This darling of the Gods was born?
Yet this is she whose chaster laws
The wanton Love shall one day fear, 15
And, under her command severe,
See his bow broke, and ensigns torn.
Happy who can
Appease this virtuous enemy of man!

O then let me in time compound 20
And parley with those conquering eyes,
Ere they have tried their force to wound;
Ere with their glancing wheels they drive
In triumph over hearts that strive,
And them that yield but more despise: 25
Let me be laid,
Where I may see the glories from some shade.

Meantime, whilst every verdant thing
Itself does at thy beauty charm,

Reform the errors of the Spring;
Make that the tulips may have share
Of sweetness, seeing they are fair,
And roses of their thorns disarm;
But most procure 5
That violets may a longer age endure.

But O young beauty of the woods,
Whom Nature courts with fruits and flowers,
Gather the flowers, but spare the buds;
Lest FLORA, angry at thy crime 10
To kill her infants in their prime,
Should quickly make th' example yours;
And ere we see —
Nip in the blossom — all our hopes and thee.

A. Marvell

CVI

CHILD AND MAIDEN

Ah, Chloris! could I now but sit 15
As unconcern'd as when
Your infant beauty could beget
No happiness or pain!
When I the dawn used to admire,
And praised the coming day, 20
I little thought the rising fire
Would take my rest away.

Your charms in harmless childhood lay
Like metals in a mine;
Age from no face takes more away 25
Than youth conceal'd in thine.
But as your charms insensibly
To their perfection prest,
So love as unperceived did fly,
And center'd in my breast. 30

My passion with your beauty grew,
While Cupid at my heart,
Still as his mother favor'd you,
Threw a new flaming dart:
Each gloried in their wanton part; 5
To make a lover, he
Employ'd the utmost of his art —
To make a beauty, she.

Sir C. Sedley

CVII

CONSTANCY

I cannot change, as others do,
Though you unjustly scorn, 10
Since that poor swain that sighs for you,
For you alone was born;
No, Phyllis, no, your heart to move
A surer way I'll try, —
And to revenge my slighted love, 15
Will still love on, and die.

When, kill'd with grief, Amintas lies,
And you to mind shall call
The sighs that now unpitied rise,
The tears that vainly fall, 20
That welcome hour that ends his smart
Will then begin your pain,
For such a faithful tender heart
Can never break in vain.

J. Wilmot,
Earl of Rochester

CVIII

COUNSEL TO GIRLS

Gather ye rosebuds while ye may, 25
Old Time is still a-flying:
And this same flower that smiles to-day,
To-morrow will be dying.

The glorious Lamp of Heaven, the Sun,
  The higher he 's a-getting
The sooner will his race be run,
  And nearer he 's to setting.

That age is best which is the first, 5
  When youth and blood are warmer;
But being spent, the worse, and worst
  Times, still succeed the former.

Then be not coy, but use your time;
  And while ye may, go marry: 10
For having lost but once your prime,
  You may forever tarry.

R. Herrick

CIX

TO LUCASTA, ON GOING TO THE WARS

Tell me not, Sweet, I am unkind
  That from the nunnery
Of thy chaste breast and quiet mind, 15
  To war and arms I fly.

True, a new mistress now I chase,
  The first foe in the field;
And with a stronger faith embrace
  A sword, a horse, a shield. 20

Yet this inconstancy is such
  As you too shall adore;
I could not love thee, Dear, so much,
  Loved I not Honor more.

Colonel Lovelace

CX

ELIZABETH OF BOHEMIA

You meaner beauties of the night, 25
  That poorly satisfy our eyes
More by your number than your light,

You common people of the skies,
What are you, when the Moon shall rise?

You curious chanters of the wood
That warble forth dame Nature's lays,
Thinking your passions understood 5
By your weak accents; what 's your praise
When Philomel her voice doth raise?

You violets that first appear,
By your pure purple mantles known
Like the proud virgins of the year, 10
As if the spring were all your own, —
What are you, when the Rose is blown?

So when my Mistress shall be seen
In form and beauty of her mind,
By virtue first, then choice, a Queen, 15
Tell me, if she were not design'd
Th' eclipse and glory of her kind?

Sir H. Wotton

CXI

TO THE LADY MARGARET LEY

Daughter to that good Earl, once President
Of England's Council and her Treasury,
Who lived in both, unstain'd with gold or fee, 20
And left them both, more in himself content,

Till the sad breaking of that Parliament
Broke him, as that dishonest victory
At Chæronea, fatal to liberty,
Kill'd with report that old man eloquent; — 25

Though later born than to have known the days
Wherein your father flourish'd, yet by you,
Madam, methinks I see him living yet;

So well your words his noble virtues praise,
That all both judge you to relate them true,
And to possess them, honor'd Margaret.

J. Milton

CXII

THE TRUE BEAUTY

He that loves a rosy cheek
  Or a coral lip admires, 5
Or from starlike eyes doth seek
  Fuel to maintain his fires;
old Time makes these decay,
is flames must waste away.

But smooth and steadfast mind, 10
  Gentle thoughts, and calm desires,
Hearts with equal love combined,
  Kindle never-dying fires: —
Where these are not, I despise
Lovely cheeks or lips or eyes. 15

T. Carew

CXIII

TO DIANEME

Sweet, be not proud of those two eyes
Which starlike sparkle in their skies;
Nor be you proud, that you can see
All hearts your captives; yours yet free:
Be you not proud of that rich hair 20
Which wantons with the lovesick air;
Whenas that ruby which you wear,
Sunk from the tip of your soft ear,
Will last to be a precious stone
When all your world of beauty 's gone. 25

R. Herrick

CXIV[1]

Love in thy youth, fair Maid, be wise;
Old Time will make thee colder,
And though each morning new arise
Yet we each day grow older.
Thou as Heaven art fair and young, 5
Thine eyes like twin stars shining;
But ere another day be sprung
All these will be declining.
Then winter comes with all his fears,
And all thy sweets shall borrow; 10
Too late then wilt thou shower thy tears,—
And I too late shall sorrow!

Anon.

CXV

Go, lovely Rose!
Tell her, that wastes her time and me,
That now she knows, 15
When I resemble her to thee,
How sweet and fair she seems to be.

Tell her that 's young
And shuns to have her graces spied,
That hadst thou sprung 20
In deserts, where no men abide,
Thou must have uncommended died.

Small is the worth
Of beauty from the light retired:
Bid her come forth, 25
Suffer herself to be desired,
And not blush so to be admired.

[1] Said to be from Walter Porter's "Madrigals and Airs," 1632.

Then die! that she
The common fate of all things rare
May read in thee:
How small a part of time they share
That are so wondrous sweet and fair! 5

E. Waller

CXVI

TO CELIA

Drink to me only with thine eyes,
And I will pledge with mine;
Or leave a kiss but in the cup
And I 'll not look for wine.
The thirst that from the soul doth rise 10
Doth ask a drink divine;
But might I of Jove's nectar sup,
I would not change for thine.

I sent thee late a rosy wreath,
Not so much honoring thee 15
As giving it a hope that there
It could not wither'd be;
But thou thereon didst only breathe
And sent'st it back to me;
Since when it grows, and smells, I swear, 20
Not of itself but thee!

B. Jonson

CXVII

CHERRY-RIPE[1]

There is a garden in her face
Where roses and white lilies blow;
A heavenly paradise is that place,
Wherein all pleasant fruits do grow; 25

[1] These verses now given to Thomas Campion, appear in his undated "Fourth Book of Airs," published after February, 1617. They had previously been published in "An Hour's Recreation in Music," 1606.

There cherries grow that none may buy,
Till Cherry-Ripe themselves do cry.

Those cherries fairly do inclose
  Of orient pearl a double row,
Which when her lovely laughter shows, 5
  They look like rose-buds fill'd with snow:
Yet them no peer nor prince may buy,
Till Cherry-Ripe themselves do cry.

Her eyes like angels watch them still;
  Her brows like bended bows do stand, 10
Threat'ning with piercing frowns to kill
  All that approach with eye or hand
These sacred cherries to come nigh,
Till Cherry-Ripe themselves do cry!

Anon.

CXVIII

CORINNA'S MAYING

Get up, get up for shame! The blooming morn 15
Upon her wings presents the god unshorn.
  See how Aurora throws her fair
  Fresh-quilted colors through the air:
  Get up, sweet Slug-a-bed, and see
  The dew bespangling herb and tree. 20
Each flower has wept, and bow'd towárd the east,
Above an hour since; yet you not drest,
  Nay! not so much as out of bed?
  When all the birds have matins said,
  And sung their thankful hymns: 't is sin, 25
  Nay, profanation, to keep in, —
Whenas a thousand virgins on this day
Spring, sooner than the lark, to fetch in May.

Rise; and put on your foliage, and be seen
To come forth, like the Spring-time, fresh and green 30

And sweet as Flora. Take no care
For jewels for your gown, or hair:
Fear not; the leaves will strew
Gems in abundance upon you:
Besides, the childhood of the day has kept, 5
Against you come, some orient pearls unwept:
Come, and receive them while the light
Hangs on the dew-locks of the night:
And Titan on the eastern hill
Retires himself, or else stands still 10
Till you come forth. Wash, dress, be brief in praying:
Few beads are best, when once we go a Maying.

Come, my Corinna, come; and coming, mark
How each field turns a street; each street a park
Made green, and trimm'd with trees: see how 15
Devotion gives each house a bough
Or branch: Each porch, each door, ere this,
An ark, a tabernacle is,
Made up of white-thorn neatly interwove;
As if here were those cooler shades of love. 20
Can such delights be in the street,
And open fields, and we not see 't?
Come we 'll abroad: and let 's obey
The proclamation made for May:
And sin no more, as we have done, by staying; 25
But, my Corinna, come, let 's go a Maying.

There 's not a budding boy, or girl, this day,
But is got up, and gone to bring in May.
A deal of youth, ere this, is come
Back, and with white-thorn laden home. 30
Some have dispatch'd their cakes and cream,
Before that we have left to dream:
And some have wept, and woo'd, and plighted troth,
And chose their priest, ere we can cast off sloth:

Many a green-gown has been given;
Many a kiss, both odd and even:
Many a glance too has been sent
From out the eye, Love's firmament:
Many a jest told of the keys betraying 5
This night, and locks pick'd: — Yet we're not a Maying.

— Come, let us go, while we are in our prime;
And take the harmless folly of the time!
We shall grow old apace, and die
Before we know our liberty. 10
Our life is short; and our days run
As fast away as does the sun: —
And as a vapor, or a drop of rain
Once lost, can ne'er be found again:
So when or you or I are made 15
A fable, song, or fleeting shade;
All love, all liking, all delight
Lies drown'd with us in endless night.
Then while time serves, and we are but decaying,
Come, my Corinna! come, let's go a Maying. 20

R. Herrick

CXIX

THE POETRY OF DRESS

I

A sweet disorder in the dress
Kindles in clothes a wantonness: —
A lawn about the shoulders thrown
Into a fine distractión, —
An erring lace, which here and there 25
Enthralls the crimson stomacher, —
A cuff neglectful, and thereby
Ribbands to flow confusedly, —
A winning wave, deserving note,

In the tempestuous petticoat, —
A careless shoe string, in whose tie
I see a wild civility, —
Do more bewitch me, than when art
Is too precise in every part. 5

R. Herrick

CXX

2

Whenas in silks my Julia goes
Then, then (methinks) how sweetly flows
That liquefaction of her clothes.

Next, when I cast mine eyes and see
That brave vibration each way free; 10
O how that glittering taketh me!

R. Herrick

CXXI[1]

3

My Love in her attire doth show her wit,
  It doth so well become her:
For every season she hath dressings fit,
  For Winter, Spring, and Summer. 15
No beauty she doth miss
When all her robes are on:
But Beauty's self she is
When all her robes are gone.

Anon.

CXXII

ON A GIRDLE

That which her slender waist confined 20
Shall now my joyful temples bind:

[1] From Davison's "Poetical Rhapsody," 1602.

No monarch but would give his crown
His arms might do what this has done.

It was my Heaven's extremest sphere,
The pale which held that lovely deer:
My joy, my grief, my hope, my love 5
Did all within this circle move.

A narrow compass! and yet there
Dwelt all that 's good, and all that 's fair:
Give me but what this ribband bound,
Take all the rest the Sun goes round. 10

E. Waller

CXXIII

A MYSTICAL ECSTASY

E'en like two little bank-dividing brooks,
That wash the pebbles with their wanton streams,
And having ranged and search'd a thousand nooks,
Meet both at length in silver-breasted Thames,
Where in a greater current they conjoin: 15
So I my Best-Belovéd's am; so He is mine.

E'en so we met; and after long pursuit,
E'en so we join'd; we both became entire;
No need for either to renew a suit,
For I was flax and he was flames of fire: 20
Our firm-united souls did more than twine;
So I my Best-Belovéd's am; so He is mine.

If all those glittering Monarchs that command
The servile quarters of this earthly ball,
Should tender, in exchange, their shares of land, 25
I would not change my fortunes for them all:
Their wealth is but a counter to my coin:
The world 's but theirs; but my Belovéd 's mine.

F. Quarles

CXXIV

TO ANTHEA WHO MAY COMMAND HIM ANYTHING

Bid me to live, and I will live
  Thy Protestant to be:
Or bid me love, and I will give
  A loving heart to thee.

A heart as soft, a heart as kind, 5
  A heart as sound and free
As in the whole world thou canst find,
  That heart I 'll give to thee.

Bid that heart stay, and it will stay,
  To honor thy decree: 10
Or bid it languish quite away,
  And 't shall do so for thee.

Bid me to weep, and I will weep
  While I have eyes to see:
And having none, yet I will keep 15
  A heart to weep for thee.

Bid me despair, and I 'll despair,
  Under that cypress tree:
Or bid me die, and I will dare
  E'en Death, to die for thee. 20

Thou art my life, my love, my heart,
  The very eyes of me,
And hast command of every part,
  To live and die for thee.

R. Herrick

CXXV[1]

Love not me for comely grace, 25
For my pleasing eye or face,
Nor for any outward part,
No, nor for my constant heart, —

[1] From John Wilbye's "Second Set of Madrigals," 1609.

For those may fail, or turn to ill,
So thou and I shall sever:
Keep therefore a true woman's eye
And love me still, but know not why—
So hast thou the same reason still 5
To dote upon me ever!

Anon.

CXXVI

Not, Celia, that I juster am
Or better than the rest;
For I would change each hour, like them,
Were not my heart at rest. 10

But I am tied to very thee
By every thought I have;
Thy face I only care to see,
Thy heart I only crave.

All that in woman is adored 15
In thy dear self I find—
For the whole sex can but afford
The handsome and the kind.

Why then should I seek further store,
And still make love anew? 20
When change itself can give no more,
'T is easy to be true.

Sir C. Sedley

CXXVII

TO ALTHEA FROM PRISON

When Love with unconfinéd wings
Hovers within my gates,
And my divine Althea brings 25
To whisper at the grates;
When I lie tangled in her hair
And fetter'd to her eye,

The Gods that wanton in the air
  Know no such liberty.

When flowing cups run swiftly round
  With no allaying Thames,
Our careless heads with roses bound, 5
  Our hearts with loyal flames;
When thirsty grief in wine we steep,
  When healths and draughts go free —
Fishes that tipple in the deep
  Know no such liberty. 10

When (like committed linnets) I
  With shriller throat shall sing
The sweetness, mercy, majesty
  And glories of my King;
When I shall voice aloud how good 15
  He is, how great should be,
Enlargéd winds, that curl the flood,
  Know no such liberty.

Stone walls do not a prison make,
  Nor iron bars a cage; 20
Minds innocent and quiet take
  That for an hermitage;
If I have freedom in my love
  And in my soul am free,
Angels alone, that soar above, 25
  Enjoy such liberty.

Colonel Lovelace

CXXVIII

TO LUCASTA, GOING BEYOND THE SEAS

If to be absent were to be
  Away from thee;
Or that when I am gone
  You or I were alone; 30

Then, my Lucasta, might I crave
Pity from blustering wind, or swallowing wave.

But I 'll not sigh one blast or gale
To swell my sail,
Or pay a tear to 'suage 5
The foaming blue-god's rage;
For whether he will let me pass
Or no, I 'm still as happy as I was.

Though seas and land betwixt us both,
Our faith and troth, 10
Like separated souls,
All time and space controls:
Above the highest sphere we meet
Unseen, unknown, and greet as Angels greet.

So then we do anticipate 15
Our after-fate,
And are alive i' the skies,
If thus our lips and eyes
Can speak like spirits unconfined
In Heaven, their earthy bodies left behind. 20

Colonel Lovelace

CXXIX

ENCOURAGEMENTS TO A LOVER

Why so pale and wan, fond lover?
Prithee, why so pale?
Will, if looking well can't move her,
Looking ill prevail?
Prithee, why so pale? 25

Why so dull and mute, young sinner?
Prithee, why so mute?
Will, when speaking well can't win her,
Saying nothing do 't?
Prithee, why so mute? 30

Quit, quit, for shame! this will not move,
This cannot take her;
If of herself she will not love,
Nothing can make her:
The D—l take her! 5

Sir J. Suckling

CXXX

A SUPPLICATION

Awake, awake, my Lyre!
And tell thy silent master's humble tale
In sounds that may prevail;
Sounds that gentle thoughts inspire:
Though so exalted she 10
And I so lowly be
Tell her, such different notes make all thy harmony.

Hark, how the strings awake!
And, though the moving hand approach not near,
Themselves with awful fear 15
A kind of numerous trembling make.
Now all thy forces try;
Now all thy charms apply;
Revenge upon her ear the conquests of her eye.

Weak Lyre! thy virtue sure 20
Is useless here, since thou art only found
To cure, but not to wound,
And she to wound, but not to cure.
Too weak too wilt thou prove
My passion to remove; 25
Physic to other ills, thou 'rt nourishment to Love.

Sleep, sleep again, my Lyre!
For thou canst never tell my humble tale
In sounds that will prevail,
Nor gentle thoughts in her inspire; 30

All thy vain mirth lay by,
Bid thy strings silent lie,
Sleep, sleep again, my Lyre, and let thy master die.

A. Cowley

CXXXI

THE MANLY HEART

Shall I, wasting in despair,
Die because a woman 's fair? 5
Or make pale my cheeks with care
'Cause another's rosy are?
Be she fairer than the day
Or the flowery meads in May —
If she think not well of me 10
What care I how fair she be?

Shall my silly heart be pined
'Cause I see a woman kind;
Or a well disposéd nature
Joinéd with a lovely feature? 15
Be she meeker, kinder than
Turtle-dove or pelican,
If she be not so to me
What care I how kind she be?

Shall a woman's virtues move 20
Me to perish for her love?
Or her well-deservings known
Make me quite forget mine own?
Be she with that goodness blest
Which may merit name of Best; 25
If she be not such to me,
What care I how good she be?

'Cause her fortune seems too high,
Shall I play the fool and die?
She that bears a noble mind 30
If not outward helps she find,

Thinks what with them he would do
Who without them dares her woo;
And unless that mind I see,
What care I how great she be?

Great or good, or kind or fair, 5
I will ne'er the more despair;
If she love me, this believe,
I will die ere she shall grieve;
If she slight me when I woo,
I can scorn and let her go; 10
For if she be not for me,
What care I for whom she be?

G. Wither

CXXXII

MELANCHOLY

Hence, all you vain delights,
As short as are the nights
Wherein you spend your folly: 15
There 's naught in this life sweet
If man were wise to see 't,
But only melancholy,
O sweetest Melancholy!
Welcome, folded arms, and fixéd eyes, 20
A sigh that piercing mortifies,
A look that 's fasten'd to the ground,
A tongue chain'd up without a sound!
Fountain-heads and pathless groves,
Places which pale passion loves! 25
Moonlight walks, when all the fowls
Are warmly housed save bats and owls!
A midnight bell, a parting groan!
These are the sounds we feed upon;
Then stretch our bones in a still gloomy valley; 30
Nothing 's so dainty sweet as lovely melancholy.

J. Fletcher

CXXXIII

FORSAKEN[1]

O waly waly up the bank,
  And waly waly down the brae,
And waly waly yon burn-side
  Where I and my Love wont to gae!
I leant my back unto an aik, 5
  I thought it was a trusty tree;
But first it bow'd, and syne it brak,
  Sae my true Love did lichtly me.

O waly waly, but love be bonny
  A little time while it is new; 10
But when 't is auld, it waxeth cauld
  And fades awa' like morning dew.
Or wherefore should I busk my head?
  Or wherefore should I kame my hair?
For my true Love has me forsook, 15
  And says he 'll never loe me mair.

Now Arthur-seat sall be my bed;
  The sheets shall ne'er be prest by me:
Saint Anton's well sall be my drink,
  Since my true Love has forsaken me. 20
Marti'mas wind, when wilt thou blaw
  And shake the green leaves aff the tree?
O gentle Death, when wilt thou come?
  For of my life I am wearíe.

'T is not the frost that freezes fell, 25
  Nor blawing snaw's inclemencie;
'T is not sic cauld that makes me cry,
  But my Love's heart grown cauld to me.
When we came in by Glasgow town
  We were a comely sight to see; 30

[1] Preserved in Percy's "Reliques of English Poetry," 1765.

My Love was clad in the black velvét,
  And I myself in cramasie.

But had I wist, before I kist,
  That love had been sae ill to win;
I had lockt my heart in a case of gowd 5
  And pinn'd it with a siller pin.
And, O! if my young babe were born,
  And set upon the nurse's knee,
And I mysell were dead and gane,
  And the green grass growing over me! 10

Anon.

CXXXIV [1]

Upon my lap my sovereign sits
And sucks upon my breast;
Meantime his love maintains my life
And gives my sense her rest.
    Sing lullaby, my little boy, 15
    Sing lullaby, mine only joy!

When thou hast taken thy repast,
Repose, my babe, on me;
So may thy mother and thy nurse
Thy cradle also be. 20
    Sing lullaby, my little boy,
    Sing lullaby, mine only joy!

I grieve that duty doth not work
All that my wishing would,
Because I would not be to thee 25
But in the best I should.
    Sing lullaby, my little boy,
    Sing lullaby, mine only joy!

Yet as I am, and as I may,
I must and will be thine, 30

[1] From Martin Peerson's "Private Music," 1620

Though all too little for thyself
Vouchsafing to be mine.
Sing lullaby, my little boy,
Sing lullaby, mine only joy!

Anon.

CXXXV

FAIR HELEN[1]

I wish I were where Helen lies; 5
Night and day on me she cries;
O that I were where Helen lies
On fair Kirconnell lea!

Curst be the heart that thought the thought,
And curst the hand that fired the shot, 10
When in my arms burd Helen dropt,
And died to succor me!

O think na but my heart was sair
When my Love dropt down and spak nae mair!
I laid her down wi' meikle care 15
On fair Kirconnell lea.

As I went down the water-side,
None but my foe to be my guide,
None but my foe to be my guide,
On fair Kirconnell lea; 20

I lighted down my sword to draw,
I hackéd him in pieces sma',
I hackéd him in pieces sma',
For her sake that died for me.

O Helen fair, beyond compare! 25
I 'll make a garland of thy hair
Shall bind my heart for evermair
Until the day I die.

[1] From Scott's "Minstrelsy of the Scottish Border," 1802–1803.

O that I were where Helen lies!
Night and day on me she cries;
Out of my bed she bids me rise,
Says, "Haste and come to me!"

O Helen fair! O Helen chaste! 5
If I were with thee, I were blest,
Where thou lies low and takes thy rest
On fair Kirconnell lea.

I wish my grave were growing green,
A winding-sheet drawn ower my een, 10
And I in Helen's arms lying,
On fair Kirconnell lea.

I wish I were where Helen lies;
Night and day on me she cries;
And I am weary of the skies, 15
Since my Love died for me.

Anon.

CXXXVI

THE TWA CORBIES[1]

As I was walking all alane
I heard twa corbies making a mane;
The tane unto the t'other say,
"Where sall we gang and dine to-day?" 20

"—In behint yon auld fail dyke,
I wot there lies a new-slain Knight;
And naebody kens that he lies there,
But his hawk, his hound, and lady fair.

"His hound is to the hunting gane, 25
His hawk to fetch the wild-fowl hame,

[1] From Scott's "Minstrelsy of the Scottish Border," 1802–1803. An older version appeared in Ravenscroft's "Melismata," 1611.

His lady 's ta'en another mate,
So we may mak our dinner sweet.

"Ye 'll sit on his white hause-bane,
And I 'll pick out his bonnie blue een:
Wi' ae lock o' his gowden hair 5
We 'll theek our nest when it grows bare.

"Mony a one for him makes mane,
But nane sall ken where he is gane;
O'er his white banes, when they are bare,
The wind sall blaw for evermair." 10

Anon.

CXXXVII

ON THE DEATH OF MR. WILLIAM HERVEY

It was a dismal and a fearful night,—
Scarce could the Morn drive on th' unwilling light,
When sleep, death's image, left my troubled breast,
By something liker death possest.
My eyes with tears did uncommanded flow, 15
And on my soul hung the dull weight
Of some intolerable fate.
What bell was that? Ah me! Too much I know!

My sweet companion, and my gentle peer,
Why hast thou left me thus unkindly here, 20
Thy end forever, and my life, to moan?
O thou hast left me all alone!
Thy soul and body, when death's agony
Besieged around thy noble heart,
Did not with more reluctance part 25
Than I, my dearest friend, do part from thee.

Ye fields of Cambridge, our dear Cambridge, say,
Have ye not seen us, walking every day?
Was there a tree about which did not know
The love betwixt us two? 30

Henceforth, ye gentle trees, forever fade,
Or your sad branches thicker join,
And into darksome shades combine,
Dark as the grave wherein my friend is laid.

Large was his soul; as large a soul as e'er 5
Submitted to inform a body here;
High as the place 't was shortly in Heaven to have,
But low and humble as his grave;
So high that all the virtues there did come
As to the chiefest seat 10
Conspicuous, and great;
So low that for me too it made a room.

Knowledge he only sought, and so soon caught,
As if for him knowledge had rather sought;
Nor did more learning ever crowded lie 15
In such a short mortality.
Whene'er the skillful youth discoursed or writ,
Still did the notions throng
About his eloquent tongue;
Nor could his ink flow faster than his wit. 20

His mirth was the pure spirits of various wit,
Yet never did his God or friends forget.
And when deep talk and wisdom came in view,
Retired, and gave to them their due.
For the rich help of books he always took, 25
Though his own searching mind before
Was so with notions written o'er,
As if wise Nature had made that her book.

With as much zeal, devotion, piety,
He always lived, as other saints do die. 30
Still with his soul severe account he kept,
Weeping all debts out ere he slept.

Then down in peace and innocence he lay,
Like the sun's laborious light,
Which still in water sets at night,
Unsullied with his journey of the day.

A. Cowley

CXXXVIII

FRIENDS IN PARADISE

They are all gone into the world of light! 5
And I alone sit lingering here;
Their very memory is fair and bright,
And my sad thoughts doth clear: —

It glows and glitters in my cloudy breast,
Like stars upon some gloomy grove, 10
Or those faint beams in which this hill is drest,
After the sun's remove.

I see them walking in an air of glory,
Whose light doth trample on my days:
My days, which are at best but dull and hoary, 15
Mere glimmering and decays.

O holy Hope! and high Humility,
High as the Heavens above!
These are your walks, and you have show'd them me,
To kindle my cold love. 20

Dear, beauteous Death! the jewel of the just,
Shining nowhere, but in the dark;
What mysteries do lie beyond thy dust,
Could man outlook that mark!

He that hath found some fledged bird's nest, may know 25
At first sight, if the bird be flown;
But what fair well or grove he sings in now,
That is to him unknown.

And yet, as Angels in some brighter dreams
Call to the soul, when man doth sleep;
So some strange thoughts transcend our wonted themes,
And into glory peep.

H. Vaughan

CXXXIX

TO BLOSSOMS

Fair pledges of a fruitful tree, 5
Why do ye fall so fast?
Your date is not so past,
But you may stay yet here awhile
To blush and gently smile,
And go at last. 10

What, were ye born to be
An hour or half's delight,
And so to bid good-night?
'T was pity Nature brought ye forth
Merely to show your worth, 15
And lose you quite.

But you are lovely leaves, where we
May read how soon things have
Their end, though ne'er so brave:
And after they have shown their pride 20
Like you, awhile, they glide
Into the grave.

R. Herrick

CXL

TO DAFFODILS

Fair Daffodils, we weep to see
You haste away so soon:
As yet the early-rising Sun 25
Has not attain'd his noon.

Stay, stay,
Until the hasting day
Has run
But to the even-song;
And, having pray'd together, we 5
Will go with you along.

We have short time to stay, as you,
We have as short a spring;
As quick a growth to meet decay
As you, or anything. 10
We die,
As your hours do, and dry
Away
Like to the summer's rain;
Or as the pearls of morning's dew 15
Ne'er to be found again.

R. Herrick

CXLI

THE GIRL DESCRIBES HER FAWN

With sweetest milk and sugar first
I it at my own fingers nursed;
And as it grew, so every day
It wax'd more white and sweet than they — 20
It had so sweet a breath! and oft
I blush'd to see its foot more soft
And white, — shall I say, — than my hand?
Nay, any lady's of the land!

It is a wondrous thing how fleet 25
'T was on those little silver feet:
With what a pretty skipping grace
It oft would challenge me the race: —
And when 't had left me far away
'T would stay, and run again, and stay: 30

For it was nimbler much than hinds,
And trod as if on the four winds.

I have a garden of my own,
But so with roses overgrown
And lilies, that you would it guess 5
To be a little wilderness:
And all the springtime of the year
It only lovéd to be there.
Among the beds of lilies I
Have sought it oft, where it should lie; 10
Yet could not, till itself would rise,
Find it, although before mine eyes:—
For in the flaxen lilies' shade
It like a bank of lilies laid.

Upon the roses it would feed, 15
Until its lips e'en seem'd to bleed:
And then to me 't would boldly trip,
And print those roses on my lip.
But all its chief delight was still
On roses thus itself to fill, 20
And its pure virgin limbs to fold
In whitest sheets of lilies cold:—
Had it lived long, it would have been
Lilies without — roses within.

A. Marvell

CXLII

THOUGHTS IN A GARDEN

How vainly men themselves amaze 25
To win the palm, the oak, or bays,
And their uncessant labors see
Crown'd from some single herb or tree,
Whose short and narrow-vergéd shade
Does prudently their toils upbraid; 30

While all the flowers and trees do close
To weave the garlands of Repose.

Fair Quiet, have I found thee here,
And Innocence thy sister dear!
Mistaken long, I sought you then 5
In busy companies of men:
Your sacred plants, if here below,
Only among the plants will grow:
Society is all but rude
To this delicious solitude. 10

No white nor red was ever seen
So amorous as this lovely green.
Fond lovers, cruel as their flame,
Cut in these trees their mistress' name:
Little, alas, they know or heed 15
How far these beauties hers exceed!
Fair trees! wheres'e'er your barks I wound,
No name shall but your own be found.

When we have run our passions' heat
Love hither makes his best retreat: 20
The gods, who mortal beauty chase,
Still in a tree did end their race;
Apollo hunted Daphne so
Only that she might laurel grow;
And Pan did after Syrinx speed 25
Not as a nymph, but for a reed.

What wondrous life is this I lead!
Ripe apples drop about my head;
The luscious clusters of the vine
Upon my mouth do crush their wine; 30
The nectarine and curious peach
Into my hands themselves do reach;
Stumbling on melons, as I pass,
Ensnared with flowers, I fall on grass.

Meanwhile the mind from pleasure less
Withdraws into its happiness;
The mind, that ocean where each kind
Does straight its own resemblance find;
Yet it creates, transcending these, 5
Far other worlds, and other seas;
Annihilating all that 's made
To a green thought in a green shade.

Here at the fountain's sliding foot
Or at some fruit tree's mossy root, 10
Casting the body's vest aside
My soul into the boughs does glide;
There, like a bird, it sits and sings,
Then whets and claps its silver wings,
And, till prepared for longer flight, 15
Waves in its plumes the various light.

Such was that happy Garden-state
While man there walk'd without a mate:
After a place so pure and sweet,
What other help could yet be meet! 20
But 't was beyond a mortal's share
To wander solitary there:
Two paradises 't were in one,
To live in Paradise alone.

How well the skillful gardener drew 25
Of flowers and herbs this dial new!
Where, from above, the milder sun
Does through a fragrant zodiac run:
And, as it works, th' industrious bee
Computes its time as well as we. 30
How could such sweet and wholesome hours
Be reckon'd, but with herbs and flowers!

A. Marvell

CXLIII

FORTUNATI NIMIUM

Jack and Joan, they think no ill,
But loving live, and merry still;
Do their week-day's work, and pray
Devoutly on the holyday:
Skip and trip it on the green, 5
And help to choose the Summer Queen;
Lash out at a country feast
Their silver penny with the best.

Well can they judge of nappy ale,
And tell at large a winter tale; 10
Climb up to the apple loft,
And turn the crabs till they be soft.
Tib is all the father's joy,
And little Tom the mother's boy: —
All their pleasure is, Content, 15
And care, to pay their yearly rent.

Joan can call by name her cows
And deck her windows with green boughs;
She can wreaths and tutties make,
And trim with plums a bridal cake. 20
Jack knows what brings gain or loss,
And his long flail can stoutly toss:
Makes the hedge which others break,
And ever thinks what he doth speak.

— Now, you courtly dames and knights, 25
That study only strange delights,
Though you scorn the homespun gray,
And revel in your rich array;
Though your tongues dissemble deep
And can your heads from danger keep; 30

Yet, for all your pomp and train,
Securer lives the silly swain!

T. Campion

CXLIV

L'ALLEGRO

Hence, loathéd Melancholy,
Of Cerberus and blackest Midnight born
In Stygian cave forlorn 5
'Mongst horrid shapes, and shrieks, and sights unholy!
Find out some uncouth cell
Where brooding Darkness spreads his jealous wings
And the night-raven sings;
There under ebon shades, and low-brow'd rocks 10
As ragged as thy locks,
In dark Cimmerian desert ever dwell.

But come, thou Goddess fair and free,
In heaven yclept Euphrosyne,
And by men, heart-easing Mirth, 15
Whom lovely Venus at a birth
With two sister Graces more
To ivy-crownéd Bacchus bore;
Or whether (as some sager sing)
The frolic wind that breathes the spring 20
Zephyr, with Aurora playing,
As he met her once a Maying —
There on beds of violets blue
And fresh-blown roses wash'd in dew
Fill'd her with thee, a daughter fair, 25
So buxom, blithe, and debonair.
Haste thee, Nymph, and bring with thee
Jest, and youthful jollity,
Quips, and cranks, and wanton wiles,
Nods, and becks, and wreathéd smiles 30
Such as hang on Hebe's cheek,

And love to live in dimple sleek;
Sport that wrinkled Care derides,
And Laughter holding both his sides: —
Come, and trip it as you go
On the light fantastic toe; 5
And in thy right hand lead with thee
The mountain-nymph, sweet Liberty;
And if I give thee honor due
Mirth, admit me of thy crew,
To live with her, and live with thee 10
In unreprovéd pleasures free;
To hear the lark begin his flight
And singing startle the dull night
From his watchtower in the skies,
Till the dappled dawn doth rise; 15
Then to come, in spite of sorrow,
And at my window bid good-morrow
Through the sweetbrier, or the vine,
Or the twisted eglantine:
While the cock with lively din 20
Scatters the rear of darkness thin,
And to the stack, or the barn door,
Stoutly struts his dames before:
Oft listening how the hounds and horn
Cheerly rouse the slumbering morn, 25
From the side of some hoar hill,
Through the high wood echoing shrill:
Sometime walking, not unseen,
By hedgerow elms, on hillocks green,
Right against the eastern gate 30
Where the great Sun begins his state
Robed in flames and amber light,
The clouds in thousand liveries dight;
While the plowman, near at hand,
Whistles o'er the furrow'd land, 35
And the milkmaid singeth blithe,

And the mower whets his scythe,
And every shepherd tells his tale
Under the hawthorn in the dale.
Straight mine eye hath caught new pleasures
Whilst the landscape round it measures; 5
Russet lawns, and fallows gray,
Where the nibbling flocks do stray;
Mountains, on whose barren breast
The laboring clouds do often rest;
Meadows trim with daisies pied, 10
Shallow brooks, and rivers wide;
Towers and battlements it sees
Bosom'd high in tufted trees,
Where perhaps some Beauty lies,
The Cynosure of neighboring eyes. 15
Hard by, a cottage chimney smokes
From betwixt two aged oaks,
Where Corydon and Thyrsis, met,
Are at their savory dinner set
Of herbs, and other country messes 20
Which the neat-handed Phillis dresses;
And then in haste her bower she leaves
With Thestylis to bind the sheaves;
Or, if the earlier season lead,
To the tann'd haycock in the mead. 25
Sometimes with secure delight
The upland hamlets will invite,
When the merry bells ring round,
And the jocund rebecks sound
To many a youth and many a maid, 30
Dancing in the checker'd shade;
And young and old come forth to play
On a sunshine holyday,
Till the livelong daylight fail:
Then to the spicy nut-brown ale, 35
With stories told of many a feat,

How Faery Mab the junkets eat: —
She was pinch'd, and pull'd, she said;
And he, by Friar's lantern led;
Tells how the drudging Goblin sweat
To earn his cream bowl duly set, 5
When in one night, ere glimpse of morn,
His shadowy flail hath thresh'd the corn
That ten day laborers could not end;
Then lies him down the lubber fiend,
And, stretch'd out all the chimney's length, 10
Basks at the fire his hairy strength;
And crop-full out of doors he flings,
Ere the first cock his matin rings.
Thus done the tales, to bed they creep,
By whispering winds soon lull'd asleep. 15
Tower'd cities please us then
And the busy hum of men,
Where throngs of knights and barons bold,
In weeds of peace, high triumphs hold,
With store of ladies, whose bright eyes 20
Rain influence, and judge the prize
Of wit or arms, while both contend
To win her grace, whom all commend.
There let Hymen oft appear
In saffron robe, with taper clear, 25
And pomp, and feast, and revelry,
With mask, and antique pageantry;
Such sights as youthful poets dream
On summer eves by haunted stream.
Then to the well-trod stage anon, 30
If Jonson's learnéd sock be on,
Or sweetest Shakespeare, Fancy's child,
Warble his native wood-notes wild.
And ever against eating cares
Lap me in soft Lydian airs 35
Married to immortal verse,

Such as the meeting soul may pierce
In notes, with many a winding bout
Of linkéd sweetness long drawn out,
With wanton heed and giddy cunning,
The melting voice through mazes running, 5
Untwisting all the chains that tie
The hidden soul of harmony;
That Orpheus' self may heave his head
From golden slumber, on a bed
Of heap'd Elysian flowers, and hear 10
Such strains as would have won the ear
Of Pluto, to have quite set free
His half-regain'd Eurydice.
These delights if thou canst give,
Mirth, with thee I mean to live. 15

J. Milton

CXLV

IL PENSEROSO

Hence, vain deluding Joys,
The brood of Folly without father bred!
How little you bestead
Or fill the fixéd mind with all your toys!
Dwell in some idle brain, 20
And fancies fond with gaudy shapes possess
As thick and numberless
As the gay motes that people the sunbeams,
Or likest hovering dreams,
The fickle pensioners of Morpheus' train. 25

But hail, thou goddess sage and holy,
Hail, divinest Melancholy!
Whose saintly visage is too bright
To hit the sense of human sight,
And therefore to our weaker view 30
O'erlaid with black, staid Wisdom's hue;

Black, but such as in esteem
Prince Memnon's sister might beseem,
Or that starr'd Ethiop queen that strove
To set her beauty's praise above
The sea nymphs, and their powers offended: 5
Yet thou art higher far descended:
Thee bright-hair'd Vesta, long of yore,
To solitary Saturn bore;
His daughter she; in Saturn's reign
Such mixture was not held a stain: 10
Oft in glimmering bowers and glades
He met her, and in secret shades
Of woody Ida's inmost grove,
While yet there saw no fear of Jove.
Come, pensive Nun, devout and pure, 15
Sober, steadfast, and demure,
All in a robe of darkest grain
Flowing with majestic train,
And sable stole of Cipres lawn
Over thy decent shoulders drawn: 20
Come, but keep thy wonted state,
With even step, and musing gait,
And looks commercing with the skies,
Thy rapt soul sitting in thine eyes:
There, held in holy passion still, 25
Forget thyself to marble, till
With a sad leaden downward cast
Thou fix them on the earth as fast:
And join with thee calm Peace, and Quiet,
Spare Fast, that oft with gods doth diet, 30
And hears the Muses in a ring
Aye round about Jove's altar sing:
And add to these retired Leisure
That in trim gardens takes his pleasure: —
But first and chiefest, with thee bring 35
Him that yon soars on golden wing

Guiding the fiery-wheelèd throne,
The cherub Contemplatión;
And the mute Silence hist along,
'Less Philomel will deign a song
In her sweetest saddest plight 5
Smoothing the rugged brow of Night,
While Cynthia checks her dragon yoke
Gently o'er the accustom'd oak.
— Sweet bird, that shunn'st the noise of folly,
Most musical, most melancholy! 10
Thee, chantress, oft, the woods among
I woo, to hear thy evensong;
And missing thee, I walk unseen
On the dry smooth-shaven green,
To behold the wandering Moon 15
Riding near her highest noon,
Like one that had been led astray
Through the heaven's wide pathless way,
And oft, as if her head she bow'd,
Stooping through a fleecy cloud. 20
Oft, on a plat of rising ground
I hear the far-off Curfew sound
Over some wide-water'd shore,
Swinging slow with sullen roar:
Or, if the air will not permit, 25
Some still removèd place will fit,
Where glowing embers through the room
Teach light to counterfeit a gloom;
Far from all resort of mirth,
Save the cricket on the hearth, 30
Or the bellman's drowsy charm
To bless the doors from nightly harm.
Or let my lamp at midnight hour
Be seen in some high lonely tower,
Where I may oft out-watch the Bear 35
With thrice-great Hermes, or unsphere

The spirit of Plato, to unfold
What worlds or what vast regions hold
The immortal mind, that hath forsook
Her mansion in this fleshly nook:
And of those demons that are found 5
In fire, air, flood, or underground,
Whose power hath a true consent
With planet, or with element.
Sometime let gorgeous Tragedy
In scepter'd pall come sweeping by, 10
Presenting Thebes, or Pelops' line,
Or the tale of Troy divine;
Or what (though rare) of later age
Ennobled hath the buskin'd stage.
But, O sad Virgin, that thy power 15
Might raise Musæus from his bower,
Or bid the soul of Orpheus sing
Such notes as, warbled to the string,
Drew iron tears down Pluto's cheek
And made Hell grant what Love did seek! 20
Or call up him that left half told
The story of Cambuscan bold,
Of Camball, and of Algarsife,
And who had Canacé to wife
That own'd the virtuous ring and glass; 25
And of the wondrous horse of brass
On which the Tartar king did ride:
And if aught else great bards beside
In sage and solemn tunes have sung
Of tourneys, and of trophies hung, 30
Of forests, and enchantments drear,
Where more is meant than meets the ear.
Thus, Night, oft see me in thy pale career,
Till civil-suited Morn appear,
Not trick'd and frounced as she was wont 35
With the Attic Boy to hunt,

But kercheft in a comely cloud
While rocking winds are piping loud,
Or usher'd with a shower still,
When the gust hath blown his fill,
Ending on the rustling leaves 5
With minute drops from off the eaves.
And when the sun begins to fling
His flaring beams, me, goddess, bring
To archéd walks of twilight groves,
And shadows brown, that Sylvan loves, 10
Of pine, or monumental oak,
Where the rude ax, with heavéd stroke,
Was never heard the nymphs to daunt
Or fright them from their hallow'd haunt.
There in close covert by some brook 15
Where no profaner eye may look,
Hide me from day's garish eye,
While the bee with honey'd thigh
That at her flowery work doth sing,
And the waters murmuring, 20
With such consort as they keep
Entice the dewy-feather'd Sleep;
And let some strange mysterious dream
Wave at his wings in airy stream
Of lively portraiture display'd, 25
Softly on my eyelids laid:
And, as I wake, sweet music breathe
Above, about, or underneath,
Sent by some Spirit to mortals good,
Or the unseen Genius of the wood. 30

But let my due feet never fail
To walk the studious cloister's pale,
And love the high-embowéd roof,
With antique pillars massy proof,
And storied windows richly dight 35
Casting a dim religious light.

There let the pealing organ blow
To the full-voiced choir below
In service high and anthems clear,
As may with sweetness, through mine ear,
Dissolve me into ecstasies, 5
And bring all Heaven before mine eyes.
And may at last my weary age
Find out the peaceful hermitage,
The hairy gown and mossy cell
Where I may sit and rightly spell 10
Of every star that heaven doth shew,
And every herb that sips the dew;
Till old experience do attain
To something like prophetic strain.

These pleasures, Melancholy, give, 15
And I with thee will choose to live.

J. Milton

CXLVI

SONG OF THE EMIGRANTS IN BERMUDA

Where the remote Bermudas ride
In the ocean's bosom unespied,
From a small boat that row'd along
The listening winds received this song. 20
"What should we do but sing His praise
That led us through the watery maze
Where He the huge sea-monsters wracks,
That lift the deep upon their backs,
Unto an isle so long unknown, 25
And yet far kinder than our own?
He lands us on a grassy stage,
Safe from the storms, and prelate's rage:
He gave us this eternal Spring
Which here enamels everything, 30
And sends the fowls to us in care

On daily visits through the air.
He hangs in shades the orange bright
Like golden lamps in a green night,
And does in the pomegranates close
Jewels more rich than Ormus shows: 5
He makes the figs our mouths to meet
And throws the melons at our feet;
But apples plants of such a price,
No tree could ever bear them twice.
With cedars chosen by His hand 10
From Lebanon He stores the land;
And makes the hollow seas that roar
Proclaim the ambergris on shore.
He cast (of which we rather boast)
The Gospel's pearl upon our coast; 15
And in these rocks for us did frame
A temple where to sound His name.
Oh! let our voice His praise exalt
Till it arrive at Heaven's vault,
Which thence (perhaps) rebounding may 20
Echo beyond the Mexique bay!"
—Thus sang they in the English boat
A holy and a cheerful note:
And all the way, to guide their chime,
With falling oars they kept the time. 25

A. Marvell

CXLVII

AT A SOLEMN MUSIC

Blest pair of Sirens, pledges of Heaven's joy,
Sphere-born harmonious Sisters, Voice and Verse!
Wed your divine sounds, and mixed power employ,
Dead things with inbreathed sense able to pierce;
And to our high-raised phantasy present 30
That undisturbéd Song of pure consent

Aye sung before the sapphire-color'd throne
To Him that sits thereon,
With saintly shout and solemn jubilee;
Where the bright Seraphim in burning row
Their loud uplifted angel-trumpets blow; 5
And the Cherubic host in thousand choirs
Touch their immortal harps of golden wires,
With those just Spirits that wear victorious palms,
Hymns devout and holy psalms
Singing everlastingly: 10
That we on Earth, with undiscording voice
May rightly answer that melodious noise;
As once we did, till disproportion'd sin
Jarr'd against nature's chime, and with harsh din
Broke the fair music that all creatures made 15
To their great Lord, whose love their motion sway'd
In perfect diapason, whilst they stood
In first obedience, and their state of good.
O may we soon again renew that Song,
And keep in tune with Heaven, till God ere long 20
To His celestial consort us unite,
To live with Him, and sing in endless morn of light!

J. Milton

CXLVIII

NOX NOCTI INDICAT SCIENTIAM

When I survey the bright
Celestial sphere:
So rich with jewels hung, that night 25
Doth like an Ethiop bride appear;

My soul her wings doth spread,
And heavenward flies,
The Almighty's mysteries to read
In the large volumes of the skies. 30

For the bright firmament
Shoots forth no flame
So silent, but is eloquent
In speaking the Creator's name.

No unregarded star 5
Contracts its light
Into so small a character,
Removed far from our human sight,

But if we steadfast look,
We shall discern 10
In it as in some holy book,
How man may heavenly knowledge learn.

It tells the Conqueror,
That far-stretch'd power
Which his proud dangers traffic for, 15
Is but the triumph of an hour.

That from the farthest North
Some nation may
Yet undiscover'd issue forth,
And o'er his new-got conquest sway. 20

Some nation yet shut in
With hills of ice,
May be let out to scourge his sin,
Till they shall equal him in vice.

And then they likewise shall 25
Their ruin have;
For as yourselves your Empires fall,
And every Kingdom hath a grave.

Thus those celestial fires,
Though seeming mute, 30
The fallacy of our desires
And all the pride of life, confute.

For they have watch'd since first
The world had birth:
And found sin in itself accursed,
And nothing permanent on earth.

W. Habington

CXLIX

HYMN TO DARKNESS

Hail thou most sacred venerable thing! 5
What Muse is worthy thee to sing?
Thee, from whose pregnant universal womb
All things, ev'n Light, thy rival, first did come.
What dares he not attempt that sings of thee,
Thou first and greatest mystery? 10
Who can the secrets of thy essence tell?
Thou, like the light of God, art inaccessible.

Before great Love this monument did raise,
This ample theater of praise;
Before the folding circles of the sky 15
Were tuned by Him, Who is all harmony;
Before the morning Stars their hymn began,
Before the council held for man,
Before the birth of either time or place,
Thou reign'st unquestion'd monarch in the empty space. 20

Thy native lot thou didst to Light resign,
But still half of the globe is thine.
Here with a quiet, but yet awful hand,
Like the best emperors thou dost command.
To thee the stars above their brightness owe, 25
And mortals their repose below:
To thy protection fear and sorrow flee,
And those that weary are of light, find rest in thee.

J. Norris
of Bemerton

CL

A VISION

I saw Eternity the other night,
Like a great ring of pure and endless light,
    All calm, as it was bright: —
And round beneath it, Time, in hours, days, years,
    Driven by the spheres, 5
Like a vast shadow moved; in which the World
    And all her train were hurl'd.

H. Vaughan

CLI

ALEXANDER'S FEAST, OR, THE POWER OF MUSIC

'Twas at the royal feast for Persia won
    By Philip's warlike son —
    Aloft in awful state 10
    The godlike hero sate
    On his imperial throne;
    His valiant peers were placed around,
    Their brows with roses and with myrtles bound,
    (So should desert in arms be crown'd); 15
    The lovely Thais by his side
    Sate like a blooming Eastern bride
    In flower of youth and beauty's pride: —
    Happy, happy, happy pair!
    None but the brave 20
    None but the brave
    None but the brave deserves the fair!

  Timotheus placed on high
Amid the tuneful choir
With flying fingers touch'd the lyre: 25
The trembling notes ascend the sky
And heavenly joys inspire.
The song began from Jove

Who left his blissful seats above —
Such is the power of mighty love!
A dragon's fiery form belied the god;
Sublime on radiant spires he rode
When he to fair Olympia prest, 5
And while he sought her snowy breast,
Then round her slender waist he curl'd,
And stamp'd an image of himself, a sovereign of the world.
— The listening crowd admire the lofty sound;
A present deity! they shout around: 10
A present deity! the vaulted roofs rebound:
With ravish'd ears
The monarch hears,
Assumes the god;
Affects to nod 15
And seems to shake the spheres.

The praise of Bacchus then the sweet musician sung,
Of Bacchus ever fair and ever young:
The jolly god in triumph comes;
Sound the trumpets, beat the drums! 20
Flush'd with a purple grace
He shows his honest face:
Now give the hautboys breath; he comes, he comes!
Bacchus, ever fair and young,
Drinking joys did first ordain; 25
Bacchus' blessings are a treasure,
Drinking is the soldier's pleasure:
Rich the treasure,
Sweet the pleasure,
Sweet is pleasure after pain. 30

Soothed with the sound, the king grew vain;
Fought all his battles o'er again,
And thrice he routed all his foes, and thrice he slew the
slain!
The master saw the madness rise,

His glowing cheeks, his ardent eyes;
And while he Heaven and Earth defied
Changed his hand and check'd his pride.
He chose a mournful Muse
Soft pity to infuse: 5
He sang Darius great and good,
By too severe a fate
Fallen, fallen, fallen, fallen,
Fallen from his high estate.
And weltering in his blood; 10
Deserted at his utmost need
By those his former bounty fed;
On the bare earth exposed he lies
With not a friend to close his eyes.
— With downcast looks the joyless victor sate, 15
Revolving in his alter'd soul
The various turns of Chance below;
And now and then a sigh he stole,
And tears began to flow.

The mighty master smiled to see 20
That love was in the next degree;
'T was but a kindred sound to move,
For pity melts the mind to love.
Softly sweet, in Lydian measures
Soon he soothed his soul to pleasures. 25
War, he sang, is toil and trouble,
Honor but an empty bubble;
Never ending, still beginning,
Fighting still, and still destroying;
If the world be worth thy winning, 30
Think, O think, it worth enjoying:
Lovely Thais sits beside thee,
Take the good the gods provide thee!
— The many rend the skies with loud applause;
So Love was crown'd, but Music won the cause. 35

The prince, unable to conceal his pain,
Gazed on the fair
Who caused his care,
And sigh'd and look'd, sigh'd and look'd,
Sigh'd and look'd, and sigh'd again: 5
At length with love and wine at once opprest
The vanquish'd victor sunk upon her breast.

Now strike the golden lyre again:
A louder yet, and yet a louder strain!
Break his bands of sleep asunder 10
And rouse him like a rattling peal of thunder.
Hark, hark! the horrid sound
Has raised up his head:
As awaked from the dead
And amazed he stares around. 15
Revenge, revenge, Timotheus cries,
See the Furies arise!
See the snakes that they rear
How they hiss in their hair,
And the sparkles that flash from their eyes! 20
Behold a ghastly band,
Each a torch in his hand!
Those are Grecian ghosts, that in battle were slain
And unburied remain
Inglorious on the plain: 25
Give the vengeance due
To the valiant crew!
Behold how they toss their torches on high,
How they point to the Persian abodes
And glittering temples of their hostile gods. 30
— The princes applaud with a furious joy:
And the King seized a flambeau with zeal to destroy;
Thais led the way
To light him to his prey,
And like another Helen, fired another Troy! 35

— Thus, long ago,
Ere heaving bellows learn'd to blow,
While organs yet were mute,
Timotheus, to his breathing flute
And sounding lyre 5
Could swell the soul to rage, or kindle soft desire.
At last divine Cecilia came,
Inventress of the vocal frame;
The sweet enthusiast from her sacred store
Enlarged the former narrow bounds, 10
And added length to solemn sounds,
With Nature's mother-wit, and arts unknown before.
— Let old Timotheus yield the prize
Or both divide the crown;
He raised a mortal to the skies; 15
She drew an angel down!

J. Dryden

BOOK THIRD

It is more difficult to characterize the English poetry of the eighteenth century than that of any other, for it was an age not only of spontaneous transition, but of bold experiment: it includes not only such absolute contrasts as distinguish the "Rape of the Lock" from the "Parish Register" [of Crabbe], but such vast contemporaneous differences as lie between Pope and Collins, Burns and Cowper. Yet we may clearly trace three leading moods or tendencies: the aspects of courtly or educated life represented by Pope and carried to exhaustion by his followers; the poetry of nature and of man, viewed through a cultivated and at the same time an impassioned frame of mind by Collins and Gray; lastly, the study of vivid and simple narrative, including natural description, begun by Gay and Thomson, pursued by Burns and others in the north, and established in England by Goldsmith, Percy, Crabbe, and Cowper. Great varieties in style accompanied these diversities in aim; poets could not always distinguish the manner suitable for subjects so far apart; and the union of conventional and of common language, exhibited most conspicuously by Burns, has given a tone to the poetry of that century which is better explained by reference to its historical origin than by naming it artificial. There is, again, a nobleness of thought, a courageous aim at high and, in a strict sense manly, excellence in many of the writers; nor can that period be justly termed tame and wanting in originality, which produced poems such as Pope's Satires, Gray's Odes and Elegy, the ballads of Gay and Carey, the songs of Burns and Cowper. In truth, poetry at this as at all times was a more or less unconscious mirror of the genius of the age; and the many complex causes which made the eighteenth century the turning time in modern European civilization are also more or less reflected in its verse. An intelligent reader will find the influence of Newton as markedly in the poems of Pope, as of Elizabeth in the plays of Shakespeare. On this great subject, however, these indications must here be sufficient. — *Transferred from Palgrave's Notes.*

CLII

ODE ON THE PLEASURE ARISING FROM VICISSITUDE

Now the golden Morn aloft
  Waves her dew-bespangled wing,
With vermeil cheek and whisper soft
  She woos the tardy Spring:
Till April starts, and calls around 5
The sleeping fragrance from the ground,

And lightly o'er the living scene
Scatters his freshest, tenderest green.

New-born flocks, in rustic dance,
  Frisking ply their feeble feet;
Forgetful of their wintry trance 5
  The birds his presence greet:
But chief, the skylark warbles high
His trembling, thrilling ecstasy;
And lessening from the dazzled sight,
Melts into air and liquid light. 10

Yesterday the sullen year
  Saw the snowy whirlwind fly;
Mute was the music of the air,
  The herd stood drooping by:
Their raptures now that wildly flow 15
No yesterday nor morrow know;
'T is Man alone that joy descries
With forward and reverted eyes.

Smiles on past misfortune's brow
  Soft reflection's hand can trace, 20
And o'er the cheek of sorrow throw
  A melancholy grace;
While hope prolongs our happier hour,
Or deepest shades, that dimly lour
And blacken round our weary way, 25
Gilds with a gleam of distant day.

Still, where rosy pleasure leads,
  See a kindred grief pursue;
Behind the steps that misery treads
  Approaching comfort view: 30
The hues of bliss more brightly glow
Chastised by sabler tints of woe,
And blended form, with artful strife,
The strength and harmony of life.

See the wretch that long has tost
  On the thorny bed of pain,
At length repair his vigor lost
  And breathe and walk again:
The meanest floweret of the vale, 5
The simplest note that swells the gale,
The common sun, the air, the skies,
To him are opening Paradise.

T. Gray

CLIII

ODE TO SIMPLICITY

O Thou, by Nature taught
To breathe her genuine thought 10
In numbers warmly pure, and sweetly strong;
Who first, on mountains wild,
In Fancy, loveliest child,
Thy babe, or Pleasure's, nursed the powers of song!

Thou, who with hermit heart, 15
Disdain'st the wealth of art,
And gauds, and pageant weeds, and trailing pall,
But com'st, a decent maid
In Attic robe array'd,
O chaste, unboastful Nymph, to thee I call! 20

By all the honey'd store
On Hybla's thymy shore,
By all her blooms and mingled murmurs dear;
By her whose lovelorn woe
In evening musings slow 25
Soothed sweetly sad Electra's poet's ear:

By old Cephisus deep,
Who spread his wavy sweep
In warbled wanderings round thy green retreat;

On whose enamell'd side,
When holy Freedom died,
No equal haunt allured thy future feet:—

O sister meek of Truth,
To my admiring youth 5
Thy sober aid and native charms infuse!
The flowers that sweetest breathe,
Though Beauty cull'd the wreath,
Still ask thy hand to range their order'd hues.

While Rome could none esteem 10
But Virtue's patriot theme,
You loved her hills, and led her laureate band;
But stay'd to sing alone
To one distinguish'd throne;
And turn'd thy face, and fled her alter'd land. 15

No more, in hall or bower,
The Passions own thy power;
Love, only Love, her forceless numbers mean:
For thou hast left her shrine;
Nor olive more, nor vine, 20
Shall gain thy feet to bless the servile scene.

Though taste, though genius, bless
To some divine excess,
Faints the cold work till thou inspire the whole;
What each, what all supply 25
May court, may charm our eye;
Thou, only thou, canst raise the meeting soul!

Of these let others ask
To aid some mighty task;
I only seek to find thy temperate vale; 30
Where oft my reed might sound
To maids and shepherds round,
And all thy sons, O Nature! learn my tale.

W. Collins

CLIV

SOLITUDE

Happy the man, whose wish and care
A few paternal acres bound,
Content to breathe his native air
In his own ground.

Whose herds with milk, whose fields with bread, 5
Whose flocks supply him with attire;
Whose trees in summer yield him shade,
In winter fire.

Blest, who can unconcern'dly find
Hours, days, and years, slide soft away 10
In health of body, peace of mind,
Quiet by day,

Sound sleep by night; study and ease
Together mixed, sweet recreation,
And innocence, which most does please 15
With meditation.

Thus let me live, unseen, unknown;
Thus unlamented let me die;
Steal from the world, and not a stone
Tell where I lie. 20

A. Pope

CLV

THE BLIND BOY

O say what is that thing call'd Light,
Which I must ne'er enjoy;
What are the blessings of the sight,
O tell your poor blind boy!

You talk of wondrous things you see, 25
You say the sun shines bright;
I feel him warm, but how can he
Or make it day or night?

My day or night myself I make
  Whene'er I sleep or play;
And could I ever keep awake
  With me 't were always day.

With heavy sighs I often hear 5
  You mourn my hapless woe;
But sure with patience I can bear
  A loss I ne'er can know.

Then let not what I cannot have
  My cheer of mind destroy: 10
Whilst thus I sing, I am a king,
  Although a poor blind boy.

C. Cibber

CLVI

ON A FAVORITE CAT, DROWNED IN A TUB OF GOLDFISHES

'T was on a lofty vase's side,
Where China's gayest art had dyed
The azure flowers that blow, 15
Demurest of the tabby kind
The pensive Selima, reclined,
Gazed on the lake below.

Her conscious tail her joy declared:
The fair round face, the snowy beard, 20
The velvet of her paws,
Her coat that with the tortoise vies,
Her ears of jet, and emerald eyes —
She saw, and purr'd applause.

Still had she gazed, but 'midst the tide 25
Two angel forms were seen to glide,
The Genii of the stream:
Their scaly armor's Tyrian hue

Through richest purple, to the view
Betray'd a golden gleam.

The hapless Nymph with wonder saw:
A whisker first, and then a claw
With many an ardent wish 5
She stretch'd, in vain, to reach the prize—
What female heart can gold despise?
What Cat 's averse to fish?

Presumptuous maid! with looks intent
Again she stretch'd, again she bent, 10
Nor knew the gulf between—
Malignant Fate sat by and smiled—
The slippery verge her feet beguiled;
She tumbled headlong in!

Eight times emerging from the flood 15
She mew'd to every watery God
Some speedy aid to send:—
No Dolphin came, no Nereid stirr'd,
Nor cruel Tom nor Susan heard—
A favorite has no friend! 20

From hence, ye Beauties! undeceived
Know one false step is ne'er retrieved,
And be with caution bold:
Not all that tempts your wandering eyes
And heedless hearts, is lawful prize, 25
Nor all that glisters, gold!

T. Gray

CLVII

TO CHARLOTTE PULTENEY

Timely blossom, Infant fair,
Fondling of a happy pair,
Every morn and every night
Their solicitous delight, 30

Sleeping, waking, still at ease,
Pleasing, without skill to please;
Little gossip, blithe and hale,
Tattling many a broken tale,
Singing many a tuneless song, 5
Lavish of a heedless tongue;
Simple maiden, void of art,
Babbling out the very heart,
Yet abandon'd to thy will,
Yet imagining no ill, 10
Yet too innocent to blush;
Like the linnet in the bush
To the mother linnet's note
Moduling her slender throat;
Chirping forth thy petty joys, 15
Wanton in the change of toys,
Like the linnet green, in May
Flitting to each bloomy spray;
Wearied then and glad of rest,
Like the linnet in the nest:— 20
This thy present happy lot
This, in time will be forgot:
Other pleasures, other cares,
Ever-busy Time prepares;
And thou shalt in thy daughter see, 25
This picture, once, resembled thee.

A. Philips

CLVIII

RULE BRITANNIA

When Britain first at Heaven's command
Arose from out the azure main,
This was the charter of her land,
And guardian angels sang the strain: 30
Rule, Britannia! Britannia rules the waves!
Britons never shall be slaves.

The nations not so blest as thee
Must in their turn to tyrants fall,
Whilst thou shalt flourish great and free
The dread and envy of them all.

Still more majestic shalt thou rise, 5
More dreadful from each foreign stroke;
As the loud blast that tears the skies
Serves but to root thy native oak.

Thee haughty tyrants ne'er shall tame;
All their attempts to bend thee down 10
Will but arouse thy generous flame,
And work their woe and thy renown.

To thee belongs the rural reign;
Thy cities shall with commerce shine;
All thine shall be the subject main, 15
And every shore it circles thine!

The Muses, still with Freedom found,
Shall to thy happy coast repair;
Blest Isle, with matchless beauty crown'd
And manly hearts to guard the fair: — 20
Rule, Britannia! Britannia rules the waves!
Britons never shall be slaves!

J. Thomson

CLIX

THE BARD

Pindaric Ode

"Ruin seize thee, ruthless King!
Confusion on thy banners wait;
Tho' fann'd by Conquest's crimson wing 25
They mock the air with idle state.
Helm, nor hauberk's twisted mail,
Nor e'en thy virtues, Tyrant, shall avail
To save thy secret soul from nightly fears,
From Cambria's curse, from Cambria's tears!" 30

— Such were the sounds that o'er the crested pride
Of the first Edward scatter'd wild dismay,
As down the steep of Snowdon's shaggy side
He wound with toilsome march his long array: —
Stout Glo'ster stood aghast in speechless trance; 5
"To arms!" cried Mortimer, and couch'd his quivering
lance.

On a rock, whose haughty brow
Frowns o'er old Conway's foaming flood,
Robed in the sable garb of woe
With haggard eyes the Poet stood; 10
(Loose his beard and hoary hair
Stream'd like a meteor to the troubled air)
And with a master's hand and prophet's fire
Struck the deep sorrows of his lyre:
"Hark, how each giant oak and desert cave 15
Sighs to the torrent's awful voice beneath!
O'er thee, oh King! their hundred arms they wave,
Revenge on thee in hoarser murmurs breathe;
Vocal no more, since Cambria's fatal day,
To highborn Hoel's harp, or soft Llewellyn's lay. 20

"Cold is Cadwallo's tongue,
That hushed the stormy main:
Brave Urien sleeps upon his craggy bed:
Mountains, ye mourn in vain
Modred, whose magic song 25
Made huge Plinlimmon bow his cloud-topt head.
On dreary Arvon's shore they lie
Smear'd with gore and ghastly pale:
Far, far aloof the affrighted ravens sail;
The famish'd eagle screams, and passes by. 30
Dear lost companions of my tuneful art,
Dear as the light that visits these sad eyes,
Dear as the ruddy drops that warm my heart,
Ye died amidst your dying country's cries —

No more I weep; They do not sleep;
  On yonder cliffs, a grisly band,
I see them sit; They linger yet,
  Avengers of their native land:
With me in dreadful harmony they join, 5
And weave with bloody hands the tissue of thy line.

"*Weave the warp and weave the woof*
  The winding sheet of Edward's race:
Give ample room and verge enough
  The characters of hell to trace. 10
Mark the year, and mark the night,
When Severn shall reëcho with affright
The shrieks of death thro' Berkley's roof that ring,
Shrieks of an agonizing king!
  She-wolf of France, with unrelenting fangs 15
That tear'st the bowels of thy mangled mate,
  From thee be born, who o'er thy country hangs
The scourge of heaven! What terrors round him wait!
Amazement in his van, with flight combined,
And sorrow's faded form, and solitude behind. 20

"*Mighty victor, mighty lord,*
  Low on his funeral couch he lies!
No pitying heart, no eye, afford
  A tear to grace his obsequies.
Is the sable warrior fled? 25
Thy son is gone. He rests among the dead.
The swarm that in thy noontide beam were born?
— Gone to salute the rising morn.
Fair laughs the Morn, and soft the zephyr blows,
  While proudly riding o'er the azure realm. 30
In gallant trim the gilded vessel goes:
  Youth on the prow, and Pleasure at the helm:
Regardless of the sweeping whirlwind's sway,
That hush'd in grim repose expects his evening prey.

"*Fill high the sparkling bowl,*
The rich repast prepare;
Reft of a crown, he yet may share the feast:
Close by the regal chair
Fell Thirst and Famine scowl 5
A baleful smile upon their baffled guest,
Heard ye the din of battle bray,
Lance to lance, and horse to horse?
Long years of havoc urge their destined course,
And thro' the kindred squadrons mow their way. 10
Ye towers of Julius, London's lasting shame,
With many a foul and midnight murder fed,
Revere his consort's faith, his father's fame,
And spare the meek usurper's holy head!
Above, below, the rose of snow, 15
Twined with her blushing foe, we spread:
The bristled boar in infant gore
Wallows beneath the thorny shade.
Now, brothers, bending o'er the accurséd loom,
Stamp we our vengeance deep, and ratify his doom. 20

"*Edward, lo! to sudden fate*
(*Weave we the woof; The thread is spun;*)
Half of thy heart we consecrate.
(*The web is wove; The work is done.*)
—Stay, oh stay! nor thus forlorn 25
Leave me unbless'd, unpitied, here to mourn:
In yon bright track that fires the western skies
They melt, they vanish from my eyes.
But oh! what solemn scenes on Snowdon's height
Descending slow their glittering skirts unroll? 30
Visions of glory, spare my aching sight,
Ye unborn ages, crowd not on my soul!
No more our long-lost Arthur we bewail:—
All hail! ye genuine kings! Britannia's issue, hail!

"Girt with many a baron bold
Sublime their starry fronts they rear;
And gorgeous dames, and statesmen old
In bearded majesty, appear.
In the midst a form divine! 5
Her eye proclaims her of the Briton line:
Her lion port, her awe-commanding face
Attemper'd sweet to virgin grace.
What strings symphonious tremble in the air,
What strains of vocal transport round her play? 10
Hear from the grave, great Taliessin, hear;
They breathe a soul to animate thy clay.
Bright Rapture calls, and soaring as she sings,
Waves in the eye of heaven her many-color'd wings.

"The verse adorn again 15
Fierce war, and faithful love,
And truth severe, by fairy fiction drest.
In buskin'd measures move
Pale grief, and pleasing pain,
With horror, tyrant of the throbbing breast. 20
A voice as of the cherub choir
Gales from blooming Eden bear,
And distant warblings lessen on my ear
That lost in long futurity expire.
Fond impious man, think'st thou yon sanguine cloud 25
Raised by thy breath, has quenched the orb of day?
To-morrow he repairs the golden flood
And warms the nations with redoubled ray.
Enough for me: with joy I see
The different doom our fates assign: 30
Be thine despair and sceptered care,
To triumph and to die are mine."
— He spoke, and headlong from the mountain's height
Deep in the roaring tide he plunged to endless night.

T. Gray

CLX

ODE WRITTEN IN 1746

How sleep the bräve, who sink to rest
By all their country's wishes blest!
When Spring, with dewy fingers cold,
Returns to deck their hallow'd mold,
She there shall dress a sweeter sod 5
Than Fancy's feet have ever trod.

By fairy hands their knell is rung,
By forms unseen their dirge is sung:
There Honor comes, a pilgrim gray,
To bless the turf that wraps their clay; 10
And Freedom shall awhile repair
To dwell a weeping hermit there!

W. Collins

CLXI

LAMENT FOR CULLODEN

The lovely lass o' Inverness,
Nae joy nor pleasure can she see;
For e'en and morn she cries, Alas! 15
And aye the saut tear blins her ee:
Drumossie moor — Drumossie day —
A waefu' day it was to me!
For there I lost my father dear,
My father dear, and brethren three. 20

Their winding-sheet the bluidy clay,
Their graves are growing green to see:
And by them lies the dearest lad
That ever blest a woman's ee!
Now wae to thee, thou cruel lord, 25
A bluidy man I trow thou be;
For mony a heart thou hast made sair
That ne'er did wrang to thine or thee.

R. Burns

CLXII

LAMENT FOR FLODDEN

I 've heard them lilting at our ewe-milking,
  Lasses a' lilting before dawn o' day;
But now they are moaning on ilka green loaning —
  The Flowers of the Forest are a' wede away.

At bughts, in the morning, nae blythe lads are scorning, 5
  Lasses are lonely and dowie and wae;
Nae daffin', nae gabbin', but sighing and sabbing,
  Ilk ane lifts her leglin and hies her away.

In har'st, at the shearing, nae youths now are jeering,
  Bandsters are lyart, and runkled, and gray; 10
At fair or at preaching, nae wooing, nae fleeching —
  The Flowers of the Forest are a' wede away.

At e'en, in the gloaming, nae younkers are roaming
  'Bout stacks wi' the lasses at bogle to play;
But ilk ane sits drearie, lamenting her dearie — 15
  The Flowers of the Forest are weded away.

Dool and wae for the order, sent our lads to the Border!
  The English, for ance, by guile wan the day;
The Flowers of the Forest, that fought aye the foremost,
  The prime of our land, are cauld in the clay. 20

We'll hear nae mair lilting at the ewe-milking;
  Women and bairns are heartless and wae;
Sighing and moaning on ilka green loaning —
  The Flowers of the Forest are a' wede away.

J. Elliot

CLXIII

THE BRAES OF YARROW

Thy braes were bonny, Yarrow stream, 25
When first on them I met my lover;

Thy braes how dreary, Yarrow stream,
When now thy waves his body cover!
Forever now, O Yarrow stream!
Thou art to me a stream of sorrow;
For never on thy banks shall I 5
Behold my Love, the flower of Yarrow!

He promised me a milk-white steed
To bear me to his father's bowers;
He promised me a little page
To squire me to his father's towers; 10
He promised me a wedding ring, —
The wedding day was fix'd to-morrow; —
Now he is wedded to his grave,
Alas, his watery grave, in Yarrow!

Sweet were his words when last we met; 15
My passion I as freely told him;
Clasp'd in his arms, I little thought
That I should nevermore behold him!
Scarce was he gone, I saw his ghost;
It vanish'd with a shriek of sorrow; 20
Thrice did the water wraith ascend,
And gave a doleful groan thro' Yarrow.

His mother from the window look'd
With all the longing of a mother;
His little sister weeping walk'd 25
The green-wood path to meet her brother;
They sought him east, they sought him west,
They sought him all the forest thorough;
They only saw the cloud of night,
They only heard the roar of Yarrow. 30

No longer from thy window look —
Thou hast no son, thou tender mother!
No longer walk, thou lovely maid; —
Alas, thou hast no more a brother!

No longer seek him east or west
And search no more the forest thorough;
For, wandering in the night so dark,
He fell a lifeless corpse in Yarrow.

The tear shall never leave my cheek, 5
No other youth shall be my marrow —
I'll seek thy body in the stream,
And then with thee I'll sleep in Yarrow.
— The tear did never leave her cheek,
No other youth became her marrow; 10
She found his body in the stream,
And now with him she sleeps in Yarrow.

J. Logan

CLXIV

WILLY DROWNED IN YARROW[1]

Down in yon garden sweet and gay
  Where bonnie grows the lily,
I heard a fair maid sighing say, 15
  "My wish be wi' sweet Willie!

"Willie 's rare, and Willie 's fair,
  And Willie 's wondrous bonny;
And Willie hecht to marry me
  Gin e'er he married ony. 20

"O gentle wind, that bloweth south
  From where my Love repaireth,
Convey a kiss frae his dear mouth
  And tell me how he fareth!

"O tell sweet Willie to come doun 25
  And hear the mavis singing,
And see the birds on ilka bush
  And leaves around them hinging.

[1] An older version, probably by several hands, of the subject treated in the preceding poem.

"The lav'rock there, wi' her white breast
And gentle throat sae narrow;
There 's sport eneuch for gentlemen
On Leader haughs and Yarrow.

"O Leader haughs are wide and braid 5
And Yarrow haughs are bonny;
There Willie hecht to marry me
If e'er he married ony.

"But Willie 's gone, whom I thought on,
And does not hear me weeping; 10
Draws many a tear frae true love's e'e
When other maids are sleeping.

"Yestreen I made my bed fu' braid,
The night I'll mak' it narrow,
For a' the live-lang winter night 15
I lie twined o' my marrow.

"O came ye by yon water-side?
Pou'd you the rose or lily?
Or came you by yon meadow green,
Or saw you my sweet Willie?" 20

She sought him up, she sought him down,
She sought him braid and narrow;
Syne, in the cleaving of a craig,
She found him drown'd in Yarrow!

Anon.

CLXV

LOSS OF THE ROYAL GEORGE

Toll for the Brave! 25
The brave that are no more!
All sunk beneath the wave
Fast by their native shore!

Eight hundred of the brave
Whose courage well was tried, 30

Had made the vessel heel
And laid her on her side.

A land breeze shook the shrouds
And she was overset;
Down went the Royal George, 5
With all her crew complete.

Toll for the brave!
Brave Kempenfelt is gone;
His last sea fight is fought,
His work of glory done. 10

It was not in the battle;
No tempest gave the shock;
She sprang no fatal leak,
She ran upon no rock.

His sword was in its sheath, 15
His fingers held the pen,
When Kempenfelt went down
With twice four hundred men.

— Weigh the vessel up
Once dreaded by our foes! 20
And mingle with our cup
The tears that England owes.

Her timbers yet are sound,
And she may float again
Full charged with England's thunder, 25
And plow the distant main:

But Kempenfelt is gone,
His victories are o'er;
And he and his eight hundred
Shall plow the wave no more. 30

W. Cowper

CLXVI

BLACK-EYED SUSAN

All in the Downs the fleet was moor'd,
  The streamers waving in the wind,
When black-eyed Susan came aboard;
  "O! where shall I my true-love find?
Tell me, ye jovial sailors, tell me true 5
If my sweet William sails among the crew."

William, who high upon the yard
  Rock'd with the billow to and fro,
Soon as her well-known voice he heard
  He sigh'd, and cast his eyes below: 10
The cord slides swiftly through his glowing hands,
And quick as lightning on the deck he stands.

So the sweet lark, high poised in air,
  Shuts close his pinions to his breast
If chance his mate's shrill call he hear, 15
  And drops at once into her nest:—
The noblest captain in the British fleet
Might envy William's lip those kisses sweet.

"O Susan, Susan, lovely dear,
  My vows shall ever true remain; 20
Let me kiss off that falling tear;
  We only part to meet again.
Change as ye list, ye winds; my heart shall be
The faithful compass that still points to thee.

"Believe not what the landmen say 25
  Who tempt with doubts thy constant mind;
They 'll tell thee, sailors, when away,
  In every port a mistress find:
Yes, yes, believe them when they tell thee so,
For Thou art present wheresoe'er I go. 30

"If to fair India's coast we sail,
  Thy eyes are seen in diamonds bright,
Thy breath is Afric's spicy gale,
  Thy skin is ivory so white.
Thus every beauteous object that I view 5
Wakes in my soul some charm of lovely Sue.

"Though battle call me from thy arms
  Let not my pretty Susan mourn;
Though cannons roar, yet safe from harms
  William shall to his Dear return. 10
Love turns aside the balls that round me fly,
Lest precious tears should drop from Susan's eye."

The boatswain gave the dreadful word,
  The sails their swelling bosom spread,
No longer must she stay aboard; 15
  They kiss'd, she sigh'd, he hung his head.
Her lessening boat unwilling rows to land;
"Adieu!" she cries; and waved her lily hand.

J. Gay

CLXVII

SALLY IN OUR ALLEY

Of all the girls that are so smart
  There's none like pretty Sally; 20
She is the darling of my heart,
  And she lives in our alley.
There is no lady in the land
  Is half so sweet as Sally;
She is the darling of my heart, 25
  And she lives in our alley.

Her father he makes cabbage nets
  And through the streets does cry 'em;
Her mother she sells laces long
  To such as please to buy 'em: 30

But sure such folks could ne'er beget
  So sweet a girl as Sally!
She is the darling of my heart,
  And she lives in our alley.

When she is by, I leave my work, 5
  I love her so sincerely;
My master comes like any Turk,
  And bangs me most severely —
But let him bang his bellyful,
  I'll bear it all for Sally; 10
She is the darling of my heart,
  And she lives in our alley.

Of all the days that 's in the week
  I dearly love but one day —
And that 's the day that comes betwixt 15
  A Saturday and Monday;
For then I'm drest all in my best
  To walk abroad with Sally;
She is the darling of my heart,
  And she lives in our alley. 20

My master carries me to church,
  And often am I blamed
Because I leave him in the lurch
  As soon as text is named;
I leave the church in sermon time 25
  And slink away to Sally;
She is the darling of my heart,
  And she lives in our alley.

When Christmas comes about again
  O then I shall have money; 30
I'll hoard it up, and box it all,
  I'll give it to my honey:

I would it were ten thousand pound,
  I'd give it all to Sally;
She is the darling of my heart,
  And she lives in our alley.

My master and the neighbors all 5
  Make game of me and Sally,
And, but for her, I'd better be
  A slave and row a galley;
But when my seven long years are out
  O then I'll marry Sally, — 10
O then we'll wed, and then we'll bed . . .
  But not in our alley!

H. Carey

CLXVIII

A FAREWELL

Go fetch to me a pint o' wine,
  An' fill it in a silver tassie;
That I may drink before I go 15
  A service to my bonnie lassie:
The boat rocks at the pier o' Leith,
  Fu' loud the wind blaws frae the ferry,
The ship rides by the Berwick-law,
  And I maun leave my bonnie Mary. 20

The trumpets sound, the banners fly,
  The glittering spears are rankéd ready;
The shouts o' war are heard afar,
  The battle closes thick and bloody;
But it 's not the roar o' sea or shore 25
  Wad make me langer wish to tarry;
Nor shout o' war that 's heard afar —
  It 's leaving thee, my bonnie Mary.

R. Burns

CLXIX

If doughty deeds my lady please
  Right soon I'll mount my steed;
And strong his arm, and fast his seat
  That bears frae me the meed.
I'll wear thy colors in my cap, 5
  Thy picture at my heart;
And he that bends not to thine eye
  Shall rue it to his smart!
    Then tell me how to woo thee, Love;
      O tell me how to woo thee! 10
    For thy dear sake, nae care I'll take
      Tho' ne'er another trow me.

If gay attire delight thine eye
  I'll dight me in array;
I'll tend thy chamber door all night, 15
  And squire thee all the day.
If sweetest sound can win thine ear,
  These sounds I'll strive to catch;
Thy voice I'll steal to woo thysell,
  That voice that nane can match. 20

But if fond love thy heart can gain,
  I never broke a vow;
Nae maiden lays her skaith to me,
  I never loved but you.
For you alone I ride the ring, 25
  For you I wear the blue;
For you alone I strive to sing,
  O tell me how to woo!
    Then tell me how to woo thee, Love;
      O tell me how to woo thee! 30
    For thy dear sake, nae care I'll take,
      Tho' ne'er another trow me.

R. Graham
of Gartmore

CLXX

TO A YOUNG LADY

Sweet stream, that winds through yonder glade,
Apt emblem of a virtuous maid —
Silent and chaste she steals along,
Far from the world's gay busy throng:
With gentle yet prevailing force, 5
Intent upon her destined course;
Graceful and useful all she does.
Blessing and blest where'er she goes;
Pure-bosom'd as that watery glass,
And Heaven reflected in her face. 10

W. Cowper

CLXXI

THE SLEEPING BEAUTY

Sleep on, and dream of Heaven awhile —
Tho' shut so close thy laughing eyes,
Thy rosy lips still wear a smile
And move, and breathe delicious sighs!

Ah, now soft blushes tinge her cheeks 15
And mantle o'er her neck of snow:
Ah, now she murmurs, now she speaks
What most I wish — and fear to know!

She starts, she trembles, and she weeps!
Her fair hands folded on her breast: 20
— And now, how like a saint she sleeps!
A seraph in the realms of rest!

Sleep on secure! Above control
Thy thoughts belong to Heaven and thee:
And may the secret of thy soul 25
Remain within its sanctuary!

S. Rogers

CLXXII

Forever, Fortune, wilt thou prove
An unrelenting foe to Love,
And when we meet a mutual heart
Come in between, and bid us part?

Bid us sigh on from day to day, 5
And wish and wish the soul away;
Till youth and genial years are flown,
And all the life of life is gone?

But busy, busy, still art thou,
To bind the loveless joyless vow, 10
The heart from pleasure to delude,
To join the gentle to the rude.

For once, O Fortune, hear my prayer,
And I absolve thy future care;
All other blessings I resign, 15
Make but the dear Amanda mine.

J. Thomson

CLXXIII

The merchant, to secure his treasure,
Conveys it in a borrow'd name:
Euphelia serves to grace my measure,
But Cloe is my real flame. 20

My softest verse, my darling lyre
Upon Euphelia's toilet lay —
When Cloe noted her desire
That I should sing, that I should play.

My lyre I tune, my voice I raise, 25
But with my numbers mix my sighs;
And whilst I sing Euphelia's praise,
I fix my soul on Cloe's eyes.

Fair Cloe blush'd: Euphelia frown'd:
I sang, and gazed; I play'd, and trembled:
And Venus to the Loves around
Remark'd how ill we all dissembled.

M. Prior

CLXXIV

LOVE'S SECRET

Never seek to tell thy love, 5
Love that never told can be;
For the gentle wind doth move
Silently, invisibly.

I told my love, I told my love,
I told her all my heart, 10
Trembling, cold, in ghastly fears: —
Ah! she did depart.

Soon after she was gone from me
A traveler came by,
Silently, invisibly: 15
He took her with a sigh.

W. Blake

CLXXV

When lovely woman stoops to folly
And finds too late that men betray, —
What charm can soothe her melancholy
What art can wash her guilt away? 20

The only art her guilt to cover,
To hide her shame from every eye,
To give repentance to her lover
And wring his bosom, is — to die.

O. Goldsmith

CLXXVI

Ye banks and braes o' bonnie Doon
  How can ye blume sae fair!
How can ye chant, ye little birds,
  And I sae fu' o' care!

Thou 'll break my heart, thou bonnie bird 5
  That sings upon the bough;
Thou minds me o' the happy days
  When my fause Luve was true.

Thou 'll break my heart, thou bonnie bird
  That sings beside thy mate; 10
For sae I sat, and sae I sang,
  And wist na o' my fate.

Aft hae I roved by bonnie Doon
  To see the woodbine twine,
And ilka bird sang o' its love; 15
  And sae did I o' mine.

Wi' lightsome heart I pu'd a rose,
  Frae aff its thorny tree;
And my fause luver staw the rose,
  But left the thorn wi' me. 20

R. Burns

CLXXVII

THE PROGRESS OF POESY

A Pindaric Ode

  Awake, Æolian lyre, awake,
And give to rapture all thy trembling strings.
From Helicon's harmonious springs
  A thousand rills their mazy progress take;
The laughing flowers that round them blow 25
Drink life and fragrance as they flow.

Now the rich stream of music winds along
Deep, majestic, smooth, and strong,
Thro' verdant vales, and Ceres' golden reign;
Now rolling down the steep amain
Headlong, impetuous, see it pour: 5
The rocks and nodding groves re-bellow to the roar.

Oh! Sovereign of the willing soul,
Parent of sweet and solemn-breathing airs,
Enchanting shell! the sullen Cares
And frantic Passions hear thy soft control. 10
On Thracia's hills the Lord of War
Has curb'd the fury of his car
And dropt his thirsty lance at thy command.
Perching on the sceptered hand
Of Jove, thy magic lulls the feather'd king 15
With ruffled plumes, and flagging wing:
Quench'd in dark clouds of slumber lie
The terror of his beak, and lightnings of his eye.

Thee the voice, the dance, obey
Temper'd to thy warbled lay. 20
O'er Idalia's velvet-green
The rosy-crownéd Loves are seen
On Cytherea's day;
With antic Sport, and blue-eyed Pleasures,
Frisking light in frolic measures; 25
Now pursuing, now retreating,
Now in circling troops they meet:
To brisk notes in cadence beating
Glance their many-twinkling feet.
Slow melting strains their Queen's approach declare: 30
Where'er she turns, the Graces homage pay:
With arms sublime that float upon the air
In gliding state she wins her easy way:
O'er her warm cheek and rising bosom move
The bloom of young Desire and purple light of Love. 35

Man's feeble race what ills await!
Labor, and Penury, the racks of Pain,
Disease, and Sorrow's weeping train,
And Death, sad refuge from the storms of fate!
The fond complaint, my song, disprove, 5
And justify the laws of Jove.
Say, has he given in vain the heavenly Muse?
Night, and all her sickly dews,
Her specters wan, and birds of boding cry
He gives to range the dreary sky: 10
Till down the eastern cliffs afar
Hyperion's march they spy, and glittering shafts of war.

In climes beyond the solar road
Where shaggy forms o'er ice-built mountains roam,
The Muse has broke the twilight gloom 15
To cheer the shivering native's dull abode.
And oft, beneath the odorous shade
Of Chili's boundless forests laid,
She deigns to hear the savage youth repeat
In loose numbers wildly sweet 20
Their feather-cinctured chiefs, and dusky loves.
Her track, where'er the goddess roves,
Glory pursue, and generous Shame,
Th' unconquerable Mind, and Freedom's holy flame.

Woods, that wave o'er Delphi's steep, 25
Isles, that crown th' Ægean deep,
Fields that cool Ilissus laves,
Or where Mæander's amber waves
In lingering labyrinths creep,
How do your tuneful echoes languish, 30
Mute, but to the voice of anguish!
Where each old poetic mountain
Inspiration breathed around;
Every shade and hallow'd fountain
Murmur'd deep a solemn sound: 35

Till the sad Nine, in Greece's evil hour
  Left their Parnassus for the Latian plains.
Alike they scorn the pomp of tyrant Power,
  And coward Vice, that revels in her chains.
When Latium had her lofty spirit lost, 5
They sought, oh Albion! next, thy sea-encircled coast.

  Far from the sun and summer gale
In thy green lap was Nature's Darling laid,
What time, where lucid Avon stray'd,
  To him the mighty Mother did unveil 10
Her awful face: the dauntless child
Stretch'd forth his little arms, and smiled.
"This pencil take" (she said), "whose colors clear
Richly paint the vernal year:
Thine, too, these golden keys, immortal Boy! 15
This can unlock the gates of joy;
Of horror that, and thrilling fears,
Or ope the sacred source of sympathetic tears."

  Nor second He, that rode sublime
Upon the seraph-wings of Ecstasy 20
The secrets of the abyss to spy:
  He pass'd the flaming bounds of place and time:
The living Throne, the sapphire-blaze
Where angels tremble while they gaze,
He saw; but blasted with excess of light, 25
Closed his eyes in endless night.
Behold where Dryden's less presumptuous car
Wide o'er the fields of glory bear
Two coursers of ethereal race,
With necks in thunder clothed, and long-resounding pace. 30

Hark, his hands the lyre explore!
Bright-eyed Fancy, hovering o'er,
Scatters from her pictured urn
Thoughts that breathe, and words that burn.

But ah! 't is heard no more—
Oh! lyre divine, what daring spirit
Wakes thee now? Tho' he inherit
Nor the pride, nor ample pinion,
  That the Theban eagle bear, 5
Sailing with supreme dominion
  Thro' the azure deep of air:
Yet oft before his infant eyes would run
  Such forms as glitter in the Muse's ray
With orient hues, unborrow'd of the sun: 10
  Yet shall he mount, and keep his distant way
Beyond the limits of a vulgar fate:
Beneath the Good how far—but far above the Great.

T. Gray

CLXXVIII

THE PASSIONS

An Ode for Music

When Music, heavenly maid, was young,
While yet in early Greece she sung, 15
The Passions oft, to hear her shell,
Throng'd around her magic cell
Exulting, trembling, raging, fainting,
Possest beyond the Muse's painting;
By turns they felt the glowing mind 20
Disturb'd, delighted, raised, refined:
'Til once, 't is said, when all were fired,
Fill'd with fury, rapt, inspired,
From the supporting myrtles round
They snatch'd her instruments of sound, 25
And, as they oft had heard apart
Sweet lessons of her forceful art,
Each (for Madness ruled the hour)
Would prove his own expressive power.

First Fear his hand, its skill to try,
  Amid the chords bewilder'd laid,
And back recoil'd, he knew not why,
  E'en at the sound himself had made.

Next Anger rush'd, his eyes on fire, 5
  In lightnings, own'd his secret stings;
In one rude clash he struck the lyre
  And swept with hurried hand the strings.

With woeful measures wan Despair,
  Low sullen sounds, his grief beguiled; 10
A solemn, strange, and mingled air,
  'T was sad by fits, by starts 't was wild.

But thou, O Hope, with eyes so fair,
  What was thy delighted measure?
Still it whisper'd promised pleasure 15
  And bade the lovely scenes at distance hail!
Still would her touch the strain prolong;
  And from the rocks, the woods, the vale
She call'd on Echo still through all the song;
  And, where her sweetest theme she chose, 20
  A soft responsive voice was heard at every close;
And Hope enchanted smiled, and waved her golden
    hair; —

And longer had she sung: — but with a frown
    Revenge impatient rose:
He threw his blood-stain'd sword in thunder down; 25
    And with a withering look
  The war-denouncing trumpet took
And blew a blast so loud and dread,
Were ne'er prophetic sounds so full of woe!
    And ever and anon he beat 30
    The doubling drum with furious heat;
And, though sometimes, each dreary pause between,

Dejected Pity at his side
Her soul-subduing voice applied,
Yet still he kept his wild unalter'd mien,
While each strain'd ball of sight seem'd bursting from his head.

Thy numbers, Jealousy, to naught were fix'd: 5
Sad proof of thy distressful state!
Of differing themes the veering song was mix'd;
And now it courted Love, now raving call'd on Hate.

With eyes upraised, as one inspired,
Pale Melancholy sat retired; 10
And from her wild sequester'd seat,
In notes by distance made more sweet,
Pour'd through the mellow horn her pensive soul:
And dashing soft from rocks around
Bubbling runnels join'd the sound; 15
Through glades and glooms the mingled measure stole,
Or, o'er some haunted stream, with fond delay,
Round an holy calm diffusing,
Love of peace, and lonely musing,
In hollow murmurs died away. 20

But O! how alter'd was its sprightlier tone
When Cheerfulness, a nymph of healthiest hue,
Her bow across her shoulder flung,
Her buskins gemm'd with morning dew,
Blew an inspiring air, that dale and thicket rung, 25
The hunter's call to Faun and Dryad known!
The oak-crown'd Sisters and their chaste-eyed Queen,
Satyrs and Sylvan Boys, were seen
Peeping from forth their alleys green:
Brown Exercise rejoiced to hear; 30
And Sport leaped up, and seized his beechen spear.

Last came Joy's ecstatic trial:
He, with viny crown advancing,
  First to the lively pipe his hand addrest:
But soon he saw the brisk awakening viol
  Whose sweet entrancing voice he loved the best: 5
They would have thought who heard the strain
    They saw, in Tempe's vale, her native maids
    Amidst the festal-sounding shades
To some unwearied minstrel dancing;
While, as his flying fingers kiss'd the strings, 10
  Love framed with Mirth a gay fantastic round:
  Loose were her tresses seen, her zone unbound;
  And he, amidst his frolic play,
  As if he would the charming air repay,
Shook thousand odors from his dewy wings. 15

O Music! sphere-descended maid,
Friend of Pleasure, Wisdom's aid!
Why, goddess! why, to us denied,
Lay'st thou thy ancient lyre aside?
As in that loved Athenian bower 20
You learn'd an all-commanding power,
Thy mimic soul, O Nymph endear'd,
Can well recall what then it heard.
Where is thy native simple heart
Devote to Virtue, Fancy, Art? 25
Arise, as in that elder time,
Warm, energic, chaste, sublime!
Thy wonders, in that godlike age,
Fill thy recording Sister's page;—
'T is said, and I believe the tale, 30
Thy humblest reed could more prevail,
Had more of strength, diviner rage,
Than all which charms this laggard age:
E'en all at once together found,
Cecilia's mingled world of sound:— 35

O bid our vain endeavors cease:
Revive the just designs of Greece:
Return in all thy simple state!
Confirm the tales her sons relate!

W. Collins

CLXXIX

THE SONG OF DAVID

He sang of God, the mighty source 5
Of all things, the stupendous force
On which all strength depends:
From Whose right arm, beneath Whose eyes,
All period, power, and enterprise
Commences, reigns, and ends. 10

The world, the clustering spheres He made,
The glorious light, the soothing shade,
Dale, champaign, grove and hill:
The multitudinous abyss,
Where secrecy remains in bliss, 15
And wisdom hides her skill.

Tell them, I AM, Jehovah said
To Moses: while Earth heard in dread,
And, smitten to the heart,
At once, above, beneath, around, 20
All Nature, without voice or sound,
Replied, "O Lord, THOU ART."

C. Smart

CLXXX

INFANT JOY

"I have no name;
I am but two days old."
—What shall I call thee? 25
"I happy am;

Joy is my name."
— Sweet joy befall thee!

Pretty joy!
Sweet joy, but two days old;
Sweet joy I call thee: 5
Thou dost smile:
I sing the while,
Sweet joy befall thee!

W. Blake

CLXXXI

A CRADLE SONG

Sleep, sleep, beauty bright,
Dreaming in the joys of night; 10
Sleep, sleep; in thy sleep
Little sorrows sit and weep.

Sweet babe, in thy face
Soft desires I can trace,
Secret joys and secret smiles, 15
Little pretty infant wiles.

As thy softest limbs I feel,
Smiles as of the morning steal
O'er thy cheek, and o'er thy breast
Where thy little heart doth rest. 20

Oh the cunning wiles that creep
In thy little heart asleep!
When thy little heart doth wake,
Then the dreadful light shall break.

W. Blake

CLXXXII

ODE ON THE SPRING

Lo! where the rosy-bosom'd Hours, 25
  Fair Venus' train, appear,
Disclose the long-expecting flowers
  And wake the purple year!

The Attic warbler pours her throat
Responsive to the cuckoo's note,
The untaught harmony of Spring:
While, whispering pleasure as they fly,
Cool Zephyrs thro' the clear blue sky 5
Their gather'd fragrance fling.

Where'er the oak's thick branches stretch
A broader, browner shade,
Where'er the rude and moss-grown beech
O'er-canopies the glade, 10
Beside some water's rushy brink
With me the Muse shall sit, and think
(At ease reclined in rustic state)
How vain the ardor of the crowd,
How low, how little are the proud, 15
How indigent the great!

Still is the toiling hand of Care;
The panting herds repose:
Yet hark, how thro' the peopled air
The busy murmur glows! 20
The insect-youth are on the wing,
Eager to taste the honeyed spring
And float amid the liquid noon:
Some lightly o'er the current skim,
Some show their gayly-gilded trim 25
Quick-glancing to the sun.

To Contemplation's sober eye
Such is the race of Man:
And they that creep, and they that fly,
Shall end where they began. 30
Alike the Busy and the Gay
But flutter thro' life's little day,
In Fortune's varying colors drest:
Brush'd by the hand of rough Mischance,

Or chill'd by Age, their airy dance
They leave, in dust to rest.

Methinks I hear in accents low
The sportive kind reply:
Poor moralist! and what art thou? 5
A solitary fly!
Thy joys no glittering female meets,
No hive hast thou of hoarded sweets,
No painted plumage to display:
On hasty wings thy youth is flown; 10
Thy sun is set, thy spring is gone —
We frolic while 't is May.

T. Gray

CLXXXIII

THE POPLAR FIELD

The poplars are fell'd; farewell to the shade
And the whispering sound of the cool colonnade;
The winds play no longer and sing in the leaves, 15
Nor Ouse on his bosom their image receives.

Twelve years have elapsed since I first took a view
Of my favorite field, and the bank where they grew:
And now in the grass behold they are laid,
And the tree is my seat that once lent me a shade! 20

The blackbird has fled to another retreat
Where the hazels afford him a screen from the heat;
And the scene where his melody charm'd me before
Resounds with his sweet-flowing ditty no more.

My fugitive years are all hasting away, 25
And I must erelong lie as lowly as they,
With a turf on my breast and a stone at my head,
Ere another such grove shall arise in its stead.

The change both my heart and my fancy employs;
I reflect on the frailty of man and his joys:
Short-lived as we are, yet our pleasures, we see,
Have a still shorter date, and die sooner than we.

W. Cowper

CLXXXIV

TO A MOUSE

ON TURNING HER UP IN HER NEST, WITH THE PLOW,
NOVEMBER, 1785

Wee, sleekit, cow'rin', tim'rous beastie, 5
O what a panic 's in thy breastie!
Thou need na start awa sae hasty,
Wi' bickering brattle!
I wad be laith to rin an' chase thee
Wi' murd'ring pattle! 10

I 'm truly sorry man's dominion
Has broken Nature's social union,
An' justifies that ill opinion
Which makes thee startle
At me, thy poor earthborn companion, 15
An' fellow mortal!

I doubt na, whiles, but thou may thieve;
What then? poor beastie, thou maun live!
A daimen-icker in a thrave
'S a sma' request: 20
I 'll get a blessin' wi' the lave,
And never miss 't!

Thy wee bit housie, too, in ruin!
Its silly wa's the win's are strewin:
And naething, now, to big a new ane, 25
O' foggage green!
An' bleak December's winds ensuin'
Baith snell an' keen!

Thou saw the fields laid bare an' waste
An' weary winter comin' fast,
An' cozie here, beneath the blast,
Thou thought to dwell,
Till, crash! the cruel colter past 5
Out thro' thy cell.

That wee bit heap o' leaves an' stibble
Has cost thee mony a weary nibble!
Now thou 's turn'd out, for a' thy trouble,
But house or hald, 10
To thole the winter's sleety dribble
An' cranreuch cauld!

But, Mousie, thou art no thy lane
In proving foresight may be vain:
The best laid schemes o' mice an' men 15
Gang aft a-gley,
An' lea'e us naught but grief an' pain,
For promised joy.

Still thou art blest, compared wi' me!
The present only toucheth thee: 20
But, Och! I backward cast my e'e
On prospects drear!
An' forward, tho' I canna see,
I guess an' fear!

R. Burns

CLXXXV

A WISH

Mine be a cot beside the hill; 25
A bee-hive's hum shall soothe my ear;
A willowy brook that turns a mill,
With many a fall shall linger near.

The swallow, oft, beneath my thatch
Shall twitter from her clay-built nest;
Oft shall the pilgrim lift the latch,
And share my meal, a welcome guest.

Around my ivied porch shall spring 5
Each fragrant flower that drinks the dew;
And Lucy, at her wheel, shall sing
In russet gown and apron blue.

The village church among the trees,
Where first our marriage vows were given, 10
With merry peals shall swell the breeze
And point with taper spire to Heaven.

S. Rogers

CLXXXVI

ODE TO EVENING

If aught of oaten stop or pastoral song
May hope, O pensive Eve, to soothe thine ear
Like thy own solemn springs, 15
Thy springs, and dying gales;

O Nymph reserved, — while now the bright-hair'd sun
Sits in yon western tent, whose cloudy skirts,
With brede ethereal wove,
O'erhang his wavy bed; 20

Now air is hush'd, save where the weak-eyed bat
With short shrill shriek flits by on leathern wing,
Or where the beetle winds
His small but sullen horn,

As oft he rises midst the twilight path, 25
Against the pilgrim borne in heedless hum, —
Now teach me, maid composed,
To breathe some soften'd strain

Whose numbers, stealing through thy darkening vale,
May not unseemly with its stillness suit;
As, musing slow, I hail
Thy genial loved return.

For when thy folding-star arising shows 5
His paly circlet, at his warning lamp
The fragrant Hours, and Elves
Who slept in buds the day,

And many a Nymph who wreathes her brows with sedge
And sheds the freshening dew, and, lovelier still, 10
The pensive Pleasures sweet,
Prepare thy shadowy car.

Then let me rove some wild and heathy scene;
Or find some ruin midst its dreary dells,
Whose walls more awful nod 15
By thy religious gleams.

Or, if chill blustering winds or driving rain
Prevent my willing feet, be mine the hut
That, from the mountain's side,
Views wilds, and swelling floods, 20

And hamlets brown, and dim-discover'd spires;
And hears their simple bell; and marks o'er all
Thy dewy fingers draw
The gradual dusky veil.

While Spring shall pour his showers, as oft he wont, 25
And bathe thy breathing tresses, meekest Eve!
While Summer loves to sport
Beneath thy lingering light;

While sallow Autumn fills thy lap with leaves;
Or Winter, yelling through the troublous air, 30
Affrights thy shrinking train
And rudely rends thy robes;

So long, regardful of thy quiet rule,
Shall Fancy, Friendship, Science, smiling Peace,
Thy gentlest influence own,
And love thy favorite name!

W. Collins

CLXXXVII

ELEGY WRITTEN IN A COUNTRY CHURCHYARD

The curfew tolls the knell of parting day, 5
The lowing herd wind slowly o'er the lea,
The plowman homeward plods his weary way,
And leaves the world to darkness and to me.

Now fades the glimmering landscape on the sight,
And all the air a solemn stillness holds, 10
Save where the beetle wheels his droning flight,
And drowsy tinklings lull the distant folds:

Save that from yonder ivy-mantled tower
The moping owl does to the moon complain
Of such as, wandering near her secret bower, 15
Molest her ancient solitary reign.

Beneath those rugged elms, that yew-tree's shade
Where heaves the turf in many a moldering heap,
Each in his narrow cell forever laid,
The rude forefathers of the hamlet sleep. 20

The breezy call of incense-breathing morn,
The swallow twittering from the straw-built shed,
The cock's shrill clarion, or the echoing horn,
No more shall rouse them from their lowly bed.

For them no more the blazing hearth shall burn 25
Or busy housewife ply her evening care:
No children run to lisp their sire's return,
Or climb his knees the envied kiss to share.

Oft did the harvest to their sickle yield,
Their furrow oft the stubborn glebe has broke;
How jocund did they drive their team afield!
How bow'd the woods beneath their sturdy stroke!

Let not ambition mock their useful toil, 5
Their homely joys, and destiny obscure;
Nor grandeur hear with a disdainful smile
The short and simple annals of the poor.

The boast of heraldry, the pomp of power,
And all that beauty, all that wealth e'er gave, 10
Awaits alike th' inevitable hour: —
The paths of glory lead but to the grave.

Nor you, ye proud, impute to these the fault
If memory o'er their tomb no trophies raise,
Where through the long-drawn aisle and fretted vault 15
The pealing anthem swells the note of praise.

Can storied urn or animated bust
Back to its mansion call the fleeting breath?
Can honor's voice provoke the silent dust,
Or flattery soothe the dull cold ear of death? 20

Perhaps in this neglected spot is laid
Some heart once pregnant with celestial fire;
Hands, that the rod of empire might have sway'd,
Or waked to ecstasy the living lyre:

But knowledge to their eyes her ample page 25
Rich with the spoils of time, did ne'er unroll;
Chill penury repress'd their noble rage,
And froze the genial current of the soul.

Full many a gem of purest ray serene
The dark unfathom'd caves of ocean bear: 30
Full many a flower is born to blush unseen,
And waste its sweetness on the desert air.

Some village Hampden, that with dauntless breast
The little tyrant of his fields withstood,
Some mute inglorious Milton here may rest,
Some Cromwell, guiltless of his country's blood.

Th' applause of listening senates to command, 5
The threats of pain and ruin to despise,
To scatter plenty o'er a smiling land,
And read their history in a nation's eyes

Their lot forbade: nor circumscribed alone
Their growing virtues, but their crimes confined; 10
Forbade to wade thro' slaughter to a throne,
And shut the gates of mercy on mankind;

The struggling pangs of conscious truth to hide,
To quench the blushes of ingenuous shame,
Or heap the shrine of luxury and pride 15
With incense kindled at the Muse's flame.

Far from the madding crowd's ignoble strife
Their sober wishes never learn'd to stray;
Along the cool sequester'd vale of life
They kept the noiseless tenor of their way. 20

Yet e'en these bones from insult to protect
Some frail memorial still erected nigh,
With uncouth rhymes and shapeless sculpture deck'd,
Implores the passing tribute of a sigh.

Their name, their years, spelled by th' unletter'd Muse, 25
The place of fame and elegy supply:
And many a holy text around she strews,
That teach the rustic moralist to die.

For who, to dumb forgetfulness a prey,
This pleasing anxious being e'er resign'd, 30
Left the warm precincts of the cheerful day,
Nor cast one longing lingering look behind?

On some fond breast the parting soul relies,
Some pious drops the closing eye requires;
E'en from the tomb the voice of nature cries,
E'en in our ashes live their wonted fires.

For thee, who, mindful of th' unhonor'd dead, 5
Dost in these lines their artless tale relate;
If chance, by lonely contemplation led,
Some kindred spirit shall inquire thy fate,

Haply some hoary-headed swain may say,
"Oft have we seen him at the peep of dawn 10
Brushing with hasty steps the dews away,
To meet the sun upon the upland lawn;

"There at the foot of yonder nodding beech
That wreathes its old fantastic roots so high,
His listless length at noontide would he stretch, 15
And pore upon the brook that babbles by.

"Hard by yon wood, now smiling as in scorn,
Muttering his wayward fancies he would rove;
Now drooping, woeful-wan, like one forlorn,
Or crazed with care, or cross'd in hopeless love. 20

"One morn I miss'd him on the custom'd hill,
Along the heath, and near his favorite tree;
Another came; nor yet beside the rill,
Nor up the lawn, nor at the wood was he;

"The next with dirges due in sad array 25
Slow through the church-way path we saw him borne, —
Approach and read (for thou canst read) the lay
Graved on the stone beneath yon aged thorn."

The Epitaph

Here rests his head upon the lap of earth
A youth, to fortune and to fame unknown; 30
Fair science frown'd not on his humble birth
And melancholy mark'd him for her own.

Large was his bounty, and his soul sincere,
Heaven did a recompense as largely send:
He gave to misery (all he had) a tear,
He gain'd from Heaven ('t was all he wish'd) a friend.

No farther seek his merits to disclose, 5
Or draw his frailties from their dread abode
(There they alike in trembling hope repose),
The bosom of his Father and his God.

T. Gray

CLXXXVIII

MARY MORISON

O Mary, at thy window be,
It is the wish'd, the trysted hour! 10
Those smiles and glances let me see
That make the miser's treasure poor:
How blithely wad I bide the stoure,
A weary slave frae sun to sun,
Could I the rich reward secure, 15
The lovely Mary Morison.

Yestreen when to the trembling string
The dance gaed thro' the lighted ha',
To thee my fancy took its wing, —
I sat, but neither heard nor saw: 20
Tho' this was fair, and that was braw,
And yon the toast of a' the town,
I sigh'd, and said amang them a',
"Ye are na Mary Morison."

O Mary, canst thou wreck his peace 25
Wha for thy sake wad gladly dee?
Or canst thou break that heart of his,
Whase only faut is loving thee?

If love for love thou wilt na gie,
At least be pity to me shown;
A thought ungentle canna be
The thought o' Mary Morison.

R. Burns

CLXXXIX

BONNIE LESLEY

O saw ye bonnie Lesley 5
As she gaed o'er the border?
She 's gane, like Alexander,
To spread her conquests farther.

To see her is to love her,
And love but her forever; 10
For Nature made her what she is,
And ne'er made sic anither!

Thou art a queen, Fair Lesley,
Thy subjects we, before thee;
Thou art divine, Fair Lesley, 15
The hearts o' men adore thee.

The Deil he could na scaith thee,
Or aught that wad belang thee;
He 'd look into thy bonnie face,
And say "I canna wrang thee!" 20

The Powers aboon will tent thee;
Misfortune sha' na steer thee;
Thou 'rt like themselves sae lovely
That ill they 'll ne'er let near thee.

Return again, Fair Lesley, 25
Return to Caledonie!
That we may brag we hae a lass
There 's nane again sae bonnie.

R. Burns

CXC

O my Luve 's like a red, red rose
That 's newly sprung in June:
O my Luve 's like the melodie
That 's sweetly play'd in tune.

As fair art thou, my bonnie lass, 5
So deep in luve am I:
And I will luve thee still, my dear,
Till a' the seas gang dry:

Till a' the seas gang dry, my dear,
And the rocks melt wi' the sun; 10
I will luve thee still, my dear,
While the sands o' life shall run.

And fare thee weel, my only Luve!
And fare thee weel awhile;
And I will come again, my Luve, 15
Tho' it were ten thousand mile.

R. Burns

CXCI

HIGHLAND MARY

Ye banks and braes and streams around
The castle o' Montgomery,
Green be your woods, and fair your flowers,
Your waters never drumlie! 20
There simmer first unfauld her robes,
And there the langest tarry;
For there I took the last fareweel
O' my sweet Highland Mary.

How sweetly bloom'd the gay green birk, 25
How rich the hawthorn's blossom,
As underneath their fragrant shade
I clasp'd her to my bosom!

The golden hours on angel wings
  Flew o'er me and my dearie;
For dear to me as light and life
  Was my sweet Highland Mary.

Wi' mony a vow and lock'd embrace 5
  Our parting was fu' tender;
And pledging aft to meet again,
  We tore oursels asunder;
But, Oh! fell Death's untimely frost,
  That nipt my flower sae early! 10
Now green's the sod, and cauld's the clay,
  That wraps my Highland Mary!

O pale, pale now, those rosy lips,
  I aft hae kiss'd sae fondly;
And closed for aye the sparkling glance 15
  That dwelt on me sae kindly;
And moldering now in silent dust
  That heart that lo'ed me dearly!
But still within my bosom's core
  Shall live my Highland Mary. 20

R. Burns

CXCII

AULD ROBIN GRAY

When the sheep are in the fauld, and the kye at hame,
And a' the world to rest are gane,
The waes o' my heart fa' in showers frae my e'e,
While my gudeman lies sound by me.

Young Jamie lo'ed me weel, and sought me for his bride; 25
But saving a croun he had naething else beside:
To make the croun a pund, young Jamie gaed to sea;
And the croun and the pund were baith for me.

He hadna been awa' a week but only twa,
When my father brak his arm, and the cow was stown awa; 30

My mother she fell sick, and my Jamie at the sea—
And auld Robin Gray came a-courtin' me.

My father couldna work, and my mother couldna spin;
I toil'd day and night, but their bread I couldna win;
Auld Rob maintain'd them baith, and wi' tears in his e'e 5
Said, Jennie, for their sakes, O, marry me!

My heart it said nay; I look'd for Jamie back;
But the wind it blew high, and the ship it was a wrack;
His ship it was a wrack—why didna Jamie dee?
Or why do I live to cry, Wae 's me? 10

My father urgit sair: my mother didna speak;
But she look'd in my face till my heart was like to break:
They gi'ed him my hand, but my heart was at the sea;
Sae auld Robin Gray he was gudeman to me.

I hadna been a wife a week but only four, 15
When mournfu' as I sat on the stane at the door,
I saw my Jamie's wraith, for I couldna think it he
Till he said, I 'm come hame to marry thee.

O sair, sair did we greet, and muckle did we say;
We took but ae kiss, and I bad him gang away; 20
I wish that I were dead, but I 'm no like to dee;
And why was I born to say, Wae 's me?

I gang like a ghaist, and I carena to spin;
I daurna think on Jamie, for that wad be a sin;
But I 'll do my best a gude wife aye to be, 25
For auld Robin Gray he is kind unto me.

Lady A. Lindsay

CXCIII

DUNCAN GRAY

Duncan Gray cam here to woo,
  Ha, ha, the wooing o't;
On blithe Yule night when we were fou,
  Ha, ha, the wooing o't: 30

Maggie coost her head fu' high,
Look'd asklent and unco skeigh,
Gart poor Duncan stand abeigh;
    Ha, ha, the wooing o't!

Duncan fleech'd, and Duncan pray'd; 5
Meg was deaf as Ailsa Craig;
Duncan sigh'd baith out and in,
Grat his een baith bleer't and blin',
Spak o' lowpin ower a linn!

Time and chance are but a tide, 10
Slighted love is sair to bide;
Shall I, like a fool, quoth he,
For a haughty hizzie dee?
She may gae to — France for me!

How it comes let doctors tell, 15
Meg grew sick — as he grew well;
Something in her bosom wrings,
For relief a sigh she brings!
And O, her een, they spak sic things!

Duncan was a lad o' grace; 20
Maggie's was a piteous case;
Duncan couldna be her death,
Swelling pity smoor'd his wrath;
Now they 're crouse and canty baith:
    Ha, ha, the wooing o't! 25

R. Burns

CXCIV

THE SAILOR'S WIFE

And are ye sure the news is true?
  And are ye sure he 's weel?
Is this the time to think o' wark?
  Ye jades, lay by your wheel;
Is this the time to spin a thread, 30
  When Colin 's at the door?

Reach down my cloak, I 'll to the quay,
  And see him come ashore.
For there 's nae luck about the house,
  There 's nae luck at a';
There 's little pleasure in the house 5
  When our gudeman 's awa'.

And gie to me my bigonet,
  My bishop's satin gown;
For I maun tell the baillie's wife
  That Colin 's in the town. 10
My Turkey slippers maun gae on,
  My stockins pearly blue;
It 's a' to pleasure our gudeman,
  For he 's baith leal and true.

Rise, lass, and mak a clean fireside, 15
  Put on the muckle pot;
Gie little Kate her button gown
  And Jock his Sunday coat;
And mak their shoon as black as slaes,
  Their hose as white as snaw; 20
It 's a' to please my ain gudeman,
  For he 's been long awa.

There 's twa fat hens upo' the coop
  Been fed this month and mair;
Mak haste and thraw their necks about, 25
  That Colin weel may fare;
And spread the table neat and clean,
  Gar ilka thing look braw,
For wha can tell how Colin fared
  When he was far awa? 30

Sae true his heart, sae smooth his speech,
  His breath like caller air;
His very foot has music in 't
  As he comes up the stair —

And will I see his face again?
  And will I hear him speak?
I 'm downright dizzy wi' the thought,
  In troth, I 'm like to greet!

If Colin 's weel, and weel content, 5
  I hae nae mair to crave:
And gin I live to keep him sae,
  I 'm blest aboon the lave:
And will I see his face again?
  And will I hear him speak? 10
I 'm downright dizzy wi' the thought,
  In troth I 'm like to greet!
For there 's nae luck about the house,
  There 's nae luck at a';
There 's little pleasure in the house 15
  When our gudeman 's awa'.

W. J. Mickle

CXCV

ABSENCE

When I think on the happy days
  I spent wi' you, my dearie;
And now what lands between us lie,
  How can I be but eerie! 20

How slow ye move, ye heavy hours,
  As ye were wae and weary!
It was na sae ye glinted by
  When I was wi' my dearie.

Anon.

CXCVI

JEAN

Of a' the airts the wind can blaw 25
  I dearly like the West,
For there the bonnie lassie lives,
  The lassie I lo'e best:

There wild woods grow, and rivers row,
  And mony a hill between;
But day and night my fancy's flight
  Is ever wi' my Jean.

I see her in the dewy flowers, 5
  I see her sweet and fair:
I hear her in the tunefu' birds,
  I hear her charm the air:
There 's not a bonnie flower that springs
  By fountain, shaw, or green, 10
There 's not a bonnie bird that sings
  But minds me o' my Jean.

O blaw ye westlin winds, blaw saft
  Amang the leafy trees;
Wi' balmy gale, frae hill and dale 15
  Bring hame the laden bees;
And bring the lassie back to me
  That 's aye sae neat and clean;
Ae smile o' her wad banish care,
  Sae charming is my Jean. 20

What sighs and vows amang the knowes
  Hae pass'd atween us twa!
How fond to meet, how wae to part
  That night she gaed awa!
The Powers aboon can only ken 25
  To whom the heart is seen,
That nane can be sae dear to me
  As my sweet lovely Jean!

R. Burns

CXCVII

JOHN ANDERSON

John Anderson my jo, John,
When we were first acquent 30
Your locks were like the raven,
Your bonnie brow was brent;

But now your brow is bald, John,
Your locks are like the snow;
But blessings on your frosty pow,
John Anderson my jo.

John Anderson my jo, John, 5
We clamb the hill thegither,
And mony a canty day, John,
We 've had wi' ane anither:
Now we maun totter down, John,
But hand in hand we 'll go, 10
And sleep thegither at the foot,
John Anderson my jo.

R. Burns

CXCVIII

THE LAND O' THE LEAL

I 'm wearing awa', Jean,
Like snaw when its thaw, Jean,
I 'm wearing awa' 15
  To the land o' the leal.
There 's nae sorrow there, Jean,
There 's neither cauld nor care, Jean,
The day is aye fair
  In the land o' the leal. 20

Ye were aye leal and true, Jean,
Your task 's ended noo, Jean,
And I 'll welcome you
  To the land o' the leal.
Our bonnie bairn 's there, Jean, 25
She was baith guid and fair, Jean;
O we grudged her right sair
  To the land o' the leal!

Then dry that tearfu' e'e, Jean,
My soul langs to be free, Jean, 30

And angels wait on me
To the land o' the leal.
Now fare ye weel, my ain Jean,
This warld's care is vain, Jean;
We 'll meet and aye be fain 5
In the land o' the leal!

Lady Nairne

CXCIX

ODE ON A DISTANT PROSPECT OF ETON COLLEGE

Ye distant spires, ye antique towers
That crown the watery glade,
Where grateful Science still adores
Her Henry's holy shade; 10
And ye, that from the stately brow
Of Windsor's heights th' expanse below
Of grove, of lawn, of mead survey,
Whose turf, whose shade, whose flowers among
Wanders the hoary Thames along 15
His silver-winding way:

Ah happy hills! ah pleasing shade!
Ah fields beloved in vain!
Where once my careless childhood stray'd,
A stranger yet to pain! 20
I feel the gales that from ye blow
A momentary bliss bestow,
As waving fresh their gladsome wing
My weary soul they seem to soothe,
And, redolent of joy and youth, 25
To breathe a second spring.

Say, Father Thames, for thou hast seen
Full many a sprightly race
Disporting on thy margent green
The paths of pleasure trace; 30
Who foremost now delight to cleave
With pliant arm, thy glassy wave?

The captive linnet which enthrall?
What idle progeny succeed
To chase the rolling circle's speed
  Or urge the flying ball?

While some on earnest business bent 5
  Their murmuring labors ply
'Gainst graver hours that bring constraint
  To sweeten liberty:
Some bold adventurers disdain
The limits of their little reign 10
And unknown regions dare descry:
Still as they run they look behind,
They hear a voice in every wind,
  And snatch a fearful joy.

Gay hope is theirs by fancy fed, 15
  Less pleasing when possest;
The tear forgot as soon as shed,
  The sunshine of the breast:
Theirs buxom health, of rosy hue,
Wild wit, invention ever new, 20
And lively cheer, of vigor born;
The thoughtless day, the easy night,
The spirits pure, the slumbers light
  That fly th' approach of morn.

Alas! regardless of their doom 25
  The little victims play;
No sense have they of ills to come
  Nor care beyond to-day:
Yet see how all around 'em wait
The ministers of human fate 30
And black Misfortune's baleful train!
Ah show them where in ambush stand
To seize their prey, the murderous band!
  Ah, tell them they are men!

These shall the fury Passions tear,
  The vultures of the mind,
Disdainful Anger, pallid Fear,
  And Shame that skulks behind;
Or pining Love shall waste their youth, 5
Or Jealousy with rankling tooth
That inly gnaws the secret heart,
And Envy wan, and faded Care,
Grim-visaged comfortless Despair,
  And Sorrow's piercing dart. 10

Ambition this shall tempt to rise,
  Then whirl the wretch from high
To bitter Scorn a sacrifice
  And grinning Infamy.
The stings of Falsehood those shall try 15
And hard Unkindness' alter'd eye,
That mocks the tear it forced to flow;
And keen Remorse with blood defiled,
And moody Madness laughing wild
  Amid severest woe. 20

Lo, in the vale of years beneath
  A grisly troop are seen,
The painful family of Death,
  More hideous than their queen:
This racks the joints, this fires the veins, 25
That every laboring sinew strains,
Those in the deeper vitals rage:
Lo! Poverty, to fill the band,
That numbs the soul with icy hand,
  And slow-consuming Age. 30

To each his sufferings: all are men,
  Condemn'd alike to groan;
The tender for another's pain,
  Th' unfeeling for his own.

Yet, ah! why should they know their fate,
Since sorrow never comes too late,
And happiness too swiftly flies?
Thought would destroy their paradise.
No more; — where ignorance is bliss, 5
'T is folly to be wise.

T. Gray

CC

THE SHRUBBERY

O happy shades! to me unblest!
Friendly to peace, but not to me!
How ill the scene that offers rest,
And heart that cannot rest, agree! 10

This glassy stream, that spreading pine,
Those alders quivering to the breeze,
Might soothe a soul less hurt than mine,
And please, if anything could please.

But fix'd unalterable Care 15
Foregoes not what she feels within,
Shows the same sadness everywhere,
And slights the season and the scene.

For all that pleased in wood or lawn
While Peace possess'd these silent bowers, 20
Her animating smile withdrawn,
Has lost its beauties and its powers.

The saint or moralist should tread
This moss-grown alley, musing, slow,
They seek like me the secret shade, 25
But not, like me, to nourish woe!

Me, fruitful scenes and prospects waste
Alike admonish not to roam;
These tell me of enjoyments past,
And those of sorrows yet to come. 30

W. Cowper

CCI

HYMN TO ADVERSITY

Daughter of Jove, relentless power,
  Thou tamer of the human breast,
Whose iron scourge and torturing hour
  The bad affright, afflict the best!
Bound in thy adamantine chain 5
The proud are taught to taste of pain,
And purple tyrants vainly groan
With pangs unfelt before, unpitied and alone.

When first thy Sire to send on earth
  Virtue, his darling child, design'd, 10
To thee he gave the heavenly birth
  And bade to form her infant mind.
Stern, rugged nurse; thy rigid lore
With patience many a year she bore;
What sorrow was, thou bad'st her know, 15
And from her own she learn'd to melt at others' woe.

Scared at thy frown terrific, fly
  Self-pleasing Folly's idle brood,
Wild Laughter, Noise, and thoughtless Joy,
  And leave us leisure to be good. 20
Light they disperse, and with them go
The summer friend, the flattering foe;
By vain Prosperity received,
To her they vow their truth, and are again believed.

Wisdom in sable garb array'd 25
  Immersed in rapturous thought profound,
And Melancholy, silent maid,
  With leaden eye, that loves the ground,
Still on thy solemn steps attend:
Warm Charity, the general friend, 30
With Justice, to herself severe,
And Pity dropping soft the sadly-pleasing tear.

Oh! gently on thy suppliant's head
    Dread goddess, lay thy chastening hand!
Not in thy Gorgon terrors clad,
    Nor circled with the vengeful band
(As by the impious thou art seen) 5
With thundering voice, and threatening mien,
With screaming Horror's funeral cry,
Despair, and fell Disease, and ghastly Poverty; —

Thy form benign, oh goddess, wear,
    Thy milder influence impart, 10
Thy philosophic train be there
    To soften, not to wound my heart.
The generous spark extinct revive,
Teach me to love and to forgive,
Exact my own defects to scan, 15
What others are to feel, and know myself a Man.

T. Gray

CCII

THE SOLITUDE OF ALEXANDER SELKIRK

I am monarch of all I survey;
My right there is none to dispute;
From the center all round to the sea
I am lord of the fowl and the brute. 20
O Solitude! where are the charms
That sages have seen in thy face?
Better dwell in the midst of alarms,
Than reign in this horrible place.

I am out of humanity's reach, 25
I must finish my journey alone,
Never hear the sweet music of speech;
I start at the sound of my own.
The beasts that roam over the plain
My form with indifference see; 30
They are so unacquainted with man,
Their tameness is shocking to me.

Society, Friendship, and Love
Divinely bestow'd upon man,
Oh, had I the wings of a dove
How soon would I taste you again!
My sorrows I then might assuage 5
In the ways of religion and truth,
Might learn from the wisdom of age,
And be cheer'd by the sallies of youth.

Ye winds that have made me your sport,
Convey to this desolate shore 10
Some cordial endearing report
Of a land I shall visit no more:
My friends, do they now and then send
A wish or a thought after me?
O tell me I yet have a friend, 15
Though a friend I am never to see.

How fleet is a glance of the mind!
Compared with the speed of its flight,
The tempest itself lags behind,
And the swift-wingéd arrows of light. 20
When I think of my own native land
In a moment I seem to be there;
But alas! recollection at hand
Soon hurries me back to despair.

But the sea-fowl is gone to her nest, 25
The beast is laid down in his lair;
Even here is a season of rest,
And I to my cabin repair.
There 's mercy in every place,
And mercy, encouraging thought! 30
Gives even affliction a grace
And reconciles man to his lot.

W. Cowper

CCIII

TO MARY UNWIN

Mary! I want a lyre with other strings,
Such aid from Heaven as some have feign'd they drew,
An eloquence scarce given to mortals, new
And undebased by praise of meaner things,

That ere through age or woe I shed my wings 5
I may record thy worth with honor due,
In verse as musical as thou art true,
And that immortalizes whom it sings:—

But thou hast little need. There is a Book
By seraphs writ with beams of heavenly light, 10
On which the eyes of God not rarely look,

A chronicle of actions just and bright—
There all thy deeds, my faithful Mary, shine;
And since thou own'st that praise, I spare thee mine.

W. Cowper

CCIV

TO THE SAME

The twentieth year is well-nigh past 15
Since first our sky was overcast;
Ah would that this might be the last!
My Mary!

Thy spirits have a fainter flow,
I see thee daily weaker grow— 20
'T was my distress that brought thee low,
My Mary!

Thy needles, once a shining store,
For my sake restless heretofore,
Now rust disused, and shine no more; 25
My Mary!

For though thou gladly wouldst fulfill
The same kind office for me still,
Thy sight now seconds not thy will,
My Mary!

But well thou play'st the housewife's part, 5
And all thy threads with magic art
Have wound themselves about this heart,
My Mary!

Thy indistinct expressions seem
Like language utter'd in a dream; 10
Yet me they charm, whate'er the theme,
My Mary!

Thy silver locks, once auburn bright,
Are still more lovely in my sight
Than golden beams of orient light, 15
My Mary!

For could I view nor them nor thee,
What sight worth seeing could I see?
The sun would rise in vain for me,
My Mary! 20

Partakers of thy sad decline
Thy hands their little force resign;
Yet, gently pressed, press gently mine,
My Mary!

Such feebleness of limbs thou prov'st 25
That now at every step thou mov'st
Upheld by two; yet still thou lov'st,
My Mary!

And still to love, though pressed with ill,
In wintry age to feel no chill, 30
With me is to be lovely still,
My Mary!

But ah! by constant heed I know
How oft the sadness that I show
Transforms thy smiles to looks of woe,
My Mary!

And should my future lot be cast 5
With much resemblance of the past,
Thy worn-out heart will break at last—
My Mary!

W. Cowper

CCV

THE CASTAWAY

Obscurest night involved the sky,
The Atlantic billows roar'd, 10
When such a destined wretch as I,
Wash'd headlong from on board,
Of friends, of hope, of all bereft,
His floating home forever left.

No braver chief could Albion boast 15
Than he with whom he went,
Nor ever ship left Albion's coast
With warmer wishes sent.
He loved them both, but both in vain,
Nor him beheld, nor her again. 20

Not long beneath the whelming brine,
Expert to swim, he lay;
Nor soon he felt his strength decline,
Or courage die away;
But waged with death a lasting strife, 25
Supported by despair of life.

He shouted: nor his friends had fail'd
To check the vessel's course,
But so the furious blast prevail'd,
That, pitiless perforce, 30

They left their outcast mate behind,
And scudded still before the wind.

Some succor yet they could afford;
  And such as storms allow,
The cask, the coop, the floated cord, 5
  Delay'd not to bestow.
But he (they knew) nor ship nor shore,
Whate'er they gave, should visit more.

Nor, cruel as it seem'd, could he
  Their haste himself condemn, 10
Aware that flight, in such a sea,
  Alone could rescue them;
Yet bitter felt it still to die
Deserted, and his friends so nigh.

He long survives, who lives an hour 15
  In ocean, self-upheld;
And so long he, with unspent power,
  His destiny repell'd;
And ever, as the minutes flew,
Entreated help, or cried "Adieu!" 20

At length, his transient respite past,
  His comrades, who before
Had heard his voice in every blast,
  Could catch the sound no more;
For then, by toil subdued, he drank 25
The stifling wave, and then he sank.

No poet wept him; but the page
  Of narrative sincere,
That tells his name, his worth, his age,
  Is wet with Anson's tear: 30
And tears by bards or heroes shed
Alike immortalize the dead.

I therefore purpose not, or dream,
  Descanting on his fate,

To give the melancholy theme
  A more enduring date:
But misery still delights to trace
Its semblance in another's case.

No voice divine the storm allay'd, 5
  No light propitious shone,
When, snatch'd from all effectual aid,
  We perish'd, each alone:
But I beneath a rougher sea,
And whelm'd in deeper gulfs than he. 10

W. Cowper

CCVI

TO-MORROW

In the downhill of life, when I find I 'm declining,
  May my fate no less fortunate be
Than a snug elbow chair will afford for reclining,
  And a cot that o'erlooks the wide sea;
With an ambling pad-pony to pace o'er the lawn, 15
  While I carol away idle sorrow,
And blithe as the lark that each day hails the dawn
  Look forward with hope for To-morrow.

With a porch at my door, both for shelter and shade too,
  As the sunshine or rain may prevail; 20
And a small spot of ground for the use of the spade too,
  With a barn for the use of the flail:
A cow for my dairy, a dog for my game,
  And a purse when a friend wants to borrow;
I 'll envy no Nabob his riches or fame, 25
  Or what honors may wait him To-morrow.

From the bleak northern blast may my cot be completely
  Secured by a neighboring hill;
And at night may repose steal upon me more sweetly
  By the sound of a murmuring rill: 30

And while peace and plenty I find at my board,
  With a heart free from sickness and sorrow,
With my friends may I share what To-day may afford,
  And let them spread the table To-morrow.

And when I at last must throw off this frail cov'ring 5
  Which I 've worn for threescore years and ten,
On the brink of the grave I 'll not seek to keep hov'ring,
  Nor my thread wish to spin o'er again:
But my face in the glass I 'll serenely survey,
  And with smiles count each wrinkle and furrow; 10
As this old worn-out stuff, which is threadbare To-day,
  May become Everlasting To-morrow.

J. Collins

CCVII

Life! I know not what thou art,
But know that thou and I must part;
And when, or how, or where we met 15
I own to me 's a secret yet.

Life! we 've been long together
Through pleasant and through cloudy weather;
'T is hard to part when friends are dear —
Perhaps 't will cost a sigh, a tear; 20
— Then steal away, give little warning,
Choose thine own time;
Say not Good Night, — but in some brighter clime
  Bid me Good Morning.

A. L. Barbauld

BOOK FOURTH

It proves sufficiently the lavish wealth of our own age in poetry, that the pieces which, without conscious departure from the standard of excellence, render this book by far the longest, were with very few exceptions composed during the first thirty years of the nineteenth century. Exhaustive reasons can hardly be given for the strangely sudden appearance of individual genius; that, however, which assigns the splendid national achievements of our recent poetry to an impulse from the France of the first Republic and Empire is inadequate. The first French Revolution was rather one result — the most conspicuous, indeed, yet itself in great measure essentially retrogressive — of that wider and more potent spirit which through inquiry and attempt, through strength and weakness, sweeps mankind round the circles (not, as some too confidently argue, of advance, but) of gradual transformation; and it is to this that we must trace the literature of modern Europe. But without attempting discussion on the motive causes of Scott, Wordsworth, Shelley, and others, we may observe that these poets carried to further perfection the later tendencies of the century preceding, in simplicity of narrative, reverence for human passion and character in every sphere, and love of nature for herself; that, while maintaining on the whole the advances in art made since the Restoration, they renewed the half-forgotten melody and depth of tone which marked the best Elizabethan writers; that, lastly, to what was thus inherited they added a richness in language and a variety in meter, a force and fire in narrative, a tenderness and bloom in feeling, an insight into the finer passages of the soul and the inner meanings of the landscape, a larger sense of humanity, hitherto scarcely attained, and perhaps unattainable even by predecessors of not inferior individual genius. In a word, the nation which, after the Greeks in their glory, may fairly claim that during six centuries it has proved itself the most richly gifted of all nations for poetry, expressed in these men the highest strength and prodigality of its nature. They interpreted the age to itself; hence the many phases of thought and style they present. To sympathize with each fervently and impartially, without fear and without fancifulness, is no doubtful step in the higher education of the soul. For purity in taste is absolutely proportionate to strength, and when once the mind has raised itself to grasp and to delight in excellence, those who love most will be found to love most wisely.

But the gallery which this book offers to the reader will aid him more than any preface. It is a royal palace of poetry which he is invited to enter:

> Adparet domus intus, et atria longa patescunt[1] —

though it is, indeed, to the sympathetic eye only that its treasures will be visible.

[1] "The interior of the house appears, and the long halls open out" (Virgil, Æneid, II, 483).

CCVIII

TO THE MUSES

Whether on Ida's shady brow,
  Or in the chambers of the East,
The chambers of the sun, that now
  From ancient melody have ceased;

Whether in Heaven ye wander fair, 5
  Or the green corners of the earth,
Or the blue regions of the air,
  Where the melodious winds have birth;

Whether on crystal rocks ye rove
  Beneath the bosom of the sea, 10
Wandering in many a coral grove, —
  Fair Nine, forsaking Poetry;

How have you left the ancient love
  That bards of old enjoy'd in you!
The languid strings do scarcely move, 15
  The sound is forced, the notes are few.

W. Blake

CCIX

ODE ON THE POETS

Bards of Passion and of Mirth,
Ye have left your souls on earth!
Have ye souls in heaven too,
Double-lived in regions new? 20

— Yes, and those of heaven commune
With the spheres of sun and moon;
With the noise of fountains wond'rous
And the parle of voices thund'rous;
With the whisper of heaven's trees 25
And one another, in soft ease

Seated on Elysian lawns
Browsed by none but Dian's fawns;
Underneath large bluebells tented,
Where the daisies are rose-scented,
And the rose herself has got 5
Perfume which on earth is not;
Where the nightingale doth sing
Not a senseless, trancéd thing,
But divine melodious truth;
Philosophic numbers smooth; 10
Tales and golden histories
Of heaven and its mysteries.

Thus ye live on high, and then
On the earth ye live again;
And the souls ye left behind you 15
Teach us, here, the way to find you,
Where your other souls are joying,
Never slumber'd, never cloying.
Here, your earthborn souls still speak
To mortals, of their little week; 20
Of their sorrows and delights;
Of their passions and their spites;
Of their glory and their shame;
What doth strengthen and what maim: —
Thus ye teach us, every day, 25
Wisdom, though fled far away.

Bards of Passion and of Mirth
Ye have left your souls on earth!
Ye have souls in heaven too,
Double-lived in regions new! 30

J. Keats

CCX

ON FIRST LOOKING INTO CHAPMAN'S HOMER

Much have I travel'd in the realms of gold
And many goodly states and kingdoms seen;
Round many western islands have I been
Which bards in fealty to Apollo hold.

Oft of one wide expanse had I been told 5
That deep-brow'd Homer ruled as his demesne:
Yet did I never breathe its pure serene
Till I heard Chapman speak out loud and bold:

— Then felt I like some watcher of the skies
When a new planet swims into his ken; 10
Or like stout Cortez, when with eagle eyes

He stared at the Pacific — and all his men
Look'd at each other with a wild surmise —
Silent, upon a peak in Darien.

J. Keats

CCXI

LOVE

All thoughts, all passions, all delights, 15
Whatever stirs this mortal frame,
All are but ministers of Love,
And feed his sacred flame.

Oft in my waking dreams do I
Live o'er again that happy hour, 20
When midway on the mount I lay,
Beside the ruin'd tower.

The moonshine stealing o'er the scene
Had blended with the lights of eve;
And she was there, my hope, my joy, 25
My own dear Genevieve!

She lean'd against the arméd man,
The statue of the arméd knight;
She stood and listen'd to my lay,
    Amid the lingering light.

Few sorrows hath she of her own, 5
My hope! my joy! my Genevieve!
She loves me best, whene'er I sing
    The songs that make her grieve.

I play'd a soft and doleful air,
I sang an old and moving story — 10
An old rude song, that suited well
    That ruin wild and hoary.

She listen'd with a flitting blush,
With downcast eyes and modest grace;
For well she knew, I could not choose 15
    But gaze upon her face.

I told her of the Knight that wore
Upon his shield a burning brand;
And that for ten long years he woo'd
    The Lady of the Land. 20

I told her how he pined: and ah!
The deep, the low, the pleading tone
With which I sang another's love
    Interpreted my own.

She listen'd with a flitting blush, 25
With downcast eyes, and modest grace;
And she forgave me, that I gazed
    Too fondly on her face!

But when I told the cruel scorn
That crazed that bold and lovely Knight, 30
And that he cross'd the mountain woods,
    Nor rested day nor night;

That sometimes from the savage den,
And sometimes from the darksome shade,
And sometimes starting up at once
    In green and sunny glade, —

There came and look'd him in the face   5
An angel beautiful and bright;
And that he knew it was a Fiend,
    This miserable Knight!

And that unknowing what he did,
He leap'd amid a murderous band,   10
And saved from outrage worse than death
    The Lady of the Land; —

And how she wept, and clasp'd his knees;
And how she tended him in vain —
And ever strove to expiate   15
    The scorn that crazed his brain; —

And that she nursed him in a cave,
And how his madness went away,
When on the yellow forest leaves
    A dying man he lay; —   20

His dying words — but when I reach'd
That tenderest strain of all the ditty,
My faltering voice and pausing harp
    Disturb'd her soul with pity!

All impulses of soul and sense   25
Had thrill'd my guileless Genevieve;
The music and the doleful tale,
    The rich and balmy eve;

And hopes, and fears that kindle hope,
An undistinguishable throng,   30

And gentle wishes long subdued,
Subdued and cherish'd long!

She wept with pity and delight,
She blush'd with love, and virgin shame;
And like the murmur of a dream, 5
I heard her breathe my name.

Her bosom heaved — she stepp'd aside,
As conscious of my look she stept —
Then suddenly, with timorous eye
She fled to me and wept. 10

She half inclosed me with her arms,
She press'd me with a meek embrace;
And bending back her head, look'd up,
And gazed upon my face.

'T was partly love, and partly fear, 15
And partly 't was a bashful art
That I might rather feel, than see,
The swelling of her heart.

I calm'd her fears, and she was calm,
And told her love with virgin pride; 20
And so I won my Genevieve,
My bright and beauteous Bride.

S. T. Coleridge

CCXII

ALL FOR LOVE

O talk not to me of a name great in story;
The days of our youth are the days of our glory;
And the myrtle and ivy of sweet two-and-twenty 25
Are worth all your laurels, though ever so plenty.

What are garlands and crowns to the brow that is wrinkled?
'T is but as a dead flower with May-dew besprinkled:
Then away with all such from the head that is hoary —
What care I for the wreaths that can only give glory?

O fame! — if I e'er took delight in thy praises, 5
'T was less for the sake of thy high-sounding phrases,
Than to see the bright eyes of the dear one discover
She thought that I was not unworthy to love her.

There chiefly I sought thee, there only I found thee;
Her glance was the best of the rays that surround thee; 10
When it sparkled o'er aught that was bright in my story,
I knew it was love, and I felt it was glory.

Lord Byron

CCXIII

THE OUTLAW

O Brignall banks are wild and fair,
And Greta woods are green,
And you may gather garlands there 15
Would grace a summer queen.
And as I rode by Dalton-Hall
Beneath the turrets high,
A Maiden on the castle wall
Was singing merrily: 20
"O Brignall banks are fresh and fair,
And Greta woods are green;
I 'd rather rove with Edmund there
Than reign our English queen."

"If, Maiden, thou wouldst wend with me, 25
To leave both tower and town,
Thou first must guess what life lead we
That dwell by dale and down.
And if thou canst that riddle read,
As read full well you may, 30

Then to the greenwood shalt thou speed
  As blithe as Queen of May."
Yet sung she, "Brignall banks are fair,
  And Greta woods are green;
I 'd rather rove with Edmund there 5
  Than reign our English queen.

"I read you, by your bugle horn
  And by your palfrey good,
I read you for a ranger sworn
  To keep the king's greenwood." 10
"A Ranger, lady, winds his horn,
  And 't is at peep of light;
His blast is heard at merry morn,
  And mine at dead of night."
Yet sung she, "Brignall banks are fair, 15
  And Greta woods are gay;
I would I were with Edmund there
  To reign his Queen of May!

"With burnish'd brand and musketoon
  So gallantly you come, 20
I read you for a bold Dragoon
  That lists the tuck of drum."
"I list no more the tuck of drum,
  No more the trumpet hear;
But when the beetle sounds his hum 25
  My comrades take the spear.
And O! though Brignall banks be fair
  And Greta woods be gay,
Yet mickle must the maiden dare
  Would reign my Queen of May! 30

"Maiden! a nameless life I lead,
  A nameless death I 'll die;
The fiend whose lantern lights the mead
  Were better mate than I!

And when I 'm with my comrades met
  Beneath the greenwood bough, —
What once we were we all forget,
  Nor think what we are now."

CHORUS

"Yet Brignall banks are fresh and fair, 5
  And Greta woods are green,
And you may gather garlands there
  Would grace a summer queen."

Sir W. Scott

CCXIV

There be none of Beauty's daughters
  With a magic like Thee; 10
And like music on the waters
  Is thy sweet voice to me:
When, as if its sound were causing
The charmed ocean's pausing,
The waves lie still and gleaming, 15
And the lull'd winds seem dreaming:

And the midnight moon is weaving
  Her bright chain o'er the deep,
Whose breast is gently heaving
  As an infant's asleep: 20
So the spirit bows before thee
To listen and adore thee;
With a full but soft emotion,
Like the swell of Summer's ocean.

Lord Byron

CCXV

THE INDIAN SERENADE

I arise from dreams of Thee 25
In the first sweet sleep of night,
When the winds are breathing low
And the stars are shining bright:

I arise from dreams of thee,
And a spirit in my feet
Hath led me — who knows how?
To thy chamber window, Sweet!

The wandering airs they faint 5
On the dark, the silent stream —
The champak odors fail
Like sweet thoughts in a dream;
The nightingale's complaint
It dies upon her heart, 10
As I must die on thine,
O belovéd as thou art!

Oh lift me from the grass!
I die, I faint, I fail!
Let thy Love in kisses rain 15
On my lips and eyelids pale.
My cheek is cold and white, alas!
My heart beats loud and fast;
Oh! press it close to thine again
Where it will break at last. 20

P. B. Shelley

CCXVI

She walks in beauty, like the night
Of cloudless climes and starry skies,
And all that 's best of dark and bright
Meet in her aspect and her eyes;
Thus mellow'd to that tender light 25
Which heaven to gaudy day denies.

One shade the more, one ray the less,
Had half impair'd the nameless grace
Which waves in every raven tress
Or softly lightens o'er her face, 30
Where thoughts serenely sweet express
How pure, how dear their dwelling place.

And on that cheek and o'er that brow
So soft, so calm, yet eloquent,
The smiles that win, the tints that glow
But tell of days in goodness spent,—
A mind at peace with all below, 5
A heart whose love is innocent.

Lord Byron

CCXVII

She was a Phantom of delight
When first she gleam'd upon my sight;
A lovely Apparition, sent
To be a moment's ornament; 10
Her eyes as stars of twilight fair;
Like Twilight's, too, her dusky hair;
But all things else about her drawn
From May-time and the cheerful dawn;
A dancing shape, an image gay, 15
To haunt, to startle, and waylay.

I saw her upon nearer view,
A Spirit, yet a Woman too!
Her household motions light and free,
And steps of virgin-liberty; 20
A countenance in which did meet
Sweet records, promises as sweet;
A creature not too bright or good
For human nature's daily food,
For transient sorrows, simple wiles, 25
Praise, blame, love, kisses, tears, and smiles.

And now I see with eye serene
The very pulse of the machine;
A being breathing thoughtful breath,
A traveler between life and death: 30
The reason firm, the temperate will,
Endurance, foresight, strength, and skill;

A perfect Woman, nobly plann'd
To warn, to comfort, and command;
And yet a Spirit still, and bright
With something of an angel light.

W. Wordsworth

CCXVIII

She is not fair to outward view 5
  As many maidens be;
Her loveliness I never knew
  Until she smiled on me.
O then I saw her eye was bright,
A well of love, a spring of light. 10

But now her looks are coy and cold,
  To mine they ne'er reply,
And yet I cease not to behold
  The love-light in her eye:
Her very frowns are fairer far 15
Than smiles of other maidens are.

H. Coleridge

CCXIX

I fear thy kisses, gentle maiden;
Thou needest not fear mine;
My spirit is too deeply laden
Ever to burthen thine. 20

I fear thy mien, thy tones, thy motion;
Thou needest not fear mine;
Innocent is the heart's devotion
With which I worship thine.

P. B. Shelley

CCXX

She dwelt among the untrodden ways 25
  Beside the springs of Dove;
A maid whom there were none to praise,
  And very few to love,

A violet by a mossy stone
  Half-hidden from the eye!
— Fair as a star, when only one
  Is shining in the sky.

She lived unknown, and few could know 5
  When Lucy ceased to be;
But she is in her grave, and, oh,
  The difference to me!

W. Wordsworth

CCXXI

I travel'd among unknown men
  In lands beyond the sea; 10
Nor, England! did I know till then
  What love I bore to thee.

'T is past, that melancholy dream!
  Nor will I quit thy shore
A second time; for still I seem 15
  To love thee more and more.

Among thy mountains did I feel
  The joy of my desire;
And she I cherish'd turn'd her wheel
  Beside an English fire. 20

Thy mornings show'd, thy nights conceal'd
  The bowers where Lucy play'd;
And thine too is the last green field
  That Lucy's eyes survey'd.

W. Wordsworth

CCXXII

THE EDUCATION OF NATURE

Three years she grew in sun and shower; 25
Then Nature said, "A lovelier flower
On earth was never sown:

This Child I to myself will take;
She shall be mine, and I will make
A lady of my own.

"Myself will to my darling be
Both law and impulse: and with me 5
The girl, in rock and plain,
In earth and heaven, in glade and bower,
Shall feel an overseeing power
To kindle or restrain.

"She shall be sportive as the fawn 10
That wild with glee across the lawn
Or up the mountain springs;
And her's shall be the breathing balm,
And her's the silence and the calm
Of mute insensate things. 15

"The floating clouds their state shall lend
To her; for her the willow bend;
Nor shall she fail to see
Ev'n in the motions of the storm
Grace that shall mold the maiden's form 20
By silent sympathy.

"The stars of midnight shall be dear
To her; and she shall lean her ear
In many a secret place
Where rivulets dance their wayward round, 25
And beauty born of murmuring sound
Shall pass into her face.

"And vital feelings of delight
Shall rear her form to stately height,
Her virgin bosom swell; 30
Such thoughts to Lucy I will give
While she and I together live
Here in this happy dell."

Thus Nature spake — The work was done —
How soon my Lucy's race was run!
She died, and left to me
This heath, this calm and quiet scene;
The memory of what has been, 5
And never more will be.

W. Wordsworth

CCXXIII

A slumber did my spirit seal;
I had no human fears:
She seem'd a thing that could not feel
The touch of earthly years. 10

No motion has she now, no force;
She neither hears nor sees;
Roll'd round in earth's diurnal course
With rocks, and stones, and trees.

W. Wordsworth

CCXXIV

A LOST LOVE

I meet thy pensive, moonlight face; 15
Thy thrilling voice I hear;
And former hours and scenes retrace,
Too fleeting, and too dear!

Then sighs and tears flow fast and free,
Though none is nigh to share; 20
And life has naught beside for me
So sweet as this despair.

There are crush'd hearts that will not break;
And mine, methinks, is one;
Or thus I should not weep and wake, 25
And thou to slumber gone.

I little thought it thus could be
  In days more sad and fair —
That earth could have a place for me,
  And thou no longer there.

Yet death cannot our hearts divide, 5
  Or make thee less my own:
'T were sweeter sleeping at thy side
  Than watching here alone.

Yet never, never can we part,
  While Memory holds her reign: 10
Thine, thine is still this wither'd heart,
  Till we shall meet again.

H. F. Lyte

CCXXV

LORD ULLIN'S DAUGHTER

A Chieftain to the Highlands bound
Cries "Boatman, do not tarry!
And I 'll give thee a silver pound 15
To row us o'er the ferry!"

"Now who be ye, would cross Lochgyle,
This dark and stormy water?"
"O I 'm the chief of Ulva's isle,
And this, Lord Ullin's daughter. 20

"And fast before her father's men
Three days we 've fled together,
For should he find us in the glen,
My blood would stain the heather.

"His horsemen hard behind us ride — 25
Should they our steps discover,
Then who will cheer my bonny bride,
When they have slain her lover?"

Out spoke the hardy Highland wight,
"I 'll go, my chief, I 'm ready:
It is not for your silver bright,
But for your winsome lady: —

"And by my word! the bonny bird 5
In danger shall not tarry;
So though the waves are raging white
I 'll row you o'er the ferry."

By this the storm grew loud apace,
The water-wraith was shrieking; 10
And in the scowl of Heaven each face
Grew dark as they were speaking.

But still as wilder blew the wind,
And as the night grew drearer,
Adown the glen rode armèd men, 15
Their trampling sounded nearer.

"O haste thee, haste!" the lady cries,
"Though tempests round us gather;
I 'll meet the raging of the skies,
But not an angry father." 20

The boat has left a stormy land,
A stormy sea before her, —
When, oh! too strong for human hand
The tempest gather'd o'er her.

And still they row'd amidst the roar 25
Of waters fast prevailing:
Lord Ullin reach'd that fatal shore, —
His wrath was changed to wailing.

For, sore dismay'd, through storm and shade
His child he did discover; — 30
One lovely hand she stretch'd for aid,
And one was round her lover.

"Come back! come back!" he cried in grief
"Across this stormy water:
And I'll forgive your Highland chief,
My daughter! — Oh, my daughter!"

'T was vain: the loud waves lash'd the shore, 5
Return or aid preventing:
The waters wild went o'er his child,
And he was left lamenting.

T. Campbell

CCXXVI

LUCY GRAY

Oft I had heard of Lucy Gray:
And when I cross'd the wild, 10
I chanced to see at break of day
The solitary child.

No mate, no comrade Lucy knew;
She dwelt on a wide moor,
The sweetest thing that ever grew 15
Beside a human door!

You yet may spy the fawn at play,
The hare upon the green;
But the sweet face of Lucy Gray
Will never more be seen. 20

"To-night will be a stormy night—
You to the town must go;
And take a lantern, Child, to light
Your mother through the snow."

"That, Father! will I gladly do: 25
'T is scarcely afternoon—
The minster clock has just struck two,
And yonder is the moon!"

At this the father raised his hook,
And snapp'd a fagot band;
He plied his work; — and Lucy took
The lantern in her hand.

Not blither is the mountain roe: 5
With many a wanton stroke
Her feet disperse the powdery snow,
That rises up like smoke.

The storm came on before its time:
She wander'd up and down; 10
And many a hill did Lucy climb:
But never reach'd the town.

The wretched parents all that night
Went shouting far and wide;
But there was neither sound nor sight 15
To serve them for a guide.

At daybreak on a hill they stood
That overlook'd the moor;
And thence they saw the bridge of wood
A furlong from their door. 20

They wept — and, turning homeward, cried
"In heaven we all shall meet!"
— When in the snow the mother spied
The print of Lucy's feet.

Then downwards from the steep hill's edge 25
They track'd the footmarks small;
And through the broken hawthorn hedge,
And by the long stonewall:

And then an open field they cross'd:
The marks were still the same; 30
They track'd them on, nor ever lost;
And to the bridge they came:

They follow'd from the snowy bank
Those footmarks, one by one,
Into the middle of the plank;
And further there were none!

— Yet some maintain that to this day 5
She is a living child;
That you may see sweet Lucy Gray
Upon the lonesome wild.

O'er rough and smooth she trips along,
And never looks behind; 10
And sings a solitary song
That whistles in the wind.

W. Wordsworth

CCXXVII

JOCK OF HAZELDEAN

"Why weep ye by the tide, ladie?
Why weep ye by the tide?
I'll wed ye to my youngest son, 15
And ye sall be his bride:
And ye sall be his bride, ladie,
Sae comely to be seen" —
But aye she loot the tears down fa'
For Jock of Hazeldean. 20

"Now let this wilfu' grief be done,
And dry that cheek so pale;
Young Frank is chief of Errington
And lord of Langley-dale;
His step is first in peaceful ha', 25
His sword in battle keen" —
But aye she loot the tears down fa'
For Jock of Hazeldean.

"A chain of gold ye sall not lack,
Nor braid to bind your hair, 30

Nor mettled hound, nor managed hawk,
  Nor palfrey fresh and fair;
And you the foremost o' them a'
  Shall ride our forest queen" —
But aye she loot the tears down fa' 5
  For Jock of Hazeldean.

The kirk was deck'd at morning-tide,
  The tapers glimmer'd fair;
The priest and bridegroom wait the bride,
  And dame and knight are there: 10
They sought her baith by bower and ha';
  The ladie was not seen!
She 's o'er the border, and awa'
  Wi' Jock of Hazeldean.

Sir W. Scott

CCXXVIII

LOVE'S PHILOSOPHY

The fountains mingle with the river 15
And the rivers with the ocean,
The winds of heaven mix forever
With a sweet emotion;
Nothing in the world is single,
All things by a law divine 20
In one another's being mingle —
Why not I with thine?

See the mountains kiss high heaven,
And the waves clasp one another;
No sister flower would be forgiven 25
If it disdain'd its brother:
And the sunlight clasps the earth,
And the moonbeams kiss the sea —
What are all these kissings worth,
If thou kiss not me? 30

P. B. Shelley

CCXXIX

ECHOES

How sweet the answer Echo makes
To Music at night
When, roused by lute or horn, she wakes,
And far away o'er lawns and lakes
Goes answering light! 5

Yet Love hath echoes truer far
And far more sweet
Than e'er, beneath the moonlight's star,
Of horn or lute or soft guitar
The songs repeat. 10

'T is when the sigh, — in youth sincere
And only then,
The sigh that 's breathed for one to hear —
Is by that one, that only Dear
Breathed back again. 15

T. Moore

CCXXX

A SERENADE

Ah! County Guy, the hour is nigh,
The sun has left the lea,
The orange flower perfumes the bower,
The breeze is on the sea.
The lark, his lay who thrill'd all day, 20
Sits hush'd his partner nigh;
Breeze, bird, and flower confess the hour,
But where is County Guy?

The village maid steals through the shade
Her shepherd's suit to hear; 25
To Beauty shy, by lattice high,
Sings highborn Cavalier.

The star of Love, all stars above,
  Now reigns o'er earth and sky,
And high and low the influence know —
  But where is County Guy?

Sir W. Scott

CCXXXI

TO THE EVENING STAR

Gem of the crimson-color'd Even, 5
Companion of retiring day,
Why at the closing gates of heaven,
Belovéd Star, dost thou delay?

So fair thy pensile beauty burns
When soft the tear of twilight flows; 10
So due thy plighted love returns
To chambers brighter than the rose;

To Peace, to Pleasure, and to Love
So kind a star thou seem'st to be,
Sure some enamor'd orb above 15
Descends and burns to meet with thee.

Thine is the breathing, blushing hour
When all unheavenly passions fly,
Chased by the soul-subduing power
Of Love's delicious witchery. 20

O! sacred to the fall of day
Queen of propitious stars, appear,
And early rise, and long delay,
When Caroline herself is here!

Shine on her chosen green resort 25
Whose trees the sunward summit crown,
And wanton flowers, that well may court
An angel's feet to tread them down: —

Shine on her sweetly scented road
Thou star of evening's purple dome,
That lead'st the nightingale abroad,
And guid'st the pilgrim to his home.

Shine where my charmer's sweeter breath 5
Embalms the soft exhaling dew,
Where dying winds a sigh bequeath
To kiss the cheek of rosy hue:—

Where, winnow'd by the gentle air,
Her silken tresses darkly flow 10
And fall upon her brow so fair,
Like shadows on the mountain snow.

Thus, ever thus, at day's decline
In converse sweet to wander far—
O bring with thee my Caroline, 15
And thou shalt be my Ruling Star!

T. Campbell

CCXXXII

TO THE NIGHT

Swiftly walk over the western wave,
Spirit of Night!
Out of the misty eastern cave
Where, all the long and lone daylight, 20
Thou wovest dreams of joy and fear
Which make thee terrible and dear,—
Swift be thy flight!

Wrap thy form in a mantle gray
Star-inwrought; 25
Blind with thine hair the eyes of Day,
Kiss her until she be wearied out:
Then wander o'er city and sea and land,
Touching all with thine opiate wand—
Come, long-sought! 30

When I arose and saw the dawn,
I sigh'd for thee;
When light rode high, and the dew was gone,
And noon lay heavy on flower and tree,
And the weary Day turn'd to his rest 5
Lingering like an unloved guest,
I sigh'd for thee.

Thy brother Death came, and cried
Wouldst thou me?
Thy sweet child Sleep, the filmy-eyed, 10
Murmur'd like a noontide bee
Shall I nestle near thy side?
Wouldst thou me? — And I replied
No, not thee!

Death will come when thou art dead, 15
Soon, too soon —
Sleep will come when thou art fled;
Of neither would I ask the boon
I ask of thee, belovéd Night —
Swift be thine approaching flight, 20
Come soon, soon!

P. B. Shelley

CCXXXIII

TO A DISTANT FRIEND

Why art thou silent? Is thy love a plant
Of such weak fiber that the treacherous air
Of absence withers what was once so fair?
Is there no debt to pay, no boon to grant? 25

Yet have my thoughts for thee been vigilant,
Bound to thy service with unceasing care —
The mind's least generous wish a mendicant
For naught but what thy happiness could spare.

Speak! — though this soft warm heart, once free to hold
A thousand tender pleasures, thine and mine,
Be left more desolate, more dreary cold

Than a forsaken bird's-nest fill'd with snow
'Mid its own bush of leafless eglantine — 5
Speak, that my torturing doubts their end may know!

W. Wordsworth

CCXXXIV

When we two parted
In silence and tears,
Half broken-hearted,
To sever for years, 10
Pale grew thy cheek and cold,
Colder thy kiss;
Truly that hour foretold
Sorrow to this!

The dew of the morning 15
Sunk chill on my brow;
It felt like the warning
Of what I feel now.
Thy vows are all broken,
And light is thy fame: 20
I hear thy name spoken
And share in its shame.

They name thee before me,
A knell to mine ear;
A shudder comes o'er me — 25
Why wert thou so dear?
They know not I knew thee
Who knew thee too well:
Long, long shall I rue thee,
Too deeply to tell. 30

In secret we met:
In silence I grieve
That thy heart could forget,
Thy spirit deceive.
If I should meet thee 5
After long years,
How should I greet thee?—
With silence and tears.

Lord Byron

CCXXXV

HAPPY INSENSIBILITY

In a drear-nighted December,
Too happy, happy tree, 10
Thy branches ne'er remember
Their green felicity:
The north cannot undo them
With a sleety whistle through them,
Nor frozen thawings glue them 15
From budding at the prime.

In a drear-nighted December,
Too happy, happy brook,
Thy bubblings ne'er remember
Apollo's summer look; 20
But with a sweet forgetting
They stay their crystal fretting,
Never, never petting
About the frozen time.

Ah! would 't were so with many 25
A gentle girl and boy!
But were there ever any
Writhed not at passéd joy?
To know the change and feel it,
When there is none to heal it 30

Nor numbéd sense to steal it —
Was never said in rhyme.

J. Keats

CCXXXVI

Where shall the lover rest
Whom the fates sever
From his true maiden's breast 5
Parted forever?
Where, through groves deep and high
Sounds the far billow,
Where early violets die
Under the willow. 10
Eleu loro
Soft shall be his pillow.

There through the summer day
Cool streams are laving:
There, while the tempests sway, 15
Scarce are boughs waving;
There thy rest shalt thou take
Parted forever,
Never again to wake
Never, O never! 20
Eleu loro
Never, O never!

Where shall the traitor rest,
He, the deceiver,
Who could win maiden's breast, 25
Ruin, and leave her?
In the lost battle,
Borne down by the flying,
Where mingles war's rattle
With groans of the dying; 30
Eleu loro
There shall he be lying.

Her wing shall the eagle flap
O'er the falsehearted;
His warm blood the wolf shall lap
Ere life be parted:
Shame and dishonor sit 5
By his grave ever;
Blessing shall hallow it
Never, O never!
Eleu loro
Never, O never! 10

Sir W. Scott

CCXXXVII

LA BELLE DAME SANS MERCI

"O what can ail thee, knight-at-arms,
Alone and palely loitering?
The sedge has wither'd from the lake,
And no birds sing.

"O what can ail thee, knight-at-arms! 15
So haggard and so woebegone?
The squirrel's granary is full,
And the harvest 's done.

"I see a lily on thy brow
With anguish moist and fever-dew, 20
And on thy cheeks a fading rose
Fast withereth too."

"I met a lady in the meads,
Full beautiful — a faery's child,
Her hair was long, her foot was light, 25
And her eyes were wild.

"I made a garland for her head,
And bracelets too, and fragrant zone;

She look'd at me as she did love,
  And made sweet moan.

"I set her on my pacing steed
  And nothing else saw all day long,
For sidelong would she bend, and sing   5
  A faery's song.

"She found me roots of relish sweet,
  And honey wild and manna-dew,
And sure in language strange she said
  'I love thee true.'   10

"She took me to her elfin grot,
  And there she wept and sigh'd full sore;
And there I shut her wild wild eyes
  With kisses four.

"And there she lullèd me asleep,   15
  And there I dream'd — Ah! woe betide!
The latest dream I ever dream'd
  On the cold hill's side.

"I saw pale kings and princes too,
  Pale warriors, death-pale were they all: 20
They cried — 'La belle Dame sans Merci
  Hath thee in thrall!'

"I saw their starved lips in the gloam
  With horrid warning gapèd wide,
And I awoke and found me here   25
  On the cold hill's side.

"And this is why I sojourn here
  Alone and palely loitering,
Though the sedge is wither'd from the lake,
  And no birds sing."   30

J. Keats

CCXXXVIII

THE ROVER

A weary lot is thine, fair maid,
  A weary lot is thine!
To pull the thorn thy brow to braid,
  And press the rue for wine.
A lightsome eye, a soldier's mien, 5
  A feather of the blue,
A doublet of the Lincoln green —
  No more of me you knew
    My Love!
No more of me you knew. 10

"This morn is merry June, I trow,
  The rose is budding fain;
But she shall bloom in winter snow
  Ere we two meet again."
He turn'd his charger as he spake 15
  Upon the river shore,
He gave the bridle reins a shake,
  Said "Adieu forevermore
    My Love!
And adieu forevermore." 20

Sir W. Scott

CCXXXIX

THE FLIGHT OF LOVE

When the lamp is shatter'd
The light in the dust lies dead —
When the cloud is scatter'd,
The rainbow's glory is shed.
When the lute is broken, 25
Sweet tones are remember'd not;
When the lips have spoken,
Loved accents are soon forgot.

As music and splendor
Survive not the lamp and the lute,
The heart's echoes render
No song when the spirit is mute—
No song but sad dirges, 5
Like the wind through a ruin'd cell,
Or the mournful surges
That ring the dead seaman's knell.

When hearts have once mingled,
Love first leaves the well-built nest; 10
The weak one is singled
To endure what it once possesst.
O Love! who bewailest
The frailty of all things here,
Why choose you the frailest 15
For your cradle, your home, and your bier?

Its passions will rock thee
As the storms rock the ravens on high;
Bright reason will mock thee
Like the sun from a wintry sky. 20
From thy nest every rafter
Will rot, and thine eagle home
Leave thee naked to laughter,
When leaves fall and cold winds come.

P. B. Shelley

CCXL

THE MAID OF NEIDPATH

O lovers' eyes are sharp to see, 25
And lovers' ears in hearing;
And love, in life's extremity,
Can lend an hour of cheering.
Disease had been in Mary's bower
And slow decay from mourning, 30

Though now she sits on Neidpath's tower
To watch her Love's returning.

All sunk and dim her eyes so bright,
Her form decay'd by pining,
Till through her wasted hand, at night, 5
You saw the taper shining.
By fits a sultry hectic hue
Across her cheek was flying;
By fits so ashy pale she grew
Her maidens thought her dying. 10

Yet keenest powers to see and hear
Seem'd in her frame residing;
Before the watch-dog prick'd his ear
She heard her lover's riding;
Ere scarce a distant form was kenn'd 15
She knew and waved to greet him,
And o'er the battlement did bend
As on the wing to meet him.

He came — he pass'd — an heedless gaze
As o'er some stranger glancing; 20
Her welcome, spoke in faltering phrase,
Lost in his courser's prancing —
The castle arch, whose hollow tone
Returns each whisper spoken,
Could scarcely catch the feeble moan 25
Which told her heart was broken.

Sir W. Scott

CCXLI

Earl March look'd on his dying child,
And, smit with grief to view her —
The youth, he cried, whom I exiled
Shall be restored to woo her. 30

She 's at the window many an hour
His coming to discover:
And he look'd up to Ellen's bower
And she look'd on her lover —

But ah! so pale, he knew her not, 5
Though her smile on him was dwelling —
And am I then forgot — forgot?
It broke the heart of Ellen.

In vain he weeps, in vain he sighs,
Her cheek is cold as ashes; 10
Nor love's own kiss shall wake those eyes
To lift their silken lashes.

T. Campbell

CCXLII

Bright Star! would I were steadfast as thou art —
Not in lone splendor hung aloft the night,
And watching, with eternal lids apart, 15
Like Nature's patient sleepless Eremite,

The moving waters at their priestlike task
Of pure ablution round earth's human shores,
Or gazing on the new soft fallen mask
Of snow upon the mountains and the moors: — 20

No — yet still steadfast, still unchangeable,
Pillow'd upon my fair Love's ripening breast
To feel forever its soft fall and swell,
Awake forever in a sweet unrest;

Still, still to hear her tender-taken breath, 25
And so live ever, — or else swoon to death.

J. Keats

CCXLIII

THE TERROR OF DEATH

When I have fears that I may cease to be
Before my pen has glean'd my teeming brain,
Before high-pilèd books, in charact'ry
Hold like rich garners the full-ripen'd grain;

When I behold, upon the night's starr'd face, 5
Huge cloudy symbols of a high romance,
And think that I may never live to trace
Their shadows, with the magic hand of chance;

And when I feel, fair Creature of an hour!
That I shall never look upon thee more, 10
Never have relish in the faery power
Of unreflecting love — then on the shore

Of the wide world I stand alone, and think
Till Love and Fame to nothingness do sink.

J. Keats

CCXLIV

DESIDERIA

Surprised by joy — impatient as the wind — 15
I turn'd to share the transport — oh! with whom
But Thee — deep buried in the silent tomb,
That spot which no vicissitude can find?

Love, faithful love recall'd thee to my mind —
But how could I forget thee? Through what power 20
Even for the least division of an hour
Have I been so beguiled as to be blind

To my most grievous loss! — That thought's return
Was the worst pang that sorrow ever bore
Save one, one only, when I stood forlorn, 25

Knowing my heart's best treasure was no more;
That neither present time, nor years unborn
Could to my sight that heavenly face restore.

W. Wordsworth

CCXLV

At the mid hour of night, when stars are weeping, I fly
To the lone vale we loved, when life shone warm in thine
eye; 5
And I think oft, if spirits can steal from the regions of air
To revisit past scenes of delight, thou wilt come to me
there
And tell me our love is remember'd, even in the sky!

Then I sing the wild song it once was rapture to hear
When our voices, commingling, breathed like one on the
ear; 10
And as Echo far off through the vale my sad orison rolls,
I think, oh my Love! 't is thy voice, from the Kingdom
of Souls
Faintly answering still the notes that once were so dear.

T. Moore

CCXLVI

ELEGY ON THYRZA

And thou art dead, as young and fair
As aught of mortal birth; 15
And forms so soft and charms so rare
Too soon return'd to Earth!
Though Earth received them in her bed,
And o'er the spot the crowd may tread
In carelessness or mirth, 20
There is an eye which could not brook
A moment on that grave to look.

I will not ask where thou liest low
Nor gaze upon the spot;

There flowers or weeds at will may grow
  So I behold them not:
It is enough for me to prove
That what I loved, and long must love,
  Like common earth can rot; 5
To me there needs no stone to tell
'T is Nothing that I loved so well.

Yet did I love thee to the last,
  As fervently as thou
Who didst not change through all the past 10
  And canst not alter now.
The love where Death has set his seal
Nor age can chill, nor rival steal,
  Nor falsehood disavow:
And, what were worse, thou canst not see 15
Or wrong, or change, or fault in me.

The better days of life were ours;
  The worst can be but mine:
The sun that cheers, the storm that lours,
  Shall never more be thine. 20
The silence of that dreamless sleep
I envy now too much to weep;
  Nor need I to repine
That all those charms have pass'd away
I might have watch'd through long decay. 25

The flower in ripen'd bloom unmatch'd
  Must fall the earliest prey;
Though by no hand untimely snatch'd,
  The leaves must drop away.
And yet it were a greater grief 30
To watch it withering, leaf by leaf,
  Than see it pluck'd to-day;
Since earthly eye but ill can bear
To trace the change to foul from fair.

I know not if I could have borne
  To see thy beauties fade;
The night that follow'd such a morn
  Had worn a deeper shade:
Thy day without a cloud hath past, 5
And thou wert lovely to the last,
  Extinguish'd, not decay'd;
As stars that shoot along the sky
Shine brightest as they fall from high.

As once I wept, if I could weep, 10
  My tears might well be shed
To think I was not near, to keep
  One vigil o'er thy bed:
To gaze, how fondly! on thy face,
To fold thee in a faint embrace, 15
  Uphold thy drooping head;
And show that love, however vain,
Nor thou nor I can feel again.

Yet how much less it were to gain,
  Though thou hast left me free, 20
The loveliest things that still remain
  Than thus remember thee!
The all of thine that cannot die
Through dark and dread Eternity
  Returns again to me, 25
And more thy buried love endears
Than aught except its living years.

Lord Byron

CCXLVII

One word is too often profaned
  For me to profane it,
One feeling too falsely disdain'd 30
  For thee to disdain it.

One hope is too like despair
For prudence to smother,
And pity from thee more dear
Than that from another.

I can give not what men call love; 5
But wilt thou accept not
The worship the heart lifts above
And the Heavens reject not:
The desire of the moth for the star,
Of the night for the morrow, 10
The devotion to something afar
From the sphere of our sorrow?

P. B. Shelley

CCXLVIII

GATHERING SONG OF DONALD THE BLACK

Pibroch of Donuil Dhu
Pibroch of Donuil
Wake thy wild voice anew, 15
Summon Clan Conuil.
Come away, come away,
Hark to the summons!
Come in your war array,
Gentles and commons. 20

Come from deep glen, and
From mountain so rocky;
The war-pipe and pennon
Are at Inverlocky.
Come every hill-plaid, and 25
True heart that wears one,
Come every steel blade, and
Strong hand that bears one.

Leave untended the herd,
The flock without shelter;
Leave the corpse uninterr'd,
The bride at the altar;
Leave the deer, leave the steer, 5
Leave nets and barges:
Come with your fighting gear,
Broadswords and targes.

Come as the winds come, when
Forests are rended, 10
Come as the waves come, when
Navies are stranded:
Faster come, faster come,
Faster and faster,
Chief, vassal, page and groom, 15
Tenant and master.

Fast they come, fast they come;
See how they gather!
Wide waves the eagle plume
Blended with heather. 20
Cast your plaids, draw your blades,
Forward each man set!
Pibroch of Donuil Dhu
Knell for the onset!

Sir W. Scott

CCXLIX

A wet sheet and a flowing sea, 25
A wind that follows fast
And fills the white and rustling sail
And bends the gallant mast;
And bends the gallant mast, my boys,
While like the eagle free 30

Away the good ship flies, and leaves
  Old England on the lee.

O for a soft and gentle wind!
  I heard a fair one cry;
But give to me the snoring breeze 5
  And white waves heaving high;
And white waves heaving high, my lads,
  The good ship tight and free—
The world of waters is our home,
  And merry men are we. 10

There 's tempest in yon hornéd moon,
  And lightning in yon cloud;
But hark the music, mariners!
  The wind is piping loud;
The wind is piping loud, my boys, 15
  The lightning flashes free—
While the hollow oak our palace is,
  Our heritage the sea.

A. Cunningham

CCL

Ye Mariners of England
That guard our native seas! 20
Whose flag has braved, a thousand years,
The battle and the breeze!
Your glorious standard launch again
To match another foe:
And sweep through the deep, 25
While the stormy winds do blow;
While the battle rages loud and long
And the stormy winds do blow.

The spirits of your fathers
Shall start from every wave— 30
For the deck it was their field of fame,
And Ocean was their grave:

Where Blake and mighty Nelson fell
Your manly hearts shall glow,
As ye sweep through the deep,
While the stormy winds do blow;
While the battle rages loud and long 5
And the stormy winds do blow.

Britannia needs no bulwarks,
No towers along the steep;
Her march is o'er the mountain waves,
Her home is on the deep. 10
With thunders from her native oak
She quells the floods below —
As they roar on the shore,
When the stormy winds do blow;
When the battle rages loud and long, 15
And the stormy winds do blow.

The meteor flag of England
Shall yet terrific burn;
Till danger's troubled night depart
And the star of peace return. 20
Then, then, ye ocean warriors!
Our song and feast shall flow
To the fame of your name,
When the storm has ceased to blow;
When the fiery fight is heard no more, 25
And the storm has ceased to blow.

T. Campbell

CCLI

BATTLE OF THE BALTIC

Of Nelson and the North
Sing the glorious day's renown,
When to battle fierce came forth
All the might of Denmark's crown, 30
And her arms along the deep proudly shone;

By each gun the lighted brand
In a bold determined hand,
And the Prince of all the land
Led them on.

Like leviathans afloat 5
Lay their bulwarks on the brine;
While the sign of battle flew
On the lofty British line:
It was ten of April morn by the chime:
As they drifted on their path 10
There was silence deep as death;
And the boldest held his breath
For a time.

But the might of England flush'd
To anticipate the scene; 15
And her van the fleeter rush'd
O'er the deadly space between.
"Hearts of oak!" our captains cried, when each gun
From its adamantine lips
Spread a death shade round the ships, 20
Like the hurricane eclipse
Of the sun.

Again! again! again!
And the havoc did not slack,
Till a feeble cheer the Dane 25
To our cheering sent us back;—
Their shots along the deep slowly boom:—
Then ceased—and all is wail,
As they strike the shatter'd sail;
Or in conflagration pale 30
Light the gloom.

Out spoke the victor then
As he hail'd them o'er the wave,

"Ye are brothers! ye are men!
And we conquer but to save:—
So peace instead of death let us bring:
But yield, proud foe, thy fleet
With the crews, at England's feet, 5
And make submission meet
To our King."

Then Denmark bless'd our chief
That he gave her wounds repose;
And the sounds of joy and grief 10
From her people wildly rose,
As death withdrew his shades from the day:
While the sun look'd smiling bright
O'er a wide and woeful sight,
Where the fires of funeral light 15
Died away.

Now joy, old England, raise!
For the tidings of thy might,
By the festal cities' blaze,
Whilst the wine cup shines in light; 20
And yet amidst that joy and uproar,
Let us think of them that sleep
Full many a fathom deep
By thy wild and stormy steep,
Elsinore! 25

Brave hearts! to Britain's pride
Once so faithful and so true,
On the deck of fame that died,
With the gallant good Riou:
Soft sigh the winds of Heaven o'er their grave! 30
While the billow mournful rolls
And the mermaid's song condoles
Singing glory to the souls
Of the brave!

T. Campbell

CCLII

ODE TO DUTY

Stern Daughter of the Voice of God!
O Duty! if that name thou love
Who art a light to guide, a rod
To check the erring, and reprove;
Thou who art victory and law 5
When empty terrors overawe;
From vain temptations dost set free,
And calm'st the weary strife of frail humanity!

There are who ask not if thine eye
Be on them; who, in love and truth 10
Where no misgiving is, rely
Upon the genial sense of youth:
Glad hearts! without reproach or blot,
Who do thy work, and know it not:
Oh! if through confidence misplaced 15
They fail, thy saving arms, dread Power! around them cast.

Serene will be our days and bright
And happy will our nature be
When love is an unerring light,
And joy its own security. 20
And they a blissful course may hold
Ev'n now, who, not unwisely bold,
Live in the spirit of this creed;
Yet seek thy firm support, according to their need.

I, loving freedom, and untried, 25
No sport of every random gust,
Yet being to myself a guide,
Too blindly have reposed my trust:
And oft, when in my heart was heard
Thy timely mandate, I deferr'd 30
The task, in smoother walks to stray;
But thee I now would serve more strictly, if I may.

Through no disturbance of my soul
Or strong compunction in me wrought,
I supplicate for thy control,
But in the quietness of thought:
Me this uncharter'd freedom tires; 5
I feel the weight of chance desires:
My hopes no more must change their name;
I long for a repose that ever is the same.

Stern Lawgiver! yet thou dost wear
The Godhead's most benignant grace; 10
Nor know we anything so fair
As is the smile upon thy face:
Flowers laugh before thee on their beds,
And fragrance in thy footing treads;
Thou dost preserve the Stars from wrong; 15
And the most ancient Heavens, through Thee, are fresh and strong.

To humbler functions, awful Power!
I call thee: I myself commend
Unto thy guidance from this hour;
Oh let my weakness have an end! 20
Give unto me, made lowly wise,
The spirit of self-sacrifice;
The confidence of reason give;
And in the light of truth thy Bondman let me live.

W. Wordsworth

CCLIII

ON THE CASTLE OF CHILLON

Eternal Spirit of the chainless Mind! 25
Brightest in dungeons, Liberty! thou art,
For there thy habitation is the heart —
The heart which love of Thee alone can bind;

And when thy sons to fetters are consign'd,
To fetters, and the damp vault's dayless gloom, 30

Their country conquers with their martyrdom,
And Freedom's fame finds wings on every wind.

Chillon! thy prison is a holy place
And thy sad floor an altar, for 't was trod,
Until his very steps have left a trace 5

Worn as if thy cold pavement were a sod,
By Bonnivard! May none those marks efface!
For they appeal from tyranny to God.

Lord Byron

CCLIV

ENGLAND AND SWITZERLAND, 1802

Two Voices are there; one is of the Sea,
One of the Mountains; each a mighty voice: 10
In both from age to age thou didst rejoice,
They were thy chosen music, Liberty!

There came a tyrant, and with holy glee
Thou fought'st against him,—but hast vainly striven:
Thou from thy Alpine holds at length art driven, 15
Where not a torrent murmurs heard by thee.

—Of one deep bliss thine ear hath been bereft;
Then cleave, O cleave to that which still is left—
For, high-soul'd Maid, what sorrow would it be

That Mountain floods should thunder as before, 20
And Ocean bellow from his rocky shore,
And neither awful Voice be heard by Thee!

W. Wordsworth

CCLV

ON THE EXTINCTION OF THE VENETIAN REPUBLIC

Once did She hold the gorgeous East in fee
And was the safeguard of the West; the worth
Of Venice did not fall below her birth, 25
Venice, the eldest child of Liberty.

She was a maiden city, bright and free;
No guile seduced, no force could violate;
And when she took unto herself a mate,
She must espouse the everlasting Sea.

And what if she had seen those glories fade, 5
Those titles vanish, and that strength decay, —
Yet shall some tribute of regret be paid

When her long life hath reach'd its final day:
Men are we, and must grieve when even the shade
Of that which once was great is pass'd away. 10

W. Wordsworth

CCLVI

LONDON, 1802

O Friend! I know not which way I must look
For comfort, being, as I am, opprest
To think that now our life is only drest
For show; mean handiwork of craftsman, cook,

Or groom! — We must run glittering like a brook 15
In the open sunshine, or we are unblest;
The wealthiest man among us is the best:
No grandeur now in nature or in book

Delights us. Rapine, avarice, expense,
This is idolatry; and these we adore: 20
Plain living and high thinking are no more:

The homely beauty of the good old cause
Is gone; our peace, our fearful innocence,
And pure religion breathing household laws.

W. Wordsworth

CCLVII

THE SAME

Milton! thou shouldst be living at this hour:
England hath need of thee: she is a fen
Of stagnant waters: altar, sword, and pen,
Fireside, the heroic wealth of hall and bower,

Have forfeited their ancient English dower 5
Of inward happiness. We are selfish men:
Oh! raise us up, return to us again;
And give us manners, virtue, freedom, power.

Thy soul was like a Star, and dwelt apart:
Thou hadst a voice whose sound was like the sea, 10
Pure as the naked heavens, majestic, free;

So didst thou travel on life's common way
In cheerful godliness; and yet thy heart
The lowliest duties on herself did lay.

W. Wordsworth

CCLVIII

When I have borne in memory what has tamed 15
Great nations; how ennobling thoughts depart
When men change swords for ledgers, and desert
The student's bower for gold, — some fears unnamed

I had, my Country! — am I to be blamed?
Now, when I think of thee, and what thou art, 20
Verily, in the bottom of my heart
Of those unfilial fears I am ashamed.

For dearly must we prize thee; we who find
In thee a bulwark for the cause of men;
And I by my affection was beguiled: 25

What wonder if a Poet now and then,
Among the many movements of his mind,
Felt for thee as a lover or a child!

W. Wordsworth

CCLIX

HOHENLINDEN

On Linden, when the sun was low,
All bloodless lay the untrodden snow; 5
And dark as winter was the flow
Of Iser, rolling rapidly.

But Linden saw another sight,
When the drum beat at dead of night
Commanding fires of death to light 10
The darkness of her scenery.

By torch and trumpet fast array'd
Each horseman drew his battle blade,
And furious every charger neigh'd
To join the dreadful revelry. 15

Then shook the hills with thunder riven;
Then rush'd the steed, to battle driven;
And louder than the bolts of Heaven
Far flash'd the red artillery.

But redder yet that light shall glow 20
On Linden's hills of stainéd snow;
And bloodier yet the torrent flow
Of Iser, rolling rapidly.

'T is morn; but scarce yon level sun
Can pierce the war clouds rolling dun, 25
Where furious Frank and fiery Hun
Shout in their sulphurous canopy.

The combat deepens. On, ye Brave
Who rush to glory, or the grave!
Wave, Munich! all thy banners wave,
And charge with all thy chivalry!

Few, few shall part, where many meet! 5
The snow shall be their winding sheet,
And every turf beneath their feet
Shall be a soldier's sepulcher.

T. Campbell

CCLX

AFTER BLENHEIM

It was a summer evening,
Old Kaspar's work was done, 10
And he before his cottage door
Was sitting in the sun;
And by him sported on the green
His little grandchild Wilhelmine.

She saw her brother Peterkin 15
Roll something large and round
Which he beside the rivulet
In playing there had found;
He came to ask what he had found
That was so large and smooth and round. 20

Old Kaspar took it from the boy
Who stood expectant by;
And then the old man shook his head,
And with a natural sigh
"'T is some poor fellow's skull," said he, 25
"Who fell in the great victory.

"I find them in the garden,
For there 's many here about;
And often when I go to plow
The plowshare turns them out. 30

For many thousand men," said he,
"Were slain in that great victory."

"Now tell us what 't was all about,"
  Young Peterkin he cries;
And little Wilhelmine looks up 5
  With wonder-waiting eyes;
"Now tell us all about the war,
And what they fought each other for."

"It was the English," Kaspar cried,
  "Who put the French to rout; 10
But what they fought each other for
  I could not well make out.
But everybody said," quoth he,
"That 't was a famous victory.

"My father lived at Blenheim then, 15
  Yon little stream hard by;
They burned his dwelling to the ground,
  And he was forced to fly:
So with his wife and child he fled,
Nor had he where to rest his head. 20

"With fire and sword the country round
  Was wasted far and wide,
And many a childing mother then
  And newborn baby died:
But things like that, you know, must be 25
At every famous victory.

"They say it was a shocking sight
  After the field was won;
For many thousand bodies here
  Lay rotting in the sun: 30
But things like that, you know, must be
After a famous victory.

"Great praise the Duke of Marlbro' won
  And our good Prince Eugene;"
'Why 't was a very wicked thing!"
  Said little Wilhelmine;
"Nay . . . nay . . . my little girl," quoth he, 5
"It was a famous victory.

"And everybody praised the Duke
  Who this great fight did win."
"But what good came of it at last?"
  Quoth little Peterkin:— 10
"Why that I cannot tell," said he,
"But 't was a famous victory."

R. Southey

CCLXI

PRO PATRIA MORI

When he who adores thee has left but the name
  Of his fault and his sorrows behind,
Oh! say wilt thou weep, when they darken the fame 15
  Of a life that for thee was resign'd!
Yes, weep, and however my foes may condemn,
  Thy tears shall efface their decree;
For, Heaven can witness, though guilty to them,
  I have been but too faithful to thee. 20

With thee were the dreams of my earliest love;
  Every thought of my reason was thine:
In my last humble prayer to the Spirit above
  Thy name shall be mingled with mine!
Oh! blest are the lovers and friends who shall live 25
  The days of thy glory to see;
But the next dearest blessing that Heaven can give
  Is the pride of thus dying for thee.

T. Moore

CCLXII

THE BURIAL OF SIR JOHN MOORE AT CORUNNA

Not a drum was heard, not a funeral note,
  As his corpse to the rampart we hurried;
Not a soldier discharged his farewell shot
  O'er the grave where our hero we buried.

We buried him darkly at dead of night, 5
  The sods with our bayonets turning;
By the struggling moonbeam's misty light
  And the lantern dimly burning.

No useless coffin inclosed his breast,
  Not in sheet or in shroud we wound him; 10
But he lay like a warrior taking his rest,
  With his martial cloak around him.

Few and short were the prayers we said,
  And we spoke not a word of sorrow;
But we steadfastly gazed on the face that was dead, 15
  And we bitterly thought of the morrow.

We thought, as we hollow'd his narrow bed
  And smoothed down his lonely pillow,
That the foe and the stranger would tread o'er his head,
  And we far away on the billow! 20

Lightly they 'll talk of the spirit that 's gone
  And o'er his cold ashes upbraid him, —
But little he 'll reck, if they let him sleep on
  In the grave where a Briton has laid him.

But half of our heavy task was done 25
  When the clock struck the hour for retiring:
And we heard the distant and random gun
  That the foe was sullenly firing.

Slowly and sadly we laid him down,
From the field of his fame fresh and gory;
We carved not a line, and we raised not a stone,
But we left him alone with his glory.

C. Wolfe

CCLXIII

SIMON LEE, THE OLD HUNTSMAN

In the sweet shire of Cardigan, 5
Not far from pleasant Ivor Hall,
An old man dwells, a little man, —
'T is said he once was tall.
Full five-and-thirty years he lived
A running huntsman merry; 10
And still the center of his cheek
Is red as a ripe cherry.

No man like him the horn could sound,
And hill and valley rang with glee,
When Echo bandied, round and round, 15
The halloo of Simon Lee.
In those proud days he little cared
For husbandry or tillage;
To blither tasks did Simon rouse
The sleepers of the village. 20

He all the country could outrun,
Could leave both man and horse behind;
And often, ere the chase was done
He reel'd and was stone-blind.
And still there 's something in the world 25
At which his heart rejoices;
For when the chiming hounds are out,
He dearly loves their voices.

But oh the heavy change! — bereft
Of health, strength, friends, and kindred, see! 30

Old Simon to the world is left
In liveried poverty: —
His master 's dead, and no one now
Dwells in the Hall of Ivor;
Men, dogs, and horses, all are dead; 5
He is the sole survivor.

And he is lean and he is sick,
His body, dwindled and awry,
Rests upon ankles swoln and thick;
His legs are thin and dry. 10
One prop he has, and only one, —
His wife, an aged woman,
Lives with him, near the waterfall,
Upon the village common.

Beside their moss-grown hut of clay, 15
Not twenty paces from the door,
A scrap of land they have, but they
Are poorest of the poor.
This scrap of land he from the heath
Inclosed when he was stronger; 20
But what to them avails the land
Which he can till no longer?

Oft, working by her husband's side,
Ruth does what Simon cannot do;
For she, with scanty cause for pride, 25
Is stouter of the two.
And, though you with your utmost skill
From labor could not wean them,
'T is little, very little, all
That they can do between them. 30

Few months of life has he in store
As he to you will tell,
For still, the more he works, the more
Do his weak ankles swell.

My gentle Reader, I perceive
How patiently you 've waited,
And now I fear that you expect
Some tale will be related.

O Reader! had you in your mind 5
Such stores as silent thought can bring,
O gentle Reader! you would find
A tale in everything.
What more I have to say is short,
And you must kindly take it: 10
It is no tale; but, should you think,
Perhaps a tale you 'll make it.

One summer day I chanced to see
This old Man doing all he could
To unearth the root of an old tree, 15
A stump of rotten wood.
The mattock totter'd in his hand;
So vain was his endeavor
That at the root of the old tree
He might have work'd forever. 20

"You 're overtask'd, good Simon Lee,
Give me your tool," to him I said;
And at the word right gladly he
Received my proffer'd aid.
I struck, and with a single blow 25
The tangled root I sever'd,
At which the poor old man so long
And vainly had endeavor'd.

The tears into his eyes were brought,
And thanks and praises seem'd to run 30
So fast out of his heart, I thought
They never would have done.

— I 've heard of hearts unkind, kind deeds
With coldness still returning;
Alas! the gratitude of men
Hath oftener left me mourning.

W. Wordsworth

CCLXIV

THE OLD FAMILIAR FACES

I have had playmates, I have had companions, 5
In my days of childhood, in my joyful school-days:
All, all are gone, the old familiar faces.

I have been laughing, I have been carousing,
Drinking late, sitting late, with my bosom cronies;
All, all are gone, the old familiar faces. 10

I loved a Love once, fairest among women:
Closed are her doors on me, I must not see her —
All, all are gone, the old familiar faces.

I have a friend, a kinder friend has no man:
Like an ingrate, I left my friend abruptly; 15
Left him, to muse on the old familiar faces.

Ghostlike I paced round the haunts of my childhood,
Earth seem'd a desert I was bound to traverse,
Seeking to find the old familiar faces.

Friend of my bosom, thou more than a brother, 20
Why wert not thou born in my father's dwelling?
So might we talk of the old familiar faces,

How some they have died, and some they have left me,
And some are taken from me; all are departed;
All, all are gone, the old familiar faces. 25

C. Lamb

CCLXV

THE JOURNEY ONWARDS

As slow our ship her foamy track
  Against the wind was cleaving,
Her trembling pennant still look'd back
  To that dear isle 't was leaving.
So loth we part from all we love, 5
  From all the links that bind us;
So turn our hearts, as on we rove,
  To those we 've left behind us!

When, round the bowl, of vanish'd years
  We talk with joyous seeming — 10
With smiles that might as well be tears,
  So faint, so sad their beaming;
While memory brings us back again
  Each early tie that twined us,
Oh, sweet 's the cup that circles then 15
  To those we 've left behind us!

And when, in other climes, we meet
  Some isle or vale enchanting,
Where all looks flowery, wild, and sweet,
  And naught but love is wanting; 20
We think how great had been our bliss
  If Heaven had but assign'd us
To live and die in scenes like this,
  With some we 've left behind us!

As travelers oft look back at eve 25
  When eastward darkly going,
To gaze upon that light they leave
  Still faint behind them glowing, —
So, when the close of pleasure's day
  To gloom hath near consign'd us, 30
We turn to catch one fading ray
  Of joy that 's left behind us.

T. Moore

CCLXVI

YOUTH AND AGE

There 's not a joy the world can give like that it takes away
When the glow of early thought declines in feeling's dull decay;
'T is not on youth's smooth cheek the blush alone, which fades
so fast,
But the tender bloom of heart is gone, ere youth itself be past.

Then the few whose spirits float above the wreck of happiness 5
Are driven o'er the shoals of guilt, or ocean of excess:
The magnet of their course is gone, or only points in vain
The shore to which their shiver'd sail shall never stretch again.

Then the mortal coldness of the soul like death itself comes down;
It cannot feel for others' woes, it dare not dream its own; 10
That heavy chill has frozen o'er the fountain of our tears,
And though the eye may sparkle still, 't is where the ice appears.

Though wit may flash from fluent lips, and mirth distract the
breast,
Through midnight hours that yield no more their former hope
of rest;
'T is but as ivy leaves around the ruin'd turret wreathe, 15
All green and wildly fresh without, but worn and gray beneath.

Oh could I feel as I have felt, or be what I have been,.
Or weep as I could once have wept o'er many a vanish'd scene,—
As springs in deserts found seem sweet, all brackish though
they be,
So midst the wither'd waste of life, those tears would flow to me! 20

Lord Byron

CCLXVII

A LESSON

There is a Flower, the lesser Celandine,
That shrinks like many more from cold and rain,
And the first moment that the sun may shine,
Bright as the sun himself, 't is out again!

When hailstones have been falling, swarm on swarm
Or blasts the green field and the trees distrest,
Oft have I seen it muffled up from harm
In close self-shelter, like a thing at rest.

But lately, one rough day, this Flower I past, 5
And recognized it, though an alter'd form,
Now standing forth an offering to the blast,
And buffeted at will by rain and storm.

I stopp'd and said, with inly-mutter'd voice,
"It doth not love the shower, nor seek the cold; 10
This neither is its courage nor its choice,
But its necessity in being old.

"The sunshine may not cheer it, nor the dew;
It cannot help itself in its decay;
Stiff in its members, wither'd, changed of hue," — 15
And, in my spleen, I smiled that it was gray.

To be a prodigal's favorite — then, worse truth,
A miser's pensioner — behold our lot!
O Man! that from thy fair and shining youth
Age might but take the things Youth needed not! 20

W. Wordsworth

CCLXVIII

PAST AND PRESENT

I remember, I remember
The house where I was born,
The little window where the sun
Came peeping in at morn;
He never came a wink too soon 25
Nor brought too long a day;
But now, I often wish the night
Had borne my breath away.

I remember, I remember
The roses, red and white,
The violets, and the lily cups —
Those flowers made of light!
The lilacs where the robin built, 5
And where my brother set
The laburnum on his birthday, —
The tree is living yet.

I remember, I remember
Where I was used to swing, 10
And thought the air must rush as fresh
To swallows on the wing;
My spirit flew in feathers then
That is so heavy now,
And summer pools could hardly cool 15
The fever on my brow.

I remember, I remember
The fir trees dark and high;
I used to think their slender tops
Were close against the sky: 20
It was a childish ignorance,
But now 't is little joy
To know I 'm farther off from Heaven
Than when I was a boy.

T. Hood

CCLXIX

THE LIGHT OF OTHER DAYS

Oft in the stilly night 25
  Ere slumber's chain has bound me,
Fond Memory brings the light
  Of other days around me:
    The smiles, the tears
    Of boyhood's years, 30

The words of love then spoken;
The eyes that shone,
Now dimm'd and gone,
The cheerful hearts now broken!
Thus in the stilly night 5
Ere slumber's chain has bound me,
Sad Memory brings the light
Of other days around me.

When I remember all
The friends so link'd together 10
I 've seen around me fall
Like leaves in wintry weather,
I feel like one
Who treads alone
Some banquet hall deserted, 15
Whose lights are fled,
Whose garlands dead,
And all but he departed!
Thus in the stilly night
Ere slumber's chain has bound me, 20
Sad Memory brings the light
Of other days around me.

T. Moore

CCLXX

STANZAS WRITTEN IN DEJECTION NEAR NAPLES

The sun is warm, the sky is clear,
The waves are dancing fast and bright,
Blue isles and snowy mountains wear 25
The purple noon's transparent might:
The breath of the moist earth is light
Around its unexpanded buds;
Like many a voice of one delight—
The winds', the birds', the ocean-floods'— 30
The city's voice itself is soft like Solitude's.

I see the deep's untrampled floor
With green and purple seaweeds strown;
I see the waves upon the shore
Like light dissolved in star showers thrown:
I sit upon the sands alone; 5
The lightning of the noontide ocean
Is flashing round me, and a tone
Arises from its measured motion —
How sweet! did any heart now share in my emotion.

Alas! I have nor hope nor health, 10
Nor peace within nor calm around,
Nor that content, surpassing wealth,
The sage in meditation found,
And walk'd with inward glory crown'd —
Nor fame, nor power, nor love, nor leisure; 15
Others I see whom these surround —
Smiling they live, and call life pleasure;
To me that cup has been dealt in another measure.

Yet now despair itself is mild
Even as the winds and waters are; 20
I could lie down like a tired child,
And weep away the life of care
Which I have borne, and yet must bear, —
Till death like sleep might steal on me,
And I might feel in the warm air 25
My cheek grow cold, and hear the sea
Breathe o'er my dying brain its last monotony.

P. B. Shelley

CCLXXI

THE SCHOLAR

My days among the Dead are past;
Around me I behold,
Where'er these casual eyes are cast, 30
The mighty minds of old:

My never-failing friends are they,
With whom I converse day by day.

With them I take delight in weal
And seek relief in woe;
And while I understand and feel 5
How much to them I owe,
My cheeks have often been bedew'd
With tears of thoughtful gratitude.

My thoughts are with the Dead; with them
I live in long-past years, 10
Their virtues love, their faults condemn,
Partake their hopes and fears,
And from their lessons seek and find
Instruction with an humble mind.

My hopes are with the Dead; anon 15
My place with them will be,
And I with them shall travel on
Through all Futurity;
Yet leaving here a name, I trust,
That will not perish in the dust. 20

R. Southey

CCLXXII

THE MERMAID TAVERN

Souls of Poets dead and gone,
What Elysium have ye known,
Happy field or mossy cavern,
Choicer than the Mermaid Tavern?
Have ye tippled drink more fine 25
Than mine host's Canary wine?
Or are fruits of Paradise
Sweeter than those dainty pies
Of venison? O generous food!
Dressed as though bold Robin Hood 30

Would, with his Maid Marian,
Sup and bowse from horn and can.

I have heard that on a day
Mine host's signboard flew away
Nobody knew whither, till 5
An astrologer's old quill
To a sheepskin gave the story,
Said he saw you in your glory,
Underneath a new-old sign
Sipping beverage divine, 10
And pledging with contented smack
The Mermaid in the Zodiac.

Souls of Poets dead and gone,
What Elysium have ye known,
Happy field or mossy cavern, 15
Choicer than the Mermaid Tavern?

J. Keats

CCLXXIII

THE PRIDE OF YOUTH

Proud Maisie is in the wood,
  Walking so early;
Sweet Robin sits on the bush,
  Singing so rarely. 20

"Tell me, thou bonny bird,
  When shall I marry me?"
— "When six braw gentlemen
  Kirkward shall carry ye."

"Who makes the bridal bed, 25
  Birdie say truly?"
— "The gray-headed sexton
That delves the grave duly.

"The glowworm o'er grave and stone
Shall light thee steady;
The owl from the steeple sing
Welcome, proud lady."

Sir W. Scott

CCLXXIV

THE BRIDGE OF SIGHS

One more Unfortunate, 5
Weary of breath,
Rashly importunate,
Gone to her death!
Take her up tenderly,
Lift her with care; 10
Fashion'd so slenderly,
Young, and so fair!

Look at her garments
Clinging like cerements;
Whilst the wave constantly 15
Drips from her clothing;
Take her up instantly,
Loving, not loathing.

Touch her not scornfully,
Think of her mournfully, 20
Gently and humanly;
Not of the stains of her—
All that remains of her
Now is pure womanly.

Make no deep scrutiny 25
Into her mutiny
Rash and undutiful:
Past all dishonor,
Death has left on her
Only the beautiful. 30

Still, for all slips of hers,
One of Eve's family —
Wipe those poor lips of hers
Oozing so clammily.

Loop up her tresses 5
Escaped from the comb,
Her fair auburn tresses;
Whilst wonderment guesses
Where was her home?

Who was her father? 10
Who was her mother?
Had she a sister?
Had she a brother?
Or was there a dearer one
Still, and a nearer one 15
Yet, than all other?

Alas! for the rarity
Of Christian charity
Under the sun!
Oh! it was pitiful! 20
Near a whole city full,
Home she had none.

Sisterly, brotherly,
Fatherly, motherly
Feelings had changed: 25
Love, by harsh evidence,
Thrown from its eminence;
Even God's providence
Seeming estranged.

Where the lamps quiver 30
So far in the river,
With many a light
From window and casement,

From garret to basement,
She stood with amazement,
Houseless by night.

The bleak wind of March
Made her tremble and shiver 5
But not the dark arch,
Or the black flowing river:
Mad from life's history,
Glad to death's mystery
Swift to be hurl'd — 10
Anywhere, anywhere
Out of the world!

In she plunged boldly,
No matter how coldly
The rough river ran, — 15
Over the brink of it,
Picture it — think of it,
Dissolute Man!
Lave in it, drink of it,
Then, if you can! 20

Take her up tenderly,
Lift her with care;
Fashion'd so slenderly,
Young, and so fair!

Ere her limbs frigidly 25
Stiffen too rigidly,
Decently, kindly,
Smooth and compose them,
And her eyes, close them,
Staring so blindly! 30

Dreadfully staring
Thro' muddy impurity,
As when with the daring

Last look of despairing
Fix'd on futurity.

Perishing gloomily,
Spurr'd by contumely,
Cold inhumanity, 5
Burning insanity,
Into her rest.
Cross her hands humbly
As if praying dumbly,
Over her breast! 10

Owning her weakness,
Her evil behavior,
And leaving, with meekness,
Her sins to her Saviour.

T. Hood

CCLXXV

ELEGY

Oh snatch'd away in beauty's bloom! 15
On thee shall press no ponderous tomb;
But on thy turf shall roses rear
Their leaves, the earliest of the year,
And the wild cypress wave in tender gloom:

And oft by yon blue gushing stream 20
Shall Sorrow lean her drooping head,
And feed deep thought with many a dream,
And lingering pause and lightly tread;
Fond wretch! as if her step disturb'd the dead!

Away! we know that tears are vain, 25
That Death nor heeds nor hears distress:
Will this unteach us to complain?
Or make one mourner weep the less?
And thou, who tell'st me to forget,
Thy looks are wan, thine eyes are wet. 30

Lord Byron

CCLXXVI

HESTER

When maidens such as Hester die
Their place ye may not well supply,
Though ye among a thousand try
With vain endeavor.
A month or more hath she been dead, 5
Yet cannot I by force be led
To think upon the wormy bed
And her together.

A springy motion in her gait,
A rising step, did indicate 10
Of pride and joy no common rate
That flush'd her spirit:
I know not by what name beside
I shall it call: if 't was not pride,
It was a joy to that allied 15
She did inherit.

Her parents held the Quaker rule,
Which doth the human feeling cool;
But she was train'd in Nature's school,
Nature had blest her. 20
A waking eye, a prying mind,
A heart that stirs, is hard to bind;
A hawk's keen sight ye cannot blind,
Ye could not Hester.

My sprightly neighbor! gone before 25
To that unknown and silent shore,
Shall we not meet, as heretofore
Some summer morning —
When from thy cheerful eyes a ray
Hath struck a bliss upon the day, 30
A bliss that would not go away,
A sweet forewarning?

C. Lamb

CCLXXVII

TO MARY

If I had thought thou couldst have died,
I might not weep for thee;
But I forgot, when by thy side,
That thou couldst mortal be:
It never through my mind had past 5
The time would e'er be o'er,
And I on thee should look my last,
And thou shouldst smile no more!

And still upon that face I look,
And think 't will smile again; 10
And still the thought I will not brook
That I must look in vain!
But when I speak — thou dost not say
What thou ne'er left'st unsaid;
And now I feel, as well I may, 15
Sweet Mary! thou art dead!

If thou wouldst stay, e'en as thou art,
All cold and all serene —
I still might press thy silent heart,
And where thy smiles have been. 20
While e'en thy chill, bleak corpse I have
Thou seemest still mine own;
But there I lay thee in thy grave —
And I am now alone!

I do not think, where'er thou art, 25
Thou hast forgotten me;
And I, perhaps, may soothe this heart,
In thinking too of thee:
Yet there was round thee such a dawn
Of light ne'er seen before, 30
As fancy never could have drawn,
And never can restore!

C. Wolfe

CCLXXVIII

CORONACH

He is gone on the mountain,
  He is lost to the forest,
Like a summer-dried fountain,
  When our need was the sorest.
The font reappearing 5
  From the raindrops shall borrow,
But to us comes no cheering,
  To Duncan no morrow!

The hand of the reaper
  Takes the ears that are hoary, 10
But the voice of the weeper
  Wails manhood in glory.
The autumn winds rushing
  Waft the leaves that are searest,
But our flower was in flushing 15
  When blighting was nearest.

Fleet foot on the correi,
  Sage counsel in cumber,
Red hand in the foray,
  How sound is thy slumber! 20
Like the dew on the mountain,
  Like the foam on the river,
Like the bubble on the fountain,
  Thou art gone; and forever!

Sir W. Scott

CCLXXIX

THE DEATH BED

We watch'd her breathing thro' the night, 25
  Her breathing soft and low,
As in her breast the wave of life
  Kept heaving to and fro.

So silently we seem'd to speak,
  So slowly moved about,
As we had lent her half our powers
  To eke her living out.

Our very hopes belied our fears, 5
  Our fears our hopes belied —
We thought her dying when she slept,
  And sleeping when she died.

For when the morn came dim and sad
  And chill with early showers, 10
Her quiet eyelids closed — she had
  Another morn than ours.

T. Hood

CCLXXX

AGNES

I saw her in childhood —
  A bright, gentle thing,
Like the dawn of the morn, 15
  Or the dews of the spring:
The daisies and harebells
  Her playmates all day;
Herself as light-hearted
  And artless as they. 20

I saw her again —
  A fair girl of eighteen,
Fresh glittering with graces
  Of mind and of mien.
Her speech was all music; 25
  Like moonlight she shone;
The envy of many,
  The glory of one.

Years, years fleeted over —
  I stood at her foot: 30

The bud had grown blossom,
  The blossom was fruit.
A dignified mother,
  Her infant she bore;
And look'd, I thought, fairer 5
  Than ever before.

I saw her once more —
  'T was the day that she died;
Heaven's light was around her,
  And God at her side; 10
No wants to distress her,
  No fears to appall —
O then, I felt, then
  She was fairest of all!

H. F. Lyte

CCLXXXI

ROSABELLE

O listen, listen, ladies gay! 15
  No haughty feat of arms I tell;
Soft is the note, and sad the lay
  That mourns the lovely Rosabelle.

"Moor, moor the barge, ye gallant crew!
  And, gentle ladye, deign to stay! 20
Rest thee in Castle Ravensheuch,
  Nor tempt the stormy firth to-day.

"The blackening wave is edged with white;
  To inch and rock the sea mews fly;
The fishers have heard the Water Sprite, 25
  Whose screams forebode that wreck is nigh.

"Last night the gifted Seer did view
  A wet shroud swathed round ladye gay;
Then stay thee, Fair, in Ravensheuch;
  Why cross the gloomy firth to-day?" 30

"'T is not because Lord Lindesay's heir
  To-night at Roslin leads the ball,
But that my ladye-mother there
  Sits lonely in her castle hall.

"'T is not because the ring they ride, 5
  And Lindesay at the ring rides well,
But that my sire the wine will chide
  If 't is not fill'd by Rosabelle."

— O'er Roslin all that dreary night
  A wondrous blaze was seen to gleam; 10
'T was broader than the watch-fire's light,
  And redder than the bright moonbeam.

It glared on Roslin's castled rock,
  It ruddied all the copse-wood glen;
'T was seen from Dryden's groves of oak, 15
  And seen from cavern'd Hawthornden.

Seem'd all on fire that chapel proud
  Where Roslin's chiefs uncoffin'd lie,
Each Baron, for a sable shroud,
  Sheathed in his iron panoply. 20

Seem'd all on fire within, around,
  Deep sacristy and altar's pale;
Shone every pillar foliage-bound,
  And glimmer'd all the dead men's mail.

Blazed battlement and pinnet high, 25
  Blazed every rose-carved buttress fair —
So still they blaze, when fate is nigh
  The lordly line of high Saint Clair.

There are twenty of Roslin's barons bold —
  Lie buried within that proud chapelle; 30
Each one the holy vault doth hold —
  But the sea holds lovely Rosabelle.

And each Saint Clair was buried there,
  With candle, with book, and with knell;
But the sea caves rung, and the wild winds sung
  The dirge of lovely Rosabelle.

Sir W. Scott

CCLXXXII

ON AN INFANT DYING AS SOON AS BORN

I saw wherein the shroud did lurk 5
A curious frame of Nature's work;
A flow'ret crushéd in the bud,
A nameless piece of Babyhood,
Was in her cradle-coffin lying;
Extinct, with scarce the sense of dying: 10
So soon to exchange the imprisoning womb
For darker closets of the tomb!
She did but ope an eye, and put
A clear beam forth, then straight up shut
For the long dark: ne'er more to see 15
Through glasses of mortality.
Riddle of destiny, who can show
What thy short visit meant, or know
What thy errand here below?
Shall we say, that Nature blind 20
Check'd her hand, and changed her mind
Just when she had exactly wrought
A finish'd pattern without fault?
Could she flag, or could she tire,
Or lack'd she the Promethean fire 25
(With her nine moons' long workings sicken'd)
That should thy little limbs have quicken'd?
Limbs so firm, they seem'd to assure
Life of health, and days mature:
Woman's self in miniature! 30
Limbs so fair, they might supply
(Themselves now but cold imagery)

The sculptor to make Beauty by.
Or did the stern-eyed Fate descry
That babe or mother, one must die;
So in mercy left the stock
And cut the branch; to save the shock 5
Of young years widow'd, and the pain
When Single State comes back again
To the lone man who, reft of wife,
Thenceforward drags a maiméd life?
The economy of Heaven is dark, 10
And wisest clerks have miss'd the mark
Why human buds, like this, should fall,
More brief than fly ephemeral
That has his day; while shrivel'd crones
Stiffen with age to stocks and stones; 15
And crabbéd use the conscience sears
In sinners of an hundred years.
Mother's prattle, mother's kiss,
Baby fond, thou ne'er wilt miss:
Rites, which custom does impose, 20
Silver bells, and baby clothes;
Coral redder than those lips
Which pale death did late eclipse;
Music framed for infants' glee,
Whistle never tuned for thee; 25
Though thou want'st not, thou shalt have them,
Loving hearts were they which gave them.
Let not one be missing; nurse,
See them laid upon the hearse
Of infant slain by doom perverse. 30
Why should kings and nobles have
Pictured trophies to their grave,
And we, churls, to thee deny
Thy pretty toys with thee to lie—
A more harmless vanity? 35

C. Lamb

CCLXXXIII

IN MEMORIAM

A child 's a plaything for an hour;
  Its pretty tricks we try
For that or for a longer space, —
  Then tire, and lay it by.

But I knew one that to itself 5
  All seasons could control;
That would have mock'd the sense of pain
  Out of a grievéd soul.

Thou straggler into loving arms,
  Young climber up of knees, 10
When I forget thy thousand ways
  Then life and all shall cease!

M. Lamb

CCLXXXIV

THE AFFLICTION OF MARGARET

Where art thou, my beloved Son,
Where art thou, worse to me than dead?
Oh find me, prosperous or undone! 15
Or if the grave be now thy bed,
Why am I ignorant of the same
That I may rest; and neither blame
Nor sorrow may attend thy name?

Seven years, alas! to have received 20
No tidings of an only child —
To have despair'd, have hoped, believed
And been forever more beguiled, —
Sometimes with thoughts of very bliss!
I catch at them, and then I miss; 25
Was ever darkness like to this?

He was among the prime in worth,
An object beauteous to behold;

Well born, well bred; I sent him forth
Ingenuous, innocent, and bold:
If things ensued that wanted grace
As hath been said, they were not base;
And never blush was on my face. 5

Ah! little doth the young one dream
When full of play and childish cares,
What power is in his wildest scream
Heard by his mother unawares!
He knows it not, he cannot guess; 10
Years to a mother bring distress;
But do not make her love the less.

Neglect me! no, I suffer'd long
From that ill thought; and being blind
Said, "Pride shall help me in my wrong: 15
Kind mother have I been, as kind
As ever breathed:" and that is true;
I 've wet my path with tears like dew,
Weeping for him when no one knew.

My Son, if thou be humbled, poor, 20
Hopeless of honor and of gain,
Oh! do not dread thy mother's door;
Think not of me with grief and pain:
I now can see with better eyes;
And worldly grandeur I despise 25
And fortune with her gifts and lies.

Alas! the fowls of heaven have wings,
And blasts of heaven will aid their flight;
They mount — how short a voyage brings
The wanderers back to their delight! 30
Chains tie us down by land and sea;
And wishes, vain as mine, may be
All that is left to comfort thee.

Perhaps some dungeon hears thee groan
Maim'd, mangled by inhuman men;
Or thou upon a desert thrown
Inheritest the lion's den;
Or hast been summon'd to the deep 5
Thou, thou, and all thy mates to keep
An incommunicable sleep.

I look for ghosts: but none will force
Their way to me; 't is falsely said
That there was ever intercourse 10
Between the living and the dead;
For surely then I should have sight
Of him I wait for day and night
With love and longings infinite.

My apprehensions come in crowds; 15
I dread the rustling of the grass;
The very shadows of the clouds
Have power to shake me as they pass:
I question things, and do not find
One that will answer to my mind; 20
And all the world appears unkind.

Beyond participation lie
My troubles, and beyond relief:
If any chance to heave a sigh
They pity me, and not my grief. 25
Then come to me, my Son, or send
Some tidings that my woes may end!
I have no other earthly friend.

W. Wordsworth

CCLXXXV

HUNTING SONG

Waken, lords and ladies gay,
On the mountain dawns the day; 30
All the jolly chase is here
With hawk and horse and hunting spear;

Hounds are in their couples yelling,
Hawks are whistling, horns are knelling,
Merrily, merrily mingle they,
"Waken, lords and ladies gay."

Waken, lords and ladies gay, 5
The mist has left the mountain gray,
Springlets in the dawn are steaming,
Diamonds on the brake are gleaming;
And foresters have busy been
To track the buck in thicket green; 10
Now we come to chant our lay,
"Waken, lords and ladies gay."

Waken, lords and ladies gay,
To the greenwood haste away,
We can show you where he lies, 15
Fleet of foot and tall of size;
We can show the marks he made
When 'gainst the oak his antlers fray'd;
You shall see him brought to bay;
"Waken, lords and ladies gay." 20

Louder, louder chant the lay
Waken, lords and ladies gay!
Tell them youth and mirth and glee
Run a course as well as we;
Time, stern huntsman! who can balk, 25
Stanch as hound and fleet as hawk;
Think of this, and rise with day,
Gentle lords and ladies gay!

Sir W. Scott

CCLXXXVI

TO THE SKYLARK

Ethereal minstrel! pilgrim of the sky!
Dost thou despise the earth where cares abound? 30
Or while the wings aspire, are heart and eye

Both with thy nest upon the dewy ground?
Thy nest which thou canst drop into at will,
Those quivering wings composed, that music still!

To the last point of vision, and beyond
Mount, daring warbler! — that love-prompted strain 5
— 'Twixt thee and thine a never-failing bond —
Thrills not the less the bosom of the plain:
Yet might'st thou seem, proud privilege! to sing
All independent of the leafy Spring.

Leave to the nightingale her shady wood; 10
A privacy of glorious light is thine,
Whence thou dost pour upon the world a flood
Of harmony, with instinct more divine;
Type of the wise, who soar, but never roam —
True to the kindred points of Heaven and Home. 15

W. Wordsworth

CCLXXXVII

TO A SKYLARK

Hail to thee, blithe Spirit!
Bird thou never wert,
That from heaven, or near it
Pourest thy full heart
In profuse strains of unpremeditated art. 20

Higher still and higher
From the earth thou springest,
Like a cloud of fire,
The blue deep thou wingest,
And singing still dost soar, and soaring ever singest. 25

In the golden lightning
Of the sunken sun
O'er which clouds are brightening,
Thou dost float and run,
Like an unbodied joy whose race is just begun. 30

The pale purple even
Melts around thy flight;
Like a star of heaven
In the broad daylight
Thou art unseen, but yet I hear thy shrill delight: 5

Keen as are the arrows
Of that silver sphere,
Whose intense lamp narrows
In the white dawn clear
Until we hardly see, we feel that it is there. 10

All the earth and air
With thy voice is loud,
As, when night is bare,
From one lonely cloud
The moon rains out her beams, and heaven is overflow'd. 15

What thou art we know not;
What is most like thee?
From rainbow clouds there flow not
Drops so bright to see
As from thy presence showers a rain of melody; — 20

Like a poet hidden
In the light of thought,
Singing hymns unbidden,
Till the world is wrought
To sympathy with hopes and fears it heeded not: 25

Like a high-born maiden
In a palace tower,
Soothing her love-laden
Soul in secret hour
With music sweet as love, which overflows her bower: 30

Like a glowworm golden
In a dell of dew,
Scattering unbeholden
Its aërial hue
Among the flowers and grass, which screen it from
the view: 5

Like a rose embower'd
In its own green leaves,
By warm winds deflower'd,
Till the scent it gives
Makes faint with too much sweet these heavy-wingéd
thieves. 10

Sound of vernal showers
On the twinkling grass,
Rain-awaken'd flowers,
All that ever was
Joyous, and clear, and fresh, thy music doth surpass. 15

Teach us, sprite or bird,
What sweet thoughts are thine:
I have never heard
Praise of love or wine
That panted forth a flood of rapture so divine. 20

Chorus hymeneal
Or triumphal chaunt
Match'd with thine, would be all
But an empty vaunt—
A thing wherein we feel there is some hidden want. 25

What objects are the fountains
Of thy happy strain?
What fields, or waves, or mountains?
What shapes of sky or plain?
What love of thine own kind? what ignorance of
pain? 30

With thy clear keen joyance
Languor cannot be:
Shadow of annoyance
Never came near thee:
Thou lovest; but ne'er knew love's sad satiety. 5

Waking or asleep
Thou of death must deem
Things more true and deep
Than we mortals dream,
Or how could thy notes flow in such a crystal stream? 10

We look before and after,
And pine for what is not:
Our sincerest laughter
With some pain is fraught;
Our sweetest songs are those that tell of saddest thought. 15

Yet if we could scorn
Hate, and pride, and fear;
If we were things born
Not to shed a tear,
I know not how thy joy we ever should come near. 20

Better than all measures
Of delightful sound,
Better than all treasures
That in books are found,
Thy skill to poet were, thou scorner of the ground! 25

Teach me half the gladness
That thy brain must know,
Such harmonious madness
From my lips would flow,
The world should listen then, as I am listening now! 30

P. B. Shelley

CCLXXXVIII

THE GREEN LINNET

Beneath these fruit-tree boughs that shed
Their snow-white blossoms on my head,
With brightest sunshine round me spread
Of Spring's unclouded weather,
In this sequester'd nook how sweet 5
To sit upon my orchard seat!
And flowers and birds once more to greet,
My last year's friends together.

One have I mark'd, the happiest guest
In all this covert of the blest: 10
Hail to Thee, far above the rest
In joy of voice and pinion!
Thou, Linnet! in thy green array
Presiding Spirit here to-day
Dost lead the revels of the May; 15
And this is thy dominion.

While birds, and butterflies, and flowers,
Make all one band of paramours,
Thou, ranging up and down the bowers,
Art sole in thy employment; 20
A Life, a Presence like the air,
Scattering thy gladness without care,
Too blest with any one to pair;
Thyself thy own enjoyment.

Amid yon tuft of hazel trees 25
That twinkle to the gusty breeze,
Behold him perch'd in ecstasies
Yet seeming still to hover;
There! where the flutter of his wings
Upon his back and body flings 30
Shadows and sunny glimmerings,
That cover him all over.

My dazzled sight he oft deceives—
A brother of the dancing leaves;
Then flits, and from the cottage eaves
Pours forth his song in gushes;
As if by that exulting strain 5
He mock'd and treated with disdain
The voiceless Form he chose to feign,
While fluttering in the bushes.

W. Wordsworth

CCLXXXIX

TO THE CUCKOO

O blithe newcomer! I have heard,
I hear thee and rejoice: 10
O Cuckoo! shall I call thee Bird,
Or but a wandering Voice?

While I am lying on the grass
Thy twofold shout I hear;
From hill to hill it seems to pass, 15
At once far off and near.

Though babbling only to the vale
Of sunshine and of flowers,
Thou bringest unto me a tale
Of visionary hours. 20

Thrice welcome, darling of the Spring!
Even yet thou art to me
No bird, but an invisible thing,
A voice, a mystery;

The same whom in my schoolboy days 25
I listen'd to; that Cry
Which made me look a thousand ways
In bush, and tree, and sky.

To seek thee did I often rove
Through woods and on the green; 30

And thou wert still a hope, a love;
Still long'd for, never seen!

And I can listen to thee yet;
Can lie upon the plain
And listen, till I do beget 5
That golden time again.

O blessèd Bird! the earth we pace
Again appears to be
An unsubstantial, faery place,
That is fit home for Thee! 10

W. Wordsworth

CCXC

ODE TO A NIGHTINGALE

My heart aches, and a drowsy numbness pains
My sense, as though of hemlock I had drunk,
Or emptied some dull opiate to the drains
One minute past, and Lethe-wards had sunk:
'T is not through envy of thy happy lot, 15
But being too happy in thine happiness, —
That thou, light-wingèd Dryad of the trees,
In some melodious plot
Of beechen green, and shadows numberless,
Singest of summer in full-throated ease. 20

O, for a draft of vintage! that hath been
Cool'd a long age in the deep-delvèd earth,
Tasting of Flora and the country green,
Dance, and Provençal song, and sunburned mirth!
O for a beaker full of the warm South, 25
Full of the true, the blushful Hippocrene,
With beaded bubbles winking at the brim,
And purple-stainèd mouth;
That I might drink, and leave the world unseen,
And with thee fade away into the forest dim: 30

Fade far away, dissolve, and quite forget
What thou among the leaves hast never known,
The weariness, the fever, and the fret
Here, where men sit and hear each other groan;
Where palsy shakes a few, sad, last gray hairs, 5
Where youth grows pale, and specter-thin, and dies;
Where but to think is to be full of sorrow
And leaden-eyed despairs;
Where Beauty cannot keep her lustrous eyes,
Or new Love pine at them beyond to-morrow. 10

Away! away! for I will fly to thee,
Not charioted by Bacchus and his pards,
But on the viewless wings of Poesy,
Though the dull brain perplexes and retards:
Already with thee! tender is the night, 15
And haply the Queen-Moon is on her throne,
Cluster'd around by all her starry Fays;
But here there is no light,
Save what from heaven is with the breezes blown
Through verdurous glooms and winding mossy ways. 20

I cannot see what flowers are at my feet,
Nor what soft incense hangs upon the boughs,
But, in embalméd darkness, guess each sweet
Wherewith the seasonable month endows
The grass, the thicket, and the fruit-tree wild; 25
White hawthorn, and the pastoral eglantine;
Fast fading violets cover'd up in leaves;
And mid-May's eldest child,
The coming musk-rose, full of dewy wine,
The murmurous haunt of flies on summer eves. 30

Darkling I listen; and for many a time
I have been half in love with easeful Death,
Call'd him soft names in many a muséd rhyme,
To take into the air my quiet breath;

Now more than ever seems it rich to die,
To cease upon the midnight with no pain,
While thou art pouring forth thy soul abroad
In such an ecstasy!
Still wouldst thou sing, and I have ears in vain — 5
To thy high requiem become a sod.

Thou wast not born for death, immortal Bird!
No hungry generations tread thee down;
The voice I hear this passing night was heard
In ancient days by emperor and clown: 10
Perhaps the selfsame song that found a path
Through the sad heart of Ruth, when, sick for home,
She stood in tears amid the alien corn;
The same that ofttimes hath
Charm'd magic casements, opening on the foam 15
Of perilous seas, in faery lands forlorn.

Forlorn! the very word is like a bell
To toll me back from thee to my sole self!
Adieu! the fancy cannot cheat so well
As she is famed to do, deceiving elf. 20
Adieu! adieu! thy plaintive anthem fades
Past the near meadows, over the still stream,
Up the hillside; and now 't is buried deep
In the next valley glades:
Was it a vision, or a waking dream? 25
Fled is that music: — Do I wake or sleep?

J. Keats

CCXCI

UPON WESTMINSTER BRIDGE, SEPT. 3, 1802

Earth has not anything to show more fair:
Dull would he be of soul who could pass by
A sight so touching in its majesty:
This City now doth like a garment wear 30

The beauty of the morning: silent, bare,
Ships, towers, domes, theaters, and temples lie
Open unto the fields, and to the sky, —
All bright and glittering in the smokeless air.

Never did sun more beautifully steep 5
In his first splendor valley, rock, or hill;
Ne'er saw I, never felt, a calm so deep!

The river glideth at its own sweet will:
Dear God! the very houses seem asleep;
And all that mighty heart is lying still! 10

W. Wordsworth

CCXCII

To one who has been long in city pent,
'T is very sweet to look into the fair
And open face of heaven, — to breathe a prayer
Full in the smile of the blue firmament.

Who is more happy, when, with heart's content, 15
Fatigued he sinks into some pleasant lair
Of wavy grass, and reads a debonair
And gentle tale of love and languishment?

Returning home at evening, with an ear
Catching the notes of Philomel, — an eye 20
Watching the sailing cloudlet's bright career,

He mourns that day so soon has glided by:
E'en like the passage of an angel's tear
That falls through the clear ether silently.

J. Keats

CCXCIII

OZYMANDIAS OF EGYPT

I met a traveler from an antique land 25
Who said: Two vast and trunkless legs of stone
Stand in the desert. Near them on the sand,
Half sunk, a shatter'd visage lies, whose frown

And wrinkled lip and sneer of cold command
Tell that its sculptor well those passions read
Which yet survive, stamp'd on these lifeless things,
The hand that mock'd them and the heart that fed;
And on the pedestal these words appear: 5
"My name is Ozymandias, king of kings:
Look on my works, ye Mighty, and despair!"
Nothing beside remains. Round the decay
Of that colossal wreck, boundless and bare,
The lone and level sands stretch far away. 10

P. B. Shelley

CCXCIV

COMPOSED AT NEIDPATH CASTLE, THE PROPERTY OF LORD QUEENSBERRY, 1803

Degenerate Douglas! oh, the unworthy lord!
Whom mere despite of heart could so far please
And love of havoc (for with such disease
Fame taxes him), that he could send forth word

To level with the dust a noble horde, 15
A brotherhood of venerable trees,
Leaving an ancient dome, and towers like these,
Beggar'd and outraged! — Many hearts deplored

The fate of those old trees; and oft with pain
The traveler at this day will stop and gaze 20
On wrongs, which Nature scarcely seems to heed:

For shelter'd places, bosoms, nooks, and bays,
And the pure mountains, and the gentle Tweed,
And the green silent pastures, yet remain.

W. Wordsworth

CCXCV

THE BEECH TREE'S PETITION

O leave this barren spot to me! 25
Spare, woodman, spare the beechen tree!
Though bush or floweret never grow
My dark unwarming shade below;

Nor summer bud perfume the dew
Of rosy blush, or yellow hue;
Nor fruits of autumn, blossom-born,
My green and glossy leaves adorn;
Nor murmuring tribes from me derive 5
Th' ambrosial amber of the hive;
Yet leave this barren spot to me:
Spare, woodman, spare the beechen tree!

Thrice twenty summers I have seen
The sky grow bright, the forest green; 10
And many a wintry wind have stood
In bloomless, fruitless solitude,
Since childhood in my pleasant bower
First spent its sweet and sportive hour;
Since youthful lovers in my shade 15
Their vows of truth and rapture made,
And on my trunk's surviving frame
Carved many a long-forgotten name.
Oh! by the sighs of gentle sound,
First breathed upon this sacred ground; 20
By all that Love has whisper'd here,
Or Beauty heard with ravish'd ear;
As Love's own altar honor me:
Spare, woodman, spare the beechen tree!

T. Campbell

CCXCVI

ADMONITION TO A TRAVELER

Yes, there is holy pleasure in thine eye! 25
— The lovely Cottage in the guardian nook
Hath stirr'd thee deeply; with its own dear brook,
Its own small pasture, almost its own sky!

But covet not the abode; forbear to sigh
As many do, repining while they look; 30
Intruders — who would tear from Nature's book
This precious leaf with harsh impiety.

— Think what the home must be if it were thine,
Even thine, though few thy wants! — Roof, window,
door,
The very flowers are sacred to the Poor,

The roses to the porch which they entwine:
Yea, all that now enchants thee, from the day 5
On which it should be touch'd, would melt away!

W. Wordsworth

CCXCVII

TO THE HIGHLAND GIRL OF INVERSNEYDE

Sweet Highland Girl, a very shower
Of beauty is thy earthly dower!
Twice seven consenting years have shed
Their utmost bounty on thy head: 10
And these gray rocks, that household lawn,
Those trees — a veil just half withdrawn,
This fall of water that doth make
A murmur near the silent lake,
This little bay, a quiet road 15
That holds in shelter thy abode;
In truth together ye do seem
Like something fashion'd in a dream;
Such forms as from their covert peep
When earthly cares are laid asleep! 20
But O fair Creature! in the light
Of common day, so heavenly bright,
I bless Thee, Vision as thou art,
I bless thee with a human heart:
God shield thee to thy latest years! 25
Thee neither know I nor thy peers:
And yet my eyes are fill'd with tears.

With earnest feeling I shall pray
For thee when I am far away;

For never saw I mien or face
In which more plainly I could trace
Benignity and home-bred sense
Ripening in perfect innocence.
Here scatter'd, like a random seed, 5
Remote from men, Thou dost not need
The embarrass'd look of shy distress,
And maidenly shamefacédness:
Thou wear'st upon thy forehead clear
The freedom of a Mountaineer: 10
A face with gladness overspread;
Soft smiles, by human kindness bred;
And seemliness complete, that sways
Thy courtesies, about thee plays;
With no restraint, but such as springs 15
From quick and eager visitings
Of thoughts that lie beyond the reach
Of thy few words of English speech:
A bondage sweetly brook'd, a strife
That gives thy gestures grace and life! 20
So have I, not unmoved in mind,
Seen birds of tempest-loving kind —
Thus beating up against the wind.

What hand but would a garland cull
For thee who art so beautiful? 25
O happy pleasure! here to dwell
Beside thee in some heathy dell;
Adopt your homely ways, and dress,
A shepherd, thou a shepherdess!
But I could frame a wish for thee 30
More like a grave reality:
Thou art to me but as a wave
Of the wild sea: and I would have
Some claim upon thee, if I could,
Though but of common neighborhood. 35

What joy to hear thee, and to see!
Thy elder brother I would be,
Thy father — anything to thee.

Now thanks to Heaven! that of its grace
Hath led me to this lonely place: 5
Joy have I had; and going hence
I bear away my recompense.
In spots like these it is we prize
Our Memory, feel that she hath eyes:
Then why should I be loath to stir? 10
I feel this place was made for her;
To give new pleasure like the past,
Continued long as life shall last.
Nor am I loth, though pleased at heart,
Sweet Highland Girl! from thee to part; 15
For I, methinks, till I grow old
As fair before me shall behold
As I do now, the cabin small,
The lake, the bay, the waterfall;
And Thee, the Spirit of them all! 20

W. Wordsworth

CCXCVIII

THE REAPER

Behold her, single in the field,
Yon solitary Highland Lass!
Reaping and singing by herself;
Stop here, or gently pass!
Alone she cuts and binds the grain, 25
And sings a melancholy strain;
O listen! for the vale profound
Is overflowing with the sound.

No nightingale did ever chaunt
More welcome notes to weary bands 30
Of travelers in some shady haunt,
Among Arabian sands:

A voice so thrilling ne'er was heard
In springtime from the cuckoo bird,
Breaking the silence of the seas
Among the farthest Hebrides.

Will no one tell me what she sings? 5
Perhaps the plaintive numbers flow
For old, unhappy far-off things,
And battles long ago:
Or is it some more humble lay,
Familiar matter of to-day? 10
Some natural sorrow, loss, or pain,
That has been, and may be again!

Whate'er the theme, the maiden sang
As if her song could have no ending;
I saw her singing at her work, 15
And o'er the sickle bending;—
I listen'd, motionless and still;
And, as I mounted up the hill,
The music in my heart I bore
Long after it was heard no more. 20

W. Wordsworth

CCXCIX

THE REVERIE OF POOR SUSAN

At the corner of Wood Street, when daylight appears,
Hangs a Thrush that sings loud, it has sung for three
years:
Poor Susan has pass'd by the spot, and has heard
In the silence of morning the song of the bird.

'T is a note of enchantment; what ails her? She sees 25
A mountain ascending, a vision of trees;
Bright volumes of vapor through Lothbury glide,
And a river flows on through the vale of Cheapside.

Green pastures she views in the midst of the dale
Down which she so often has tripp'd with her pail; 30

And a single small cottage, a nest like a dove's,
The one only dwelling on earth that she loves.

She looks, and her heart is in heaven: but they fade,
The mist and the river, the hill and the shade;
The stream will not flow, and the hill will not rise, 5
And the colors have all pass'd away from her eyes!

W. Wordsworth

CCC

TO A LADY, WITH A GUITAR

Ariel to Miranda: — Take
This slave of music, for the sake
Of him, who is the slave of thee;
And teach it all the harmony 10
In which thou canst, and only thou,
Make the delighted spirit glow,
Till joy denies itself again
And, too intense, is turn'd to pain.
For by permission and command 15
Of thine own Prince Ferdinand,
Poor Ariel sends this silent token
Of more than ever can be spoken;
Your guardian spirit, Ariel, who
From life to life must still pursue 20
Your happiness, for thus alone
Can Ariel ever find his own.
From Prospero's enchanted cell,
As the mighty verses tell,
To the throne of Naples he 25
Lit you o'er the trackless sea,
Flitting on, your prow before,
Like a living meteor.
When you die, the silent Moon
In her interlunar swoon 30
Is not sadder in her cell
Than deserted Ariel: —

When you live again on earth,
Like an unseen Star of birth
Ariel guides you o'er the sea
Of life from your nativity: —
Many changes have been run 5
Since Ferdinand and you begun
Your course of love, and Ariel still
Has track'd your steps and served your will.
Now in humbler, happier lot,
This is all remember'd not; 10
And now, alas! the poor Sprite is
Imprison'd for some fault of his
In a body like a grave —
From you he only dares to crave,
For his service and his sorrow 15
A smile to-day, a song to-morrow.

The artist who this idol wrought
To echo all harmonious thought,
Fell'd a tree, while on the steep
The woods were in their winter sleep, 20
Rock'd in that repose divine
On the wind-swept Apennine;
And dreaming, some of Autumn past,
And some of Spring approaching fast,
And some of April buds and showers, 25
And some of songs in July bowers,
And all of love: And so this tree, —
Oh that such our death may be! —
Died in sleep, and felt no pain,
To live in happier form again: 30
From which, beneath heaven's fairest star,
The artist wrought this loved Guitar;
And taught it justly to reply
To all who question skillfully
In language gentle as thine own; 35
Whispering in enamor'd tone

Sweet oracles of woods and dells,
And summer winds in sylvan cells:
— For it had learned all harmonies
Of the plains and of the skies,
Of the forests and the mountains, 5
And the many-voicéd fountains;
The clearest echoes of the hills,
The softest notes of falling rills,
The melodies of birds and bees,
The murmuring of summer seas, 10
And pattering rain, and breathing dew,
And airs of evening; and it knew
That seldom-heard mysterious sound
Which, driven on its diurnal round,
As it floats through boundless day, 15
Our world enkindles on its way:
— All this it knows, but will not tell
To those who cannot question well
The Spirit that inhabits it;
It talks according to the wit 20
Of its companions; and no more
Is heard than has been felt before
By those who tempt it to betray
These secrets of an elder day.
But, sweetly as its answers will 25
Flatter hands of perfect skill,
It keeps its highest holiest tone
For our beloved Friend alone.

P. B. Shelley

CCCI

THE DAFFODILS

I wander'd lonely as a cloud
That floats on high o'er vales and hills, 30
When all at once I saw a crowd,
A host of golden daffodils,

Beside the lake, beneath the trees,
Fluttering and dancing in the breeze.

Continuous as the stars that shine
And twinkle on the milky way,
They stretch'd in never-ending line 5
Along the margin of a bay:
Ten thousand saw I at a glance
Tossing their heads in sprightly dance.

The waves beside them danced, but they
Outdid the sparkling waves in glee:— 10
A Poet could not but be gay
In such a jocund company!
I gazed—and gazed—but little thought
What wealth the show to me had brought;

For oft, when on my couch I lie 15
In vacant or in pensive mood,
They flash upon that inward eye
Which is the bliss of solitude;
And then my heart with pleasure fills,
And dances with the daffodils. 20

W. Wordsworth

CCCII

TO THE DAISY

With little here to do or see
Of things that in the great world be,
Sweet Daisy! oft I talk to thee
For thou art worthy,
Thou unassuming Commonplace 25
Of Nature, with that homely face,
And yet with something of a grace
Which Love makes for thee!

Oft on the dappled turf at ease
I sit and play with similes,
Loose types of things through all degrees,
　　Thoughts of thy raising;
And many a fond and idle name 5
I give to thee, for praise or blame
As is the humor of the game,
　　While I am gazing.

A nun demure, of lowly port;
Or sprightly maiden, of Love's court, 10
In thy simplicity the sport
　　Of all temptations;
A queen in crown of rubies drest;
A starveling in a scanty vest;
Are all, as seems to suit thee best, 15
　　Thy appellations.

A little Cyclops, with one eye
Staring to threaten and defy,
That thought comes next — and instantly
　　The freak is over, 20
The shape will vanish, and behold!
A silver shield with boss of gold
That spreads itself, some faery bold
　　In fight to cover.

I see thee glittering from afar — 25
And then thou art a pretty star,
Not quite so fair as many are
　　In heaven above thee!
Yet like a star, with glittering crest,
Self-poised in air thou seem'st to rest; — 30
May peace come never to his nest
　　Who shall reprove thee!

Sweet Flower! for by that name at last
When all my reveries are past

I call thee, and to that cleave fast,
Sweet silent Creature!
That breath'st with me in sun and air,
Do thou, as thou art wont, repair
My heart with gladness, and a share 5
Of thy meek nature!

W. Wordsworth

CCCIII

ODE TO AUTUMN

Season of mists and mellow fruitfulness,
Close bosom friend of the maturing sun;
Conspiring with him how to load and bless
With fruit the vines that round the thatch eaves run; 10
To bend with apples the moss'd cottage trees,
And fill all fruit with ripeness to the core;
To swell the gourd, and plump the hazel shells
With a sweet kernel; to set budding more,
And still more, later flowers for the bees, 15
Until they think warm days will never cease;
For Summer has o'erbrimm'd their clammy cells.

Who hath not seen thee oft amid thy store?
Sometimes whoever seeks abroad may find
Thee sitting careless on a granary floor, 20
Thy hair soft-lifted by the winnowing wind;
Or on a half-reap'd furrow sound asleep,
Drowsed with the fume of poppies, while thy hook
Spares the next swath and all its twinéd flowers:
And sometimes like a gleaner thou dost keep 25
Steady thy laden head across a brook;
Or by a cider-press, with patient look,
Thou watchest the last oozings, hours by hours.

Where are the songs of Spring? Aye, where are they?
Think not of them, thou hast thy music too, — 30

While barréd clouds bloom the soft-dying day
And touch the stubble-plains with rosy hue;
Then in a wailful choir the small gnats mourn
Among the river sallows, borne aloft
Or sinking as the light wind lives or dies; 5
And full-grown lambs loud bleat from hilly bourn;
Hedge crickets sing; and now with treble soft
The redbreast whistles from a garden croft;
And gathering swallows twitter in the skies.

J. Keats

CCCIV

ODE TO WINTER

GERMANY, DECEMBER, 1800

When first the fiery-mantled Sun 10
His heavenly race began to run,
Round the earth and ocean blue
His children four the Seasons flew.
First, in green apparel dancing,
The young Spring smiled with angel grace; 15
Rosy Summer next advancing,
Rush'd into her sire's embrace —
Her bright-hair'd sire, who bade her keep
Forever nearest to his smiles,
On Calpe's olive-shaded steep 20
Or India's citron-cover'd isles:
More remote, and buxom-brown,
The Queen of vintage bow'd before his throne;
A rich pomegranate gemm'd her crown,
A ripe sheaf bound her zone. 25

But howling Winter fled afar
To hills that prop the polar star;
And loves on deer-borne car to ride
With barren darkness by his side,

Round the shore where loud Lofoden
  Whirls to death the roaring whale,
Round the hall where Runic Odin
  Howls his war song to the gale;
Save when adown the ravaged globe 5
  He travels on his native storm,
Deflowering Nature's grassy robe
  And trampling on her faded form:—
Till light's returning Lord assume
  The shaft that drives him to his polar field, 10
Of power to pierce his raven plume
  And crystal-cover'd shield.

Oh, sire of storms! whose savage ear
The Lapland drum delights to hear,
When Frenzy with her bloodshot eye 15
Implores thy dreadful deity—
Archangel! Power of desolation!
  Fast descending as thou art,
Say, hath mortal invocation
  Spells to touch thy stony heart? 20
Then, sullen Winter! hear my prayer,
And gently rule the ruin'd year;
Nor chill the wanderer's bosom bare
Nor freeze the wretch's falling tear:
To shuddering Want's unmantled bed 25
  Thy horror-breathing agues cease to lend,
And gently on the orphan head
  Of Innocence descend.

But chiefly spare, O king of clouds!
The sailor on his airy shrouds, 30
When wrecks and beacons strew the steep,
And specters walk along the deep.
Milder yet thy snowy breezes
  Pour on yonder tented shores,

Where the Rhine's broad billow freezes,
  Or the dark-brown Danube roars.
Oh, winds of Winter! list ye there
  To many a deep and dying groan?
Or start, ye demons of the midnight air, 5
  At shrieks and thunders louder than your own?
Alas! ev'n your unhallow'd breath
  May spare the victim fallen low;
But Man will ask no truce to death, —
  No bounds to human woe. 10

T. Campbell

CCCV

YARROW UNVISITED, 1803

From Stirling Castle we had seen
The mazy Forth unravel'd,
Had trod the banks of Clyde and Tay
And with the Tweed had travel'd;
And when we came to Clovenford, 15
Then said my "winsome Marrow,"
"Whate'er betide, we 'll turn aside,
And see the Braes of Yarrow."

"Let Yarrow folk, frae Selkirk town,
Who have been buying, selling, 20
Go back to Yarrow, 't is their own,
Each maiden to her dwelling!
On Yarrow's banks let herons feed,
Hares couch, and rabbits burrow;
But we will downward with the Tweed, 25
Nor turn aside to Yarrow.

"There 's Gala Water, Leader Haughs,
Both lying right before us;
And Dryburgh, where with chiming Tweed
The lintwhites sing in chorus; 30

There 's pleasant Tiviot-dale, a land
Made blithe with plow and harrow:
Why throw away a needful day
To go in search of Yarrow?

"What 's Yarrow but a river bare 5
That glides the dark hills under?
There are a thousand such elsewhere
As worthy of your wonder."
— Strange words they seem'd of slight and scorn;
My True-love sigh'd for sorrow, 10
And look'd me in the face, to think,
I thus could speak of Yarrow!

"O green," said I, "are Yarrow's holms,
And sweet is Yarrow flowing!
Fair hangs the apple frae the rock, 15
But we will leave it growing.
O'er hilly path and open strath
We 'll wander Scotland thorough;
But, though so near, we will not turn
Into the dale of Yarrow. 20

"Let beeves and home-bred kine partake
The sweets of Burn-mill meadow;
The swan on still Saint Mary's Lake
Float double, swan and shadow!
We will not see them; will not go 25
To-day, nor yet to-morrow;
Enough if in our hearts we know
There 's such a place as Yarrow.

"Be Yarrow stream unseen, unknown!
It must, or we shall rue it: 30
We have a vision of our own,
Ah! why should we undo it?
The treasured dreams of times long past,
We 'll keep them, winsome Marrow!

For when we 're there, although 't is fair,
'T will be another Yarrow!

"If Care with freezing years should come
And wandering seem but folly, —
Should we be loath to stir from home, 5
And yet be melancholy;
Should life be dull, and spirits low,
'T will soothe us in our sorrow
That earth has something yet to show,
The bonny holms of Yarrow!" 10

W. Wordsworth

CCCVI

YARROW VISITED

September, 1814

And is this — Yarrow? — This the stream
Of which my fancy cherish'd
So faithfully, a waking dream,
An image that hath perish'd?
O that some minstrel's harp were near 15
To utter notes of gladness
And chase this silence from the air,
That fills my heart with sadness!

Yet why? — a silvery current flows
With uncontroll'd meanderings; 20
Nor have these eyes by greener hills
Been soothed, in all my wanderings.
And, through her depths, Saint Mary's Lake
Is visibly delighted;
For not a feature of those hills 25
Is in the mirror slighted.

A blue sky bends o'er Yarrow Vale,
Save where that pearly whiteness
Is round the rising sun diffused,
A tender hazy brightness; 30

Mild dawn of promise! that excludes
All profitless dejection;
Though not unwilling here to admit
A pensive recollection.

Where was it that the famous Flower
Of Yarrow Vale lay bleeding? 5
His bed perchance was yon smooth mound
On which the herd is feeding:
And haply from this crystal pool,
Now peaceful as the morning, 10
The Water wraith ascended thrice,
And gave his doleful warning.

Delicious is the lay that sings
The haunts of happy lovers,
The path that leads them to the grove, 15
The leafy grove that covers:
And pity sanctifies the verse
That paints, by strength of sorrow,
The unconquerable strength of love;
Bear witness, rueful Yarrow! 20

But thou that didst appear so fair
To fond imagination,
Dost rival in the light of day
Her delicate creation:
Meek loveliness is round thee spread, 25
A softness still and holy:
The grace of forest charms decay'd,
And pastoral melancholy.

That region left, the vale unfolds
Rich groves of lofty stature, 30
With Yarrow winding through the pomp
Of cultivated nature;
And rising from those lofty groves
Behold a ruin hoary,

The shatter'd front of Newark's towers,
Renown'd in Border story.

Fair scenes for childhood's opening bloom,
For sportive youth to stray in,
For manhood to enjoy his strength, 5
And age to wear away in!
Yon cottage seems a bower of bliss,
A covert for protection
Of tender thoughts that nestle there —
The brood of chaste affection. 10

How sweet on this autumnal day
The wildwood fruits to gather,
And on my True-love's forehead plant
A crest of blooming heather!
And what if I enwreathed my own? 15
'T were no offense to reason;
The sober hills thus deck their brows
To meet the wintry season.

I see — but not by sight alone,
Loved Yarrow, have I won thee; 20
A ray of Fancy still survives —
Her sunshine plays upon thee!
Thy ever-youthful waters keep
A course of lively pleasure;
And gladsome notes my lips can breathe 25
Accordant to the measure.

The vapors linger round the heights,
They melt, and soon must vanish;
One hour is theirs, nor more is mine —
Sad thought! which I would banish, 30
But that I know, where'er I go,
Thy genuine image, Yarrow!
Will dwell with me, to heighten joy,
And cheer my mind in sorrow.

W. Wordsworth

CCCVII

THE INVITATION

Best and brightest, come away,—
Fairer far than this fair Day,
Which, like thee, to those in sorrow
Comes to bid a sweet good morrow
To the rough year just awake 5
In its cradle on the brake.
The brightest hour of unborn Spring
Through the winter wandering,
Found, it seems, the halcyon morn
To hoar February born; 10
Bending from heaven, in azure mirth,
It kiss'd the forehead of the earth,
And smiled upon the silent sea,
And bade the frozen streams be free,
And waked to music all their fountains, 15
And breathed upon the frozen mountains,
And like a prophetess of May
Strew'd flowers upon the barren way,
Making the wintry world appear
Like one on whom thou smilest, dear. 20

Away, away, from men and towns,
To the wildwood and the downs—
To the silent wilderness
Where the soul need not repress
Its music, lest it should not find 25
An echo in another's mind,
While the touch of Nature's art
Harmonizes heart to heart.

Radiant Sister of the Day,
Awake! arise! and come away! 30
To the wildwoods and the plains,
To the pools where winter rains

Image all their roof of leaves,
Where the pine its garland weaves
Of sapless green, and ivy dun,
Round stems that never kiss the sun;
Where the lawns and pastures be 5
And the sandhills of the sea;
Where the melting hoarfrost wets
The daisy star that never sets,
And windflowers and violets
Which yet join not scent to hue 10
Crown the pale year weak and new;
When the night is left behind
In the deep east, dim and blind,
And the blue noon is over us,
And the multitudinous 15
Billows murmur at our feet,
Where the earth and ocean meet,
And all things seem only one
In the universal Sun.

P. B. Shelley

CCCVIII

THE RECOLLECTION

Now the last day of many days 20
All beautiful and bright as thou,
The loveliest and the last, is dead:
Rise, Memory, and write its praise!
Up — to thy wonted work! come, trace
The epitaph of glory fled, 25
For now the earth has changed its face,
A frown is on the heaven's brow.

We wander'd to the Pine Forest
 That skirts the Ocean's foam;
The lightest wind was in its nest, 30
 The tempest in its home.

The whispering waves were half asleep,
  The clouds were gone to play,
And on the bosom of the deep
  The smile of heaven lay;
It seem'd as if the hour were one 5
  Sent from beyond the skies
Which scatter'd from above the sun
  A light of Paradise!

We paused amid the pines that stood
  The giants of the waste, 10
Tortured by storms to shapes as rude
  As serpents interlaced, —
And soothed by every azure breath
  That under heaven is blown,
To harmonies and hues beneath, 15
  As tender as its own:
Now all the treetops lay asleep
  Like green waves on the sea,
As still as in the silent deep
  The ocean woods may be. 20

How calm it was! — The silence there
  By such a chain was bound,
That even the busy woodpecker
  Made stiller with her sound
The inviolable quietness; 25
  The breath of peace we drew
With its soft motion made not less
  The calm that round us grew.
There seem'd, from the remotest seat
  Of the white mountain waste 30
To the soft flower beneath our feet,
  A magic circle traced, —
A spirit interfused around,
  A thrilling silent life;

To momentary peace it bound
  Our mortal nature's strife; —
And still I felt the center of
  The magic circle there
Was one fair form that fill'd with love 5
  The lifeless atmosphere.

We paused beside the pools that lie
  Under the forest bough;
Each seem'd as 't were a little sky
  Gulf'd in a world below; 10
A firmament of purple light
  Which in the dark earth lay,
More boundless than the depth of night
  And purer than the day —
In which the lovely forests grew 15
  As in the upper air,
More perfect both in shape and hue
  Than any spreading there.
There lay the glade and neighboring lawn,
  And through the dark-green wood 20
The white sun twinkling like the dawn
  Out of a speckled cloud.
Sweet views which in our world above
  Can never well be seen
Were imaged in the water's love 25
  Of that fair forest green:
And all was interfused beneath
  With an Elysian glow,
An atmosphere without a breath,
  A softer day below. 30
Like one beloved, the scene had lent
  To the dark water's breast
Its every leaf and lineament
  With more than truth exprest;
Until an envious wind crept by, 35
  Like an unwelcome thought

Which from the mind's too faithful eye
Blots one dear image out.
— Though thou art ever fair and kind,
The forests ever green,
Less oft is peace in Shelley's mind 5
Than calm in waters seen!

P. B. Shelley

CCCIX

BY THE SEA

It is a beauteous evening, calm and free;
The holy time is quiet as a Nun
Breathless with adoration; the broad sun
Is sinking down in its tranquillity; 10

The gentleness of heaven is on the Sea:
Listen! the mighty Being is awake,
And doth with his eternal motion make
A sound like thunder — everlastingly.

Dear child! dear girl! that walkest with me here, 15
If thou appear untouch'd by solemn thought
Thy nature is not therefore less divine:

Thou liest in Abraham's bosom all the year,
And worship'st at the Temple's inner shrine,
God being with thee when we know it not. 20

W. Wordsworth

CCCX

SONG TO THE EVENING STAR

Star that bringest home the bee,
And sett'st the weary laborer free!
If any star shed peace, 't is Thou
That send'st it from above,
Appearing when Heaven's breath and brow 25
Are sweet as hers we love.

Come to the luxuriant skies,
Whilst the landscape's odors rise,
Whilst far-off lowing herds are heard
  And songs when toil is done,
From cottages whose smoke unstirr'd 5
  Curls yellow in the sun.

Star of love's soft interviews,
Parted lovers on thee muse;
Their remembrancer in Heaven
  Of thrilling vows thou art, 10
Too delicious to be riven
  By absence from the heart.

T. Campbell

CCCXI

DATUR HORA QUIETI

The sun upon the lake is low,
  The wild birds hush their song,
The hills have evening's deepest glow, 15
  Yet Leonard tarries long.
Now all whom varied toil and care
  From home and love divide,
In the calm sunset may repair
  Each to the loved one's side. 20

The noble dame, on turret high,
  Who waits her gallant knight,
Looks to the western beam to spy
  The flash of armor bright.
The village maid, with hand on brow 25
  The level ray to shade,
Upon the footpath watches now
  For Colin's darkening plaid.

Now to their mates the wild swans row,
By day they swam apart,
And to the thicket wanders slow
The hind beside the hart.
The woodlark at his partner's side 5
Twitters his closing song—
All meet whom day and care divide,
But Leonard tarries long!

Sir W. Scott

CCCXII

TO THE MOON

Art thou pale for weariness
Of climbing heaven, and gazing on the earth, 10
Wandering companionless
Among the stars that have a different birth,—
And ever-changing, like a joyless eye
That finds no object worth its constancy?

P. B. Shelley

CCCXIII

TO SLEEP

A flock of sheep that leisurely pass by 15
One after one; the sound of rain, and bees
Murmuring; the fall of rivers, winds and seas,
Smooth fields, white sheets of water, and pure sky;

I 've thought of all by turns, and yet do lie
Sleepless; and soon the small birds' melodies 20
Must hear, first utter'd from my orchard trees,
And the first cuckoo's melancholy cry.

Even thus last night, and two nights more I lay,
And could not win thee, Sleep! by any stealth:
So do not let me wear to-night away: 25

Without Thee what is all the morning's wealth?
Come, blessèd barrier between day and day,
Dear mother of fresh thoughts and joyous health!

W. Wordsworth

CCCXIV

THE SOLDIER'S DREAM

Our bugles sang truce, for the night cloud had lower'd,
And the sentinel stars set their watch in the sky; 5
And thousands had sunk on the ground overpower'd,
The weary to sleep, and the wounded to die.

When reposing that night on my pallet of straw
By the wolf-scaring fagot that guarded the slain,
At the dead of the night a sweet Vision I saw; 10
And thrice ere the morning I dreamed it again.

Methought from the battle-field's dreadful array
Far, far, I had roam'd on a desolate track:
'T was Autumn, — and sunshine arose on the way
To the home of my fathers, that welcomed me back. 15

I flew to the pleasant fields traversed so oft
In life's morning march, when my bosom was young;
I heard my own mountain goats bleating aloft,
And knew the sweet strain that the corn reapers sung.

Then pledged we the wine cup, and fondly I swore 20
From my home and my weeping friends never to part;
My little ones kiss'd me a thousand times o'er,
And my wife sobb'd aloud in her fullness of heart.

"Stay — stay with us! — rest! — thou art weary and worn!" —
And fain was their war-broken soldier to stay; — 25
But sorrow return'd with the dawning of morn,
And the voice in my dreaming ear melted away.

T. Campbell

CCCXV

A DREAM OF THE UNKNOWN

I dream'd that as I wander'd by the way
  Bare Winter suddenly was changed to Spring,
And gentle odors led my steps astray,
  Mix'd with a sound of waters murmuring
Along a shelving bank of turf, which lay 5
  Under a copse, and hardly dared to fling
Its green arms round the bosom of the stream,
But kiss'd it and then fled, as Thou mightest in dream.

There grew pied windflowers and violets,
  Daisies, those pearl'd Arcturi of the earth, 10
The constellated flower that never sets;
  Faint oxlips; tender bluebells, at whose birth
The sod scarce heaved; and that tall flower that wets —
  [Like a child, half in tenderness and mirth —][1]
Its mother's face with heaven-collected tears, 15
When the low wind, its playmate's voice, it hears.

And in the warm hedge grew lush eglantine,
  Green cow-bind and the moonlight-color'd May,
And cherry blossoms, and white cups, whose wine
  Was the bright dew yet drain'd not by the day; 20
And wild roses, and ivy serpentine
  With its dark buds and leaves, wandering astray;
And flowers azure, black, and streak'd with gold,
Fairer than any waken'd eyes behold.

And nearer to the river's trembling edge 25
  There grew broad flag-flowers, purple prank'd with
      white,
And starry river buds among the sedge,
  And floating water lilies, broad and bright,

[1] Omitted from Palgrave's text and early editions of Shelley. Cf. Hutchinson's edition, p. 684.

Which lit the oak that overhung the hedge
With moonlight beams of their own watery light;
And bulrushes, and reeds of such deep green
As soothed the dazzled eye with sober sheen.

Methought that of these visionary flowers 5
I made a nosegay, bound in such a way
That the same hues, which in their natural bowers
Were mingled or opposed, the like array
Kept these imprison'd children of the Hours
Within my hand, — and then, elate and gay, 10
I hasten'd to the spot whence I had come
That I might there present it — O! to Whom?

P. B. Shelley

CCCXVI

KUBLA KHAN

In Xanadu did Kubla Khan
A stately pleasure-dome decree:
Where Alph, the sacred river, ran 15
Through caverns measureless to man
Down to a sunless sea.
So twice five miles of fertile ground
With walls and towers were girdled round:
And there were gardens bright with sinuous rills 20
Where blossom'd many an incense-bearing tree;
And here were forests ancient as the hills,
Enfolding sunny spots of greenery.

But oh! that deep romantic chasm which slanted
Down the green hill athwart a cedarn cover! 25
A savage place! as holy and enchanted
As e'er beneath a waning moon was haunted
By woman wailing for her demon-lover!
And from this chasm, with ceaseless turmoil seething,
As if this earth in fast thick pants were breathing, 30
A mighty fountain momently was forced:
Amid whose swift half-intermitted burst

Huge fragments vaulted like rebounding hail,
Or chaffy grain beneath the thresher's flail:
And mid these dancing rocks at once and ever
It flung up momently the sacred river.
Five miles meandering with a mazy motion 5
Through wood and dale the sacred river ran,
Then reach'd the caverns measureless to man,
And sank in tumult to a lifeless ocean:
And 'mid this tumult Kubla heard from far
Ancestral voices prophesying war! 10

The shadow of the dome of pleasure
Floated midway on the waves;
Where was heard the mingled measure
From the fountain and the caves.
It was a miracle of rare device, 15
A sunny pleasure dome with caves of ice!
A damsel with a dulcimer
In a vision once I saw:
It was an Abyssinian maid,
And on her dulcimer she play'd, 20
Singing of Mount Abora.
Could I revive within me
Her symphony and song,
To such a deep delight 't would win me
That with music loud and long, 25
I would build that dome in air,
That sunny dome! those caves of ice!
And all who heard should see them there,
And all should cry, Beware! Beware!
His flashing eyes, his floating hair! 30
Weave a circle round him thrice,
And close your eyes with holy dread,
For he on honeydew hath fed,
And drunk the milk of Paradise.

S. T. Coleridge

CCCXVII

THE INNER VISION

Most sweet it is with unuplifted eyes
To pace the ground, if path be there or none,
While a fair region round the traveler lies
Which he forbears again to look upon;

Pleased rather with some soft ideal scene, 5
The work of Fancy, or some happy tone
Of meditation, slipping in between
The beauty coming and the beauty gone.

— If Thought and Love desert us, from that day
Let us break off all commerce with the Muse: 10
With Thought and Love companions of our way —

Whate'er the senses take or may refuse, —
The Mind's internal heaven shall shed her dews
Of inspiration on the humblest lay.

W. Wordsworth

CCCXVIII

THE REALM OF FANCY

Ever let the Fancy roam; 15
Pleasure never is at home:
At a touch sweet Pleasure melteth,
Like to bubbles when rain pelteth;
Then let wingéd Fancy wander
Through the thought still spread beyond her: 20
Open wide the mind's cage door,
She 'll dart forth, and cloudward soar.
O sweet Fancy! let her loose;
Summer's joys are spoiled by use,
And the enjoying of the Spring 25
Fades as does its blossoming;
Autumn's red-lipp'd fruitage too,
Blushing through the mist and dew,

Cloys with tasting: What do then?
Sit thee by the ingle, when
The sear fagot blazes bright,
Spirit of a winter's night;
When the soundless earth is muffled, 5
And the cakéd snow is shuffled
From the plowboy's heavy shoon;
When the Night doth meet the Noon
In a dark conspiracy
To banish Even from her sky. 10
Sit thee there, and send abroad,
With a mind self-overaw'd,
Fancy, high-commission'd: — send her!
She has vassals to attend her:
She will bring, in spite of frost, 15
Beauties that the earth hath lost;
She will bring thee, all together,
All delights of summer weather;
All the buds and bells of May,
From dewy sward or thorny spray; 20
All the heapéd Autumn's wealth,
With a still, mysterious stealth:
She will mix these pleasures up
Like three fit wines in a cup,
And thou shalt quaff it: — thou shalt hear 25
Distant harvest carols clear;
Rustle of the reapéd corn;
Sweet birds antheming the morn:
And, in the same moment — hark!
'T is the early April lark, 30
Or the rooks, with busy caw,
Foraging for sticks and straw.
Thou shalt, at one glance, behold
The daisy and the marigold;
White-plumed lilies, and the first 35
Hedge-grown primrose that hath burst;

Shaded hyacinth, alway
Sapphire queen of the mid-May;
And every leaf, and every flower
Pearléd with the selfsame shower.
Thou shalt see the field mouse peep 5
Meager from its celléd sleep;
And the snake all winter-thin
Cast on sunny bank its skin;
Freckled nest eggs thou shalt see
Hatching in the hawthorn tree, 10
When the hen-bird's wing doth rest
Quiet on her mossy nest;
Then the hurry and alarm
When the beehive casts its swarm;
Acorns ripe down-pattering, 15
While the autumn breezes sing.

Oh, sweet Fancy! let her loose;
Everything is spoiled by use:
Where 's the cheek that doth not fade,
Too much gazed at? Where 's the maid 20
Whose lip mature is ever new?
Where 's the eye, however blue,
Doth not weary? Where 's the face
One would meet in every place?
Where 's the voice, however soft, 25
One would hear so very oft?
At a touch sweet Pleasure melteth
Like to bubbles when rain pelteth.
Let then wingéd Fancy find
Thee a mistress to thy mind: 30
Dulcet-eyed as Ceres' daughter,
Ere the God of Torment taught her
How to frown and how to chide;
With a waist and with a side
White as Hebe's, when her zone 35

Slipped its golden clasp, and down
Fell her kirtle to her feet,
While she held the goblet sweet,
And Jove grew languid. — Break the mesh
Of the Fancy's silken leash; 5
Quickly break her prison-string,
And such joys as these she 'll bring.
— Let the wingéd Fancy roam,
Pleasure never is at home.

J. Keats

CCCXIX

WRITTEN IN EARLY SPRING

I heard a thousand blended notes 10
While in a grove I sate reclined,
In that sweet mood when pleasant thoughts
Bring sad thoughts to the mind.

To her fair works did Nature link
The human soul that through me ran; 15
And much it grieved my heart to think
What Man has made of Man.

Through primrose tufts, in that sweet bower,
The periwinkle trail'd its wreaths;
And 't is my faith that every flower 20
Enjoys the air it breathes.

The birds around me hopp'd and play'd,
Their thoughts I cannot measure, —
But the least motion which they made
It seem'd a thrill of pleasure. 25

The budding twigs spread out their fan
To catch the breezy air;
And I must think, do all I can,
That there was pleasure there.

If this belief from heaven be sent,
If such be Nature's holy plan,
Have I not reason to lament
What Man has made of Man?

W. Wordsworth

CCCXX

RUTH: OR THE INFLUENCES OF NATURE

When Ruth was left half desolate 5
Her father took another mate;
And Ruth, not seven years old,
A slighted child, at her own will
Went wandering over dale and hill,
In thoughtless freedom, bold. 10

And she had made a pipe of straw,
And music from that pipe could draw
Like sounds of winds and floods;
Had built a bower upon the green,
As if she from her birth had been 15
An infant of the woods.

Beneath her father's roof, alone
She seem'd to live; her thoughts her own;
Herself her own delight:
Pleased with herself, nor sad nor gay; 20
And passing thus the livelong day,
She grew to woman's height.

There came a youth from Georgia's shore, —
A military casque he wore
With splendid feathers dressed; 25
He brought them from the Cherokees;
The feathers nodded in the breeze
And made a gallant crest.

From Indian blood you deem him sprung:
But no! he spake the English tongue 30

And bore a soldier's name;
And, when America was free
From battle and from jeopardy,
He 'cross the ocean came.

With hues of genius on his cheek, 5
In finest tones the youth could speak:
—While he was yet a boy
The moon, the glory of the sun,
And streams that murmur as they run
Had been his dearest joy. 10

He was a lovely youth! I guess
The panther in the wilderness
Was not so fair as he;
And when he chose to sport and play,
No dolphin ever was so gay 15
Upon the tropic sea.

Among the Indians he had fought;
And with him many tales he brought
Of pleasure and of fear;
Such tales as, told to any maid 20
By such a youth, in the green shade,
Were perilous to hear.

He told of girls, a happy rout!
Who quit their fold with dance and shout,
Their pleasant Indian town, 25
To gather strawberries all day long;
Returning with a choral song
When daylight is gone down.

He spake of plants that hourly change
Their blossoms, through a boundless range 30
Of intermingling hues;
With budding, fading, faded flowers,
They stand the wonder of the bowers
From morn to evening dews.

He told of the magnolia, spread
High as a cloud, high overhead!
The cypress and her spire;
— Of flowers that with one scarlet gleam
Cover a hundred leagues, and seem 5
To set the hills on fire.

The youth of green savannahs spake,
And many an endless, endless lake
With all its fairy crowds
Of islands, that together lie 10
As quietly as spots of sky
Among the evening clouds.

"How pleasant," then he said, "it were
A fisher or a hunter there,
In sunshine or in shade 15
To wander with an easy mind,
And build a household fire, and find
A home in every glade!

"What days and what bright years! Ah me!
Our life were life indeed, with thee 20
So pass'd in quiet bliss;
And all the while," said he, "to know
That we were in a world of woe,
On such an earth as this!"

And then he sometimes interwove 25
Fond thoughts about a father's love,
"For there," said he, "are spun
Around the heart such tender ties,
That our own children to our eyes
Are dearer than the sun. 30

"Sweet Ruth! and could you go with me
My helpmate in the woods to be,
Our shed at night to rear;

Or run, my own adopted bride,
A sylvan huntress at my side,
And drive the flying deer!

"Beloved Ruth!"— No more he said.
The wakeful Ruth at midnight shed 5
A solitary tear:
She thought again—and did agree
With him to sail across the sea,
And drive the flying deer.

"And now, as fitting is and right, 10
We in the church our faith will plight,
A husband and a wife."
Even so they did; and I may say
That to sweet Ruth that happy day
Was more than human life. 15

Through dream and vision did she sink,
Delighted all the while to think
That, on those lonesome floods
And green savannahs, she should share
His board with lawful joy, and bear 20
His name in the wild woods.

But, as you have before been told,
This Stripling, sportive, gay, and bold,
And with his dancing crest
So beautiful, through savage lands 25
Had roam'd about, with vagrant bands
Of Indians in the West.

The wind, the tempest roaring high,
The tumult of a tropic sky
Might well be dangerous food 30
For him, a youth to whom was given
So much of earth—so much of heaven,
And such impetuous blood.

Whatever in those climes he found
Irregular in sight or sound
Did to his mind impart
A kindred impulse, seem'd allied
To his own powers, and justified 5
The workings of his heart.

Nor less, to feed voluptuous thought,
The beauteous forms of Nature wrought,—
Fair trees and gorgeous flowers;
The breezes their own languor lent; 10
The stars had feelings, which they sent
Into those favor'd bowers.

Yet, in his worst pursuits, I ween
That sometimes there did intervene
Pure hopes of high intent: 15
For passions link'd to forms so fair
And stately, needs must have their share
Of noble sentiment.

But ill he lived, much evil saw,
With men to whom no better law 20
Nor better life was known;
Deliberately and undeceived
Those wild men's vices he received,
And gave them back his own.

His genius and his moral frame 25
Were thus impair'd, and he became
The slave of low desires:
A man who without self-control
Would seek what the degraded soul
Unworthily admires. 30

And yet he with no feign'd delight
Had woo'd the maiden, day and night
Had loved her, night and morn:

What could he less than love a maid
Whose heart with so much nature play'd—
So kind and so forlorn?

Sometimes most earnestly he said,
"O Ruth! I have been worse than dead; 5
False thoughts, thoughts bold and vain
Encompass'd me on every side
When I, in confidence and pride,
Had cross'd the Atlantic main.

"Before me shone a glorious world 10
Fresh as a banner bright, unfurl'd
To music suddenly:
I look'd upon those hills and plains,
And seem'd as if let loose from chains
To live at liberty! 15

"No more of this—for now, by thee,
Dear Ruth! more happily set free,
With nobler zeal I burn;
My soul from darkness is released
Like the whole sky when to the east 20
The morning doth return."

Full soon that better mind was gone;
No hope, no wish remain'd, not one,—
They stirr'd him now no more;
New objects did new pleasure give, 25
And once again he wish'd to live
As lawless as before.

Meanwhile, as thus with him it fared,
They for the voyage were prepared,
And went to the seashore: 30
But, when they thither came, the youth
Deserted his poor bride, and Ruth
Could never find him more.

God help thee, Ruth! — Such pains she had
That she in half a year was mad
And in a prison housed;
And there, with many a doleful song
Made of wild words, her cup of wrong 5
She fearfully caroused.

Yet sometimes milder hours she knew,
Nor wanted sun, nor rain, nor dew,
Nor pastimes of the May,
— They all were with her in her cell; 10
And a clear brook with cheerful knell
Did o'er the pebbles play.

When Ruth three seasons thus had lain,
There came a respite to her pain;
She from her prison fled; 15
But of the Vagrant none took thought;
And where it liked her best she sought
Her shelter and her bread.

Among the fields she breathed again:
The master-current of her brain 20
Ran permanent and free;
And, coming to the banks of Tone,
There did she rest; and dwell alone
Under the greenwood tree.

The engines of her pain, the tools 25
That shaped her sorrow, rocks and pools,
And airs that gently stir
The vernal leaves — she loved them still,
Nor ever tax'd them with the ill
Which had been done to her. 30

A barn her Winter bed supplies;
But, till the warmth of Summer skies
And Summer days is gone,

(And all do in this tale agree)
She sleeps beneath the greenwood tree,
And other home hath none.

An innocent life, yet far astray!
And Ruth will, long before her day, 5
Be broken down and old.
Sore aches she needs must have! but less
Of mind, than body's wretchedness,
From damp, and rain, and cold.

If she is pressed by want of food 10
She from her dwelling in the wood
Repairs to a roadside;
And there she begs at one steep place,
Where up and down with easy pace
The horsemen-travelers ride. 15

That oaten pipe of hers is mute
Or thrown away: but with a flute
Her loneliness she cheers;
This flute, made of a hemlock stalk,
At evening in his homeward walk 20
The Quantock woodman hears.

I, too, have pass'd her on the hills
Setting her little water mills
By spouts and fountains wild —
Such small machinery as she turn'd 25
Ere she had wept, ere she had mourn'd, —
A young and happy child!

Farewell! and when thy days are told,
Ill-fated Ruth! in hallow'd mold
Thy corpse shall buried be; 30
For thee a funeral bell shall ring,
And all the congregation sing
A Christian psalm for thee.

W. Wordsworth

CCCXXI

WRITTEN AMONG THE EUGANEAN HILLS

Many a green isle needs must be
In the deep wide sea of Misery,
Or the mariner, worn and wan,
Never thus could voyage on
Day and night, and night and day, 5
Drifting on his dreary way,
With the solid darkness black
Closing round his vessel's track;
Whilst above, the sunless sky
Big with clouds, hangs heavily, 10
And behind the tempest fleet
Hurries on with lightning feet,
Riving sail, and cord, and plank,
Till the ship has almost drank
Death from the o'erbrimming deep; 15
And sinks down, down, like that sleep
When the dreamer seems to be
Weltering through eternity;
And the dim low line before
Of a dark and distant shore 20
Still recedes, as ever still
Longing with divided will,
But no power to seek or shun,
He is ever drifted on
O'er the unreposing wave, 25
To the haven of the grave.

Ah, many flowering islands lie
In the waters of wide Agony:
To such a one this morn was led
My bark, by soft winds piloted. 30
—'Mid the mountains Euganean
I stood listening to the pæan
With which the legion'd rooks did hail

The Sun's uprise majestical:
Gathering round with wings all hoar,
Through the dewy mist they soar
Like gray shades, till the eastern heaven
Bursts; and then, — as clouds of even 5
Fleck'd with fire and azure, lie
In the unfathomable sky, —
So their plumes of purple grain
Starr'd with drops of golden rain
Gleam above the sunlight woods, 10
As in silent multitudes
On the morning's fitful gale
Through the broken mist they sail;
And the vapors cloven and gleaming
Follow down the dark steep streaming, 15
Till all is bright, and clear, and still
Round the solitary hill.

Beneath is spread like a green sea
The waveless plain of Lombardy,
Bounded by the vaporous air, 20
Islanded by cities fair;
Underneath Day's azure eyes,
Ocean's nursling, Venice lies, —
A peopled labyrinth of walls,
Amphitrite's destined halls, 25
Which her hoary sire now paves
With his blue and beaming waves.
Lo! the sun upsprings behind,
Broad, red, radiant, half-reclined
On the level quivering line 30
Of the waters crystalline;
And before that chasm of light,
As within a furnace bright,
Column, tower, and dome, and spire,
Shine like obelisks of fire, 35

Pointing with inconstant motion
From the altar of dark ocean
To the sapphire-tinted skies;
As the flames of sacrifice
From the marble shrines did rise 5
As to pierce the dome of gold
Where Apollo spoke of old.

Sun-girt City! thou hast been
Ocean's child, and then his queen;
Now is come a darker day, 10
And thou soon must be his prey,
If the power that raised thee here
Hallow so thy watery bier.
A less drear ruin then than now,
With thy conquest-branded brow 15
Stooping to the slave of slaves
From thy throne among the waves
Wilt thou be, — when the sea mew
Flies, as once before it flew,
O'er thine isles depopulate, 20
And all is in its ancient state,
Save where many a palace gate
With green sea flowers overgrown
Like a rock of ocean's own,
Topples o'er the abandon'd sea 25
As the tides change sullenly.
The fisher on his watery way
Wandering at the close of day,
Will spread his sail and seize his oar
Till he pass the gloomy shore, 30
Lest thy dead should, from their sleep,
Bursting o'er the starlight deep,
Lead a rapid mask of death
O'er the waters of his path.

Noon descends around me now:
'T is the noon of autumn's glow,
When a soft and purple mist
Like a vaporous amethyst,
Or an air-dissolvéd star 5
Mingling light and fragrance, far
From the curved horizon's bound
To the point of heaven's profound,
Fills the overflowing sky;
And the plains that silent lie 10
Underneath; the leaves unsodden
Where the infant Frost has trodden
With his morning-wingéd feet
Whose bright print is gleaming yet;
And the red and golden vines 15
Piercing with their trellised lines
The rough, dark-skirted wilderness;
The dun and bladed grass no less,
Pointing from this hoary tower
In the windless air; the flower 20
Glimmering at my feet; the line
Of the olive-sandal'd Apennine
In the south dimly islanded;
And the Alps, whose snows are spread
High between the clouds and sun; 25
And of living things each one;
And my spirit, which so long
Darken'd this swift stream of song, —
Interpenetrated lie
By the glory of the sky; 30
Be it love, light, harmony,
Odor, or the soul of all
Which from heaven like dew doth fall,
Or the mind which feeds this verse,
Peopling the lone universe. 35

Noon descends, and after noon
Autumn's evening meets me soon,
Leading the infantine moon
And that one star, which to her
Almost seems to minister 5
Half the crimson light she brings
From the sunset's radiant springs:
And the soft dreams of the morn
(Which like wingéd winds had borne
To that silent isle, which lies 10
'Mid remember'd agonies,
The frail bark of this lone being),
Pass, to other sufferers fleeing,
And its ancient pilot, Pain,
Sits beside the helm again. 15

Other flowering isles must be
In the sea of Life and Agony:
Other spirits float and flee
O'er that gulf: Ev'n now, perhaps,
On some rock the wild wave wraps, 20
With folded wings they waiting sit
For my bark, to pilot it
To some calm and blooming cove;
Where for me, and those I love,
May a windless bower be built, 25
Far from passion, pain, and guilt,
In a dell 'mid lawny hills
Which the wild sea murmur fills,
And soft sunshine, and the sound
Of old forests echoing round, 30
And the light and smell divine
Of all flowers that breathe and shine,
— We may live so happy there,
That the Spirits of the Air
Envying us, may ev'n entice 35
To our healing paradise

The polluting multitude:
But their rage would be subdued
By that clime divine and calm,
And the winds whose wings rain balm
On the uplifted soul, and leaves 5
Under which the bright sea heaves;
While each breathless interval
In their whisperings musical
The inspired soul supplies
With its own deep melodies; 10
And the Love which heals all strife
Circling, like the breath of life,
All things in that sweet abode
With its own mild brotherhood: —
They, not it, would change; and soon 15
Every sprite beneath the moon
Would repent its envy vain,
And the Earth grow young again.

P. B. Shelley

CCCXXII

ODE TO THE WEST WIND

O wild West Wind, thou breath of Autumn's being,
Thou, from whose unseen presence the leaves dead 20
Are driven, like ghosts from an enchanter fleeing,
Yellow, and black, and pale, and hectic red,
Pestilence-stricken multitudes! O thou
Who chariotest to their dark wintry bed
The wingéd seeds, where they lie cold and low, 25
Each like a corpse within its grave, until
Thine azure sister of the Spring shall blow
Her clarion o'er the dreaming earth, and fill
(Driving sweet buds like flocks to feed in air)
With living hues and odors plain and hill: 30
Wild Spirit, which art moving everywhere;
Destroyer and Preserver; Hear, oh hear!

Thou on whose stream, 'mid the steep sky's commotion,
Loose clouds like earth's decaying leaves are shed,
Shook from the tangled boughs of heaven and ocean,
Angels of rain and lightning! there are spread
On the blue surface of thine airy surge, 5
Like the bright hair uplifted from the head
Of some fierce Mænad, ev'n from the dim verge
Of the horizon to the zenith's height—
The locks of the approaching storm. Thou dirge
Of the dying year, to which this closing night 10
Will be the dome of a vast sepulcher,
Vaulted with all thy congregated might
Of vapors, from whose solid atmosphere
Black rain, and fire, and hail, will burst: Oh hear!

Thou who didst waken from his summer dreams 15
The blue Mediterranean, where he lay,
Lull'd by the coil of his crystalline streams,
Beside a pumice isle in Baiæ's bay,
And saw in sleep old palaces and towers
Quivering within the wave's intenser day, 20
All overgrown with azure moss, and flowers
So sweet, the sense faints picturing them! Thou
For whose path the Atlantic's level powers
Cleave themselves into chasms, while far below
The sea-blooms and the oozy woods which wear 25
The sapless foliage of the ocean, know
Thy voice, and suddenly grow gray with fear
And tremble and despoil themselves: Oh hear!

If I were a dead leaf thou mightest bear;
If I were a swift cloud to fly with thee; 30
A wave to pant beneath thy power, and share
The impulse of thy strength, only less free
Than Thou, O uncontrollable! If even
I were as in my boyhood, and could be
The comrade of thy wanderings over heaven, 35

As then, when to outstrip thy skyey speed
Scarce seem'd a vision, — I would ne'er have striven
As thus with thee in prayer in my sore need.
Oh! lift me as a wave, a leaf, a cloud!
I fall upon the thorns of life! I bleed! 5
A heavy weight of hours has chain'd and bow'd
One too like thee — tameless, and swift, and proud.

Make me thy lyre, ev'n as the forest is:
What if my leaves are falling like its own!
The tumult of thy mighty harmonies 10
Will take from both a deep autumnal tone,
Sweet though in sadness. Be thou, Spirit fierce,
My spirit! be thou me, impetuous one!
Drive my dead thoughts over the universe,
Like wither'd leaves, to quicken a new birth: 15
And, by the incantation of this verse,
Scatter, as from an unextinguish'd hearth
Ashes and sparks, my words among mankind!
Be through my lips to unawaken'd earth
The trumpet of a prophecy! O Wind, 20
If Winter comes, can Spring be far behind?

P. B. Shelley

CCCXXIII

NATURE AND THE POET

Suggested by a Picture of Peele Castle in a Storm painted by Sir George Beaumont

I was thy neighbor once, thou rugged Pile!
Four summer weeks I dwelt in sight of thee:
I saw thee every day; and all the while
Thy Form was sleeping on a glassy sea. 25

So pure the sky, so quiet was the air!
So like, so very like, was day to day!
Whene'er I look'd, thy image still was there;
It trembled, but it never pass'd away.

How perfect was the calm! It seem'd no sleep,
No mood, which season takes away, or brings:
I could have fancied that the mighty Deep
Was even the gentlest of all gentle things.

Ah! then — if mine had been the painter's hand 5
To express what then I saw; and add the gleam,
The light that never was on sea or land,
The consecration, and the Poet's dream, —

I would have planted thee, thou hoary pile,
Amid a world how different from this! 10
Beside a sea that could not cease to smile;
On tranquil land, beneath a sky of bliss.

Thou shouldst have seem'd a treasure house divine
Of peaceful years; a chronicle of heaven; —
Of all the sunbeams that did ever shine 15
The very sweetest had to thee been given.

A picture had it been of lasting ease,
Elysian quiet, without toil or strife;
No motion but the moving tide; a breeze;
Or merely silent Nature's breathing life. 20

Such, in the fond illusion of my heart,
Such picture would I at that time have made;
And seen the soul of truth in every part,
A steadfast peace that might not be betray'd.

So once it would have been, — 't is so no more; 25
I have submitted to a new control:
A power is gone, which nothing can restore;
A deep distress hath humanized my soul.

Not for a moment could I now behold
A smiling sea, and be what I have been: 30
The feeling of my loss will ne'er be old;
This, which I know, I speak with mind serene.

Then, Beaumont, Friend! who would have been the friend
If he had lived, of Him whom I deplore,
This work of thine I blame not, but commend;
This sea in anger, and that dismal shore.

O 't is a passionate work! — yet wise and well, 5
Well chosen is the spirit that is here;
That hulk which labors in the deadly swell,
This rueful sky, this pageantry of fear!

And this huge Castle, standing here sublime,
I love to see the look with which it braves, 10
— Cased in the unfeeling armor of old time —
The lightning, the fierce wind, and trampling waves.

— Farewell, farewell the heart that lives alone,
Housed in a dream, at distance from the Kind!
Such happiness, wherever it be known, 15
Is to be pitied; for 't is surely blind.

But welcome fortitude, and patient cheer,
And frequent sights of what is to be borne!
Such sights, or worse, as are before me here: —
Not without hope we suffer and we mourn. 20

W. Wordsworth

CCCXXIV

THE POET'S DREAM

On a Poet's lips I slept
Dreaming like a love-adept
In the sound his breathing kept;
Nor seeks nor finds he mortal blisses,
But feeds on the aërial kisses 25
Of shapes that haunt Thought's wildernesses.
He will watch from dawn to gloom
The lake-reflected sun illume
The yellow bees in the ivy-bloom,

Nor heed nor see what things they be —
But from these create he can
Forms more real than living Man,
Nurslings of Immortality!

P. B. Shelley

CCCXXV

GLEN-ALMAIN, THE NARROW GLEN

In this still place, remote from men, 5
Sleeps Ossian, in the Narrow Glen;
In this still place, where murmurs on
But one meek streamlet, only one:
He sang of battles, and the breath
Of stormy war, and violent death; 10
And should, methinks, when all was past,
Have rightfully been laid at last
Where rocks were rudely heap'd, and rent
As by a spirit turbulent;
Where sights were rough, and sounds were wild, 15
And everything unreconciled;
In some complaining, dim retreat,
For fear and melancholy meet;
But this is calm; there cannot be
A more entire tranquillity. 20
Does then the Bard sleep here indeed?
Or is it but a groundless creed?
What matters it? — I blame them not
Whose fancy in this lonely spot
Was moved; and in such way express'd 25
Their notion of its perfect rest.
A convent, even a hermit's cell,
Would break the silence of this Dell:
It is not quiet, is not ease;
But something deeper far than these: 30
The separation that is here
Is of the grave; and of austere

Yet happy feelings of the dead:
And, therefore, was it rightly said
That Ossian, last of all his race!
Lies buried in this lonely place.

W. Wordsworth

CCCXXVI

The World is too much with us; late and soon, 5
Getting and spending, we lay waste our powers;
Little we see in Nature that is ours;
We have given our hearts away, a sordid boon!

This Sea that bares her bosom to the moon,
The winds that will be howling at all hours 10
And are upgather'd now like sleeping flowers,
For this, for everything, we are out of tune;

It moves us not. — Great God! I 'd rather be
A Pagan suckled in a creed outworn, —
So might I, standing on this pleasant lea, 15

Have glimpses that would make me less forlorn;
Have sight of Proteus rising from the sea;
Or hear old Triton blow his wreathéd horn.

W. Wordsworth

CCCXXVII

WITHIN KING'S COLLEGE CHAPEL, CAMBRIDGE

Tax not the royal Saint with vain expense,
With ill-match'd aims the Architect who plann'd 20
(Albeit laboring for a scanty band
Of white-robed Scholars only) this immense

And glorious work of fine intelligence!
— Give all thou canst; high Heaven rejects the lore
Of nicely calculated less or more: — 25
So deem'd the man who fashion'd for the sense

These lofty pillars, spread that branching roof
Self-poised, and scoop'd into ten thousand cells
Where light and shade repose, where music dwells

Lingering — and wandering on as loth to die;
Like thoughts whose very sweetness yieldeth proof 5
That they were born for immortality.

W. Wordsworth

CCCXXVIII

ODE ON A GRECIAN URN

Thou still unravish'd bride of quietness,
  Thou foster-child of silence and slow time,
Sylvan historian, who canst thus express
  A flowery tale more sweetly than our rhyme: 10
What leaf-fringed legend haunts about thy shape
  Of deities or mortals, or of both,
    In Tempé or the dales of Arcady?
What men or gods are these? What maidens loth?
  What mad pursuit? What struggle to escape? 15
    What pipes and timbrels? What wild ecstasy?

Heard melodies are sweet, but those unheard
  Are sweeter; therefore, ye soft pipes, play on;
Not to the sensual ear, but, more endear'd,
  Pipe to the spirit ditties of no tone: 20
Fair youth, beneath the trees, thou canst not leave
  Thy song, nor ever can those trees be bare;
    Bold Lover, never, never canst thou kiss,
Though winning near the goal — yet, do not grieve;
  She cannot fade, though thou hast not thy bliss, 25
    Forever wilt thou love, and she be fair!

Ah, happy, happy boughs! that cannot shed
  Your leaves, nor ever bid the Spring adieu;
And, happy melodist, unwearièd,
  Forever piping songs forever new; 30

More happy love! more happy, happy love!
Forever warm and still to be enjoy'd,
Forever panting, and forever young;
All breathing human passion far above,
That leaves a heart high-sorrowful and cloy'd, 5
A burning forehead, and a parching tongue.

Who are these coming to the sacrifice?
To what green altar, O mysterious priest,
Lead'st thou that heifer lowing at the skies,
And all her silken flanks with garlands drest? 10
What little town by river or seashore,
Or mountain-built with peaceful citadel,
Is emptied of this folk, this pious morn?
And, little town, thy streets forevermore
Will silent be; and not a soul to tell 15
Why thou art desolate, can e'er return.

O Attic shape! Fair attitude! with brede
Of marble men and maidens overwrought,
With forest branches and the trodden weed;
Thou, silent form, dost tease us out of thought 20
As doth eternity: Cold Pastoral!
When old age shall this generation waste,
Thou shalt remain, in midst of other woe
Than ours, a friend to man, to whom thou say'st,
"Beauty is truth, truth beauty," — that is all 25
Ye know on earth, and all ye need to know.

J. Keats

CCCXXIX

YOUTH AND AGE

Verse, a breeze 'mid blossoms straying,
Where Hope clung feeding, like a bee —
Both were mine! Life went a-maying
With Nature, Hope, and Poesy, 30
When I was young!

When I was young? — Ah, woeful when!
Ah! for the change 'twixt Now and Then!
This breathing house not built with hands,
This body that does me grievous wrong,
O'er aëry cliffs and glittering sands 5
How lightly then it flash'd along:
Like those trim skiffs, unknown of yore,
On winding lakes and rivers wide,
That ask no aid of sail or oar,
That fear no spite of wind or tide! 10
Naught cared this body for wind or weather
When Youth and I lived in 't together.

Flowers are lovely; Love is flowerlike;
Friendship is a sheltering tree;
O! the joys, that came down showerlike, 15
Of Friendship, Love, and Liberty,
Ere I was old!
Ere I was old? Ah woeful Ere,
Which tells me, Youth 's no longer here!
O Youth! for years so many and sweet, 20
'T is known that Thou and I were one,
I 'll think it but a fond conceit —
It cannot be, that Thou art gone!
Thy vesper bell hath not yet toll'd: —
And thou wert aye a masker bold! 25
What strange disguise hast now put on
To make believe that Thou art gone?
I see these locks in silvery slips,
This drooping gait, this alter'd size:
But Springtide blossoms on thy lips, 30
And tears take sunshine from thine eyes!
Life is but Thought: so think I will
That Youth and I are housemates still.

Dewdrops are the gems of morning,
But the tears of mournful eve! 35

Where no hope is, life 's a warning
That only serves to make us grieve
When we are old:
— That only serves to make us grieve
With oft and tedious taking-leave, 5
Like some poor nigh-related guest
That may not rudely be dismist,
Yet hath outstay'd his welcome while,
And tells the jest without the smile.

S. T. Coleridge

CCCXXX

THE TWO APRIL MORNINGS

We walk'd along, while bright and red 10
Uprose the morning sun;
And Matthew stopp'd, he look'd, and said
"The will of God be done!"

A village schoolmaster was he,
With hair of glittering gray; 15
As blithe a man as you could see
On a spring holiday.

And on that morning, through the grass
And by the steaming rills
We travel'd merrily, to pass 20
A day among the hills.

"Our work," said I, "was well begun;
Then, from thy breast what thought,
Beneath so beautiful a sun,
So sad a sigh has brought?" 25

A second time did Matthew stop;
And fixing still his eye
Upon the eastern mountain top,
To me he made reply:

"Yon cloud with that long purple cleft
Brings fresh into my mind
A day like this, which I have left
Full thirty years behind.

"And just above yon slope of corn 5
Such colors, and no other,
Were in the sky that April morn,
Of this the very brother.

"With rod and line I sued the sport
Which that sweet season gave, 10
And to the churchyard come, stopp'd short
Beside my daughter's grave.

"Nine summers had she scarcely seen,
The pride of all the vale;
And then she sang, — she would have been 15
A very nightingale.

"Six feet in earth my Emma lay;
And yet I loved her more —
For so it seem'd — than till that day
I e'er had loved before. 20

"And turning from her grave, I met,
Beside the churchyard yew,
A blooming Girl, whose hair was wet
With points of morning dew.

"A basket on her head she bare; 25
Her brow was smooth and white:
To see a child so very fair,
It was a pure delight!

"No fountain from its rocky cave
E'er tripp'd with foot so free; 30
She seem'd as happy as a wave
That dances on the sea.

"There came from me a sigh of pain
Which I could ill confine;
I look'd at her, and look'd again:
And did not wish her mine!"

— Matthew is in his grave, yet now 5
Methinks I see him stand
As at that moment, with a bough
Of wilding in his hand.

W. Wordsworth

CCCXXXI

THE FOUNTAIN

A Conversation

We talk'd with open heart, and tongue
Affectionate and true, 10
A pair of friends, though I was young,
And Matthew seventy-two.

We lay beneath a spreading oak,
Beside a mossy seat;
And from the turf a fountain broke 15
And gurgled at our feet.

"Now, Matthew!" said I, "let us match
This water's pleasant tune
With some old border-song, or catch
That suits a summer's noon; 20

"Or of the church clock and the chimes
Sing here beneath the shade
That half-mad thing of witty rhymes
Which you last April made!"

In silence Matthew lay, and eyed 25
The spring beneath the tree;
And thus the dear old man replied,
The gray-hair'd man of glee:

"No check, no stay, this Streamlet fears,
How merrily it goes!
'T will murmur on a thousand years
And flow as now it flows.

"And here, on this delightful day, 5
I cannot choose but think
How oft, a vigorous man, I lay
Beside this fountain's brink.

"My eyes are dim with childish tears,
My heart is idly stirr'd, 10
For the same sound is in my ears
Which in those days I heard.

"Thus fares it still in our decay:
And yet the wiser mind
Mourns less for what Age takes away, 15
Than what it leaves behind.

"The blackbird amid leafy trees,
The lark above the hill,
Let loose their carols when they please,
Are quiet when they will. 20

"With Nature never do they wage
A foolish strife; they see
A happy youth, and their old age
Is beautiful and free:

"But we are press'd by heavy laws; 25
And often, glad no more,
We wear a face of joy, because
We have been glad of yore.

"If there be one who need bemoan
His kindred laid in earth, 30
The household hearts that were his own, —
It is the man of mirth.

"My days, my friend, are almost gone,
My life has been approved,
And many love me; but by none
Am I enough beloved."

"Now both himself and me he wrongs, 5
The man who thus complains!
I live and sing my idle songs
Upon these happy plains:

"And Matthew, for thy children dead
I'll be a son to thee!" 10
At this he grasp'd my hand and said,
"Alas! that cannot be."

— We rose up from the fountain side;
And down the smooth descent
Of the green sheep track did we glide; 15
And through the wood we went;

And ere we came to Leonard's rock
He sang those witty rhymes
About the crazy old church clock,
And the bewilder'd chimes. 20

W. Wordsworth

CCCXXXII

THE RIVER OF LIFE

The more we live, more brief appear
  Our life's succeeding stages:
A day to childhood seems a year,
  And years like passing ages.

The gladsome current of our youth, 25
  Ere passion yet disorders,
Steals lingering like a river smooth
  Along its grassy borders.

But as the careworn cheek grows wan,
  And sorrow's shafts fly thicker, 30

Ye Stars, that measure life to man,
  Why seem your courses quicker?

When joys have lost their bloom and breath
  And life itself is vapid,
Why, as we reach the Falls of Death, 5
  Feel we its tide more rapid?

It may be strange — yet who would change
  Time's course to slower speeding,
When one by one our friends have gone
  And left our bosoms bleeding? 10

Heaven gives our years of fading strength
  Indemnifying fleetness;
And those of youth, a seeming length,
  Proportion'd to their sweetness.

T. Campbell

CCCXXXIII

THE HUMAN SEASONS

Four Seasons fill the measure of the year; 15
There are four seasons in the mind of man:
He has his lusty Spring, when fancy clear
Takes in all beauty with an easy span:

He has his Summer, when luxuriously
Spring's honey'd cud of youthful thought he loves 20
To ruminate, and by such dreaming high
Is nearest unto heaven: quiet coves

His soul has in its Autumn, when his wings
He furleth close; contented so to look
On mists in idleness — to let fair things 25
Pass by unheeded as a threshold brook.

He has his Winter too of pale misfeature,
Or else he would forego his mortal nature.

J. Keats

CCCXXXIV

A DIRGE

Rough wind, that moanest loud
   Grief too sad for song;
Wild wind, when sullen cloud
   Knells all the night long;
Sad storm whose tears are vain, 5
Bare woods whose branches stain,
Deep caves and dreary main, —
   Wail for the world's wrong!

P. B. Shelley

CCCXXXV

THRENOS

O World! O Life! O Time!
On whose last steps I climb, 10
   Trembling at that where I had stood before;
When will return the glory of your prime?
   No more — Oh, nevermore!

Out of the day and night
A joy has taken flight: 15
   Fresh spring, and summer, and winter hoar
Move my faint heart with grief, but with delight
   No more — Oh, nevermore!

P. B. Shelley

CCCXXXVI

THE TROSACHS

There 's not a nook within this solemn Pass,
But were an apt confessional for One 20
Taught by his summer spent, his autumn gone,
That Life is but a tale of morning grass

Wither'd at eve. From scenes of art which chase
That thought away, turn, and with watchful eyes

Feed it 'mid Nature's old felicities,
Rocks, rivers, and smooth lakes more clear than glass

Untouch'd, unbreathed upon: — Thrice happy quest,
If from a golden perch of aspen spray
(October's workmanship to rival May), 5

The pensive warbler of the ruddy breast
That moral sweeten by a heaven-taught lay,
Lulling the year, with all its cares, to rest!

W. Wordsworth

CCCXXXVII

My heart leaps up when I behold
A rainbow in the sky: 10
So was it when my life began,
So is it now I am a man,
So be it when I shall grow old
Or let me die!
The Child is father of the Man: 15
And I could wish my days to be
Bound each to each by natural piety.

W. Wordsworth

CCCXXXVIII

ODE ON INTIMATIONS OF IMMORTALITY FROM RECOLLECTIONS OF EARLY CHILDHOOD

There was a time when meadow, grove, and stream,
The earth, and every common sight
To me did seem 20
Apparel'd in celestial light,
The glory and the freshness of a dream.
It is not now as it hath been of yore; —
Turn wheresoe'er I may,
By night or day, 25
The things which I have seen I now can see no more.

The rainbow comes and goes,
And lovely is the rose;
The moon doth with delight
Look round her when the heavens are bare;
Waters on a starry night 5
Are beautiful and fair;
The sunshine is a glorious birth;
But yet I know, where'er I go,
That there hath passed away a glory from the earth.

Now, while the birds thus sing a joyous song, 10
And while the young lambs bound
As to the tabor's sound,
To me alone there came a thought of grief:
A timely utterance gave that thought relief,
And I again am strong. 15
The cataracts blow their trumpets from the steep; —
No more shall grief of mine the season wrong:
I hear the echoes through the mountains throng,
The winds come to me from the fields of sleep,
And all the earth is gay; 20
Land and sea
Give themselves up to jollity,
And with the heart of May
Doth every beast keep holiday; —
Thou child of joy 25
Shout round me, let me hear thy shouts, thou happy
Shepherd boy!

Ye blessèd Creatures, I have heard the call
Ye to each other make; I see
The heavens laugh with you in your jubilee;
My heart is at your festival, 30
My head hath its coronal,
The fullness of your bliss, I feel — I feel it all.

Oh evil day! if I were sullen
While Earth herself is adorning
This sweet May morning;
And the children are culling
On every side 5
In a thousand valleys far and wide,
Fresh flowers; while the sun shines warm
And the babe leaps up on his mother's arm:—
I hear, I hear, with joy I hear!
— But there 's a tree, of many, one, 10
A single field which I have look'd upon,
Both of them speak of something that is gone:
The pansy at my feet
Doth the same tale repeat:
Whither is fled the visionary gleam? 15
Where is it now, the glory and the dream?

Our birth is but a sleep and a forgetting;
The Soul that rises with us, our life's Star,
Hath had elsewhere its setting
And cometh from afar; 20
Not in entire forgetfulness,
And not in utter nakedness,
But trailing clouds of glory do we come
From God, who is our home:
Heaven lies about us in our infancy! 25
Shades of the prison house begin to close
Upon the growing Boy,
But he beholds the light, and whence it flows,
He sees it in his joy;
The Youth, who daily farther from the east 30
Must travel, still is Nature's priest,
And by the vision splendid
Is on his way attended;
At length the Man perceives it die away,
And fade into the light of common day. 35

Earth fills her lap with pleasures of her own;
Yearnings she hath in her own natural kind,
And, even with something of a mother's mind
And no unworthy aim,
The homely nurse doth all she can 5
To make her foster-child, her inmate, Man,
Forget the glories he hath known,
And that imperial palace whence he came.

Behold the Child among his newborn blisses,
A six years' darling of a pigmy size! 10
See, where 'mid work of his own hand he lies,
Fretted by sallies of his mother's kisses,
With light upon him from his father's eyes!
See, at his feet, some little plan or chart,
Some fragment from his dream of human life, 15
Shaped by himself with newly learnéd art;
A wedding or a festival,
A mourning or a funeral;
And this hath now his heart,
And unto this he frames his song: 20
Then will he fit his tongue
To dialogues of business, love, or strife;
But it will not be long
Ere this be thrown aside,
And with new joy and pride 25
The little actor cons another part;
Filling from time to time his "humorous stage"
With all the Persons, down to palsied Age,
That life brings with her in her equipage;
As if his whole vocation 30
Were endless imitation.

Thou, whose exterior semblance doth belie
Thy soul's immensity;
Thou best philosopher, who yet dost keep
Thy heritage, thou eye among the blind, 35

That, deaf and silent, read'st the eternal deep,
Haunted forever by the eternal Mind, —
Mighty Prophet! Seer blest!
On whom those truths do rest
Which we are toiling all our lives to find, 5
In darkness lost, the darkness of the grave;
Thou, over whom thy Immortality
Broods like the day, a master o'er a slave,
A Presence which is not to be put by;
Thou little child, yet glorious in the might 10
Of heaven-born freedom on thy being's height,
Why with such earnest pains dost thou provoke
The years to bring the inevitable yoke,
Thus blindly with thy blessedness at strife?
Full soon thy soul shall have her earthly freight, 15
And custom lie upon thee with a weight
Heavy as frost, and deep almost as life!

O joy! that in our embers
Is something that doth live,
That Nature yet remembers 20
What was so fugitive!
The thought of our past years in me doth breed
Perpetual benediction: not indeed
For that which is most worthy to be blest,
Delight and liberty, the simple creed 25
Of Childhood, whether busy or at rest,
With new-fledged hope still fluttering in his breast: —
Not for these I raise
The song of thanks and praise;
But for those obstinate questionings 30
Of sense and outward things,
Fallings from us, vanishings;
Blank misgivings of a creature
Moving about in worlds not realized,
High instincts, before which our mortal nature 35
Did tremble like a guilty thing surprised:

But for those first affections,
Those shadowy recollections,
Which, be they what they may,
Are yet the fountain-light of all our day,
Are yet a master-light of all our seeing; 5
Uphold us, cherish, and have power to make
Our noisy years seem moments in the being
Of the eternal Silence: truths that wake,
To perish never;
Which neither listlessness, nor mad endeavor, 10
Nor man nor boy
Nor all that is at enmity with joy,
Can utterly abolish or destroy!
Hence, in a season of calm weather
Though inland far we be, 15
Our souls have sight of that immortal sea
Which brought us hither;
Can in a moment travel thither —
And see the children sport upon the shore,
And hear the mighty waters rolling evermore. 20

Then, sing ye birds, sing, sing a joyous song!
And let the young lambs bound
As to the tabor's sound!
We, in thought, will join your throng
Ye that pipe and ye that play, 25
Ye that through your hearts to-day
Feel the gladness of the May!
What though the radiance which was once so bright
Be now forever taken from my sight,
Though nothing can bring back the hour 30
Of splendor in the grass, of glory in the flower;
We will grieve not, rather find
Strength in what remains behind;
In the primal sympathy
Which having been must ever be; 35
In the soothing thoughts that spring

Out of human suffering;
In the faith that looks through death,
In years that bring the philosophic mind.

And O, ye Fountains, Meadows, Hills, and Groves,
Forebode not any severing of our loves! 5
Yet in my heart of hearts I feel your might;
I only have relinquish'd one delight
To live beneath your more habitual sway:
I love the brooks which down their channels fret
Even more than when I tripp'd lightly as they; 10
The innocent brightness of a newborn day
Is lovely yet;
The clouds that gather round the setting sun
Do take a sober coloring from an eye
That hath kept watch o'er man's mortality; 15
Another race hath been, and other palms are won.
Thanks to the human heart by which we live,
Thanks to its tenderness, its joys, and fears,
To me the meanest flower that blows can give
Thoughts that do often lie too deep for tears. 20

W. Wordsworth

CCCXXXIX

Music, when soft voices die,
Vibrates in the memory —
Odors, when sweet violets sicken,
Live within the sense they quicken.

Rose leaves, when the rose is dead, 25
Are heap'd for the beloved's bed;
And so thy thoughts, when Thou art gone,
Love itself shall slumber on.

P. B. Shelley

BIOGRAPHICAL NOTES

FRANCIS TURNER PALGRAVE, the anthologist of the "Golden Treasury," was born at Great Yarmouth, September 28, 1824. His father was Sir Francis Palgrave, a noted historian and antiquary, and the home in which he grew up was one of great culture as well as scholarship. The remarkable taste, therefore, which made so valuable the selection of the poems in the "Golden Treasury," was the inheritance of his family. After five years at Charterhouse he went to Balliol College, Oxford, where he distinguished himself and won an Exeter fellowship.

For some months in 1846 Palgrave was a private secretary to W. E. Gladstone; from 1850 to 1855 he was vice principal of a training school for teachers at Twickenham, where Tennyson then lived. From this time dates their close friendship. It was on one of many summer trips together that Palgrave evolved the plan of his great anthology. In his recollections of Tennyson, in the "Memoir" by Hallam Tennyson, he says:

"I had put the scheme of my 'Golden Treasury' before him during a walk near the Land's End in the late summer of 1860, and he encouraged me to proceed, barring only any poems by himself from insertion in an anthology whose title claimed excellence for its contents. And at the Christmastide following, the gathered materials, already submitted to the judgment of two friends of taste (one, the very able sculptor, T. Woolner, lately taken from us), were laid before Tennyson for final judgment."

The anthology was published in 1861, and took its place among lyrical collections as second only to the "Greek Anthology." Until 1884 Palgrave was an industrious public servant in the education department of the government. He had also written volumes of verse and had made other less famous anthologies. From 1885 to 1895 he was professor of poetry at Oxford, and his last publication was his well-known collection of University lectures, "Landscape in Poetry." He died October 24, 1897.

ANNA LETITIA AIKIN was born in Leicestershire in 1743. Her reputation as a poet dates from 1773. After her marriage to Mr. Barbauld she and her husband kept a school, to which her genius gave something like fame. For the school she wrote her best work, the "Hymns in Prose for Children." She died in 1825 at Stoke Newington. These lines, No. 207, taken from her "Ode to Life," were greatly admired by Wordsworth.

SIR WILLIAM ALEXANDER was born at Menstrie, Scotland, probably in 1567. He was private tutor to the king's sons, and assisted James in a metrical version of the Psalms. Scholar, courtier, poet, — he was also a trusted statesman. Toward the end of his life he was Secretary of State for Scotland, having been raised to the peerage as Earl of Sterling. He died in London in 1640.

LADY ANNE BARNARD, eldest daughter of James Lindsay, fifth earl of Balcarres, was born December 8, 1750. She was early introduced to the literary life of Edinburgh, and met Dr. Johnson on his visit there in 1773. For a while she lived with a sister in London, and there married, in 1793, Andrew Barnard, son of Thomas, Bishop of Limerick. Her first husband died at the Cape of Good Hope in 1807. She returned to London, and five years later married Sir James Bland Burges. Sheridan and Burke were among her friends. She had written "Auld Robin Gray" anonymously in 1771, and though it became very popular, its authorship was not generally known till Scott revealed it incidentally in "The Pirate," 1823. Lady Anne then wrote Scott an account of its composition, which he edited and published for the Bannatyne Club in 1824. She died the following year, May 6.

RICHARD BARNFIELD was born at Norbury, Shropshire, and was baptized June 13, 1574. He was educated at Brasenose College, Oxford. This poem, No. 45, which in a longer form appeared in "The Passionate Pilgrim," and was attributed to Shakespeare, is in Barnfield's "Poems in Divers Humours," 1598. As it is printed here, it appeared in "England's Helicon," 1600, over the name "Ignoto." Barnfield died at Stone, Staffordshire, March, 1627.

FRANCIS BEAUMONT, associated in English poetry with John Fletcher, was born at Grace-Dieu in Leicestershire, in 1584. Little is known of him except that he was for a time at Oxford and at the Inner Temple, that for a while he lived with Fletcher in London, and that he married in 1613 and died March 6, 1616.

WILLIAM BLAKE, poet and engraver, was born of an eccentric family in London, November 28, 1757. He was a passionate, strange child, disposed to see visions. He became a remarkable illustrator of imaginative poems; his designs for the Book of Job are his masterpiece. His own poems he illustrated with singular energy and grandeur. He was influenced by Swedenborg, and much of his writing shows, besides, a tendency to insanity. His memorable work for the general public is chiefly in "The Songs of Innocence," 1789, and "The Songs of Experience," 1794. He died in London, August 12, 1827.

ROBERT BURNS, best loved of modern British poets, was born at Alloway, Ayrshire, January 25, 1759. He was brought up a farmer, in poverty, but his mind was stored with old Scotch songs. His genius for love-making was his reason for writing his first songs; his independence of spirit led him to make his satires on the Church and on conventional authority. Besides ranking as perhaps the most passionate of modern lyrists and one of the best of satirists, he is also distinguished as a realistic painter of Scottish life. His first volume of poems, 1786, brought him immediate fame. Through the weakness of his character his last years were unhappy. He died at Dumfries, July 21, 1796.

GEORGE GORDON BYRON, Lord Byron, was born in London, January 22, 1788. After an unhappy boyhood he was educated at Harrow and at Cambridge. In 1807 he published his first book, "Hours of Idleness," and two years later replied to his critics in "English Bards and Scotch Reviewers." His fame began with the first two cantos of "Childe Harold's Pilgrimage," February, 1812, written after his first visit to the Mediterranean. In the next four years he wrote his oriental tales, such as "The Giaour" and "The Bride of Abydos." In 1816 he left England and lived on the Continent, chiefly in Italy. During these years he completed "Childe Harold," wrote his dramas, and began his unfinished masterpiece, "Don Juan." He engaged in the war of Greek independence, and died of fever at Missolonghi, April 19, 1824. No other modern English poet has achieved so world-wide a fame.

THOMAS CAMPBELL, who excelled as the writer of battle poems, was born at Glasgow, July 27, 1777. His reputation was established by "The Pleasures of Hope," 1799. A visit to the Continent the next year inspired such martial poems as "Hohenlinden." Other publications were "Gertrude of Wyoming," 1809; "Theodoric," 1824; and "The Pilgrim of Glencoe," 1842. He died at Boulogne, June 15, 1844.

The date and place of THOMAS CAMPION's birth are unknown. He studied at Cambridge, and at one time was a member of Gray's Inn, but later became a physician. He was the friend of Thomas Nash and John Dowland, the lutanist. All the words and most of the music of Dowland's "First Book of Airs," 1601, were written by Campion. From that time the latter was the chief writer of "airs" or short songs in Jacobean England. He also wrote masques, and in 1602 published his important "Observations in the Art of English Poesy." He died, probably of the plague, March 1, 1619.

THOMAS CAREW was born probably at Wickham, Kent, in 1598. He was educated at Westminster School and at Corpus Christi, Oxford. He was a favorite of Charles I, a friend of Ben Jonson, and the most artistic of the courtly poets of the time. Little else is known of him, but he seems to have died not later than April 17, 1638, probably at the end of March.

HENRY CAREY is supposed to have been the son of George Savile, Marquis of Halifax. Nothing more definite is known of his birth. He began his career as a teacher of music, but soon acquired some fame as a writer of songs and burlesques. The song here given, No. 167, first published about 1715, was a favorite of Addison's and is the only work of Carey's now generally remembered. He died October 4, 1743.

COLLEY CIBBER was born in London, November 6, 1671. After some soldiering he became an actor and playwright of considerable fame. He was poet laureate, wrote a famous autobiography, and was made the later hero of Pope's "Dunciad." He died in London, December 12, 1757.

HARTLEY COLERIDGE, son of the more famous Samuel Taylor Coleridge, was born near Bristol, September 19, 1796. He was educated at Oxford, but early showed the tendency to drink which ruined his career. He spent his life in miscellaneous literary work. A small volume of his poems appeared in 1833, a posthumous complete edition in 1851. He died at Grasmere, January 6, 1849.

SAMUEL TAYLOR COLERIDGE was born at Ottery St. Mary, Devonshire, October 21, 1772. He was educated at Christ's Hospital and at Jesus College, Cambridge. He became the brother-in-law of Southey and the friend of Wordsworth. To the "Lyrical Ballads," 1798, he contributed "The Ancient Mariner." "Christabel," written at this time, was not published till 1816. In 1817 a collection of his poems called "Sibylline Leaves" appeared. Complete editions of his poems appeared in 1828 and 1834. His slavery to opium ruined his splendid genius. He died at Highgate, July 25, 1834. As poet, critic, student of philosophy and theology, lecturer, and conversationalist Coleridge is one of the most variously gifted and seminal of modern men of letters.

JOHN COLLINS was born at Bath in the first half of the eighteenth century. He was probably a tailor's son. He became an actor and appeared in Dublin and London with moderate success. Later he invented a composite form of entertainment, — lecture, song, and story, — which brought him some wealth. He invested his earnings in *The Birmingham Chronicle*, where his poems appeared. He died May 2, 1808.

WILLIAM COLLINS was born at Chichester, Christmas Day, 1721. He was educated at Winchester and at Oxford. He published his first poems before he left school. Later he lived in London, in Richmond, and in Chichester, where he died June 12, 1759. His mind had long been clouded, and during his early life he had suffered the effects of poverty. Dr. Johnson was his friend, and wrote a sympathetic notice of him in the "Lives of the Poets." His name is now associated with that of Gray to represent the best poetry of the mid-eighteenth century.

ABRAHAM COWLEY was born in London toward the end of 1618. He was educated at Westminster and at Trinity College, Cambridge. He was secretary to Queen Henrietta Maria after her flight to the Continent, but returned to England during Cromwell's lifetime. After the Restoration he lived in retirement, generally regarded as the greatest poet of his day. His poetry is now seldom read, but his charming "Essays" help to preserve his fame. He died at Chertsey, July 28, 1667.

WILLIAM COWPER was born November 15, 1731, at Great Berkhampstead, where his father was rector of the parish. During a somewhat unhappy boyhood, spent chiefly at Westminster School, he developed his love of literature. In 1748 he was entered at the Middle Temple, where he remained until 1759, when he removed to the Inner Temple and became a commissioner of bankrupts. A few years later he grew so nervous over an examination which was to qualify him for a government appointment, that he temporarily lost his reason and made several attempts at suicide. After a brief confinement in an asylum Cowper recovered and removed to Huntingdon, where he formed his famous friendship for the Unwins. After Mr. Unwin's death in 1767 his wife and Cowper lived at Olney, where the poet wrote with Newton the "Olney Hymns." Cowper's friends devoted themselves to keeping him in a sane state of mind, and the remainder of his life is important only for his writings, which include many forms of poetry and some of the most charming letters in the language. The "Poems" appeared in 1782, "John Gilpin" in 1783, "The Task" in 1785. After establishing his fame as the greatest living English poet and undergoing much mental wretchedness, Cowper died at East Dereham, April 25, 1800.

RICHARD CRASHAW was born in London, probably in 1613. His father was a Puritan minister. He was educated at the Charterhouse School, and at Cambridge, where he held a Fellowship until he was ejected by Parliament in 1643. He went to Paris, where he received some assistance from Cowley and from Queen Henrietta Maria. His poems appeared in 1646, under the title "Steps to the Temple," and gave him a high rank among the religious poets of the seventeenth century. He entered the Roman Church and died a canon of Loretto, 1649.

ALLAN CUNNINGHAM was born at Keir, Dumfriesshire, December 7, 1784. His father was later the friend and neighbor of Burns, and the son walked in Burns's funeral procession. Allan was brought up as a stonemason, but his fondness for old Scotch songs led him to perpetrate a sort of hoax on a London publisher by bringing out his original compositions under the title of "Remains of Nithsdale and Galloway Song," 1810. At this time he came to London and became the secretary of Francis Chantrey, the sculptor. His chief later publications were "Traditional Tales of the English and Scottish Peasantry," 1822; a four-volume collection, "Songs of Scotland, Ancient and Modern," 1825, in which this fine song, "A Wet Sheet and a Flowing Sea," No. 249, was included; and from 1829 to 1833, the "Lives of the Most Eminent British Painters, Sculptors, and Architects." He died in London, October 30, 1842.

SAMUEL DANIEL was born near Taunton, 1562, of a musical family. He was educated at Magdalen, Oxford, and became famous for the beauty of his diction and his versification. He was much honored during his lifetime, succeeded Spenser as unofficial poet laureate, and died at Beckington in October, 1619.

THOMAS DEKKER was born about 1570, in London. He may have attended the Merchant Tailors' School. He was one of the hack writers employed by the theatrical manager Henslowe, who, when he was imprisoned for debt in 1598, procured his freedom. He was a most prolific writer of plays and pamphlets, but died poor about 1641. The poem here given, No. 75, is from "The Pleasant Comedy of Patient Grissell," 1599.

ROBERT DEVEREUX, second Earl of Essex, was born at Netherwood, Herefordshire, November 19, 1566. He was the brother of that Penelope Devereux whom Sidney loved. He attended Trinity College, Cambridge, and embarked on the career of courtier, soldier, and queen's favorite, for which he is remembered in history. In 1590 he married the widow of Sir Philip Sidney. In 1596 he captured Cadiz. Then in 1599 he was appointed Governor-General of Ireland, and after a disastrous campaign there he fell into disfavor with Elizabeth, whereupon he tried to start a rebellion, and was executed for treason, February 25, 1601.

JOHN DONNE, grandson of John Heywood and kin to Sir Thomas More, was born in London about 1573. Probably because his family were Roman Catholics, he took no degree at the universities, though he attended both. After some foreign travel he became secretary to Chancellor Sir Thomas Egerton, and eloped with Anne More, Lady Egerton's niece. He took orders in 1615, became a famous preacher, and was made Dean of St. Paul's in November, 1621. He died March 31, 1631. For the most part his poems — noted for their subtle imagination — were written in his youth, and became famous through circulation in manuscript.

MICHAEL DRAYTON was born at Hartshill, Warwickshire, 1563. He was the friend of Spenser and of most of the great Elizabethans. He wrote voluminous historical poems, and busied himself with some dramatic writing, but he is chiefly remembered for this sonnet, No. 49, for "Nimphidia," and for "The Ballad of Agincourt," one of the most martial ballads in English. He died in London, 1631.

WILLIAM DRUMMOND was born at Hawthornden, December 13, 1585. He attended the famous high school at Edinburgh and graduated from the university there. After some foreign travel he lived chiefly at his home, writing love poems in the fashions prevailing in London. He entertained Ben Jonson in 1618, and recorded their oft-quoted conversations about contemporary English poets. He died December 4, 1649.

JOHN DRYDEN, the chief man of letters of the Restoration, was born at Aldwinkle All Saints, Northamptonshire, August 9, 1631. He attended Westminster School and Trinity College, Cambridge. He is popularly remembered for his great odes, — the "Song for St. Cecilia's Day," 1687, and "Alexander's Feast," 1697, — and for his remarkable satires, "Absalom and Achitophel," 1681, and "MacFlecknoe," 1682; but he also wrote a large number of comedies and heroic plays and an important body of narrative verse, and he was the best critic of his age. He died in London, May 1, 1700.

JANE OR JEAN ELLIOT was born in 1727 at Minto House, Teviotdale. Her father, Sir Gilbert Elliot, and her brother Gilbert were literary in their tastes. One evening in 1756 the brother bet Jean "a pair of gloves or a set of ribbons" that she could not write a ballad on the subject of Flodden Field. Jean won the wager with the verses here given, No. 162. The poem was published anonymously in 1756, and for some time it was thought to be a "genuine relic of the past." Among the first to discover the modern note in it was Burns. Scott included it as a modern poem in the "Minstrelsy of the Scottish Border," 1803. Jean Elliot lived in Edinburgh from 1782 to 1804. She was the last lady in the town to make regular use of her sedan chair, and in other ways she cultivated old fashions. She died at Teviot House or at Minto House, March 29, 1805.

JOHN FLETCHER was born at Rye, Sussex, in December, 1579. He seems to have been educated at Cambridge, and he later collaborated in writing plays with his friend Francis Beaumont. He excelled in the writing of comedy, and in his lyrics. The song here given, No. 132, from "The Nice Valour," may have influenced Milton's "Il Penseroso." Fletcher died in London and was buried August 29, 1625.

JOHN GAY was born at Barnstaple, probably in September, 1685. After a brief experience as a London apprentice he began his literary career under circumstances not known. His first poem is said to have been published in 1708. His collected poems appeared in 1720. He became one of the important men of letters in his age, with varied kinds of success to his credit, and he was the close friend of Pope and Swift. Besides several admirable songs, he wrote "Trivia," 1716; the "Fables," 1727; and "The Beggar's Opera," 1728. He died in London, December 4, 1732.

OLIVER GOLDSMITH was born in Ireland, November 10, 1728. He was educated at Trinity College, Dublin. After much miscellaneous experience he became a sort of hack writer to the editor of the *Monthly Review*. "The Traveller," 1764; "The Vicar of Wakefield," 1766; "The Deserted Village," 1770; and "She Stoops to Conquer," 1773, are his best-known works and have made him a favorite writer. He died in London, April 4, 1774.

ROBERT GRAHAM, afterwards Cunninghame-Graham, was educated at Glasgow University, for a time was a planter in Jamaica, and in 1785 was elected rector of Glasgow University. From 1794 to 1796 he was in Parliament. He was well known for his songs, which made their way without the help of any systematic publishing. He died about 1797.

THOMAS GRAY was born at Cornhill, December 26, 1716. He was educated at Eton and at Peterhouse, Cambridge. In 1739 and 1740 he traveled abroad with Horace Walpole. After a short residence at Stoke Poges he went to Cambridge, where he remained, first at Peterhouse and afterwards at Pembroke. He wrote, besides his famous "Elegy," comparatively few poems, but, in compensation, made himself one of the most learned men in England, and wrote letters to his friends which are delightful in their kind. He was one of the first Englishmen to take journeys for the sake of romantic scenery. He died at Cambridge, July 30, 1771.

ROBERT GREENE was born in Norwich, 1558. The date of his baptism is July 11. He was educated at Cambridge, and after the customary Elizabethan travel abroad, settled into a life in London that he himself has described as vicious in the extreme. He is famous for his romances, dramas, and charming poems, for his pamphlets on roguery of all sorts, and for his highly emotional repentance. He died in extreme want, in the house of a London shoemaker, September 3, 1592. The poem here given, No. 60, is from "Menaphon," 1589, one of his romances.

WILLIAM HABINGTON was born at Hindlip on November 4, 1605. After being educated in St. Omers and at Paris, he became a courtier, and wrote Platonic verse after the French fashion. He died November 30, 1654.

GEORGE HERBERT, one of the best known of English religious poets, was born of a noble Welsh family in the Castle of Montgomery, Wales,

April 3, 1593. His elder brother, Edward, Lord Herbert of Cherbury, was also a poet, but better known as a diplomatist, philosopher, and historian, and as the writer of an interesting autobiography. George Herbert was educated at Westminster and at Cambridge. After graduating he became Public Orator of the University, and was ambitious of a political career. A change in his character, possibly brought about by increasing ill health, or by the death of several friends, turned him to the religious life. In 1630 he became Vicar of Bemerton, near Salisbury, where he led a life famous for its quiet piety. He died of consumption, and was buried March 3, 1633. Shortly afterwards "The Temple," his one volume of poems, was published by his friends.

ROBERT HERRICK, the model of English lyrical poets of the less elaborate type, was born in London, August 24, 1591. He was educated at Cambridge, at St. John's College and Trinity Hall, and after some miscellaneous adventures took orders before 1627. On September 30, 1629, he became vicar of Dean Prior, in Devonshire. In 1647 Parliament ejected him from his living, whereupon he went to London and shortly afterward published his one collection, "Hesperides." After the Restoration Herrick returned to his vicarage in Dean Prior, August 24, 1662. He died in October, 1674, and was buried on the fifteenth of the month.

THOMAS HEYWOOD, a hack writer employed by the manager Henslowe, was born in Lincolnshire, some time before 1575. His best known play is "A Woman Killed with Kindness," 1603. Heywood died after 1648. The present song, No. 73, comes from "The Rape of Lucrece."

THOMAS HOOD, humorist and humanitarian, was born in London, May 23, 1799. His life was spent chiefly in editing magazines, to which he contributed his poems, and in a vain search for health. He edited successively the *London Magazine*, the *Comic Annual*, 1830–1840, the *New Monthly Magazine*, 1841–1843, and *Hood's Magazine* during the last year of his life. His humorous poems are remarkable for their brilliant punning; the three serious poems in the present collection and "The Song of the Shirt" seem now the basis of his permanent reputation. He died in London, May 3, 1845.

BEN JONSON, Shakespeare's great contemporary in the drama, was born in London, 1573. He was educated at Westminster School, but it is not known that he attended either Oxford or Cambridge. After some experience as a bricklayer, and later as a soldier in the Netherlands, he turned to the stage, and wrote "Every Man in His Humour," some time before 1598. For the rest of his life he shared with Shakespeare the leadership of the drama, and also wrote short poems in a manner so perfect that they became the models for Herrick and for minor poets ever since. After being for many years a sort of literary dictator, much looked up to by young writers, he died in London, August 6, 1637.

JOHN KEATS was born in London, October 31, 1795, of humble parentage. His father died in 1804 and his mother in 1810. In the latter year he was apprenticed to a surgeon, and for some time he pursued his medical studies conscientiously. But about 1812 the reading of Spenser's "Faerie Queene" inspired him to write poetry. His great sonnet "On First Looking into Chapman's Homer" was written in 1815. In 1817 appeared his first volume of "Poems," in 1818 "Endymion," and in 1820 his last volume, containing "Lamia," "Isabella," "The Eve of St. Agnes," the famous odes, and the fragment of "Hyperion." In September, 1820, Keats left England for Italy, in an attempt to recover from consumption. He died in Rome, February 23, 1821, and in a few years his fame began to spread rapidly. He is now generally regarded as one of the truest and greatest of the English poets.

CHARLES LAMB was born in London, February 10, 1775. He was educated at Christ's Hospital, where he met Coleridge, as he has beautifully told us in a famous essay. He became a clerk in the South Sea House, and then, in 1792, in the East India Company, where he remained until he retired on a pension in 1825. His life was devoted to his sister Mary, and literature was his chief recreation. He is best known for the "Essays of Elia," which appeared first in the *London Magazine* and then in two collections in 1823 and 1833. Almost as famous are the "Tales from Shakespeare," which he wrote in collaboration with Mary Lamb. Few of his poems are important, but the three in the present collection are famous. "The Old Familiar Faces" appeared in "Blank Verse, by Charles Lamb and Charles Lloyd," 1798. He died at Edmonton, December 27, 1834.

MARY LAMB was born in London, 1764. She had a tendency toward insanity, which suddenly developed in 1796 in a most tragic manner. Her brother Charles made himself responsible for her conduct, and their pathetic devotion to each other is one of the romantic passages in the literary history of England. Besides collaborating in the "Tales from Shakespeare," 1807, Charles and Mary Lamb published "Poetry for Children," 1809, from which this poem, No. 283, is taken. Mary Lamb died at Edmonton, May 20, 1847.

THOMAS LODGE was born about 1558, at West Ham, or at London. His father was Lord Mayor. He entered Trinity College, Oxford, in 1573. On his numerous voyages, perhaps buccaneering expeditions, he wrote several romances, notably that one from which this song, No. 19, is taken, "Rosalynde, Euphues' Golden Legacie," 1590. This romance is the source of Shakespeare's "As You Like It." Lodge later became a convert to Roman Catholicism, practiced medicine, and published prose translations. He died in London of the plague, 1625.

JOHN LOGAN was born at Soutra, Fala, Midlothian, in 1748. He was educated at Musselburgh and at the University of Edinburgh. In 1770 he was licensed to preach in the Scottish Church, and in 1773 he was ordained. His "Poems" were published in 1781. His connection with the stage, through the composition of a tragedy, "Runnymede," produced in Edinburgh in 1783, made him unpopular with his church. He died in London, December 25, 1788. He is probably the author of the charming and famous "Ode to the Cuckoo," more often attributed to his friend Michael Bruce.

RICHARD LOVELACE was born at Woolwich, Kent, in 1618. He was educated at the Charterhouse School, and at Gloucester Hall, Oxford. By his personal charms he early attracted the attention of the Court. He became a soldier, and was chosen to present the Kentish Petition to the House of Commons. For this act he was thrown into prison. He spent his fortune in the cause of Charles, and, later, served the French king. He died in obscurity in London, in April, 1658.

JOHN LYLY was born between October 9, 1553, and October 8, 1554, in Kent. He was educated at Oxford. The first part of "Euphues," the most famous and influential Elizabethan novel, appeared in 1579; the second part in 1580. Lyly also wrote plays for the children of St. Paul's and the children of the Chapel Royal, and it is from these plays that his lyrics are taken, the present song, No. 72, coming from "Alexander and Campaspe," 1584. He died in November, 1606.

HENRY FRANCIS LYTE was born at Ednam, June 1, 1793. He was educated at Trinity College, Dublin, and became a minister in the Established Church. His poor health compelled him to travel much on the Continent. In 1826 he published his "Tales in Verse"; his "Poems, Chiefly Religious" appeared in 1833, and his literary "Remains" in 1850. He is best known by his famous hymn, "Abide With Me," but others of his hymns are only less popular. He died at Nice, November 20, 1847.

CHRISTOPHER MARLOWE is ranked as Shakespeare's chief predecessor in the drama. The son of a Canterbury shoemaker, he was christened February 26, 1564. He was educated at the King's School and at Cambridge. From that time till his death in a tavern brawl, June 1, 1593, his only record is the brief series of important plays, "Tamburlaine," in 1587, and, in close sequence, "Doctor Faustus," "The Jew of Malta," and "Edward II." The first two dramas and his translation of "Hero and Leander" proved him one of the most musical and exquisite of poets. The famous song here given, No. 7, appeared in "The Passionate Pilgrim," 1599. See note on Shakespeare, p. 390.

ANDREW MARVELL, Milton's assistant in the Latin secretaryship, was born at Winestead, March 31, 1621. He was educated at Hull and at Trinity College, Cambridge. After some travel on the Continent and private tutoring at the home of Lord Fairfax he was recommended by Milton to a post under the Commonwealth, and in 1657 he became Milton's assistant. In January, 1659, he was elected a member of Parliament for Hull, and at the Restoration he used his influence to protect Milton. He continued to take a highly honorable part in politics until his death in London, August 18, 1678. He is remembered as a political satirist and controversialist, and as a lyric poet of great charm.

WILLIAM JULIUS MICKLE, usually thought though not certainly proved to be the author of No. 194, was born September 28, 1735, at Langholm, Dumfriesshire. Educated at Langholm and in the schools of Edinburgh, he became clerk in a brewery, which by 1757 he owned. But his literary interests led to neglect of business and to failure. In 1765 he became corrector to the Clarendon Press, and six years later began his translation of the "Lusiads" of Camoens, finished in 1775. After some attempts at dramatic writing and a visit to Portugal, where he was elected a member of the Royal Academy, he settled into a government sinecure. To Evans's "Old Ballads, Historical and Narrative, With Some of Modern Date," 1777–1784, he contributed his beautiful "Cumnor Hall," mentioned by Scott in the Introduction to "Kenilworth." He died at Forest Hill, near Oxford, October 28, 1788. "The Sailor's Wife" has sometimes been given, on very insufficient evidence, to a certain Jean Adam or Jane Adams, a Scotch schoolmistress.

JOHN MILTON, usually regarded as the greatest English nondramatic poet, was born in London, December 9, 1608. He was fortunate in his home. His father enabled him to spend several years in leisure and travel after he had completed his studies at Cambridge, and to these happy years belong his lovely early poems. Then he taught a few pupils, continued his own deep studies, and began the series of his great prose pamphlets. At the beginning of the Commonwealth he was appointed Latin Secretary to the Committee on Foreign Affairs, and lost his sight through overwork. At the Restoration he was in danger of his life and went into hiding. "Paradise Lost" was begun in 1658 and published in 1667. "Paradise Regained" and "Samson Agonistes" appeared together in 1671. Milton died November 8, 1674. The present poem, No. 85, was composed at the end of 1629, when Milton had just passed his twenty-first birthday, — an extraordinary achievement for so young a man.

THOMAS MOORE, the friend of Byron, was born in Dublin, May 28, 1779. He came to London with some fame as a rising poet, and became celebrated for his "Irish Melodies," published from 1807 to 1834. "Lalla Rookh," a pseudo-oriental tale in verse, 1817, expressed the same interest in the East that made Byron's oriental poems popular. Moore died at Sloperton Cottage, Wiltshire, February 25, 1852. He won some distinction as a satirist and as a prose writer by his biographies, particularly his "Life, Letters, and Journals of Lord Byron."

THOMAS NASH, the youngest of the Elizabethan university wits, was born at Lowestoft in November, 1567. He studied at Cambridge from 1582 to 1586, and became the friend and defender of Greene and Marlowe. His important works are "Jack Wilton," a novel, 1594, and the play "Summer's Last Will and Testament," 1600, from which this song, No. 1, is taken. He was dead by 1601.

JOHN NORRIS was born at Collingbourne-Kingston, Wiltshire, 1657. He was educated at Winchester and at Exeter College, Oxford, and became fellow of All Souls. He entered the ministry and wrote much in a religious or mystical vein. In 1692 he became rector of Bemerton, near Salisbury, the parish that George Herbert had made famous. Norris died there in 1711.

CAROLINA OLIPHANT, Baroness Nairne, was born at Gask, Perthshire, August 16, 1766. She was inspired by Burns's poems to imitate and revise old Scotch songs, and under an assumed name contributed to the collections of the time. "The Land o' the Leal," 1798, No. 198, was sent for comfort to Mrs. Campbell Colquhoun, who had lost a child. The latter part of Lady Nairne's life was spent in travel for the health of her own son. She died at Gask, October 26, 1845.

AMBROSE PHILIPS was born in Shropshire about 1675. He was educated at Shrewsbury and at St. John's College, Cambridge. His famous "Pastorals," 1709, which excited Pope's jealousy, were perhaps written while he was in college. He was befriended by Swift, Addison, and Steele. In 1724 he became secretary to the Bishop of Armagh, and later rose to be judge of the prerogative court. He died in London, June 18, 1749. He was ridiculed by Henry Carey (see p. 379) as "Namby Pamby."

ALEXANDER POPE was born in London, May 21, 1688. He was brought up a Roman Catholic, and spent a sickly childhood and youth in retirement. His literary career began with his "Pastorals," 1709, and his fame was assured by "The Rape of the Lock," 1714. He died at Twickenham, May 30, 1744. He had long since become the chief poet of the age, but as his work lay chiefly in the fields of satiric and didactic verse, he is represented in this volume by only the present poem, No. 154, which he claimed to have written when he was twelve years old. The piece is remarkably Horatian in tone.

Matthew Prior was born in Dorsetshire, July 21, 1664. He was educated at St. John's College, Cambridge, and afterwards had a distinguished diplomatic career, especially at the time of the Peace of Utrecht. He is considered by many to be the best English writer of society verse. He died September 18, 1721.

Francis Quarles was born at Romford, Essex, where he was baptized May 8, 1592. He was educated at Christ's College, Cambridge, and studied law at Lincoln's Inn. After a short residence abroad he settled in London and published poems of an eccentric and religious character. Before 1629 he became secretary to the Bishop of Armagh, Ireland. Before 1633 he was in England again, at Roxwell, Essex. In 1635 he published his famous book, the "Emblems." He died September 8, 1644.

Samuel Rogers was born at Stoke Newington, July 30, 1763. He entered the banking business at his father's wish, but his real interest was in literature. In 1781 he made his first appearance in print with a paper reminiscent of Johnson's "Rambler." His first volume of poems was published in 1786. In 1792 appeared "The Pleasures of Memory." From that year his reputation constantly increased. He was the friend of most of the prominent statesmen, artists, and poets who flourished during his long life. He died in London, December 18, 1855.

Sir Walter Scott, whom Tennyson called the greatest man of letters of the nineteenth century, was born at Edinburgh, August 15, 1771. After graduating from Edinburgh University he became a lawyer, but managed to do much writing in addition to his public duties. His "Border Minstrelsy" was published in 1802, "The Lay of the Last Minstrel" in 1805, "Marmion" in 1808, "The Lady of the Lake" in 1810, "Rokeby" in 1813. After 1814 Scott devoted himself to his novels, but the incidental poems in his stories are among the best short lyrics in the language. He died at Abbotsford, September 21, 1832.

Sir Charles Sedley was born about 1639 at Aylesford, Kent. He was for a while at Wadham College, Oxford, and after the Restoration was a member of Parliament. Although once noted as a dramatist, a wit, and a man of taste, he is chiefly remembered for his dissolute life. His best trait seems to have been his gift of song writing. He died August 20, 1701.

William Shakespeare, greatest of English dramatists, was born at Stratford-on-Avon, April 23, 1564. His early life is the subject of much conjecture; recent discoveries have made his later years a little less legendary than they were. He married Anne Hathaway when he was little more than a boy, and shortly afterwards he went to London and became connected with the stage as actor and playwright, and shareholder in two theaters. He died at Stratford, April 23, 1616. The songs in this anthology are taken from his various dramas and from "The Passionate Pilgrim," 1599, a collection of poems, of which five are known to be Shakespeare's. The sonnets are from the collection printed in 1609.

PERCY BYSSHE SHELLEY was born at Field Place, Sussex, August 4, 1792. He was educated at Eton and at University College, Oxford, but was expelled by the college authorities in 1811 for the publication of his tract, "The Necessity of Atheism." His father practically disowned him, and the radical nature of his poems and his conduct caused his virtual exile from England. His last years were spent in Italy. He published "Queen Mab" in 1813, "Alastor" in 1816, "The Revolt of Islam" in 1817, "Prometheus Unbound" in 1820, and "The Cenci" in the same year. He was drowned in the Mediterranean, July 8, 1822. Like Wordsworth, he is now praised by his admirers almost as much for his personality as for his poems.

JAMES SHIRLEY was born in London, September 18, 1596. He was educated at the Merchant Tailors School, at St. John's College, Oxford, and at Catherine Hall, Cambridge. He took orders in the English Church, but later became a Roman Catholic and devoted his life to writing plays. He was a prolific dramatist and ranks as the last of the great Elizabethan playwrights. No. 91 is from his masque "Cupid and Death"; No. 92 is from his "Contention of Ajax and Ulysses." He died of exposure during the fire of London, October, 1666.

SIR PHILIP SIDNEY was born of noble parentage at Penshurst, Kent, November 29, 1554. At Shrewsbury School he formed his famous friendship with Fulke Greville, his biographer. For a time he studied at Christ Church, Oxford, and later traveled on the Continent. Returning to Elizabeth's court, he was the friend of Spenser and other poets. By the nobility of his character and by his romantic death he became the ideal English courtier. At the battle of Zutphen, September 22, 1586, he was fatally wounded, and died on October 17. He was only incidentally a writer, but in each of his works, "Astrophel and Stella," "The Countess of Pembroke's Arcadia," "The Apologie for Poetrie," he had the fortune to set the standard for Elizabethan sonnet sequences, romances, and criticism. For his contemporaries he was the model of the perfect gentleman, and such he remains to us.

CHRISTOPHER SMART was born at Shipbourne, Kent, April 11, 1722. He was educated at Pembroke Hall, Cambridge, and became a fellow of that college in 1745. Later he removed to London and published an unimportant volume of poems. He lost his reason, but in a sane interval wrote the "Song to David," 1763, from which these lines,

No. 179, are taken. But for this extraordinary poem, one of the most imaginative of the century, Smart would be known, if at all, mainly as a hack writer. He died in London, May 21, 1771.

ROBERT SOUTHEY was born at Bristol, August 12, 1774. He was educated at Westminster School and at Balliol, Oxford. With Coleridge he took a deep interest in the French Revolution, and was for a while a decided Radical. After his marriage to the sister of Coleridge's wife, the necessity of supporting the Coleridges as well as his own large family developed the steadier qualities in his fine character. His home for the chief part of his life was at Keswick. Besides much reviewing and historical writing and general literary work, he wrote some ambitious epics like "Thalaba," 1801, and "The Curse of Kehama," 1810, and a few memorable short poems. In 1813 he became poet laureate. He died at Keswick, March 21, 1843.

EDMUND SPENSER, one of the greatest of English poets, was born in London, in 1552. He was educated at Pembroke Hall, Cambridge, and joined the group of young poets at Elizabeth's court. In 1579 appeared "The Shepheardes Calendar," the most important poem since Chaucer's day. In 1580 Spenser was appointed secretary to the Lord Deputy of Ireland. In 1590 he issued the first three books of "The Faerie Queene"; in 1595 "Colin Clouts Come Home Againe," the "Amoretti," and the "Epithalamion"; and in 1596, the fourth, fifth, and sixth books of "The Faerie Queene." He died in London, January 16, 1599.

SIR JOHN SUCKLING was born at Whitton, Middlesex, February, 1609. He was a precocious child, and early became distinguished for his wit. After attending Trinity College, Cambridge, he traveled much on the Continent. He was popular at the English Court for his verses and plays, and was also noted as a gamester and a gallant. The song here given, No. 129, his most famous piece, occurs in his play "Aglaura," 1638. For political reasons he was obliged to leave the country. The manner of his death is uncertain. One story is that he committed suicide in Paris, probably before the end of 1642.

JOSHUA SYLVESTER, born in Kent, 1563, was a business man who made literature his avocation. In 1606 he was attached to the Court as a poet. His translations from the French poet Du Bartas had great fame and much influence, but are now forgotten. He died at Middelburg, September 28, 1618.

JAMES THOMSON was born at Ednam, Roxburghshire, probably on September 7, 1700. He was educated at Jedburgh and at the University of Edinburgh. In 1725 he came to London in search of a literary career. His fame was secured by "The Seasons," published in four parts between 1726 and 1730. Aside from some dramatic writing, his only other considerable work was the "Castle of Indolence," of 1748. His most famous poem, No. 158, appeared in "The Masque of Alfred," produced in collaboration with David Mallet on August 1 and 2, 1740, for which Dr. Arne wrote the music. There has been some question as to Thomson's authorship of the song, but it is almost certainly his. Some have also questioned its inclusion in the "Golden Treasury" on the assumption that it lacks the higher qualities of lyric poetry. To this it may be replied that it rings true to the patriotic heart and is full of dignity, facts which Lord Tennyson and Mr. Palgrave doubtless perceived. Thomson died August 27, 1748.

THE SHEPHERD TONIE. This pen name has not been definitely assigned, but it is supposed to represent Anthony Munday, a hack writer of whose life little is known. He was born in 1553, was apprenticed to a stationer, wrote plays for Henslowe, and died in 1633. If this poem, No. 20, is his, he wrote no other lyric like it, so far as we know.

HENRY VAUGHAN, "Silurist," was born at Newton S. Bridget, Wales, April 17, 1622. From other Vaughans he distinguished himself by this title derived from the ancient tribe of Silures. He was educated at Jesus College, Oxford, and spent his life in literary leisure, although to some extent practicing as a physician. He came to be the chief disciple of George Herbert, but occasionally showed far more imaginative power than his master. He died April 23, 1695.

EDMUND WALLER, one of the chief literary figures of seventeenth-century England, was born at Coleshill, Buckinghamshire, March 3, 1606. He was educated at Eton and at King's College, Cambridge. While still very young he was returned to Parliament for Amersham. His long political career is not altogether to his credit, but as an orator and wit he deserved his immense reputation. He is important as a forerunner of the formal restrained poets of the eighteenth century, and a few of his poems still possess great charm. He died at Hall Barn, Beaconsfield, October 21, 1687.

JOHN WEBSTER, one of the hack writers employed by Henslowe, was born in London, perhaps in 1580. He wrote several plays in partnership with other writers. No. 66 occurs in "The White Devil," one of his two great tragedies, 1612. The other, "The Duchess of Malfi," was produced in 1616. Webster died toward the end of 1625.

JOHN WILMOT, second Earl of Rochester, was the chief of those dissolute, gifted youths who adorned and disgraced the court of Charles II. He was born at Ditchley, Oxfordshire, April 10, 1647. For a short time he attended Wadham College, Oxford, and he then traveled in France and Italy. After a brief military experience he settled down to a career of brilliant depravity. He died at Woodstock Park, July 26, 1680.

George Wither or Withers was born at Bentworth, Hampshire, June 11, 1588. After two years at Magdalen College, Oxford, he studied law in London and entered Lincoln's Inn. His fame rests on his lyrics and his satires. For one of his satires he was imprisoned. Under the Commonwealth he was a not very successful soldier, and the end of his long life was unhappy. He died in London, May 2, 1667.

Charles Wolfe was born at Blackhall, Kildare, December 14, 1791. Educated at Trinity College, Dublin, he took orders in the Established Church and became curate of Donoughmore, Ireland. His famous poem, No. 262, was published in the *Newry Telegraph*, April 19, 1817. Various claimants to its authorship have arisen, but Wolfe's right to the honor seems established. He died at Queenstown, February 21, 1823.

William Wordsworth was born at Cockermouth, Cumberland, April 7, 1770. He was educated at St. John's College, Cambridge. Filled with revolutionary fervor, he visited France during the Terror and incurred some personal danger. His "Lyrical Ballads," 1798, with the famous preface added later (Second Series, 1800), marked the beginning of a new kind of poetry, which aimed at extreme naturalness in diction and thought. Almost as much as for his poetry, Wordsworth is affectionately remembered for the life of noble poverty which he led with his sister Dorothy, chiefly at Grasmere. On October 4, 1802, he married his cousin, Mary Hutchinson. In March, 1843, upon the death of Southey, Wordsworth succeeded to the office of poet laureate. He died at Rydal Mount, April 23, 1850. His poetry attained comparative popularity only toward the end of his life, but he has been regarded by two generations as one of the very greatest of the English poets.

Sir Henry Wotton, in his later years the friend of Milton, was born in Boughton, Kent, April 9, 1568. He was educated at Winchester and at Oxford, and traveled on the Continent from 1590 to 1599. He was an ambassador to Venice and to Germany under James I, and on his retirement from public life became Provost of Eton College. He died at Eton, December, 1639.

Sir Thomas Wyat, the earliest of the famous "courtly makers" of Tudor times, was born at Allington Castle, Kent, in 1503. He was graduated from St. John's College, Cambridge, at a very early age, and after some travel took up the life of a courtier. Toward the end of 1540 he was accused of treason and imprisoned, but he cleared himself at his trial. He died at Sherborne, in Dorsetshire, on October 10 or 11, 1542. His poems, which followed Italian models, circulated in manuscript, and were first printed in "Tottel's Miscellany," 1557.

NOTES

(The notes in brackets are Palgrave's.)

2 1 **The palm and may**: the great sallow, or goat willow, and the hawthorn. See the Century Dictionary.—10 This and the following song are sung by Ariel in "The Tempest." Compare Act V, scene i, and Act I, scene ii.—20 [**whist**: hushed, quieted.]—21 **featly**: daintily.—22 **burthen**: undersong.

3 7 [**Rouse Memnon's mother**: Awaken the Dawn from the dark Earth and the clouds where she is resting. This is one of that limited class of early myths which may be reasonably interpreted as representations of natural phenomena. Aurora in the old mythology is mother of Memnon (the East), and wife of Tithonus (the appearances of Earth and Sky during the last hours of night). She leaves him every morning in renewed youth, to prepare the way for Phœbus (the Sun), whilst Tithonus remains in perpetual old age and grayness.]—14 **decore**: decorate.—30 [**by Penéus' streams**: Phœbus loved the Nymph Daphne whom he met by the river Penéus in the vale of Tempe.]

4 3 [**Amphion's lyre**: He was said to have built the walls of Thebes to the sound of his music.]—8 **chair**: chariot.—11 [**Night like a drunkard reels**: Compare "Romeo and Juliet," Act II, scene iii: "The grey-eyed morn smiles," etc. It should be added that three lines, which appeared hopelessly misprinted, have been omitted in this poem.]—14 **orient**: bright.—17 This and the following poem are the sixty-fourth and sixty-fifth of Shakespeare's sonnets.—20 **eternal**: should be construed with *brass*.—25 **state**: condition. In the next line it seems to mean *magnificence, greatness*.

5 1 **which**: since it (that is, the *thought*).—12 [**Time's chest**: in which he is figuratively supposed to lay up past treasures. So in "Troilus," Act III, scene iii, "Time hath a wallet at his back," etc. In the "Arcadia," *chest* is used to signify *tomb*.] 17 [A fine example of the high-wrought and conventional Elizabethan pastoralism, which it would be unreasonable to criticize on the ground of the unshepherdlike or unreal character of some images suggested. Stanza 6 was perhaps inserted by Izaak Walton.]

6 1 **kirtle**: gown with a skirt, petticoat.—19 [This beautiful lyric is one of several recovered from the very rare Elizabethan songbooks, for the publication of which our thanks are due to Mr. A. H. Bullen (1887, 1888).] The title means (*Love*) *conquers All Things*.

7 11 This is one of those pieces in the "Passionate Pilgrim" (1599), which are generally assigned to Shakespeare. — 17 **brave**: finely dressed.

8 1 This song is sung by Amiens in "As You Like It," Act II, scene v. — 3 **turn**: return, give back. — 17 This song is sung by the two pages in "As You Like It," Act V, scene iii. — 18 The refrain is meaningless, at least to-day. — 20 **ring time**: season for dancing in a ring. — 29 **prime**: usually means *spring* (compare **11** 3), but here it may mean *supreme happiness*. If it means *spring*, there should be at least a comma after it.

9 3 [One stanza has been here omitted, in accordance with the principle noticed in the Preface. Similar omissions occur in a few other poems. The more serious abbreviation by which it has been attempted to bring Crashaw's "Wishes" and Shelley's "Euganean Hills," with one or two more, within the scheme of this selection, is commended with much diffidence to the judgment of readers acquainted with the original pieces.] — 6 This line seems to convey a challenge. — 21 [Sidney's poetry is singularly unequal; his short life, his frequent absorption in public employment, hindered doubtless the development of his genius. His great contemporary fame, second only, it appears, to Spenser's, has been hence obscured. At times he is heavy and even prosaic; his simplicity is rude and bare; his verse unmelodious. These, however, are the "defects of his merits." In a certain depth and chivalry of feeling, — in the rare and noble quality of disinterestedness (to put it in one word), — he has no superior, hardly perhaps an equal, amongst our poets; and after or beside Shakespeare's sonnets, his "Astrophel and Stella," in the editor's judgment, offers the most intense and powerful picture of the passion of love in the whole range of our poetry.]

10 8 [**Hundreds of years**: "The very rapture of love," says Mr. Ruskin; "A lover like this does not believe his mistress can grow old or die."] The title means *The Way of Love*. — 9 This is the fifty-seventh of Shakespeare's sonnets. — 21 **in your will**: so far as concerns your intent. — 23 This is the ninety-seventh of Shakespeare's sonnets.

11 1 **removed**: of removal, of absence. — 9 **cheer**: countenance. — 11 This is the twenty-ninth of Shakespeare's sonnets. The last six lines have rarely been surpassed, even by him. — 16 **with**: of. — 20 **state**: Here and in the fourth line below, both meanings of the word, *condition* and *magnificence*, may be combined.

12 1 This is the one hundred and ninth of Shakespeare's sonnets. — 2 **qualify**: diminish. — 7 **exchanged**: changed. — 10 **blood**: disposition. — 12 **To**: as to. — 15 This is the one hundred and fourth of Shakespeare's sonnets. — 22 **which**: who (refers to *you*). — 24 **his**: its.

13 1 [Readers who have visited Italy will be reminded of more than one picture by this gorgeous Vision of Beauty, equally sublime and pure in its Paradisaical naturalness. Lodge wrote it on a voyage to "the Islands of Terceras and the Canaries"; and he seems to have caught, in those southern seas, no small portion of the qualities which marked the almost contemporary art of Venice, — the glory and the glow of Veronese, Titian, or Tintoret. From the same romance is No. 71, — a charming picture in the purest style of the later Renaissance. — 1 **the clear**: is the crystalline or outermost heaven of the old cosmography.] — 8 **whenas**: when. — 13 **shroud**: covering; that is, probably, a cloud. — 31 **orient**: bright.

14 9 **muse**: wonder. — 11 [**for a fair there 's fairer none**: If you desire a Beauty, there is none more beautiful than Rosaline.] — 26 **fond**: foolish. 28 **her fashion**: the way she was fashioned, her form or shape.

15 12 **thou art woe-begone thee**: Fowler explains this as a confusion of two constructions, *thee is woe-begone* ("to thee has woe closed round") and the more modern *thou art woe-begone*. — 13 [Another gracious lyric from an Elizabethan songbook . . . reprinted . . . in Mr. W. J. Linton's "Rare Poems," 1883] and in Arber's "English Garner," 1882 (Fowler). — 14 **What**: why (as often in the older poets).

16 6 This is the eighteenth of Shakespeare's sonnets. — 13 **untrimm'd**: stripped of its trim (its beauty or adornment). — 15 [**that fair thou owest**: that beauty thou ownest.] — 20 This is the one hundred and sixth of Shakespeare's sonnets. — 22 **making beautiful old rhyme**: making old rhymes beautiful. — 24 **blazon**: description.

17 5 **for**: since, because. — 9 [From one of the three songbooks of T. Campion, who appears to have been author of the words which he set to music. His merit as a lyrical poet (recognized in his own time, but since then forgotten) has been again brought to light by Mr. Bullen's taste and research.] — 13 **still**: ever. Compare the sixth and eighth lines below. — 24 **which**: of which. — 27 [**swerving**: is Mr. Bullen's conjecture for *changing* in the text of 1601.] The title means *Kisses;* it is the plural of the Latin *basium*.

18 5 **as discontent**: as the result of being discontented (probably). In the older writers *as* often means *as if*. — 19 This poem is read by Dumain in "Love's Labour 's Lost," Act IV, scene iii. — 24 **'gan**: began (but not a contraction of that word). The Globe edition reads *can*. — 25 **That**: so that.

19 9 **for Jove**: as Jove (deny his existence as a god). — 16 **whan**: when. — 19 **assays**: endeavors. — 27 **thine own approved**: him who has been proved thine own.

20 7 **in**: into. — 15 The title means *Into Tears*. Compare Æneid, IV, 413 (Bates). — 17 **keep**: abide. — 20 **parts**: qualities.

21 2 **leave off in time to grieve**: cease grieving in due time. — 7 This is the one hundred and sixteenth of Shakespeare's sonnets. — 11 **mark**: sea-mark. — 14 [**Whose worth 's unknown, although his height be taken**: apparently, Whose stellar influence is uncalculated, although his angular altitude from the plane of the astrolabe or artificial horizon used by astrologers has been determined.] — 15 **Time's fool**: the sport of Time

(Beeching). — 21 [This lovely song appears, as here given, in Puttenham's "Arte of English Poesie," 1589. A longer and inferior form was published in the "Arcadia" of 1590; but Puttenham's prefatory words clearly assign his version to Sidney's own authorship.]

23 7 This song is sung by the clown in "Twelfth Night," Act II, scene iii. The title, from Horace's Odes, Book I, ode xi, means *Seize the Day*. — 19 The title alludes to Autolycus, the amusing, rascally peddler in Shakespeare's "A Winter's Tale." — 19 **brave**: fine looking.

24 4 **orient'st**: brightest. — 7 This song is found at the very close of "Love's Labour 's Lost." — 15 [**keel**: keep cooler by stirring round.] — 17 **saw**: sermon full of pious maxims. — 20 **crabs**: crab apples. — 25 This is the seventy-third of Shakespeare's sonnets.

25 6 **That**: as. — 6 **his**: its. — 11 This is the thirtieth of Shakespeare's sonnets. — 18 [**expense**: loss.] — 20 **tell**: count.

26 1 This is the thirty-ninth of Sidney's famous "Astrophel and Stella" sonnets. Compare Sidney Lee's "Elizabethan Sonnets," Vol. I, in the revised "English Garner." The Elizabethan poets vied with one another in paying tributes to sleep. Compare Daniel's sonnet, p. 30, and for a modern comparison, Wordsworth's sonnet, p. 331. — 2 **baiting place**: feeding place. — 4 **indifferent**: impartial. — 5 **proof**: tested metal. — 5 [**prease**: press.] — 10 **deaf of**: Lee reads *deaf to*, which seems preferable. — 13 **heavy grace**: favor slow to grant itself. — 15 This is the sixtieth of Shakespeare's sonnets. — 19 [**Nativity, once in the main of light**: when a star has risen and entered on the full stream of light; — another of the astrological phrases no longer familiar.] — 21 [**Crooked eclipses**: as coming athwart the sun's apparent course] and producing malignant effects. [Wordsworth, thinking probably of the "Venus" and the "Lucrece," said finely of Shakespeare: "Shakespeare *could* not have written an epic; he would have died of plethora of thought." This prodigality of nature is exemplified equally in his sonnets. The copious selection here given (which, from the wealth of the material, required greater consideration than any other portion of the editor's task), contains many that will not be fully felt and understood without some earnestness of thought on the reader's part. But he is not likely to regret the labor.] — 23 **flourish**: "outward painting" (Beeching).

27 3 **in hope**: that are to be expected to come. — 5 This is the eighty-seventh of Shakespeare's sonnets. — 7 **charter**: in addition to the play upon legal terms, there is here the meaning of *privilege*. — 8 **determinate**: canceled, expired. — 15 [**upon misprision growing**: either, granted in error, or, upon the growth of contempt.] — 19 This is the ninety-fourth of Shakespeare's sonnets. [With the tone of this sonnet compare Hamlet's "Give me that man That is not passion's slave," etc. Shakespeare's writings show the deepest sensitiveness to passion; hence the attraction he felt in the contrasting effects of apathy.] — 24 **expense**: waste.

28 4 **outbraves**: surpasses in a showy manner. — 4 **his**: its. — 10 [**grame**: sorrow. Renaissance influences long impeded the return of English poets to the charming realism of this and a few other poems by Wyat.] — 15 **wealth**: well-being (Fowler). — 15 **among**: in the midst of.

29 10 **up-till**: against. — 10 **thorn**: hawthorn. Compare p. 30, l. 18. — 23 [Pandion in the ancient fable was father to Philomela.] — 24 **lapp'd in lead**: wrapped in, covered by leaden coffins.

30 6 **ill-adventured youth**: youth which put forth upon an unfortunate voyage of life. — 7 **their**: of them (the objective use). — 11 **approve**: prove. — 13 **embracing clouds**: the allusion seems to be to the legend of Ixion, but it would be a pity to consider the sonnet as a mere complaint of a lover. Compare ll. 5–6. — 15 [In the old legend it is now Philomela, now Procne (the swallow), who suffers violence from Tereus. This song has a fascination in its calm intensity of passion, — that "sad earnestness and vivid exactness" which Cardinal Newman ascribes to the masterpieces of ancient poetry.] Tereus was the mythical king of Thrace. — 28 **wroken**: wreaked.

31 6 **woe**: This may be an adjective, equivalent to *woeful*, but it may also be a noun. — 11 This beautiful song is sung by a boy at the opening of the fourth act of "Measure for Measure." The title means *In Vain*. — 22 **cleanly**: completely.

32 7 The title is from Psalms xxxix, 6: "man walketh in a vain shew" (Bates). — 18 **turneth**: though the form is singular, the subject is *beams*. — 26 [**proved**: approved.]

33 1 This is the one hundred and forty-eighth of Shakespeare's sonnets. — 4 [**censures**: judges.] — 8 Is there a pun in this line? — 15 [Exquisite in its equably balanced metrical flow.] — 21 **secure**: this probably, but not certainly, means *free from care* rather than *free from danger*.

34 1 [Judging by its style, this beautiful example of old simplicity and feeling may, perhaps, be referred to the earlier years of Elizabeth.] — 3 [**late forgot**: lately.]

35 26 **mere**: pure.

36 4 **were**: even were. — 7 For the turn at the end of this poem, compare Drayton's famous sonnet, p. 31. — 9 This song is sung by Amiens in "As You Like It," Act II, scene vii.

37 1 [Printed in a little Anthology by Nicholas Breton, 1597. It is, however, a stronger and finer piece of work than any known to be his.] — 1 [**silly**: simple.] — 3 **doubt**: conjecture. — 3 [**dole**: grief.] — 4 [**chief**: chiefly.] — 5 **lap**: wrap. — 15 [**If there be any**: obscure; perhaps, if there be any who speak harshly of thee, thy pain may plead for pity from Fate]; or, *That* may be taken as a demonstrative pronoun referring to the preceding clause. [This poem, with 60 and 143, are each graceful variations of a long popular theme.] — 18 **the time**: probably, the while, meanwhile. — 21 **purchase**: acquire. — 26 The construction is mixed, but the sense is clear. — 30 **purchased**: acquired.

38 4 **in town**: What is to be said of the poetical quality of this phrase? — 6 **hath**: singular form with plural noun. — 9 **rascal**: of low origin. — 18 "In consideration of thy father's nobility" (Fowler). — 19 This is the thirty-first of Sidney's "Astrophel and Stella" sonnets. — 22 [**That busy archer**: Cupid.] — 26 [**descries**: used actively — *points out.*] — 27 **of**: on account of.

39 2 ["The last line of this poem is a little obscured by transposition. He means, *Do they call ungratefulness there a virtue?*" (C. Lamb).] — 3 The title means *O Cruel Love.* — 6 [**White Iopé**: suggested, Mr. Bullen notes, by a passage in Propertius (iii, 20) describing Spirits in the lower world: Vobiscum est Iopé, vobiscum candida Tyro.] The line means *Iopé is with you, with you is the fair white Tyro.* Compare Müller's edition, III, xxvi (Teubner, 1885). — 6 **Helen**: Helen of Troy. — 7 **finish'd**: completed, over and done with. — 15 **wanton**: playful pet. — 21 **woe**: woeful.

40 1 **stint**: cease. — 3 **by course**: continuously. — 4 **That**: so that. — 27 **caitiffs**: cowards, yielders.

41 1 This song is sung by the clown in "Twelfth Night," Act II, scene iv. — 2 [**cypres** or cyprus: used by the old writers for *crape*: whether from the French *crespe* or from the island whence it was imported. Its accidental similarity in spelling to *cypress* has, here and in Milton's "Penseroso," probably confused readers.] The Cambridge Shakespeare, however, reads *cypress*, which spelling has been followed in the text. — 19 **immelodious**: unmelodious. — 20 [**ramage**: confused noise.] — 22 **wont**: was accustomed, or were accustomed, as it is parsed with *voice* or *sounds.* — 25 **be**: are. Compare the modern use three lines below.

42 2 **turtle**: turtle dove, poetically noted for its constancy. — 2 **still**: ever. — 3 This dirge is sung by Guiderius and Arviragus in "Cymbeline," Act IV, scene ii. The title, the name which the disguised Imogen assumed, means *Faithful.* — 16 **thunderstone**: thunderbolt. — 20 **Consign to thee**: be bound in a like compact with thee. — 21 This dirge is sung by Ariel, in "The Tempest," Act I, scene ii.

43 4 ["I never saw anything like this funeral dirge," says Charles Lamb, "except the ditty which reminds Ferdinand of his drowned father in "The Tempest." As that is of the water, watery; so this is of the earth, earthy. Both have that intenseness of feeling, which seems to resolve itself into the element which it contemplates."] — 8 **dole**: lament. — 14 This is the thirty-second of Shakespeare's sonnets. — 14 **well-contented**: the day of his death will bring him content, or will find him contented to die. — 17 **lover**: friend. — 20 **Reserve**: preserve. — 21 **height of happier men**: higher achievements of men more fortunately endowed. — 25 **equipage**: equipment.

44 1 This is the seventy-first of Shakespeare's sonnets. — 8 **woe**: Is this a noun or an adjective? — 15 This song is sung in "The Merchant of Venice," Act III, scene iii, while Bassanio is making his choice of the caskets. — 15 **Fancy**: love, as Palgrave's title shows.

45 1 [Paraphrased from an Italian madrigal

. . . Non so conoscer poi
Se voi le rose, o sian le rose in voi.]

— 24 **Whist**: be still.

46 14 **like of**: the *of* is superfluous. — 17 **Campaspé**: a beautiful captive whom Alexander the Great gave to the painter Apelles, who sings the song in Lyly's play, "Alexander and Campaspé." — 20 **doves, sparrows**: birds sacred to Venus. — 24 [**crystal**: fairness.]

47 7 **prune**: preen. — 16 [**Stare**: starling.] — 21 [This "Spousal Verse" was written in honor of the Ladies Elizabeth and Katherine Somerset. Nowhere has Spenser more emphatically displayed himself as the very poet of beauty; the Renaissance impulse in England is here seen at its highest and purest. The genius of Spenser, like Chaucer's, does itself justice only in poems of some length. Hence it is impossible to represent it in this volume by other pieces of equal merit, but of impracticable dimensions. And the same applies to such poems as the "Lover's Lament" or the "Ancient Mariner."] — 23 **lightly did delay**: gently or easily mitigated.

48 3 **rutty**: Hales takes this as equivalent to *rooty*, hence *flower-producing*. This is pretty, but Fowler seems right in suggesting that it means "seamed with tracks of streams," which is an elegant expression for "full of ruts." — 4 **variable**: various. — 6 **bowers**: private apartments. — 7 **paramours**: lovers. — 8 **Against**: in anticipation of. — 8 **long**: far off. — 12 **thereby**: at hand. — 14 **As**: as if. — 16 [**entrailèd**: twisted.] — 17 **flasket**: little flask, or vase to hold flowers. — 18 [**feateously**: elegantly.] — 24 **vermeil**: vermilion. — 25 **posies**: bouquets. — 29 **Lee**: a river that flows into the Thames, near Greenwich. — 31 **Pindus**: a mountain in Thessaly. — 34 **Leda**: see a classical dictionary.

49 12 **Eftsoons**: soon afterwards. — 13 **all**: modifies *in haste*. — 17 **Them seem'd**: it seemed to them.

50 21 **virtue**: power. — 22 **love's dislike**: dislike of love. — 23 **assoil**: remove. — 24 **accord**: bring together in harmony. — 33 They sang the burden or refrain in tune with her.

51 10 [**shend**: shame.] — 19 Spenser thought that he was related to the Spencers of Althorpe, Northamptonshire (Fowler). — 21 **whereas**: where. — 24 **whilom**: formerly. The buildings here referred to were on the south side of Fleet Street. At the suppression of the Knights Templars in 1313 the property passed to the Crown, thence to the Earl of Pembroke, thence to the Knights of St. John, and thence, in 1346, by lease to the students of the common law. It has ever since been the site of a school of law, at least that portion of it known as the Inner and the Middle Temple, which was granted to the benchers by James I in 1609. Compare Baedeker's "London," 1905, p. 183.—28 **great lord**: the Earl of Leicester.—29 **want**: the object of *feels*.—34 [**a noble peer**: Robert Devereux, second Lord Essex, then at the height of his brief triumph after taking Cadiz: hence the allusion following to the Pillars of Hercules, placed near Gades by ancient legend] and marking the western limit of his wanderings.

52 6 **thy**: caused by thee.—11 [**Elisa**: Elizabeth.]—13 **Muse**: poet. Compare p. 74, l. 5.—18 **Hesper**: the evening star.—27 [**twins of Jove**: the stars Castor and Pollux.]—28 [**baldric**: belt; the zodiac.]—31 **tide**: time.

53 6 **numbers**: coins.

54 1 **dispossest**: deprived of activity, "put out of commission."—17 This is the one hundred and forty-sixth of Shakespeare's sonnets.—17 **earth**: body. The text here is corrupt. The quartos, in modernized spelling, read "My sinful earth those rebel powers that thee array." Various attempts have been made to emend, including the substitution of phrases like "Foil'd by," "Starv'd by," etc. for the repeated words, and the omission of the words "that thee." Compare Beeching, pp. 128–129. *Array* may mean *beleaguer* or *afflict*, with a play on the sense of *adorn*. The whole passage is obscure, partly on account of an apparent change in the metaphor—the house is first an assailed castle and then a decaying mansion—and partly on account of the suddenness with which the metaphor is dropped and then taken up again.—21 **cost**: expensive outlay. —26 **aggravate**: increase.

55 1 **terms**: periods. The word is probably suggested by the idea that instead of having an earthly estate for a term of years, the soul can secure a heavenly estate forever.—3 "By withdrawing food from what dies and so diminishing the diet of death, we are said to 'feed on death'" (Beeching).—5 [This lyric may with very high probability be assigned to Campion, in whose first Book of Airs it appeared (1601). The evidence sometimes quoted ascribing it to Lord Bacon appears to be valueless.] Compare Horace, Odes, Book I, ode xxii, "Integer vitae."

56 8 **period of**: limit to.—22 **Ply**: make their toilsome way.

57 1 This is the sixty-sixth of Shakespeare's sonnets.—3 **trimm'd**: adorned.—4 **forsworn**: renounced.—8 **disabled**: pronounce as four syllables. Fowler takes the word as equivalent to *undervalued*, which may be right.—11 **simplicity**: silliness.—15 **he**: he who.—16 **unhaunted**: not the haunt of men.—20 **hip**: the fruit of the rosebush.—20 **haws**: sloes (perhaps).—21 **still**: ever.

59 6 That he should remit the penalty of spiritual death imposed on us for our sins.

60 3 **wont**: was accustomed. — 4 **the midst of**: in the midst of. — 8 **vein**: mood. — 17 **prevent**: anticipate. — 18 **lowly**: in lowly wise. — 21 **secret**: withdrawn from the common gaze. — 23 **While**: at the time when. The present *lies* goes more naturally with *while*, and also serves to lend vividness to the passage. — 26 **doff'd her gaudy trim**: This may mean, as Mr. Bell explains, *put off her holiday attire* (gaudy-day, a festival); but it seems more likely that Milton meant that nature was no longer showily attired as in summer, when she plays with her lover (paramour, l. 29) the sun.

61 2 **Pollute**: polluted. — 6 **cease**: cause to cease. — 9 **sphere**: the poet is using the Ptolemaic system of astronomy, in which the earth was regarded as the center of a system of heavenly spheres. — 11 **turtle**: like that of a dove, the bird of constancy and meekness. — 20 **awful**: full of awe or fear. — 21 **sovran**: Milton's usual spelling of *sovereign*. — 25 [**whist**: **hushed.**] — 29 **birds of calm**: halcyons. See a classical dictionary under *Alcyone*. — 32 **influence**: used in its astrological sense.

62 2 **Lucifer**: the morning star. — 3 **orbs**: orbits (probably). — 4 **bespake**: Compare "Lycidas," p. 76, l. 28. — 9 **As**: as if. — 14 **Or ere**: before. — 15 **simply**: innocently. — 16 [**than**: obsolete for *then*.] — 17 [**Pan**: used here for the Lord of all.] Christ is regarded as the true Pan, the god of all things, the old Pan of the Greek mythology having died at the time of the Crucifixion, according to a well-known legend. — 20 **silly**: innocent. — 28 **close**: final cadence. — 31 **Cynthia's**: the moon's. The passage is obscure, but if we conceive the poet to have imagined the moon as riding upon a throne through the heavens, and place commas after *sound* and *seat*, we may suppose that the sound thrills the space between the moon and the earth.

63 1 **alone**: by itself, without her assistance. — 8 **display'd**: outspread. — 10 **unexpressive**: inexpressible. — 26 [**consort**: Milton's spelling of this word, here and elsewhere, has been followed, as it is uncertain whether he used it in the sense of *accompanying*, or simply for *concert*.]

64 3 **like**: similar. — 15 **ychain'd**: chained. *y* is what remains of the original *ge* prefixed to the past participle. — 17–19 The comparison is made with the phenomena that accompanied the giving of the tables of the law to Moses. Compare Exodus xix. — 23 **last sessión**: Last Judgment. — 25–32 After the judgment there will be no more earthly life with its ills; the bliss of the Christian will be perfect. This bliss has now begun with the nativity of the Saviour and the greater restraint put upon Satan. — 32 **Swinges**: swings to and fro.

65 5 **divine**: utter prophecies. — 6 **Delphos**: Delphi, the seat of the chief temple of Apollo. — 9 **o'er**: overhead (probably). — 14 **parting**: departing. — 14 **Genius**: spirit presiding over spring or dale. — 19 [**Lars and Lemurés**: household gods and spirits of dead relations.] — 22 [**Flamens**: Roman priests.] — 24 **peculiar**: special. — 25 **Peor and Baalim**: Phœnician deities. — 27 [**that twice-batter'd god**: Dagon.] Compare 1 Samuel v, 3, where allusion is made to Dagon's twice falling before the ark of God (Bell). — 28 **Ashtaroth**: Astarte, goddess of the moon, a Semitic divinity. — 31 **Lybic Hammon**: the Ethiopian deity Ammon, identified by the Greeks with their Zeus. — 31 **shrinks**: draws in through fear. The god was represented as having horns like those of a ram. — 32 **Thammuz**: Adonis. — 33 **Moloch**: the god of the Ammonites, to whom frightful human sacrifices were made.

66 6 **Isis**: mother of Horus (Orus), a goddess of the earth, identified by the Greeks with Demeter. — 6 **Anubis**: brother of Horus. — 7 [**Osiris**: the Egyptian god of agriculture (here, perhaps by confusion with Apis, figured as a bull), who was torn to pieces by Typho and embalmed after death in a sacred chest. This myth, reproduced in Syria or Greece in the legends of Thammuz, Adonis, and perhaps Absyrtus, may have originally signified the annual death of the Sun or the Year under the influences of the winter darkness. Horus, the son of Osiris, as the New Year, in his turn overcomes Typho.] — 8 **Memphian**: from Memphis, the famous Egyptian city. — 9 [**unshower'd grass**: as watered by the Nile only.] — 13 **timbrel'd**: The timbrel was an ancient musical instrument resembling a tambourine. — 13 **dark**: obscure, unintelligible (probably). — 14 **sable-stoléd**: wearing black stoles. Whether Milton used *stole* here in the sense of robe, or hood, or ecclesiastical scarf, is hard to determine. — 17 **eyn**: an old plural of eye. — 18 **the gods beside**: the other gods. — 20 **Typhon**: brother of Osiris (compare note **66** 7), sometimes represented as a crocodile. — 23–25 A good example of the far-fetched or inappropriate figures of speech — "conceits" — that often marred the poetry of this period. — 25 **orient**: bright, or eastern. — 28 **several**: separate. — 29 **fays**: fairies. — 30 **maze**: intricate dance.

67 1 [**youngest-teeméd**: last born.] — 4 **courtly**: the stable with its kingly occupants suggests a court. — 5 [**Bright-harness'd**: armored.] — 6–20 This is a poetical statement of the main idea of the Pythagorean philosophy. See some encyclopedia. — 20 **diapason**: the octave in Greek music. — 21 **passion**: emotion. — 22 **Jubal**: see Genesis iv, 21. — 22 **chorded shell**: The tradition was that the first stringed instrument was made by stretching cords over a tortoise shell. — 26 **Less**: anything less. It is the subject of the infinitive *dwell*.

68 2 **mortal alarms**: alarums, incitements to deadly conflicts. — 8 **discovers**: makes known. — 12 **Their**: the lovers'. — 22 **Orpheus**: the fabulous Greek musician. See a classical dictionary. — 24 **Sequacious of**: following. — 25 **Cecilia**: St. Cecilia, the patron saint of music, was a noble Roman lady who lived in the fourth century, and suffered martyrdom for her Christian faith. Her festival occurs on November 22.

69 5 [**The Late Massacre**: the Vaudois persecution, carried on in 1655 by the Duke of Savoy. No more mighty sonnet than this "collect in verse," as it has been justly named, probably can be found in any language. Readers should observe that it is constructed on the original Italian or Provençal model. This form, in a language such as ours, not affluent in rime, presents great difficulties; the rimes are apt to be forced, or the substance commonplace. But, when successfully handled, it has a unity and a beauty of effect which place the strict sonnet above the less compact and less lyrical systems adopted by Shakespeare, Sidney, Spenser, and other Elizabethan poets.] It should be added that here and in some other sonnets Milton omitted the full stop which comes regularly at the eighth line of the Petrarchan sonnet, and which divides that form into two parts known as the octave and the sestet. The result of this omission of the pause is the imparting to the sonnet of a sonorous unity which harmonizes with the poet's mood, and justifies Wordsworth's famous lines to the effect that in Milton's hands the sonnet became a trumpet. — 13 **redoubled**: reëchoed. — 16 **The triple Tyrant**: the Pope, so called because he controlled the Church and wore a triple crown or tiara. — 18 **the Babylonian woe**: the Church of Rome, regarded as idolatrous by the Puritans. — 19 [Cromwell returned from Ireland in 1650, and Marvell probably wrote his lines soon after, whilst living at Nunappleton in the Fairfax household. It is hence not surprising that (stanzas 21–24) he should have been deceived by Cromwell's professed submissiveness to the Parliament which, when it declined to register his decrees, he expelled by armed violence: one despotism, by natural law, replacing another. The poet's insight has, however, truly prophesied that result in his last two lines. This ode, beyond doubt one of the finest in our language, and more in Milton's style than has been reached by any other poet, is occasionally obscure from imitation of the condensed Latin syntax. The meaning of stanza 5 is "rivalry or hostility are the same to a lofty spirit, and limitation more hateful than opposition." The allusion in stanza 11 is to the old physical doctrines of the nonexistence of a vacuum and the impenetrability of matter; in stanza 17 to the omen traditionally connected with the foundation of the Capitol at Rome, — *forced*, fated. The ancient belief that certain years in life complete natural periods and are hence peculiarly exposed to death is introduced in stanza 26 by the word *climacteric*]; that is, *dangerous*. This ode, which approximates the felicity and dignity of the odes of Horace at their highest excellence, is in all probability the work of Marvell, but the external evidence of his authorship is weaker than one likes to have it. See Birrell's "Andrew Marvell," pp. 63–66. — 19 **appear**: appear distinguished. The word *forward* is not used, of course, in its unpleasant sense. It means *aspiring*.

70 1 **cease**: linger. — 4 **star**: of destiny, that is, his genius. — 7 **thorough**: through. — 23 **his highest plot**: his chief concern were. — 24 **bergamot**: a sort of pea.

71 7 **Hampton:** Hampton Court, where Charles was for a time a prisoner, where he cherished vain hopes of final success, and whence he escaped only to be soon imprisoned in Carisbrook Castle. See below, l. 12. — 26 **forcéd power:** the power of the Commonwealth acquired by force. In his note above on this poem Palgrave took *forcéd* as equivalent to *fated*. — 28 **The Capitol:** "The Capitol or Temple of Jupiter at Rome is said to have been so called because in digging its foundations a human head was found in a fresh condition. This was at once accepted as an omen that Rome should be the *head* of the world (Latin *caput*, 'head')" (Bell).

72 10 Loyal in his service to the Commonwealth. — 14 **A Kingdom:** Ireland. — 15 **what:** as far as. — 32 **climacteric:** dangerous.

73 1 **The Pict:** the Scots. — 2 Scotland was believed by the supporters of the Commonwealth to have acted treacherously in rising for Charles I in 1648, and in supporting his son, Charles II. — 3 **valor sad:** rendered sad by Cromwell's valor. — 6 **mistake:** fail to find. — 11 Perhaps this line is equivalent to "and as the ultimate arbiter." — 14 A poetical way of referring to the treasonable attempts that might be expected against the Commonwealth.—17 [**Lycidas:** The person here lamented is Milton's college contemporary, Edward King, drowned in 1637 whilst crossing from Chester to Ireland.] The poem was contributed by Milton to a volume of elegies in King's memory published in 1638. [Strict pastoral poetry was first written or perfected by the Dorian Greeks settled in Sicily, but the conventional use of it, exhibited more magnificently in "Lycidas" than in any other pastoral, is apparently of Roman origin. Milton, employing the noble freedom of a great artist, has here united ancient mythology, with what may be called the modern mythology of Camus and St. Peter, to direct Christian images. Yet the poem, if it gains in historical interest, suffers in poetry by the harsh intrusion of the writer's narrow and violent theological politics.] On this point opinions differ. See note to **77** 11 below. [The metrical structure of this glorious elegy is partly derived from Italian models.] — 17–24 The poet, having written little of late and feeling himself not yet ripe for great poetry, will nevertheless lament his lost friend. — 21 **Shatter:** scatter. — 22 **dear:** intimate. — 23 **disturb your season due:** pluck you prematurely. — 29 **welter:** roll about. — 30 Without the tribute of some melodious poem that brings tears to the eyes.

74 1 [**Sisters of the sacred well:** the Muses, said to frequent the Pierian spring at the foot of Mount Olympus.] — 5 **Muse:** poet. — 11–22 A description in pastoral terms of the life led by Milton and King at Cambridge. — 14 **What time the gray-fly winds:** the trumpet fly when she winds. — 15 **Battening:** fattening. — 19 **oaten:** made of reeds (straw). — 20 **Satyrs, Fauns:** Cambridge students. See a classical dictionary. — 22 **Damœtas:** some Cambridge teacher. — 23, 24 Notice the repeated phrase. — 24 **must**: expresses certainty, not necessity. — 26 **gadding**: straggling. — 28 **copses**: woods filled with undergrowth. — 31 **canker**: cankerworm. — 32 **taintworm**: generally, but doubtfully, explained as a small red spider. — 34 **whitethorn blows**: hawthorn blossoms.

75 5 [**Mona**: Anglesey, called by the Welsh poets the Dark Island, from its dense forests.] — 6 [**Deva**: the Dee; a river which may have derived its magical character from Celtic traditions; it was long the boundary of Briton and English. These places are introduced as being near the scene of the shipwreck.] — 9 **the Muse**: Calliope, the muse of epic poetry, was the mother of Orpheus. — 9 [**Orpheus**: was torn to pieces by Thracian women.] — 12 **rout**: wild crowd. — 14 **Hebrus**: a Thracian river said not to be *swift*. The legend ran that the head of Orpheus, thrown into the river by angry Bacchanals, was floated to the island of Lesbos and there buried. For this pious act the Lesbians were made preëminent in song, the compatriots of Sappho. — 15 **boots it**: profits it. — 15 **uncessant**: incessant. — 16 **shepherd's trade**: not the scholar's profession, as might be supposed here, but the poet's. — 17 **meditate**: apply one's self to. — 18 **use**: are accustomed to do. — 19 [**Amaryllis**, 20 **Neæra**: names used here for the love idols of poets: as *Damoetas* previously for a shepherd.] — 21 **clear**: noble. — 21 **spirit**: object of *raise*. — 22 This line is in apposition to *Fame*. — 24 **guerdon**: reward. — 26 [**the blind Fury**: Atropos, fabled to cut the thread of life.] — 28 **touch'd . . . ears**: Masson says that we have here "a fine poetical appreciation of the popular superstition that the tingling of a person's ears is a sign that people are talking of him." It seems more likely that touching the ear is a symbolic act intended to impress the memory, and that Milton trembles because he is in the presence of the God of Song. — 30 **glistering foil**: glittering show. *Foil* is literally a thin sheet or leaf of metal put under a jewel to set off its luster. The figurative language is mixed, but the general meaning is clear. — 32 **by**: by means of (probably). — 33 **witness**: judgment (perhaps).

76 1 [**Arethuse**, 2 **Mincius**: Sicilian and Italian waters here alluded to as representing the pastoral poetry of Theocritus and Vergil.] — 4 [**oat**: pipe, used here like Collins's *oaten stop*, p. 184, l. 13, for *song*.] — 5 **herald of the sea**: Triton. — 6 **plea**: defense, that is, to present a plea for Neptune. — 12 [**Hippotadés**: Æolus, god of the winds.] — 13 **his**: This may refer to *Hippotadés* or to *blast*. If to the latter, it means *its*. — 15 [**Panopé**: a Nereid. Certain names of local deities in the Hellenic mythology render some feature in the landscape, which the Greeks studied and analyzed with their usual unequaled insight and feeling. *Panope* seems to express the boundlessness of the ocean horizon when seen from a height, as compared with the limited sky line of the land in hilly countries such as Greece or Asia Minor.] — 19 [**Camus**:

the Cam, put for King's university.] — 19 **went footing slow**: wended his way slowly, approached with deliberate pace. — 22 [**that sanguine flower**: the Hyacinth of the ancients, probably our Iris.] — 23 **reft**: taken away. — 25 [**The Pilot**: Saint Peter, probably introduced as head of the Church on earth, to foretell "the ruin of our corrupted clergy," as Milton regarded them, "then in their heighth" under Laud's primacy.] — 27 **amain**: with force. — 28 **mitered**: crowned with a bishop's miter. — 28 **stern bespake**: spoke out sternly. — 30 **Enow**: a considerable number; it is an old plural of *enough*. — 35 **mouths**: gluttons — conscienceless clergy eager only for earthly gain and ease.

77 3 **recks it them**: do they care. — 3 **are sped**: have gained what they wanted. — 4 **list**: please. — 4 **flashy**: insipid. — 5 [**scrannel**: screeching; apparently Milton's coinage (Masson).] — 9 [**wolf**: the Puritans of the time were excited to alarm and persecution by a few conversions to Roman Catholicism which had recently occurred.] — 11, 12 No one knows surely what this instrument of vengeance is. It is more important to remark that in this indignant speech of Saint Peter, which is often condemned by critics as being too harsh to suit the tender mood in which elegies are usually written, we probably have the central passage, the core of the poem. Milton seems not to have known King specially well, but there is every reason to believe that he did know that King was a very promising young clergyman, whose loss could be ill afforded by the Church at that time. This knowledge was sufficient to inspire him with that sincere regret which must underlie the true elegy, and it was, moreover, sufficient to rouse him to a burst of indignant scorn which lifts the elegy out of the region of mild pastoral into that of the passionate ode, the loftiest form of lyric poetry. That he fuses rather than mixes mechanically the elements of elegy, pastoral, and ode into an artistic whole, may be inferred from the fact that "Lycidas" has seemed to exigent critics and poets like Lord Tennyson one of the most consummate achievements of English poetry. The poem is conventional, as befitted a contribution to an academic volume; it is also sincere and noble, because Milton, looking beyond the fate of an individual to the perilous state of the Church, treated his theme in a large and lofty manner. — 13 [**Alphéus**: a stream in southern Greece, supposed to flow underseas to join the Arethuse.] — 17 **use**: have their abodes. — 19 [**swart star**: Dog Star, called swarthy because its heliacal rising in ancient times occurred soon after midsummer.] — 20 **eyes**: blossoms. — 22 **purple**: probably an imperative — give color to; but as Palgrave does not put a comma after *showers*, the word must, as the text stands, be considered an indicative. — 23 [**rathe**: early.] — 24 **crowtoe**: crowfoot. — 27 **well-attired**: with a beautiful headdress. — 30 **amaranthus**: Greek for *unfading*. — 32 **laureat hearse**: The best explanation is that which refers to the custom of attaching laudatory verses to the hearse, a platform hung with black and containing an effigy of the deceased. Some think that *laureate* is used because King was a poet, or else because he had taken a degree.

78 2 **Hebrides:** the Western Isles, along the west coast of Scotland. — 5 [**moist vows:** either tearful prayers, or prayers for one at sea.] — 6 [**Bellerus:** a giant, apparently created by Milton to personify Belerium, the ancient title of the Land's End.] — 7 [**great Vision:** the story was that the Archangel Michael had appeared on the rock by Marazion in Mount's Bay which bears his name. Milton calls on him to turn his eyes from the south homeward, and to pity Lycidas, if his body has drifted into the troubled waters off the Land's End.] Some editors, however, hold that Lycidas himself is the person addressed. [Finisterre being the land due south of Marazion, two places in that district (then through our trade with Corunna probably less unfamiliar to English ears) are named. — 8 **Namancos:** now Mujio in Galicia. — 8 **Bayona:** north of the Minho, or perhaps a fortified rock (one of the *Cies* Islands) not unlike Saint Michael's Mount, at the entrance of Vigo Bay.] — 8 **hold:** castle. — 10 **dolphins:** an allusion to the saving, by these fish, of the Greek poet Arion. See a classical dictionary. — 12 **your sorrow:** the cause of your sorrow. — 14 **day star:** the sun. — 16 **tricks:** displays. — 16 [**ore:** rays of golden light.] — 22 **unexpressive:** inexpressible. — 29 **Genius:** The ancients fancied that a drowned person might become a guardian spirit at the spot where he met his fate, and warn others from the threatened doom. — 30 **thy:** to thee. — 32 **uncouth:** unknown (probably). — 35 **Doric lay:** Sicilian pastoral.

79 1 The shadows of the hills had lengthened as the sun declined. — 9 **had:** who had. — 17 **birth:** Apparently this means *high birth*, but why the bones of the great should use "they" instead of "we" in the next verse, is hard to see. — 22 **once dead by fate:** Mr. W. Bell explains *once* as equivalent to *once for all;* yet might it not mean *when once?*

80 8 **quaint:** fine, exquisite. — 11 **blood:** lineage. — 29 **purple:** blood-stained (probably).

81 5 [*The assault* was an attack on London expected in] the autumn of [1642, when the troops of Charles I reached Brentford. "Written on his door" was the original title of this sonnet. Milton was then living in Aldersgate Street.] — 5 **Colonel:** three syllables. — 6 **Whose chance:** whose lot it may be to, who by chance. — 9 **charms:** magical rites or verses, incantations. — 13 **bower:** house. — 14 [**Emathian conqueror:** When Thebes was destroyed (B.C. 335) and the citizens massacred by thousands, Alexander ordered the house of Pindar to be spared.] Emathia was a province of Macedonia. Pindar (B.C. 522–443) was a great lyric poet. — 16, 17 [**the repeated air Of sad Electra's poet:** Plutarch has a tale that when the Spartan confederacy in 404 B.C. took Athens, a proposal to demolish it was rejected through the effect produced on the commanders by hearing part of a chorus from the *Electra* of Euripides] B.C. 480–406 [sung at a feast. There is, however, no apparent congruity between the lines quoted (167, 168, edition Dindorf) and the result ascribed to them.] Readers of Browning will recall his poem "Balaustion's Adventure." — 20 **Ere half my days**: Milton was blind at middle age, by the time he was forty-four. — 21 For the parable in Milton's mind see Matthew xxv. The *one talent* is Milton's ability, of which he has long been conscious, — to write a great poem which the world would not willingly let die. If *to hide* preceded *which*, the construction would be plainer. — 24 **returning**: in return. — 26 **fondly**: foolishly.

82 2 **gifts**: to man. — 4 **thousands**: of angels, of heavenly ministers. — 7 [A fine example of a peculiar class of poetry, — that written by thoughtful men who practiced this art but little. Jeremy Taylor, Bishop Berkeley, Dr. Johnson, Lord Macaulay, have left similar specimens.] — 12 **still**: always. — 14 **private breath**: current opinion expressed by individuals — in its worst form, gossip. — 18 **Nor**: supply some such word as *follows*. — 21 **state**: possessions, way of living. — 22 **Nor**: The construction is mixed. We may simplify it as follows: Whose state, on the one hand, cannot feed flatterers, nor his ruin, on the other, make oppressors great. — 25 **entertains**: beguiles. — 27 **bands**: bonds.

83 3 These lines are taken from the long pindaric ode "To the Immortal Memory and Friendship of that Noble Pair, Sir Lucius Cary and Sir Henry Morison," to be found in the collection of miscellaneous verses called by Jonson "Underwoods." — 13 Herbert himself gave this poem the quaint name of "The Pulley." — 20 **stay**: pause.

84 6 [These beautiful verses should be compared with Wordsworth's great ode on Immortality] see p. 370, l. 18; [and a copy of Vaughan's very rare little volume] "Silex Scintillans," 1650 [appears in the list of Wordsworth's library. In imaginative intensity Vaughan stands beside his contemporary Marvell.] — 10 **fancy**: conceive, or exercise its powers in. — 13 **Love**: God. — 23 **several**: separate. — 31 heaven, paradise.

85 6 **In**: It is difficult to say whether this means *in* or *into*, and on our answer will depend the phrase we insert after *state* in order to make the meaning clear. There seems to be little doubt that *state* means the innocence of infancy. — 7 This sonnet, written when Milton was about forty-seven years of age, was addressed to a son of an important member of Cromwell's government. — 10 **Help waste**: help each other to spend in a sociable way time that hangs heavy on our hands. — 12 [**Favonius**: the spring wind.] — 14 Compare Matthew vi, 28. — 15 **neat**: attractive in its setting. — 16 **Attic**: refined as were the better classes of the Athenians. — 17 **artful**: trained according to the rules of musical art. — 18 **Tuscan**: Here Tuscany, of which Florence is the chief city, is used to represent the whole of Italy. — 19 **spare**: refrain from making an inordinate use of them. — 21 A companion sonnet to the one preceding, addressed to the grandson of the famous lawyer, Sir Edward Coke (1552–1634), who is referred to in the first four lines. — 22 [**Themis**: the goddess of justice. Skinner was grandson by his mother to Sir Edward Coke; hence, as pointed out by Mr. Keightley, Milton's allusion to the *bench*.] — 23 **volumes**: for example, the famous *Coke upon Littleton*, that is, "Commentaries on Littleton," etc. — 25 **resolve**: an imperative. *Thoughts* is the object of *drench*. — 26 **after**: afterwards, or after it.

86 1 Do not occupy yourself with problems of mathematics and physics. Euclid was the great Alexandrian geometer who flourished about 300 B.C. Archimedes, who flourished half a century later, was a great mathematician and physicist of Syracuse. — 2 **Swede**: plural. [Sweden was then at war with Poland, and France with the Spanish Netherlands.] — 4 The involved syntax of this line is very characteristic of Milton, but a little thought resolves its difficulties. — 8 **refrains**: neglects to use it. In connection with each of these sonnets two points should be remembered. They show that Milton was not altogether austere, that he possessed that crowning grace of middle and old age, the sympathetic charm of a rounded personality that comprehends and appeals to youth. They throw light also both on Milton's tastes and, probably, on a curious personal idiosyncrasy, his apparent inability to work steadily and copiously during the colder part of the year. It is at least certain that a few years after the date of these sonnets this inability affected him in the composition of "Paradise Lost." — 13 **scaly nation**: a periphrastic way of saying *fishes*. — 19 **Tritons**: attendants of Neptune, who had by Amphitrite a son Triton, trumpeter to his father. — 24 **Sirens**: see a classical dictionary and consult the Odyssey. — 27 **noise**: In the older poets this word is frequently employed of sounds that have no disagreeable character. — 28 **empery**: imperial rule.

87 1 This song is from "Cynthia's Revels," Act V, scene iii. — 5 **Hesperus**: the evening star, who is the singer of this song. — 11 **wishéd**: wished for. — 19 Palgrave condensed this poem by about one half. — 24 That is, in the obscure book of fate. — 27 **tread**: to tread.

88 7 **her**: for her. — 8 **duty**: the homage paid to it. — 9 **tire**: head-dress. — 11 **Taffeta**: a thin stuff, partly of silk. — 11 **tissue**: cloth interwoven with gold or silver. — 11 **can**: know how to make up (perhaps). — 15 **alone**: by itself. — 19 [**Sidneian showers**: either in allusion to the conversations in the "Arcadia," or to Sidney himself as a model of "gentleness" in spirit and demeanor.] — 24 **give down to**: render sleep-giving. — 28–30 Days that can salute us in a pleasant manner, free from the effects of any previous night wasted in suffering.

89 5 **his**: its. — 5 **end**: death. — 6 **say**: dependent on *dares*. — 8 **may**: which may. — 8, 9 **poor Of wishes**: with nothing left to wish for. — 12 **them**: for themselves. — 21 **determine them to**: give them the form of. — 24 **her story**: be true in her.

90 1 Under the ocean. — 10 **fast**: tight. — 14 **for**: with respect to. — 21 **lose**: get rid of. — 29, 30 This is used as an impossibility which is nevertheless not so impossible as to control love. The eagle cannot be trained like a hawk for the purposes of hunting. — 30 **stoop**: to pounce or swoop down on. — 30 **to your fist**: since it is used with *stoop*, the object of which is the prey, this probably means "at a signal given by your hand."

91 4 [Delicate humor, delightfully united to thought, at once simple and subtle. It is full of conceit and paradox, but these are imaginative, not as with most of our seventeenth-century poets, intellectual only.] — 17 **ensigns**: banners, flags. — 19 **virtuous**: There seems to be no means of determining whether Marvell uses this epithet in the sense of *powerful*, or whether he means rather *chaste* and *pure*. — 29 Enchants itself at thy beauty.

92 12 Treat you as you have treated them. — 15 Mr. W. Bell notes that Palgrave follows the version of this song given in Allan Ramsay's "Tea Table Miscellany," 1724. The song appeared originally in Sedley's comedy "The Mulberry Garden," 1668.

93 3 **Still**: even. With this song should be read Marvell's "Young Love" and Prior's inimitable "To a Child of Quality Five Years Old," neither of which is given by Palgrave.

94 11 **having lost but**: only having lost. — 25 [**Elizabeth of Bohemia**: daughter to James I, and ancestor of Sophia of Hanover. These lines are a fine specimen of gallant and courtly compliment.]

95 7 **Philomel**: The nightingale. See a classical dictionary, under *Philomela*. — 18 [Lady M. Ley was daughter to Sir J. Ley, afterwards Earl of Marlborough, who died March, 1629, coincidently with the dissolution of the third parliament of Charles's reign. Hence Milton poetically compares his death to that of the orator Isocrates of Athens, after Philip's victory in 328 B.C.] This sonnet was published in Milton's earliest collection of poems, 1645; it is therefore dated ten or more years earlier than the sonnet tributes to friends already given. — 21 Supply after *content* some such phrase as "than he had been with political honors heaped upon him." — 22 The idea is that from the dissolution of this parliament dated the arbitrary conduct of the king that led to the Civil War. — 26 **later born**: Milton was a very young man when the earl died.

96 2 Notice the irregular position of *both*. — 4 For some inscrutable reason Carew, the most perfect master of courtly compliment in verse, is represented in the "Golden Treasury" by only this lovely poem. Students should turn to the more adequate selections from his work given in the second volume of Ward's "English Poets," or to the edition of his poems in the "Muses Library." Perhaps his masterpiece is the famous "Ask me no more where Jove bestows." — 22 **Whenas**: since, in view of the fact that.

97 10 **borrow**: take away. — 16 **resemble**: compare.

98 6 "From the (prose) love letters of Philostratus the younger (about 250 A.D.)" (note in Ward's "English Poets"). The song appeared in 1616 in Jonson's collection "The Forest." — 13 **change**: exchange.

99 4 **orient**: bright. — 5 **Which when**: and when them (object of shows). — 9 **still**: always. — 15 [A masterpiece of humor, grace, and gentle feeling, all, with Herrick's unfailing art, kept precisely within the peculiar field which he chose — or Nature chose for him — in his Pastorals.] — 16 [**the god unshorn**: Imberbis Apollo] the sun. — 18 **Fresh-quilted**: freshly-stitched, combined. — 27 **Whenas**: since, seeing that.

100 6 **Against you come**: in anticipation of your coming. — 6 **orient**: bright. — 8 **dew-locks**: dewy locks. — 9 **Titan**: the sun. — 12 [**beads**: prayers.] — 13–26 "On the calands or first of May, commonly called May-day, the juvenile part of both sexes were wont to rise a little after midnight and walk to some neighboring wood, accompanied with music and blowing of horns, where they brake down branches from the trees and adorn them with nosegays and crowns of flowers; when this is done, they return with their booty homewards about the rising of the sun, and make their doors and windows to triumph with their flowery spoils; and the after part of the day is chiefly spent in dancing round a tall poll, which is called a may-poll" (quoted in Strutt, "Sports and Pastimes of the People of England"). — 18 **tabernacle**: a tent, a transient shelter. In Jewish history, the portable sanctuary of the race in its wanderings. Compare Exodus xxv–xxvii and xxxvi–xxxviii, and in particular Leviticus xxiii, 40–43. — 32 **left to**: ceased to.

101 1 **green-gown**: "a romp in the new-mown hay or on the grass" (W. Bell). — 8 **take**: take advantage of. This last stanza marks Herrick's highest flight into the heaven of poetry, but it is essentially a pagan stanza. — 22 **Kindles**: excites, calls out, produces. See the Century Dictionary. — 24 With charming negligence. — 24 **distractión**: four syllables, as often in the older poets, especially the dramatists. — 25 **erring**: wandering, stray. — 27 **neglectful**: not looked after. — 27 **thereby**: by its side.

102 3 **wild civility**: a spontaneous touch of the sort of grace that is usually associated with studied fashion. It is the figure of speech known as *oxymoron*, the joining of words of more or less opposite meaning. — 6 **Whenas**: when. — 8 The poet is alluding to the flow and the shimmering of the silk dress. — 10 **brave**: fine. — 12 **wit**: intelligence. — 16 **miss**: want, lack.

103 4 **pale**: inclosure. — 11 [With better taste, and less diffusiveness, Quarles might (one would think) have retained more of that high place which he held in popular estimate among his contemporaries.] — 18 **entire**: one whole. — 27 **counter to**: imitation coin as compared with.

104 2 **Protestant**: Perhaps this means champion, but, as Professor Saintsbury suggests, it is better to leave the meaning somewhat indefinite. It is a fine, mouth-filling word.

105 4, 5 **still**: does this word mean the same thing in both verses? And note the meanings of *so* in lines 2 and 5. — 13 **face I only**: face alone I. — 19 **further store**: that is, for more sweethearts. — 23 [**From Prison**: to which his active support of Charles I twice brought the high-spirited writer.]

106 1 [**Gods**: thus in the original; Lovelace, in his fanciful way, making here a mythological allusion. *Birds*, commonly substituted, is without authority.] — 1 **wanton**: sport. — 4 Undiluted with water of the river. — 5 **careless**: free from care. — 11 [**committed**: to prison.]

107 5 **'suage**: assuage. — 6 [**blue-god**: Neptune.] — 9 Supply *be* or *lie*. The student will do well to compare this poem with 109, and to note how the perfect simplicity and lack of effort discernible in the shorter piece have helped to make it much the better known. — 21 This famous song appeared in the drama "Aglaura," published in 1638. — 21 **fond**: foolish.

108 6 This song is taken from the third book of Cowley's epic "Davideis, a Sacred Poem of the Troubles of David." — 15 **awful**: full of awe, not awe-inspiring. — 16 **numerous**: musical. — 20 **virtue**: power (a frequent meaning of the word in the early poets).

109 12 **silly**: simple, innocent. — 12 **pined**: made to pine or suffer. — 17 **pelican**: This bird was supposed to allow its young to feed upon its own lifeblood. — 31 **outward helps**: apparently, social advantages possessed by the lover.

110 21 **mortifies**: chastens. — 26 **fowls**: birds. — 28 **parting**: of one departing, dying. — 30 **still gloomy**: ever gloomy.

111 1 [**Waly waly**: an exclamation of sorrow] pronounced wáw-ly [the root and the pronunciation of which are preserved in the word *caterwaul*.] — 2 [**brae**: hillside.] — 3 **burn**: brook. — 7 **syne**: after that. — 8 **lichtly**: make light of. — 13 [**busk**: adorn.] — 19 [**Saint Anton's well**: below Arthur's Seat by Edinburgh.] — 21 **Marti'mas**: Martinmas, the festival of St. Martin of France, formerly celebrated on November 11. — 25 **fell**: cruelly. — 27 **sic**: such.

112 2 [**cramasie**: crimson.] — 3 **wist**: known. — 5 **gowd**: gold. Compare *siller* (silver) in the next line. — 11 [These stanzas are by Richard Verstegan (*fl.* 1565–1620), a poet and antiquarian, published in his rare "Odes" (1601), under the title "Our Blessed Ladies Lullaby," and reprinted by Mr. Orby Shipley in his beautiful "Carmina Mariana" (1893). The four verses here given form the opening of a hymn of twenty-four.] These verses also appear in Martin Peerson's "Private Music," a songbook of 1620. — 14 **my sense her rest**: my emotions or sensations some repose.

113 1 **for**: in return for. — 5 Tradition says that the lovers were Adam Fleming and Helen Irving (or Bell), daughter of the Laird of Kirconnell. The rival suitor, starting up on the other side of the river Kirtle by which the lovers were walking, shot Helen in Adam's arms. — 11 [**burd**: maiden.] — 15 **meikle**: much.

114 10 **een**: eyes. — 17 **alane**: alone. — 18 [**corbies**: crows.] — 18 **mane**: moan. — 19 **The tane**: the one. — 21 [**fail**: turf.]

115 3 [**hause**: neck.] — 3 **bane**: bone. — 5 **ae**: one. — 5 **gowden**: golden. — 6 [**theek**: thatch. If not in their origin, in their present form this, with the preceding poem and 133, appear due to the seventeenth century, and have therefore been placed in Book II.] — 11 [The poetical and the prosaic, after Cowley's fashion, blend curiously in this deep-felt elegy.] — 19 **peer**: equal. — 24 **around**: To be construed with *besieged*.

116 6 **inform**: give life to. — 21 **spirits**: distillation.

118 5 **pledges**: children. — 7 **date**: span of life. — 7 **so past**: so far gone that you may not. — 19 **brave**: fine. — 20 **pride**: glory.

119 17 [Perhaps no poem in this collection is more delicately fancied, more exquisitely finished. By placing his description of the Fawn in a young girl's mouth, Marvell has, as it were, legitimated that abundance of "imaginative hyperbole" to which he is always partial: he makes us feel it natural that a maiden's favorite should be whiter than milk, sweeter than sugar — "lilies without, roses within." The poet's imagination is justified in its seeming extravagance by the intensity and unity with which it invests his picture.] Palgrave has given only about a third of this beautiful poem, which goes by the title of "The Nymph Complaining for the Death of her Fawn."

120 14 **laid**: lay. — 19 **still**: ever. — 25 [The remark quoted in the note to No. 65 applies equally to these truly wonderful verses. Marvell here throws himself into the very soul of the "Garden" with the imaginative intensity of Shelley in his "West Wind." This poem appears also as a translation in Marvell's works. The most striking verses in it, here quoted as the book is rare, answer more or less to stanzas 2 and 6:

> Alma Quies, teneo te! et te, germana Quietis,
> Simplicitas! vos ergo diu per templa, per urbes
> Quaesivi, regum perque alta palatia, frustra:
> Sed vos hortorum per opaca silentia, longe
> Celarunt plantae virides, et concolor umbra.]

— 25 **amaze**: perplex. — 26 The rewards of soldier, public-spirited citizen, and poet or scholar. — 27 **uncessant**: incessant. — 29 **narrow-vergéd**: brought into small compass.

121 9 **all but rude**: little short of barbarous. — 10 **To**: in comparison with. — 13 **Fond**: silly (perhaps). — 22 **Still**: always. — 23 **Daphne**: see a classical dictionary (also for Syrinx, line 25). — 31 **curious**: suiting a dainty taste.

122 1 **pleasure less:** a pleasure that is worthless (physical, sensuous pleasure). — 3 **kind:** nature, disposition, or perhaps, object. — 4 **straight:** straightway. — 7, 8 The poet, says Bell, in an ecstasy of imaginative delight, almost becomes one with the scene he contemplates. But is this a true interpretation of the mental state indicated by these not very clear lines in a not very clear but exquisitely beautiful stanza? The poet really seems to reduce the tangible world to nothingness in comparison with the ideal world which is the result of a "green thought in a green shade," that is, of his meditations in the garden. — 14 **whets:** prunes. — 20 **meet:** proper, fitting. — 21 **share:** of happiness. — 23, 24 A conceit, not specially worthy of Marvell, depending on a play upon two senses of the word "paradise." — 27 **milder:** comparatively mild. This construction is known as the absolute comparative.

123 1 The title means "Too Happy." It is an allusion to Vergil's line, *Georgics* ii, 458. — 2 **still:** always. — 7 **Lash out:** spend freely. — 8 **silver penny:** a coin weighing twenty-two and one-half and later twenty grains. The copper penny was first struck at the beginning of the seventeenth century. There used to be gold pennies. See the Century Dictionary. — 9 **nappy:** strong. — 12 **crabs:** crab apples. — 16 **care:** all their care is. — 19 [**tutties:** nosegays.] — 23 **Makes:** either, makes the hedge with the result that others, trespassers or hunters, break it down; or, repairs the hedge which others in their carelessness have broken down.

124 1 **for:** despite. — 2 **Securer:** more free from care. — 2 [**silly:** simple.] — 3 [" L'Allegro " and " Il Penseroso." It is a striking proof of Milton's astonishing power, that these, the earliest great lyrics of the landscape in our language, should still reign supreme in their style for range, variety, and melodious beauty. The bright and the thoughtful aspects of nature and of life are their subjects: but each is preceded by a mythological introduction in a mixed classical and Italian manner. With that of " L'Allegro " may be compared a similar myth in the first section of the first book of Shackerley Marmion's graceful "Cupid and Psyche," 1637.] — 4 **Cerberus:** the three-headed dog that guarded the gates of hell. — 5 **Stygian:** The Styx was the river encircling Hades, over which souls were ferried by Charon. Cerberus had a den beyond the Styx. — 7 **uncouth:** unknown and repulsive. — 12 **Cimmerian:** The Cimmerians are mentioned in the Odyssey (xi, 14) as dwelling in gloom and cloud at the ends of the ocean. — 14 **yclept:** called (a past participle of an obsolete verb). — 14 **Euphrosyne:** one of the three Graces. See a classical dictionary. — 26 So "full of life, joy, and easy grace." — 29 Clever sayings, humorous turns of speech, and playful tricks. — 31 **Hebe:** the goddess of youth who poured out nectar for the gods.

125 2 **Care:** The direct object of *derides*. — 7 [**The mountain-nymph:** compare Wordsworth's sonnet, No. 254.] — 9 **of:** to. Palgrave says that this line "is in *apposition* with the preceding, by a syntactical license not uncommon with Milton." He must have miscounted. Perhaps he meant to refer to lines 12 and 16, which may be taken as infinitives in apposition with the *unreprovéd* (unreprovable) *pleasures* of line 11. — 16 **to come**: who is to come, the bird or the poet? On this question the commentators have expended much energy, involving themselves in tangled syntactical exegesis and in a discussion of the habits of larks. It is more natural for a poet to go to his own window than for a lark to come down to salute him. — 18 **sweetbrier**: eglantine, or wild rose. The real eglantine is not twisted, and the *twisted eglantine* of line 19 may be the honeysuckle. — 24 **listening**: refers to L'Allegro himself. — 30 **Right against**: toward. — 33 **dight**: clad.

126 4 **Straight**: straightway. — 5 **round**: generally construed with *measures*, but it seems rather to go with *landscape*. — 6 **lawns**: open, grass-grown fields. — 6 **fallows**: unsown ground. — 9 **laboring**: about to bring forth rain. — 10 **pied**: variegated. — 13 **Bosom'd**: inclosed, contained. — 15 **Cynosure**: In Greek the word meant "dog's tail," and it was used to designate the stars making up the tail of the Lesser Bear, including the pole star. Hence it has the general meaning of anything that attracts great attention. — 18 [**Corydon, Thyrsis**: shepherd names from the old idylls.] — 21 **neat-handed**: skillful. — 26 **secure**: free from care. — 27 **upland**: out of the way, remote. — 29 [**rebecks**: an elementary form of violin.] — 32 **come**: It seems best to treat this as an indicative, not as a participle agreeing with *young and old*, treated as objects of "to" understood. — 35 This line refers to a drink composed of hot ale, nutmeg, roasted apples, and other ingredients.

127 1 **Mab**: supposed to bestow dreams. Compare "Romeo and Juliet," Act I, scene iv, ll. 53–95. — 1 **junkets eat**: ate the sweetmeats. — 2 The women and men servants tell of their experiences with the fairies, who were supposed to pinch lazy menials. The construction here and two lines below is awkward. Perhaps the subject of *Tells* is another servant. — 3 **Friar's lantern**: the will-o'-the-wisp or jack-o'-lantern. — 4 **Goblin**: Robin Goodfellow or Hobgoblin, who would perform services if paid in milk or cream. — 9 **lubber**: strong and clumsy. — 12 **crop-full**: gorged with food. — 13 **matin**: salutation to the morning. — 16 In the following lines, critics are divided as to whether L'Allegro actually goes to the city to seek its pleasures, or only reads plays and hears music. — 19 **weeds**: garments. — 20 **store of**: abundance of. — 23 **her**: refers to the chief favorite among the ladies. — 24 **Hymen**: the god of marriage. — 26 **pomp**: a solemn procession. — 30 **anon**: soon after. — 31 [**Jonson's learnéd sock**: his comedies are deeply colored by classical study.] The actors in ancient comedy wore a low shoe, the *soccus*; in tragedy, a higher buskin or *cothurnus*. — 33 This line, and indeed the passage, should not be construed, as is sometimes done, to lend countenance to the view that Milton did not thoroughly appreciate

Shakespeare's greatness, and thought him lacking in art. He is contrasting Shakespeare's comedies with those of Ben Jonson, and the language he employs accomplishes well his purpose. Besides, some almost contemporary lines, by Sir John Suckling, who was a great admirer of Shakespeare, contrast the two dramatists in much the same fashion, which quite possibly represents the usual criticism of the day. — 35 [**Lydian airs**: used here to express a light and festive style of ancient music. The "Lydian Mode," one of the seven original Greek scales, is nearly identical with our "Major."]

128 1 **pierce**: a true rime to *verse*, though not so in modern pronunciation, except occasionally when the word is used as a proper name. — 2 **bout**: turn in the music. — 4 This line illustrates the figure known as *oxymoron*, the epithets being, literally speaking, inapplicable to the nouns they accompany. — 5 **mazes**: difficult passages of the music. — 8 **That**: so that. — 8 **Orpheus**: compare "Lycidas," p. 75, lines 9–14. — 10 **Elysian**: The Elysian Fields were the abode of the blessed after death. — 12 **Pluto**: the ruler of the underworld or Hades. Milton describes the music as so beautiful that, if he had heard it instead of the music of Orpheus, Pluto would have released unconditionally the latter's wife. — 18 [**bestead**: avail.] — 19 **toys**: trifles. — 21 **fond**: foolish. — 21 **possess**: occupy — with either *fancies* or *yourselves* (understood) as object. In the latter case, the meaning is "occupy yourselves with fancies," etc.— 25 **pensioners**: followers.— 25 **Morpheus**: the god of sleep.

129 1 **esteem**: estimation. — 2 **Prince Memnon's sister**: Himera. Nothing is known of her beauty, but the poet infers that she was more beautiful than her brother, the king of the Ethiopians. See a classical dictionary for *Memnon* and the other names in this passage. — 2 **beseem**: suit. — 3 [**starr'd Ethiop queen**: Cassiopeia, the legendary queen of Ethiopia, and thence translated amongst the constellations.] — 17 **grain**: purple. — 19 **Cipres**: This is generally printed *cypress*, a word of unknown origin, meaning a sort of crape. It is often confused with Cyprus, where the crape was supposed to be made. Palgrave first read *cypres*. — 20 **decent**: comely. — 23 **commercing**: having communion. — 25 **still**: motionless. — 32 **Aye**: always.

130 3 **hist**: allure by quiet calls. — 4 **Philomel**: the nightingale. — 5 **plight**: strain (or else, mood). — 7 [**Cynthia**: the moon. Milton seems here to have transferred to her chariot the dragons anciently assigned to Demeter and to Medea.] — 22 **Curfew**: the bell that sounded about eight or nine o'clock in the evening to warn householders to extinguish fires and lights. From the French *couvre-feu*. — 26 **still removéd**: quiet and removed. — 28 Make "darkness visible." Compare "Paradise Lost," i, 63. — 35 **out-watch the Bear**: study till daybreak, when the constellation of the Great Bear is no longer visible. — 36 [**Hermes**: called Trismegistus, a mystical writer of the Neo-Platonist school.] Il

Penseroso will study his writings as well as those of the great Greek philosopher, Plato, in order to learn the secrets of the spiritual universe.

131 7 **consent**: affinity. — 11 [**Thebes**, etc.: subjects of Athenian tragedy.] — 13 Milton is almost certainly alluding to Shakespeare's tragedies. — 14 [**buskin'd**: tragic, in opposition to *sock* above], the word used in the corresponding passage in "L'Allegro." — 16 [**Musaeus**: a poet in mythology.] — 21 [**him that left half-told**: Chaucer, in his incomplete "Squire's Tale."] — 28 [**great bards**: Ariosto, Tasso, and Spenser, are here presumably intended.] — 30 **trophies**: arms or banners of the foe hung up in sign of victory. — 34 **civil-suited**: simply clad. — 35 [**frounced**: curled.] — 36 [**the Attic Boy**: Cephalus.]

132 3 **still**: probably an adjective qualifying *shower* and = gentle. — 4 **his**: its. — 6 **minute drops**: drops that fall at the rate of about one a minute (not *minúte* drops). — 10 **Sylvan**: Sylvanus, the Roman god of woods and fields. — 16 **profaner**: less sympathetic. — 17 **garish**: glaring, staring. — 21 **consort**: company of consonant sounds. — 23–25 A very obscure passage; *his wings* may be those of sleep or of the dream. — 27 **breathe**: how should this be parsed? — 30 **Genius**: presiding or guardian spirit. — 32 **pale**: inclosure. — 34 **massy proof**: massive, and hence able to bear the weight of the roof. — 35 **storied**: telling in pictures a Biblical story. — 35 **dight**: arrayed.

133 3 **clear**: clearly sung, or pure. — 10 **spell**: con, reflect upon; not necessarily *read*. — 17 [Emigrants supposed to be driven towards America by the government of Charles I.] Marvell doubtless heard much of the Bermudas, or Somers Islands, from his friend John Oxenbridge, who had taken refuge there from Laud's tyranny. — 23 **wracks**: wrecks, destroys. — 30 **enamels**: makes bright.

134 5 **Jewels**: seeds. — 5 **Ormus**: a small kingdom at the mouth of the Persian Gulf notable for its commerce and wealth. — 7 **throws**: Notice the imaginative effect produced by this concrete verb, — how it increases our sense of the natural profusion. — 8 [**But apples**: A fine example of Marvell's imaginative hyperbole.] — 21 **Mexique bay**: Gulf of Mexico. — 29 **pierce**: Note again that this word makes a good rime with *verse*. — 30 **phantasy**: imagination. — 31 [**consent**: harmony.]

135 1 **Aye**: ever. — 12 **noise**: This word in this connection did not offend our early poets. — 17 **diapason**: compare p. 67, l. 20. — 21 **consort**: harmony. — 23 The title means, "night unto night sheweth knowledge." See the nineteenth Psalm. — 26 Compare p. 129, l. 3.

136 7 **character**: form of print or handwriting, the metaphor of the "volume" (p. 135, l. 30) being continued (see below, p. 136, l. 11).

137 5 [A lyric of a strange, fanciful, yet solemn beauty: Cowley's style intensified by the mysticism of Henry More.] — 13 [**monument**: the world.] — 18 **council**: compare "Paradise Lost," vii, 516 seq. — 20 **reign'st**: the sequence of tenses suggests "reigned'st."

138 1 This is the opening strophe of a much longer poem.—8 [Entitled "A Song in Honor of St. Cecilia's Day: 1697."] This is one of the most perfectly constructed odes in English, and is specially notable for combining with consummate lyric power and felicity a moving dramatic and a vivid descriptive quality. It is one of the supreme triumphs of English poetry, a fact not sufficiently remembered by those who think of Dryden chiefly as a satirist.—8 **Persia won**: the winning of Persia.—10 **awful**: awe inspiring.—16 **Thais**: For this companion of Alexander and for the hero himself see a classical dictionary.—23 **Timotheus**: a Theban *flute* player whose music did greatly affect Alexander.

139 3 **belied**: disguised.—4 **Sublime**: aloft.—5 **Olympia**: Alexander's mother, Olympias.—11 **rebound**: reëcho.—14 **god**: the part of a god.—21 **purple**: rosy (probably).—22 **honest**: good-looking and kindly.—23 **hautboys**: oboes (wooden wind instruments of soprano compass). From the French *haut bois*, literally "high wood."

140 3 **his hand**: Timotheus's.—4 **Muse**: nearly equivalent here to "musical mood."—6 **Darius**: the third of that name to rule over Persia. See a classical dictionary or a manual of ancient history.—24 **Lydian**: see above, p. 127, l. 35.—34 **The many**: compare the Greek *οἱ πολλοί*.

141 6 **at once**: at one and the same time.—14 **As**: as if.—24 **unburied**: To remain unburied was, in the opinion of the ancients, to continue in a state of spiritual wretchedness. Compare the "Antigone" of Sophocles, and Horace, Book I, ode xxviii.—30 **their hostile gods**: The gods of the Persians would be hostile to the Greeks. It is most probable that *their* refers to the Persians.—32 **flambeau**: torch.

142 8 **vocal frame**: the organ.—9 **store**: musical knowledge (perhaps).

143 3 **vermeil**: vermilion.

144 26 **Gilds**: Its object is *shades*, l. 24, and its subject is *hope*, l. 23.—27 **Still**: always.—32 **Chastised**: when, or because, chastised.—33 **blended**: when blended.

145 8 **opening**: Is this a participle or an adjective?—9 [We have no poet more marked by rapture, by the ecstasy which Plato held the note of genuine inspiration, than Collins. Yet but twice or thrice do his lyrics reach that simplicity, that *sinceram sermonis Attici gratiam*] true grace of Attic utterance [to which this ode testifies his enthusiastic devotion. His style, as his friend Dr. Johnson truly remarks, was obscure; his diction often harsh and unskillfully labored; he struggles nobly against the narrow, artificial manner of his age, but his too scanty years did not allow him to reach perfect mastery.]—11 **numbers**: verses.—17 **gauds**: ornaments.—18 **decent**: comely.—22 [**Hybla**: near Syracuse.] A Sicilian mountain noted for its honey.—24 [**her whose . . . woe**: the nightingale, "for which Sophocles seems to have entertained a peculiar fondness"; Collins here refers to the famous chorus in the "Œdipus at Colonus."] — 26 **sweetly**: Does this limit *soothed* or *sad?* Do you like such a number of sibilants in a line? If *sweetly* be construed with *sad*, is the cadence of the line satisfactory? — 26 **sad Electra's poet**: Sophocles, not Euripides, to whom Milton had applied the phrase; see above, p. 81, l. 17. Both these Greek dramatists wrote tragedies about Electra. — 27 [**Cephisus**: the stream encircling Athens on the north and west, passing Colonus.]

146 1 **enamell'd**: gay with flowers. — 13 [**stay'd to sing**: stayed her song when Imperial tyranny was established at Rome.] This interpretation will not hold. The meaning is that Simplicity, that is, poetic sincerity and singleness of aim and treatment, waited to sing to only one throne, that of Augustus. This age of Augustus, when Vergil, Horace, and Ovid flourished, was the golden age of Latin poetry. — 15 **her**: Rome's. This line is a very poor one. — 16 [Stanza 7 refers to the Italian amorist poetry of the Renaissance. In Collins's day Dante was almost unknown in England.] — 27 [**meeting soul**: which moves sympathetically towards Simplicity as she comes to inspire the poet.] Compare above, p. 128, l. 1. — 28 [**Of these**: taste and genius.]

148 3 **ever**: always. — 15 **blow**: bloom. — 17 Selima belonged to Gray's friend Horace Walpole. The poem was written in 1747. — 28 **Tyrian hue**: A famous purple was made at Tyre from a sort of shellfish.

149 18 **Dolphin**: According to legend the Greek poet Arion was saved from drowning by dolphins. — 18 **Nereid**: sea nymph. — 26 Compare "Merchant of Venice," Act II, scene vii, 65. — 28 **happy pair**: Daniel Pulteney and his wife. Pulteney was a politician of some standing and opposed to Sir Robert Walpole. Philips addressed another ode to Margaret Pulteney, but neither girl lived to fulfill the happy auguries of the poet.

150 14 **Moduling**: tuning.

151 11 **flame**: of indignation. — 13 **rural reign**: of agriculture, as opposed to *commerce*, in the next line. — 17 **still**: ever. — 23 [**The Bard**: In 1757, when this splendid ode was completed,] and published along with "The Progress of Poesy" from Horace Walpole's private press [so very little had been printed, whether in Wales or in England, in regard to Welsh poetry, that it is hard to discover whence Gray drew his Cymric allusions. The fabled massacre of the bards (shown to be wholly groundless in Stephens's "Literature of the Kymry") appears first in the family history of Sir John Wynn of Gwydir (cir. 1600), not published till 1773; but the story seems to have passed in manuscript to Carte's History, whence it may have been taken by Gray. The references to *high-born Hoel* and *soft Llewellyn;* to *Cadwallo* and *Urien;* may, similarly, have been derived from the "Specimens" of early Welsh poetry, by the Rev. E. Evans: — as, although not published till

1764, the manuscript, we learn from a letter to Dr. Wharton, was in Gray's hands by July, 1760, and may have reached him by 1757. It is, however, doubtful whether Gray (of whose acquaintance with Welsh we have no evidence) must not have been also aided by some Welsh scholar. He is one of the poets least likely to scatter epithets at random: "soft" or gentle is the epithet emphatically and specially given to Llewellyn in contemporary Welsh poetry, and is hence here used with particular propriety. Yet, without such assistance as we have suggested, Gray could hardly have selected the epithet, although applied to the King among a crowd of others, in Llygad Gwr's Ode, printed by Evans.—After lamenting his comrades (st. 2, 3) the Bard prophesies the fate of Edward II, and the conquests of Edward III (4); his death and that of the Black Prince (5); of Richard II, with the wars of York and Lancaster, the murder of Henry VI (*the meek usurper*), and of Edward V and his brother (6). He turns to the glory and prosperity following the accession of the Tudors (7), through Elizabeth's reign (8): and concludes with a vision of the poetry of Shakespeare and Milton.] —23 **ruthless King**: Edward I, who according to a false tradition put to death all the bards that fell into his hands during the conquest of Wales. Gray's Odes were at first regarded as obscure, but if we understand that this is in the main a dramatic monologue by one of the bards, much of the obscurity disappears.—30 **Cambria's**: of Wales.

152 3 **Snowdon**: the name given to an extensive mountainous tract in Wales. The time is 1283 A.D.—5 [**Glo'ster**: Gilbert de Clare, son-in-law to Edward.]—6 [**Mortimer**: one of the Lords Marchers of Wales.] —12 Gray refers to "Paradise Lost," i, 537.—20 [**high-born Hoel, soft Llewellyn**: the "Dissertatio de Bardis" of Evans names the first as son to the King Owain Gwynedd; Llewellyn, last king of North Wales, was murdered 1282.]—21 [**Cadwallo**: Cadwallon (died 631) and Urien Rheged (early kings of Gwynedd and Cumbria respectively) are mentioned by Evans as bards none of whose poetry is extant.]—25 [**Modred**: Evans supplies no *data* for this name which Gray (it has been supposed) uses for Merlin (Myrddin Wyllt), held prophet as well as poet.]—27 [**Arvon**: the shores of Carnarvonshire opposite Anglesey. Whether intentionally or through ignorance of the real dates, Gray here seems to represent the Bard as speaking of these poets, all of earlier days, Llewellyn excepted, as his own contemporaries at the close of the thirteenth century. Gray, whose penetrating and powerful genius rendered him in many ways an initiator in advance of his age, is probably the first of our poets who made some acquaintance with the rich and admirable poetry in which Wales from the sixth century has been fertile,—before and since his time so barbarously neglected, not in England only. Hence it has been thought worth while here to enter into a little detail upon his Cymric allusions.]

153 2 **grisly**: frightful. — 5 **join**: pronounced so as to make a perfect rime with *line*. — 7 [The italicized lines mark where the Bard's song is joined by that of his predecessors departed.] — 10 **characters**: the figures or letters in which the doom is expressed. — 13 **Berkley's roof**: At this castle in Gloucestershire Edward II was murdered in 1327. The edition of 1768 has *roofs*. — 15 [**She-wolf**: Isabel of France, adulterous queen of Edward II.] — 17 **who**: Edward III, during whose reign the English won notable victories in France. — 17 **thy country**: France. — 17 **hangs**: seems to be transitive, with *scourge* for its object. — 19, 20 In the edition of 1768 *flight* is printed with a capital, but the nouns *sorrow* and *solitude* are not so printed. Yet all are apparently personifications. — 20 **solitude**: desolation. — 25 **sable warrior**: Edward the Black Prince. — 30 **azure realm**: the inflated, eighteenth-century way of not saying water. — 30–34 Gray explained that these lines refer to the magnificence of Richard II's reign. — 34 **his**: the whirlwind's, which in the edition of 1768 is printed with a capital.

154 3 **he**: Richard II. Gray notes that he was starved to death. — 7 **din of battle**: Gray's note is, "Ruinous civil wars of York and Lancaster." — 11 [**Towers of Julius**: the Tower of London, built in part, according to tradition, by Julius Cæsar.] — 12 **murder**: Gray noted that Henry VI, George Duke of Clarence, Edward V, Richard Duke of York, etc. were believed to have been secretly murdered in the Tower. — 13 **consort's**: Margaret of Anjou, wife of Henry VI. — 13 **father's fame**: Henry V, the victor of Agincourt. — 14 **meek usurper's**: Henry VI was mild and holy. He is called a usurper because, in Gray's words, "The line of Lancaster had no right of inheritance to the crown." — 16 **blushing foe**: the red rose of Lancaster, which may be considered as twined with the white rose of York through the marriage of Edward IV with Lady Grey. One would naturally think of Henry VII's marriage, but for the fact that these lines *precede* those which refer to Richard III. — 17 [**bristled boar**: the badge of Richard III] who murdered his nephews. — 23 [**Half of thy heart**: Queen Eleanor died soon after the conquest of Wales.] — 25 Here the Bard addresses the vanishing ghosts. — 33 [**Arthur**: Henry VII named his eldest son thus, in deference to native feeling and story.] — Gray's note is as follows: "It was the common belief of the Welsh nation, that King Arthur was still alive in Fairy Land, and should return again to reign over Britain." — 34 **All hail**: Gray's note, — "Both Merlin and Taliessin had prophesied that the Welsh should regain their sovereignty over this island; which seemed to be accomplished in the house of Tudor."

155 2 **Sublime**: on high. — 2 **they**: Henry VII and Henry VIII. Gray hardly had in mind the young Edward VI. — 5 **midst**: If the reference is to the preceding lines, those lines give a picture of Elizabeth's court. But the punctuation seems to make those lines a group covering the reigns before Elizabeth's. If this be the case, *midst* probably refers to the entire procession of monarchs.—9, 10 The glorious poetry of Elizabeth's reign is recalled.—11 **Taliessin**: "Chief of the Bards, flourished in the sixth century. His works are still preserved, and his memory held in high veneration among his countrymen" (Gray).—15 **adorn**: The subjects are *war*, *love*, and *truth*. The style of the passage leaves much to be desired.—16 Gray's note shows that the reference is to the poetry of Spenser. He quotes from the proem to the "Faerie Queene" the line "Fierce wars and faithful loves shall moralize my song." The fact that Spenser is here alluded to suggests that the preceding lines may refer specifically to lyric poetry. It seems scarcely well, however, to indulge in such minute exegesis, and, if we do, we must remember that the best Elizabethan lyric poetry did not precede the poetry of Spenser.—18 The allusion, as Gray notes, is to Shakespeare, and the word *buskin'd* shows that it is his tragedies that are meant.—21 Gray's note, "Milton," is scarcely needed.—23 Gray notes, "The succession of poets after Milton's time."—25 **man**: Edward I.—25 **sanguine**: blood-red. The allusion is to the bards the king has slain.—27 **repairs**: renews. Compare "Lycidas" above, p. 78, l. 15.

156 1 Collins states that this ode, which is ranked as one of the most beautiful short poems in the language, was written in the beginning of the year 1746. From this fact it has been argued that the ode refers specially to the soldiers who fell in the battle of Falkirk, won by the Young Pretender. It may also refer to the battles of Preston Pans and Fontenoy, lost in 1745 (perhaps more probably to the latter).—17 [The Highlanders called the battle of Culloden, Drumossie.] In this battle, April 16, 1756, the Duke of Cumberland defeated the Young Pretender and finally put down the rising of 1745. Culloden is a moor not far from Inverness.—25 **lord**: the Duke of Cumberland. Compare Campbell's "Lochiel": "Proud Cumberland prances insulting the slain."

157 1 Flodden Field, the battle in Northumberland in which the Earl of Surrey and the English defeated King James IV of Scotland, in September, 1513.—1 [**lilting**: singing blithely.]—3 [**loaning**: broad lane.]—4 **wede away**: weeded out.—5 [**bughts**: pens.]—5 [**scorning**: rallying.]—6 [**dowie**: dreary.]—7 [**daffin', gabbin'**: joking and chattering.]—8 [**leglin**: milk pail.]—9 [**shearing**: reaping.]—10 [**Bandsters**: sheaf binders.]—10 [**lyart**: grizzled.]—10 [**runkled**: wrinkled.]—11 [**fleeching**: coaxing.]—13 [**gloaming**: twilight.]—14 [**bogle**: ghost.]—17 [**Dool**: sorrow.]—25 **Yarrow**: a stream in Selkirkshire famous in Scotch poetry. Compare Wordsworth's poems in the Fourth Book, pp. 320, 322.—25 **braes**: banks, hillsides.—25 **bonny**: fair.

158 21 **water wraith**: apparition of the drowned man rising from the water.—28 **thorough**: through.

159 10 **marrow**: husband, companion. — 13 [The editor has found no authoritative text of this poem, to his mind superior to any other of its class in melody and pathos. Part is probably not later than the seventeenth century; in other stanzas a more modern hand, much resembling Scott's, is traceable. Logan's poem (163) exhibits a knowledge rather of the old legend than of the old verses.] — 19 [**hecht**: promised (the obsolete *hight*).] — 26 [**mavis**: thrush.] — 27 [**ilka**: every.]

160 1 [**lav'rock**: lark.] — 4 [**haughs**: valley-meadows.] — 16 [**twined**: parted from.] — 16 [**marrow**: mate.] — 22 **braid and narrow**: widely and carefully, minutely. — 23 [**Syne**: then.] — 25 [The *Royal George*, of 108 guns, whilst undergoing a partial careening at Spithead, was overset about 10 A.M., August 29, 1782. The total loss was believed to be nearly 1000 souls. This little poem might be called one of our trial pieces, in regard to taste. The reader who feels the vigor of description and the force of pathos underlying Cowper's bare and truly Greek simplicity of phrase, may assure himself *se valde profecisse* in poetry.] The Latin means "that he has made great progress." — 28 **Fast by**: hard by, near.

161 8 Richard Kempenfelt, 1718–1782, a rear admiral who had seen considerable service, particularly in the East Indies.

162 1 **Downs**: the sea off the eastern coast of Kent. — 15 **chance**: probably *it* is omitted.

163 19 [A little masterpiece in a very difficult style: Catullus himself could hardly have bettered it. In grace, tenderness, simplicity, and humor, it is worthy of the Ancients; and even more so, from the completeness and unity of the picture presented.] — 27 **cabbage nets**: nets in which cabbages were boiled. — 29 **laces**: either shoe laces, or laces for stays.

165 14 **tassie**: goblet. — 17 **Leith**: the port of Edinburgh. — 19 **Berwick-law**: "a conspicuous hill near the shore by North Berwick, and a landmark for sailors" (J. G. Dow).

166 12 **trow**: believe. — 14 **dight**: attire. — 23 **skaith**: injury. — 25 **ride the ring**: as in the modern tournament.

168 1 [Perhaps no writer who has given such strong proofs of the poetic nature has left less satisfactory poetry than Thomson. Yet this song, with "Rule Britannia" and a few others, must make us regret that he did not more seriously apply himself to lyrical writing.] — 3 **mutual**: kindred, sharing our feelings, returning our affection. — 14 **absolve thy**: excuse thee from. — 18 **Conveys**: has it sent. — 18 **in a borrow'd name**: This seems ambiguous. The treasure might be sent as something less valuable, or to or by some one not likely to have his goods confiscated. — 19 **measure**: verses. — 23 **noted**: made known.

169 5 [With what insight and tenderness, yet in how few words, has this painter poet here himself told *Love's Secret!*] — 14 **traveler**: This seems to be a symbol for a recognition of the fact that she was loved, or else for the sudden springing up of love in her own heart. — 17 This little poem is from the "Vicar of Wakefield," Chapter XXIV.

170 1 Burns wrote three versions of this song. Mr. Palgrave has selected the most beautiful, but not the most popular, and he has slightly changed his version. See G. A. Aitken's edition of Burns in the "New Aldine Poets," Vol. III, pp. 19–27. — 21 This ode was labored on for several years, was finished in 1754, and was first published in 1757. — 21 [**Æolian lyre**: the Greeks ascribed the origin of their lyrical poetry to the colonies of Æolis in Asia Minor.] Gray, as his note and his poem show, was thinking of the poetry of Pindar, of Thebes in Bœotia, rather than of the Æolian lyric poets, Sappho and Alcæus. His phrase has nothing to do with the Æolian harp. — 23 **Helicon's harmonious springs**: Aganippe and Hippocrene, fountains sacred to the Muses, which were situated in the mountain range of Helicon in Bœotia. — 25 **blow**: bloom.

171 3 **Ceres' golden reign**: the realm of the goddess of agriculture. — 7–18 "Power of harmony to calm the turbulent sallies of the soul. The thoughts are borrowed from the first Pythian of Pindar" (Gray). — — 9 **shell**: lyre (which was supposed to have been invented by Mercury, who stretched strings across a tortoise shell). — 11 [**Thracia's hills**: supposed a favorite resort of Mars.] — 15 [**feather'd king**: the eagle of Jupiter, admirably described by Pindar in a passage here imitated by Gray.] — 20 **Temper'd**: attuned. — 21 [**Idalia**: in Cyprus, where *Cytherea* (Venus) was especially worshiped.] — 24 **antic**: quaint, but with no unpleasant suggestion. — 32 **sublime**: lifted high. — 34–35 Gray's note shows that he was imitating a verse of the Greek tragic poet, Phrynichus.

172 1–12 "To compensate the real and imaginary ills of life, the Muse was given to mankind by the same Providence that sends the day by its cheerful presence to dispel the gloom and terror of the night" (Gray). — 5 **fond**: foolish, unfounded. — 10 **gives**: allows. — 11, 12 Gray quotes: "Or seen the morning's well-appointed star Come marching up the eastern hills afar" (Cowley). — 12 [**Hyperion**: the sun.] — 13 Gray's note runs: "Extensive influence of poetic Genius over the remotest and most uncivilized nations: its connection with liberty, and the virtues that naturally attend on it (see the Erse, Norwegian, and Welsh fragments, the Lapland and American songs)." Gray also showed that in l. 13 he was utilizing phrases found in Vergil and Petrarch. — 19 **repeat**: recite the names and qualities of. — 22 **track**: the object of *pursue*, which has for subjects *Glory*, *Shame*, etc. — 25 [The following stanzas allude to the poets of the islands and mainland of Greece, to those of Rome and of England.] For the proper names, see a classical dictionary. — 28 **amber**: yellow.

173 5 **Latium**: the part of ancient Italy in which Rome was situated. — 7 **the sun**: of more southern lands, like Greece and Italy. — 8 **Nature's Darling**: Shakespeare is represented as owing more to natural endowment and to observation than to study. — 14 **year**: season. — 19 **Nor**: Notice that Gray was unwilling to make Milton second even to Shakespeare. — 20 **Ecstasy**: inspired imagination. — 23 Gray referred to Ezekiel i, 20, 26, 28. — 28 **bear**: The subject is *coursers* and the object is *car*. Does Gray seem always happy in his style in passages marked by similar grammatical characteristics? — 30 "Meant to express the stately march and sounding energy of Dryden's rimes" (Gray). Pope had already written of Dryden's "long majestic march, and energy divine." — 31 **his**: Gray seems to be speaking of Dryden in his capacity of lyric poet, for in his note to l. 1, p. 174, he writes: "We have had in our language no other odes of the sublime kind, than that of Dryden on St. Cecilia's Day."

174 2 **daring spirit**: Gray himself. — 5 [**Theban eagle**: Pindar.] — 10 **orient**: bright. — 12 **vulgar fate**: the fate that may be expected by the crowd of ordinary men. — 16 **shell**: see above, note to l. 9, p. 171. — 19 **Possessed**: inspired by a spirit. — 24 **myrtles**: associated with song by the Greeks, who held boughs of myrtle when they sang at banquets.

175 1 Professor Bronson seems to be right in holding that Fear signifies, not cowardice, but imaginative and sublime apprehension of the terrible. — 10 **sounds**: in apposition with *measures*. — 27 **war-denouncing**: threatening war.

176 25 **that**: so that. — 26 **Faun**: follower of the Roman god Faunus. — 26 **Dryad**: forest nymph. — 27 **Sisters**: followers of Diana. — 27 [**chaste-eyed Queen**: Diana.] — 28 **Satyrs**: followers of Pan. — 28 **Sylvan Boys**: followers of the forest god of the Romans, Sylvanus.

177 4 **viol**: a medieval stringed instrument, precursor of the violin. — 7 **Tempe's vale**: situated in Thessaly and famous in poetry. — 11 **fantastic**: full of the freedom of fancy. — 16 **sphere-descended**: Compare the phrase "music of the spheres," and give an explanation of it. — 20–21 Collins wrote an ode, never printed and undiscovered, on the "Music of the Grecian Theater." Perhaps it is to this music that reference is here made. — 22 **mimic**: Compare Aristotle's view as to the origin of all art. — 27 **Warm, energic**: full of passion and energy. — 29 **page**: that of history. — 31 **reed**: pipe. — 32 **rage**: inspiration. — 35 The reference is to the varied musical powers of the organ.

178 5 [From that wild rhapsody of mingled grandeur, tenderness, and obscurity, that "medley between inspiration and possession," which poor Smart is believed to have written whilst in confinement for madness.] — 9 **period**: this probably means *cessation of things* or else is equivalent to "epoch," according as the three verbs in the next line form predicates in inverse or in direct order to the three nouns in this line.

179 24 [**the dreadful light**: of life and experience.] — 25 **Hours**: goddesses of the seasons. — 28 **purple year**: "bright season" (Fowler).

180 1 [**Attic warbler**: the nightingale.] — 23 **liquid**: clear. — 25 **trim**: attire.

181 4 **kind**: race of insects. — 16 **Ouse**: There are three rivers of this name in England. This is the Great Ouse, and two of Cowper's homes, at Huntingdon and at Olney, were in its vicinity.

182 1–4 This is the form Cowper finally gave the last stanza. The original form, which is better and is usually given, runs:

> 'Tis a sight to engage me, if anything can,
> To muse on the perishing pleasures of man;
> Though his life be a dream, his enjoyments, I see,
> Have a being less durable even than he.

— 5 [**sleekit**: sleek.] — 8 [**bickering brattle**: flittering flight.] — 9 [**laith**: loath.] — 10 [**pattle**: plow staff.] — 17 [**whiles**: at times.] — 19 [**daimen-icker**: a corn ear now and then.] — 19 [**thrave**: shock.] — 21 [**lave**: rest.] — 24 **silly wa's**: weak walls. — 25 **big**: build. — 26 [**foggage**: after-grass.] — 28 [**snell**: biting.]

183 5 **colter**: plow share. — 10 [**But**: without.] — 10 [**hald**: dwelling place.] — 11 [**thole**: bear.] — 12 [**cranreuch**: hoarfrost.] — 13 [**thy lane**: alone.] — 16 [**a-gley**: off the right line, awry.]

184 13 **oaten stop**: shepherd's pipe. — 14 This line originally stood and is often printed, "May hope, chaste Eve, to soothe thy modest ear." — 19 **brede**: braid. — 20 **wavy bed**: the sun is sinking into the sea.

185 5 **folding-star**: the star that indicates the time for the cattle to return to the fold. — 7 **Hours**: Are these the *Hours* of Gray's "Ode on the Spring." See above, p. 179, l. 25. — 25 **wont**: is accustomed.

186 2 **Fancy**: This probably includes both the Imagination and the Fancy, as these terms are generally used. — 5 **parting**: departing. — 10 **air**: object of *holds*. — 20 **rude**: uneducated.

187 5 **toil**: made a true rime with *smile*. — 11 **Awaits**: Are those editors necessarily correct who note that *hour* is the subject, not the object, of this verb? Sometimes the text is misprinted *Await*. — 15 **fretted**: For this technical word see some good dictionary. — 17 **storied**: telling the life story in an inscription. — 19 **provoke**: call forth. — 27 **rage**: enthusiasm.

188 1 **Hampden**: John Hampden, who refused to pay the ship money exacted during the reign of Charles I. — 12 **shut**: an infinitive dependent on *forbade*. *Their lot* is the subject of all the finite verbs in this stanza. The infinitives in the next stanza still depend on *forbade*. — 13, 14 Whose are the *pangs* and *blushes?* — 17 **madding**: carried away by enthusiasm. — 17, 18 Explain the syntax of these lines. — 19 **sequester'd**: secluded, retired. — 21–24 Explain the syntax of this stanza.

— 28 **teach**: Why is this verb in the plural? — 28 **to die**: how to die. — 29 **to dumb forgetfulness a prey**: this phrase describes the result of resigning *This pleasing anxious being*. The syntax is ambiguous. — 31 **precincts**: probably used in the sense of *boundaries*.

189 7 **chance**: compare above, p. 162, l. 15. — 27 The parenthesis seems to indicate that the old swain cannot read. — 28 **thorn**: hawthorn tree. — 32 Perhaps Gray meant not much more than we should mean by the expression "a subdued and pensive man."

190 13 [**stoure**: dust storm.] — 18 **ha'**: hall. — 21 [**braw**: smart.]

191 17 [**scaith**: hurt.] — 18 **wad belang thee**: would, or rather, could belong to thee. — 21 **aboon**: above. — 21 [**tent**: guard.] — 22 [**steer**: molest.]

192 18 "Coilsfield House (in Ayrshire) is meant, occupied in 1786 by a family of the name of Montgomery" (Robertson). "Highland Mary" was a domestic servant named Mary Campbell, with whom Burns fell deeply in love. She died in the autumn of the same year, 1786. — 20 [**drumlie**: muddy.] — 25 [**birk**: birch.]

193 21 [There can hardly exist a poem more truly tragic in the highest sense than this, nor, perhaps, Sappho excepted, has any poetess equaled it.] — 21 **kye**: cattle.

194 17 **Jamie's wraith**: apparition of Jamie. — 19 [**greet**: cry.] — 24 [**daurna**: dare not.] — 29 **Yule**: Christmas. — 29 [**fou**: merry with drink.]

195 1 [**coost**: carried.] — 2 [**unco skeigh**: very proud.] — 3 [**Gart**: forced.] — 3 [**abeigh**: aside.] — 5 **fleech'd**: coaxed, besought. — 6 [**Ailsa Craig**: a rock in the Firth of Clyde.] — 8 [**Grat his een bleer't**: cried till his eyes were bleared.] — 9 [**lowpin**: leaping.] — 9 [**linn**: waterfall.] — 10 **tide**: a flux and reflux like the tides of the ocean. — 11 [**sair**: sore.] — 23 [**smoor'd**: smothered.] — 24 [**crouse and canty**: blithe and gay.] — 26 [Burns justly named this "one of the most beautiful songs in the Scots or any other language." One stanza, interpolated by Beattie, is here omitted; it contains two good lines, but is out of harmony with the original poem.]

196 7 [**bigonet**: little cap, — probably altered from *béguinette*.] — 8 **bishop's satin**: satin of the quality used in a bishop's gown. Compare the phrase "bishop's lawn." Compare also the following passage from "An Epistle to the Terrible Priests" (one of the Marprelate tracts), 1588, ed. Peterham, p. 21: "And yet I hope he may weare as brave a sattin gowne as my Lord of Winchester weareth, and be as cholericke as he." — 9 **baillie's**: bailiff's. — 14 **leal**: loyal. — 16 **muckle**: big. — 19 **slaes**: sloes. — 25 [**thraw**: twist.] — 28 **Gar**: make. — 28 **braw**: fine. — 32 [**caller**: fresh.]

197 1 **will**: shall. — 4 **greet**: weep. — 7 **gin**: if. — 8 **lave**: rest. — 17 [Burns himself, despite two attempts, failed to improve this little absolute masterpiece of music, tenderness, and simplicity: this "Romance of a life" in eight lines.] But the two stanzas seem to be the two best stanzas in Burns's "How long and dreary is the night" (Fowler). See Aitken's edition of Burns, II, 187. The text of the Oxford complete edition (p. 360) varies somewhat. — 20 [**eerie**: strictly, scared: uneasy.] — 23 **glinted**: sped swiftly. — 25 [**airts**: quarters.]

198 1 [**row**: roll.] — 10 [**shaw**: small wood in a hollow, spinney.] — 13 [The last two stanzas are not by Burns.] They are by John Hamilton, a music dealer of Edinburgh. — 13 **westlin**: westland, western. — 21 [**knowes**: knolls.] — 29 [**jo**: sweetheart.] — 32 [**brent**: smooth,] high.

199 3 [**pow**: head.] — 7 **canty**: delightful. — 9 **maun**: must. — 16 [**leal**: faithful.]

200 5 [**fain**: happy.] — 9 **Science**: all knowledge, not merely natural science. — 10 [Henry VI founded Eton.] — 19 **careless**: probably used in the sense of "free from care." — 29 **margent**: margin.

201 7 They were preparing for coming classes. — 19 **buxom**: vigorous. — 21 **cheer**: Does this necessarily refer to the expression of the countenance?

202 22 **grisly**: frightful. — 23 **painful family**: pain-causing attendants.

203 7 [Written in 1773, toward the beginning of Cowper's second attack of melancholy madness, — a time when he altogether gave up prayer, saying, "For him to implore mercy would only anger God the more." Yet had he given it up when sane, it would have been "major insania."]

204 1 Compare with this noble poem Wordsworth's "Ode to Duty," in the Fourth Book, p. 258. — 11 **birth**: child.

205 3 **Gorgon**: see a classical dictionary. — 4 **band**: of the Furies. — 13 **extinct**: though practically extinct. — 15 **Exact**: Does this mean *exactly*, or is it a verb in the imperative? — 17 Alexander Selkirk was a sailor who after a quarrel with his captain was put ashore on the uninhabited island of Juan Fernandez, where he remained five years (1704–1709) before he was rescued. His adventures suggested to Defoe the writing of "Robinson Crusoe."

206 8 At this point a stanza is omitted.

207 1 [The editor would venture to class in the very first rank this sonnet, which, with (204), records Cowper's gratitude to the lady whose affectionate care for many years gave what sweetness he could enjoy to a life radically wretched. Petrarch's sonnets have a more ethereal grace and a more perfect finish; Shakespeare's more passion; Milton's stand supreme in stateliness; Wordsworth's in depth and delicacy. But Cowper's unite with an exquisiteness in the turn of thought which the ancients would have called Irony, an intensity of pathetic tenderness peculiar to his loving and ingenuous nature. There is much mannerism, much that is unimportant or of now exhausted interest in his poems; but where he is great, it is with that elementary greatness which rests on the most universal human feelings. Cowper is our highest master in simple pathos.] — 9 **Book**: compare Revelation xx, 12.

209 9 [Cowper's last original poem, founded upon a story told in Anson's "Voyages." It was written March, 1799; he died in next year's April.] — 16 **he**: George Lord Anson, who sailed around the world, 1740–1744. — 20 **Nor him beheld**: nor did he behold him. — 26 **despair of life**: What is the exact meaning of this phrase as used here?

210 13 **still**: Notice the position of this adverb.

211 11 [Very little except his name appears recoverable with regard to the author of this truly noble poem, which appeared in the "Scripscrapologia, or Collins' Doggerel Dish of All Sorts," with three or four other pieces of merit, Birmingham, 1804.] — 15 **pad-pony**: road pony, one trained to pace the roads easily. — 25 **Nabob**: any Englishman who had sought his fortune in India and returned home.

212 8 **thread**: of life. Compare the thread spun by the Fates. — 12 [**Everlasting**: used with side allusion to a cloth so named at the time when Collins wrote.]

214 1 [This beautiful lyric, printed in 1783, seems to anticipate in its imaginative music that return to our great early age of song, which in Blake's own lifetime was to prove, — how gloriously! that the English Muses had resumed their "ancient melody": Keats, Shelley, Byron, — he overlived them all.] — 1 **Ida's**: probably the famous mountain in the Troad. — 24 **parle**: speech.

215 3 **tented**: covered, as with tents, by the flowers. — 8 **trancéd**: It would be pleasant to think that Keats thought of the nightingale as enchanted with its own sweet song, but the use of *senseless* makes one think he may have meant to emphasize the bird's lack of feeling. — 10 **numbers**: verses. — 18 Never slumbering (put to sleep) or satiated.

216 1 **realms of gold**: of great books, chiefly of poetry. — 6 **demesne**: sovereign estate. — 8 Chapman, George (1557–1634), the Elizabethan dramatist and translator. — 12 [**stout Cortez**: History would here suggest *Balboa* (A. T.). It may be noticed that to find in Chapman's Homer the "pure serene" of the original, the reader must bring with him the imagination of the youthful poet; he must be "a Greek himself," as Shelley finely said of Keats.]

218 25 **sense**: sensation.

219 23 [The most tender and true of Byron's smaller poems.] — 25 **myrtle and ivy**: compare the second line of "Lycidas," p. 73.

220 2 Bathing in May dew was supposed to produce beauty. — 7 **discover**: reveal, show. — 13 [This poem exemplifies the peculiar skill with which Scott employs proper names: a rarely misleading sign of true poetical genius.] This poem is an imitation of the famous ballad of "The Nut-brown Maid." It is from "Rokeby," III, xvi, xvii. The place names belong to Yorkshire. — 16 **Would**: which would.

221 7 **read you**: guess who you are. — 19 **brand**: saber. — 19 **musketoon**: short musket. — 22 **tuck**: beating. — 29 **mickle**: much. — 30 **Would**: who would.

223 7 **champak**: an Indian flower of the magnolia type. — 24 **Meet**: Explain the use of the plural. — 28 **Had**: would have.

224 7 This poem was inspired by Wordsworth's wife and composed about two years after his marriage.

225 24 **thine**: heart or devotion? — 26 **Dove**: The locality is not certainly identified.

227 16 **state**: stateliness. — 24 **secret**: secluded.

228 15 **moonlight**: suggestive of the calm beauty of moonlight.

229 2 **more sad and fair**: perhaps, once fairer than the present, but now sadder when viewed in the light of memory. Fowler suggests the paraphrase, "In days which, even when fuller of pain, were dearer to me than the present." — 15 **silver pound**: The pound is now a gold coin, but its twenty shillings were originally equivalent to a *pound* of silver. The pound Scots was, however, only a twelfth of the pound sterling. See the Century Dictionary. — 17 **Lochgyle**: an arm of the sea on the west coast of Mull (Fowler).

230 1 **wight**: man, fellow, person. — 4 **winsome**: pleasant and gracious. — 10 **water-wraith**: apparition ascending from the water.

231 9 [Simple as "Lucy Gray" seems, a mere narrative of what "has been, and may be again," yet every touch in the child's picture is marked by the deepest and purest ideal character. Hence, pathetic as the situation is, this is not strictly a pathetic poem, such as Wordsworth gives us in 221, Lamb in 264, and Scott in his "Maid of Neidpath," — "almost more pathetic," as Tennyson once remarked, "than a man has the right to be." And Lyte's lovely stanzas (224) suggest, perhaps, the same remark.] One may ask whether some criticism is not more critical than any criticism has a right to be. — 27 **minster clock**: cathedral clock. The incident on which the poem is founded occurred near Halifax, in Yorkshire.

232 1, 2 Loosened a bundle of sticks and twigs with a lopping tool. — 6 **wanton**: sportive.

233 3 This is almost as unadorned a line as Wordsworth ever wrote, and the entire poem is as severely simple as poetry can well be. Yet many capable readers — not all readers — feel it to be one of the most moving and truly noble poems ever written by an English poet. To appreciate it is to make one's calling and election as a lover of poetry about as sure as such an unspectacular consecration can be made. — 19 **loot**: let. — 24 **Langley-dale**: in the county of Durham.

234 1 **mettled**: full of spirit. — 1 **managed**: well trained. — 7 **morning-tide**: "tide" here means *time;* in the first two lines of this poem it means waterside, where the tide rises.

235 5 **light**: Parse this word. — 16 This song is from the fourth chapter of "Quentin Durward." — 16 **County**: Count. — 20 **nis lay**: notice the position in the clause. — 22 **confess**: bear manifest witness to the influence of.

236 9 **pensile**: hanging. — 27 **wanton**: luxuriantly growing.

237 6 **Embalms**: converts to balm. — 27 **her**: compare with *his*, p. 238, l. 5.

240 9 [In this and in other instances the addition (or the change) of a title has been risked, in hope that the aim of the piece following may be grasped more clearly and immediately.] — 22 **fretting**: Is this word used in a physical (= ruffling) or in a metaphysical sense? — 28 **Writhed**: supply "who."

241 3 From the third canto of "Marmion." — 3–6 Should these lines be as bare of punctuation as they are? — 11 **Eleu loro**: a Highland (Gaelic) lament. — 14 **laving**: Perhaps "their banks" is understood.

242 11 The title, which is that of an old French poem written by Alain Chartier, means "the beautiful lady without compassion." Keats owed little or nothing to any preceding poem. — 12 **palely**: a questionable use of the adverb in place of the adjective, yet the poetic effect is striking.

243 1 **as**: as if. — 3–6 Notice the picture. What is the effect of mounting her on the steed? — 17 **latest**: very last, the dream from which he only half awoke. — 23 **gloam**: Is this noun often used? — 24 **gapéd**: Is this a verb or a participle?

244 1 From "Rokeby," III, xxviii. — 4 **rue**: This bitter plant was a symbol for repentance. — 7 **Lincoln**: a town famous for its dyeing of green cloth. — 11 **trow**: suppose. — 12 **fain**: joyously.

245 11 **singled**: Fowler thinks that this means "left single," "left alone," rather than "selected," picked out. Is this explanation too subtle? — 12 An obscure line. Perhaps the sense is that, after love has first left its well-built nest in an unstable heart, then that heart is left to endure the person it has once loved, or else the fact that it has loved and proved inconstant. — 15 **the frailest**: Fowler explains this as meaning "the human heart." Perhaps it means the singer himself. — 22 **eagle**: lofty. — 25 Neidpath Castle was the residence of the earls of March (compare p. 246, l. 27), near Peebles. The tradition which occasioned Scott's and Campbell's poems is made sufficiently clear by their treatment of it.

246 20 **As**: as if. Parse *glancing*.

247 8 **Ellen**: a bad rime, but it would be an affectation to contend that it is a serious blemish in an exquisitely tender and beautiful poem.

—13 [This beautiful sonnet was the last word of a youth, in whom, if the fulfillment may ever safely be prophesied from the promise, England lost one of the most rarely gifted in the long roll of her poets. Shakespeare and Milton, had their lives been closed at twenty-five, would (so far as we know) have left poems of less excellence and hope than the youth who, from the petty school and the London surgery, passed at once to a place with them of "high collateral glory."]—16 **Eremite**: hermit.

248 3 **charact'ry**: printed characters.—6 **romance**: that of creation, of the wonders of the infinite universe.—8 **magic hand of chance**: inspiration.—15 The title means *Absent things longed for*.—17 **Thee**: Wordsworth's daughter Catharine, who died in early childhood.

249 4 [It is impossible not to regret that Moore has written so little in this sweet and genuinely national style.]—4 **weeping**: Dew was the tears of the stars.—11 **orison**: prayer.—14 [A masterly example of Byron's command of strong thought and close reasoning in verse: as the next is equally characteristic of Shelley's wayward intensity.]

250 7 What I loved so well has now become nothing—not literally, however. Compare p. 251, ll. 23–25.

251 26 **endears**: What is the subject of this verb?—28 **One word**: love. Compare the second stanza, which explains the first.

252 4 **that**: Fowler says that here *that* "must mean love." But must it? It may not be very great poetry which Shelly gives us if *that* stands for *pity*; but even Shelley may have ended a stanza in a weak fashion, and even he is not exempt from obedience to the rules of grammar.—13 **Pibroch**: martial music on the bagpipe. The time of these verses is 1431 A.D.; the scene the northern Highlands.—23 **pennon**: pennant, flag.

253 22 **man set**: How is this phrase used? Does it make a good rime with *onset?* Does the blemish seriously mar the splendidly spirited war song? Would it not be well if some modern critics were to revise their unflattering opinions of Scott as a poet?—25 **sheet**: a rope or chain used to move a sail.—25 **flowing**: rising.

255 1 Robert Blake (1599–1657) and Horatio Nelson (Lord Nelson, 1758–1805), two of the greatest of England's naval heroes.—8 **steep**: doubtless used for the cliffs that line the coast of England.—27 The battle of the Baltic commemorated in this stirring ode was fought under Nelson on April 2, 1801. For its results on England's relations with the northern nations see some English history.

256 21 **hurricane eclipse**: eclipse, blotting out by a great storm.

257 15 **funeral light**: light that lit up the spectacle of destruction.—19, 20 These lines show how the *joy* of l. 17 is to be exhibited.—25 **Elsinore**: a Danish seaport. Compare "Hamlet."—29 Edward Riou (1758?–1801), a captain killed in the battle.—32 **mermaid's song**: This touch has been objected to as artificial. Is this criticism or hypercriticism? In other words, does the fact that the mermaid is an accepted figure of poetical mythology minimize, to a considerable extent, the incongruity and artificiality?

258 1 **Daughter of the Voice**: echo. De Quincey, quoted by Fowler. — 12 **sense**: perhaps nearly equivalent to "intuitions." — 15, 16 Many readers may prefer another reading of these lines:

> Long may the kindly impulse last!
> But Thou, if they should totter, teach them to stand fast.

— 24 Is this better than the reading, "Yet find that other strength, according to their need"?

259 5 **uncharter'd**: unregulated. The poet perhaps had in mind the charters that helped to reduce to order the lawlessness of the Middle Ages. — 9–16 This stanza should be carefully studied as an illustration of the working of a noble imagination. — 25 [Bonnivard, a Genevese, was imprisoned by the Duke of Savoy in Chillon on the lake of Geneva for his courageous defense of his country against the tyranny with which Piedmont threatened it during the first half of the seventeenth century. This noble sonnet is worthy to stand near Milton's on the Vaudois massacre.]

260 9 [Switzerland was usurped by the French under Napoleon in 1800; Venice in 1797 (255)]. — 13 **tyrant**: Napoleon. — 23 **in fee**: as a fief or dependency. See a sketch of the history of Venice in some good encyclopedia.

261 3, 4 A reference to the custom of the doge going out to espouse the Adriatic. — 11 Poets have not infrequently bemoaned the condition of their country in terms of unwarranted severity. Cowper had done it before Wordsworth. Yet, on the whole, noble faultfinding is more stimulating than most praise, which so often and easily tends to be chauvinistic and fatuous. And Wordsworth apologizes finely in 258. — 22 **cause**: of home and fatherland. — 23 **fearful**: full of fear lest it do wrong.

262 3 **pen**: used with reference to writers and students in general. — 8 **manners**: good habits that make character.

263 4 [This battle was fought December 3, 1800, between the Austrians under Archduke John and the French under Moreau, in a forest near Munich. *Hohen Linden* means *High Limetrees*.] — 25 **dun**: dark.

264 3 **Munich**: the Bavarian capital.

265 6 **wonder-waiting**: waiting in wonder to hear the story. — 15 **Blenheim**: a village on the Danube, near the Nebel (referred to in the next line), where on August 13, 1704, the Duke of Marlborough and Prince Eugene of Savoy, commanding the allies (England, Holland, and the Empire), defeated the French in one of the most famous of battles. — 16 **hard by**: near that little stream. — 23 **childing**: with child.

266 2 **our**: Prince Eugene (1663–1736) was a Frenchman, who through indignation at his treatment by France, entered the Austrian service. He was a very able soldier and statesman. — 13 The title is from Horace's Odes, Book III, ode ii, 13, and is the conclusion of the line, which translated means "It is sweet and glorious to die for the fatherland." — 17 **my**: These lines, addressed to Ireland, are put in the mouth of Robert Emmet (1778–1803), who was executed for his share in the Irish uprising of 1803.

267 1 [After the capture of Madrid by Napoleon, Sir John Moore retreated before Soult and Ney to Corunna, and was killed whilst covering the embarkation of his troops], January 16, 1809.

268 5 **Cardigan**: in Wales. — 29 **But oh the heavy change**: a reminiscence of "Lycidas."

271 1 **deeds**: the object of *returning*, which participle is construed with *hearts unkind*. — 2 **still**: ever. — 14 **friend**: the poet, Charles Lloyd (Fowler).

274 16 **that it was gray**: a clause giving the reason for *smiled*. — 17 **prodigal's**: Youth and the season of spring. — 18 **miser's**: Age and the season of winter.

275 13 **in feathers**: with flight like that of birds.

277 13 **The sage**: It is not clear what special sage, if any, Shelley had in mind. — 27 Compare the manner of Shelley's death. A fifth stanza has been omitted from the poem as it was originally written in December, 1818. Note that if each of the first eight lines had an additional foot, this poem would be in Spenserian stanzas.

278 24 [The Mermaid was the clubhouse of Shakespeare, Ben Jonson, and other choice spirits of that age.] — 30 **Robin Hood**: See "Ivanhoe."

279 2 **bowse**: booze, drink heavily. — 12 **Zodiac**: "An imaginary belt encircling the heavens . . . within which are the larger planets. It is divided into twelve parts, called signs of the Zodiac, which formerly corresponded to twelve constellations bearing the same name" (The Students' Standard Dictionary). See some almanac. Are the poets in the Zodiac, or is the Mermaid there, as a new constellation, or are both there? — 17 [Scott has given us nothing more complete and lovely than this little song] from "The Heart of Midlothian," Chapter XL [which unites simplicity and dramatic power to a wild-wood music of the rarest quality. No moral is drawn, far less any conscious analysis of feeling attempted; the pathetic meaning is left to be suggested by the mere presentment of the situation. A narrow criticism has often named this, which may be called the Homeric manner, superficial, from its apparent simple facility; but first-rate excellence in it is in truth one of the least common triumphs of poetry. This style should be compared with what is not less perfect in its way, the searching out of inner feeling, the expression of hidden meanings, the revelation of the heart of nature and of the soul within the soul, — the analytical method, in short, — most completely represented by Wordsworth and by Shelley.] — 23 **braw**: handsome. — 24 **Kirkward**: toward the church.

280 14 **cerements**: waxed clothes in which the dead were buried.

283 4 **contumely**: Notice the accentuation.

284 32 **forewarning**: of heaven.

285 1 [Wolfe resembled Keats, not only in his early death by consumption and the fluent freshness of his poetical style, but in beauty of character — brave, tender, energetic, unselfish, modest. Is it fanciful to find some reflex of these qualities in the "Burial" and "Mary"? Out of the abundance of the *heart* . . .]

286 1 **Coronach**: dirge. — 15 **in flushing**: full bloom. — 17 [**correi**: covert on a hillside.] — 18 [**cumber**: trouble.]

287 3 **As**: as if. — 13 [This book has not a few poems of greater power and more perfect execution than "Agnes" and the extract which we have ventured to make from the deep-hearted author's "Sad Thoughts" (224). But none are more emphatically marked by the note of exquisiteness.] Nevertheless it should be noted that ll. 3, 4, p. 288, come perilously near to being doggerel, although they have the merit of representing British respectability in a most adequate manner.

288 24 [**inch**: island.] — 27, 28 This is an illustration of the phenomenon known as second-sight, long believed in by the Highlanders. Compare Defoe's "Duncan Campbell."

289 2 **Roslin**: "Roslin Castle now consists of a ruined keep, and a mansion of more modern date. It stands on a steep eminence, overlooking the Esk. Roslin Chapel . . . is, though of small size, one of the richest and most perfect specimens of church architecture in Scotland" (Palgrave's note in the Globe Scott). — 16 **Hawthornden**: the residence of William Drummond, some of whose poems are included in this volume.

290 25 **Promethean**: see a classical dictionary. — 31 What is the meaning of this and the next two lines?

291 11 **clerks**: scholars.

292 1 [From "Poetry for Children" (1809), by Charles and Mary Lamb. This tender and original little piece seems clearly to reveal the work of that noble-minded and afflicted sister, who was at once the happiness, the misery, and the life-long blessing of her equally noble-minded brother.] — 5–8 Note the splendid poetic quality of this stanza.

293 12 **love**: a noun or an infinitive? — 13 **Neglect me**: Did I brood over his neglect, or rather, shall I brood now, or some such paraphrase seems needed.

295 25 **Time**: object of *balk*, deprive of his prey.

296 30 **unbodied**: disembodied.

298 21 **hymeneal**: relating to marriage.

299 21 **measures**: musical strains.

300 18 **paramours**: lovers.

301 9 [This poem has an exaltation and a glory, joined with an exquisiteness of expression, which place it in the highest rank among the many masterpieces of its illustrious author.]

302 14 **Lethe-wards**: toward the river of forgetfulness. — 17 **Dryad**: see a classical dictionary. — 23 **Flora**: the Roman goddess of flowers. — 24 **Provençal song**: the poetry of the troubadours of Provence, in the south of France. — 26 **Hippocrene**: the spring of the Muses on Mt. Helicon. — 27 **winking**: hard to render in prose; sparkling gleefully, perhaps.

303 12 **pards**: tigers or lynxes that drew the wine god's chariot. — 31 **Darkling**: hidden in the dark.

304 10 **clown**: rustic.

305 17 **debonair**: Perhaps this means here charming rather than elegant. — 20 **Philomel**: the nightingale.— 25 This sonnet is probably due more or less to Shelley's own invention.

306 11 **Neidpath Castle**: see above, poems 240 and 241.

308 26 **peers**: those of equal station.

311 28 **Cheapside**: for these streets see Baedeker's "London."

312 7 **Ariel to Miranda**: see Shakespeare's "The Tempest." — 30 [**interlunar swoon**: interval of the moon's invisibility.]

315 17, 18 These lines were supplied to the poet by his wife.

316 1 **dappled**: spotted, variegated, with the daisies. — 9 **port**: bearing. — 17 **Cyclops**: see a classical dictionary and the Odyssey.

318 1 **barréd clouds**: that suggest bars (probably). — 1 **bloom**: reflect the rosy glow of, or give a glowing quality to. — 4 **river sallows**: willows by the river. — 6 **hilly bourn**: boundary of hills. — 8 **garden croft**: inclosure that serves as a garden. — 10 **fiery-mantled**: covered with fire, as the cheek with blushes. — 20 [**Calpe**: Gibraltar.] — 22 **buxom-brown**: brown with health. — 23 **Queen of vintage**: autumn. In this stanza Campbell is apparently affected by the style of Collins.

319 1 [**Lofoden**: the maelstrom whirlpool off the northwest coast of Norway.] See Poe's "The Descent of the Maelstrom." — 3 **Runic Odin**: the chief god of the northern mythology, celebrated in runic poetry. — 11 **Of power**: which (the shaft) has the power. — 34 **tented**: This ode was written when war was widespread.

320 11 [This lovely poem refers here and there to a ballad by Hamilton on the subject, better treated in 163 and 164.] — 16 **Marrow**: mate, companion, — his sister, Dorothy Wordsworth. — 18 **Braes**: slopes. — 27 **Leader Haughs**: the meadows along the river Leader. — 29 **Dryburgh**: the seat of the abbey. — 30 **lintwhites**: linnets.

321 1 **Tiviot-dale**: also Teviot. — 13 **holms**: alluvial fields. — 17 **strath**: valley.

323 5–12 Compare above, poems 163 and 164.

325 1 This poem is not given in its complete form. — 3, 4 Note the influence of Milton's "L'Allegro." — 9 **halcyon**: calm. See a classical dictionary under "Alcyone."

326 3 **dun**: dark. — 8 **never sets**: blooms at all seasons. — 21 **thou**: Shelley's friend, Mrs. Jane Williams.

327 27 **With**: Fowler notes that Palgrave follows W. M. Rossetti's edition, other editions reading *by*.

329 18 **Abraham's bosom**: see Luke xvi, 22.

331 15 See above, poem 58.

332 5 **sentinel stars**: Lovelace had already employed this phrase.

333 6 **copse**: thicket. — 9 **pied**: variegated. — 10 [**Arcturi**: seemingly used for *northern stars*.] — 10, 11 Compare p. 326, l. 8. — 13 **tall flower**: What flower did Shelley mean? — 21 [**And wild roses**: Our language has perhaps no line modulated with more subtle sweetness.] — 26 **prank'd**: adorned, decked.

334 9 **Kept**: the subject is *children*; the objects are *hues* and *array*. Would a comma after *array* help the awkward passage? — 13 [Coleridge describes this poem as the fragment of a dream vision — perhaps, an opium dream? — which composed itself in his mind when fallen asleep after reading a few lines about "the Khan Kubla" in Purchas's "Pilgrimage."] Kubla Khan, founder of the Mongol Dynasty and builder of Peking, lived in the thirteenth century of this era. — 25 **cover**: wood.

335 1 **vaulted**: leaped up. — 13 **measure**: music. — 17 **dulcimer**: a stringed instrument played with two padded hammers. — 21 **Mount Abora**: in Abyssinia.

336 19, 20 The rimes suggest the remark that editors who are eloquently censorious with regard to the faulty rimes of Byron and Campbell accept those of Keats and Shelley with a gaping gratitude of silence.

337 2 **ingle**: fireplace. — 7 **shoon**: old plural of shoes.

338 1 **Shaded**: that has grown up in the shade (probably). — 31 [**Ceres' daughter**: Proserpine.] — 32 [**God of Torment**: Pluto.] — 35 **Hebe**: see a classical dictionary.

339 2 **kirtle**: a garment with a skirt. — 7 The comparison of this poem with "L'Allegro" is inevitable. Despite the wealth of beauty lavished by the romantic poet, the student will do well to note the superiority of the more restrained poet, who is the supreme English representative of classical art.

340 5 This poem shows Nature's influence in the formation of an evil character, as poem 222 shows her power to train a noble soul. — 26 **Cherokees**: The student need not be surprised that, although he was an Englishman, Wordsworth selected the name of a tribe of Indians who were really found in the southern states. He had read such books as William Bartram's "Travels," and had caught from them some notions of the beauty of semitropical nature.

341 20–22 Compare Othello's wooing of Desdemona.

342 7 **savannahs:** meadows (Spanish). Compare the name of the Georgia city.

343 2 **sylvan:** forest. — 20–27 Do these lines represent the prosaic Wordsworth? — 27 **West:** Is Wordsworth's geography becoming hazy?

346 4–6 These lines seem labored when compared with the following more appropriate close of the stanza:

> And there she sang tumultuous songs,
> By recollection of her wrongs
> To fearful passion roused.

— 11 **clear:** This once read *wild*. — 17 **it liked her:** note the archaic touch. — 22 **Tone:** a small river in Somersetshire, near the Quantock Hills (see p. 347, l. 21). — 25 **engines:** Wordsworth seems to assume that Ruth had as philosophic an insight into the effects of free nature as had the thoughtful but in this case rather fantastic poet.

348 1 [The leading idea of this beautiful description of a day's landscape in Italy appears to be: On the voyage of life are many moments of pleasure, given by the sight of nature, who has power to heal even the worldliness and the uncharity of man.] The poem has been shortened. — 14 **drank:** strictly the preterite form. — 31 **Euganean:** hills between Padua and Verona. — 32 **pæan:** choral song addressed to Apollo.

349 8 **grain:** dye or color. See above, "Il Penseroso," p. 129, l. 17. — 25 [**Amphitrite:** daughter to Ocean.] — 33 **As:** as if.

350 13 **watery bier:** a phrase used by Milton in "Lycidas," p. 73, l. 28. — 16 **slave of slaves:** Napoleon, — a moral rather than historical judgment. — 33 **mask:** dance.

351 5 **air-dissolvéd:** dissolved into air, whatever that phenomenon may be. — 8 **profound:** depth. — 18 **dun:** dark. — 22 **olive-sandal'd:** The reference is to the olive trees lining the foot of the mountains.

353 7 **interval:** object of *supplies*, two lines below. — 15 **it:** the "healing paradise" of p. 352, l. 36. Are *they* the "Spirits" of p. 352, l. 34, or the "polluting multitude" of p. 353, l. 1?

354 7 [**Mænad:** a frenzied nymph, attendant on Dionysus in the Greek mythology. May we not call this the most vivid, sustained, and impassioned amongst all Shelley's magical personifications of nature?] — 18 **Baiæ's bay:** a resort of the Romans at the western end of the Bay of Naples. — 25 [Plants under water sympathize with the seasons of the land, and hence with the winds which affect them.]

355 22 [Written soon after the death by shipwreck, of Wordsworth's brother John] see p. 356, l. 28. [This poem may be profitably compared with Shelley's following it. Each is the most complete expression of the innermost spirit of his art given by these great poets, — of that Idea which, as in the case of the true painter (to quote the words of

Reynolds), "subsists only in the mind; the sight never beheld it, nor has the hand expressed it; it is an idea residing in the breast of the artist, which he is always laboring to impart, and which he dies at last without imparting."] Sir George Beaumont of Coleorton Hall was a cultivated friend of Wordsworth's. Peele Castle is "a ruined keep on a small island close to the modern town of Barrow, in Furness, Lancashire" (Fowler).

356 5–8 One of the most famous passages in Wordsworth's poetry.

357 7 **hulk**: dismantled vessel. — 14 [**the Kind**: the human race.] — 21 From "Prometheus Unbound," Act I, scene i. — 22 **love-adept**: one versed in love.

358 6 **Ossian**: the ancient Gaelic poet.

359 17 **Proteus**: the old man of the sea in Grecian mythology, who kept Amphitrite's seals, and could change himself into any form, — whence the adjective "protean." — 18 **Triton**: the trumpeter who raised or calmed the waves. Compare Spenser's lines in "Colin Clout's Come Home Againe":

> Of them the shepheard which hath charge in chief,
> Is Triton blowing loud his wreathed horne.

— 19 [**royal Saint**: Henry VI.] — 22 **white-robed**: wearing surplices. — 26 **sense**: of beauty.

360 7 [Every one knows the general story of the Italian Renaissance, of the revival of letters. From Petrarch's day to our own, that ancient world has renewed its youth; poets and artists, students and thinkers, have yielded themselves wholly to its fascination, and deeply penetrated its spirit. Yet perhaps no one more truly has vivified, whilst idealizing, the picture of Greek country life in the fancied Golden Age, than Keats in these lovely (if somewhat unequally executed) stanzas; his quick imagination, by a kind of "natural magic," more than supplying the scholarship which his youth had no opportunity of gaining.] — 13 **Tempé**: the famous vale in Thessaly. — 13 **Arcady**: in the Peloponnesus, famous for pastoral life. — 16 **timbrels**: tambourines. — 19 **sensual**: not used with an unpleasant connotation.

361 4 **passion**: object of *above*. — 13 [**this folk**: *its* has been here plausibly, but perhaps unnecessarily, conjectured.]

362 7 **unknown of yore**: save in poetry. — 22 **it**: that Thou art gone (see following line). — 22 **fond conceit**: foolish fancy. — 28 **slips**: strips. — 30 **blossoms**: a verb.

364 9 **sued**: Does this mean wooed, courted, or followed?

365 8 **wilding**: crab apple. — 19 **catch**: snatch.

369 3 **cloud**: thundercloud. — 6 **stain**: almost meaningless. Shelley probably meant to write *strain*. — 19 **Trosachs**: a mountain pass in Perthshire, Scotland.

370 18 The fundamental idea of this great ode — already expressed in Vaughan's beautiful poem (see above, p. 84) — is Platonic. Wordsworth held it true only in a poetic sense.

371 12 **tabor**: a small drum. — 31 **coronal**: wreath. Do you like the cadence of this line?

373 9 **the Child**: Hartley Coleridge. There are lines in this stanza which to some readers come near to being doggerel. Despite the truth to nature of the description, the poet's style seems to drop distressingly far below the splendid level maintained in the stanzas that precede and follow. Lines 12, 13, are unamenable to this criticism; but in contrast see ll. 30, 31.

375 14–20 A splendid illustration of Wordsworth's imagination at its height, — the power of seeing and making others see "the light that never was on sea or land."

376 4–20 These lines are both nobly calm and piercingly pathetic. Which seems in excess, the calm or the pathos? — 21 This snatch of suggestive melody forms a lovely epilogue to the most beautiful volume of lyric poetry in the English language. Coming as it does after the deep harmony of Wordsworth's concluding stanza, it helps us to comprehend the range of our lyric verse.

INDEX OF WRITERS

AND

INDEX OF FIRST LINES

INDEX OF WRITERS

WITH DATES OF BIRTH AND DEATH

INDEX OF FIRST LINES

ANNOUNCEMENTS

STANDARD ENGLISH CLASSICS

(*Continued*)

Macaulay: Essays on Addison and Milton (in one volume) (Smith) $0.40
Macaulay: Essays on Lord Clive and Warren Hastings (Gaston) .44
Macaulay: Lays of Ancient Rome, The Armada, Ivry, and The Battle of Naseby (Daniell) 40
Macaulay: Life of Samuel Johnson (Hanson) 32
Macaulay: Speeches on Copyright, with Lincoln's Address at Cooper Union (Gaston) 32
Milton: L'Allegro, Il Penseroso, Comus, and Lycidas (Huntington) 32
Milton: Paradise Lost, Books I and II, and Lycidas (Sprague) . .40
Old Testament: Selections (Snyder) 40
Palgrave: Golden Treasury. First Series (Trent and Erskine) . .60
Palgrave: Golden Treasury: Poems of Wordsworth, Shelley, and Keats (Trent and Erskine) 32
Parkman: Oregon Trail (Leonard) 56
Poe: Select Poems and Tales (Gambrill) 40
Pope: Iliad, Books I, VI, XXII, and XXIV (Tappan) 32
Pope: Rape of the Lock and Other Poems (Parrott) 40
Ruskin: Selected Essays and Letters (Hufford) 72
Ruskin: Sesame and Lilies (Hufford) 32
Scott: Ivanhoe (Lewis) 72
Scott: Lady of the Lake (Ginn) 44
Scott: Quentin Durward (Bruère) 60
Smith: Short Stories, Old and New 56
Spenser: Faerie Queene. Selections (Litchfield) 52
Stevenson: Inland Voyage and Travels with a Donkey (Snow) . .44
Stevenson: Treasure Island (Hersey) 60
Tennyson: Coming of Arthur, Gareth and Lynette, Lancelot and Elaine, Quest of the Holy Grail, and Passing of Arthur (Boughton) .40
Tennyson: The Princess (Cook) 40
Thackeray: English Humorists (Young) 44
Thackeray: History of Henry Esmond, Esq. (Moore) 72
Washington's Farewell Address and Webster's First Bunker Hill Oration (Gaston) 32

GINN AND COMPANY PUBLISHERS

REFERENCE BOOKS ON POETRY

Alexander: Introduction to the Poetry of Robert Browning. 212 pages $1.25
Bright and Miller: Elements of English Versification. 166 pages 1.20
Cook's Addison: Criticisms on Paradise Lost. xxiv + 200 pages 1.36
Cook: Art of Poetry. The Poetical Treatises of Horace, Vida, and Boileau, with the translations by Howes, Pitt, and Soame. lviii + 303 pages 1.40
Cook: Cardinal Newman's Essay on Poetry, with reference to Aristotle's Poetics. 36 pages 40
Cook: Hunt's "What is Poetry?" 98 pages 72
Cook: Shelley's Defense of Poetry. 86 pages 72
Cook: Sidney's Defense of Poesy. xlv + 103 pages . .88
Cooper: Aristotle on the Art of Poetry. xxix+101 pages 1.00
Corson: Primer of English Verse. 232 pages . . . 1.25
Gayley: Classic Myths in English Literature and in Art. xlii + 597 pages 1.80
Gayley and Flaherty: Poetry of the People. 403 pages .60
Gayley and Kurtz: Methods and Materials of Literary Criticism: Lyric, Epic, and Allied Forms of Poetry . . . . [*In press*]
Gummere: Handbook of Poetics. 250 pages 1.40
Gummere: Old English Ballads. xcviii + 380 pages . 1.00
Hudson: Life, Art, and Characters of Shakespeare. Two volumes, 1003 pages, cloth, $4.00; half morocco 8.00
Long: American Literature. xxi + 481 pages . . . 1.48
Long: English Literature. 582 pages 1.48
Long: Outlines of English and American Literature . 1.52
Manly: English Poetry. xxviii + 580 pages 1.80
Schelling: Elizabethan Lyrics. lxix + 327 pages 90
Schelling: Seventeenth Century Lyrics. lxix + 314 pages .90
Sneath: Wordsworth — Poet of Nature and Poet of Man. 320 pages 2.40